GODLESS INTELLECTUALS?

Godless Intellectuals?

The Intellectual Pursuit of the Sacred Reinvented

Alexander Tristan Riley

Berghahn Books

New York • Oxford

First published in 2010 by

Berghahn Books

www.berghahnbooks.com

©2010, 2012 Alexander Tristan Riley
First paperback edition published in 2012

Library of Congress Cataloging-in-Publication Data

Riley, Alexander Tristan.
　Godless intellectuals? : the intellectual pursuit of the sacred reinvented /
Alexander Tristan Riley.
　　p. cm.
　Includes bibliographical references and index.
　ISBN 978-1-84545-670-2 (hbk.)– ISBN 978-0-85745-805-6 (pbk.)
　1. Durkheimian school of sociology. 2. Poststructuralism. 3. Holy, The. I. Title.
　HM465.R56 2010
　301.0943–dc22

2010006673

British Library Cataloguing in Publication Data

A catalogue record for this book is available from the British Library

Printed in the United States on acid-free paper.

ISBN: 978-0-85745-805-6 (paperback)　　ISBN: 978-0-85745-821-6 (ebook)

… no biography, no depiction of the growth and development of an intellectual life, could properly be written without taking its subject back to the pupil stage, to the period of his beginnings in life and art, when he listened, learned, divined, gazed, and ranged now afar, now close at hand.

—Thomas Mann, *Doctor Faustus*

Contents

Acknowledgements

Two mentors (or, to use the borrowed terminology I use in this book, two *masters of ceremonies*) were essential in the completion of the research on which this book is based. Harvey Goldman influenced and shaped it in more ways than I can begin to list. Very simply, this book would not have existed, at least not in this form, if I had not had the tremendous good fortune to come to work with him as a graduate student. He convinced an impetuous and hot-headed young man to settle down and do a little work, no small task. He has also been the most generous of friends. Philippe Besnard encouraged this project during my time digging in the Paris archives and gave tremendous practical aid in finding and accessing many documents. Both Harvey and Philippe shared with me the supreme scholarly gift: honesty. Though they both became my friends as well as my teachers, they unflinchingly let me know when I was talking about things I did not well understand, and they suggested ways to amend the problem. Philippe died, far too early, in 2003, and I greatly regret that he will not be able to read and criticize this book.

Willie Watts Miller and Bill Pickering have long spiritually supported the work on which this book is based. Jeffrey Alexander and Philip Smith also provided encouragement and asked me to submit a chapter for their *Cambridge Companion to Durkheim* which wound up being a condensed version of the core argument in the book. Ed Tiryakian's *Sociologism and Existentialism* and Mike Gane's writings on Durkheim, Mauss, and Baudrillard have been a tremendous inspiration and example to me. Ed also shared some very kind words with me over lunch in Montréal back in 1998 that I will not soon forget. Marcel Hénaff provided boundless encouragement and enthusiasm, as well as inspiration, for this work.

Thanks to all the archivists at the Collège de France, the Laboratoire d'Anthropologie Sociale, and IMEC and to the staff at the Bibliothèque Nationale Richelieu and François-Mitterrand sites. What a pleasure it has been to work in your facilities and reap the benefits of your expertise.

Thanks also go to Marion Berghahn for her support and patience in the process of getting this into print.

Some parts of the arguments in Chapters 2, 8, 9, 10, and 13 have previously appeared in other forms in articles and one book chapter published by Cambridge University Press, the *Revue européene des sciences sociales,* and the University of California Press.

This book is dedicated to my wife Esmeralda and our daughter Valeria, who are currently engaged in the difficult task of teaching me about the virtue of hope.

1   The Intellectual Pursuit of the Sacred

The central goal of this book is to map the emergence, trajectory, and influence of a very particular kind of intellectual project that I call *mystic Durkheimianism,* which unites two seemingly very strange bedfellows: Durkheimian sociology and poststructuralism. An understanding of its existence and influence in the French intellectual world will contribute to a better understanding of some otherwise fairly mysterious facts in intellectual history. Moreover, there are to date no treatments of this important piece of the history of French social theory by a sociologist using sociological terms and tools, and I hope to contribute to the work of filling that considerable hole in the scholarly literature.

A second and closely related goal of the book involves the presentation and test-driving of a research method for thinking about intellectual works and identities. How can we understand the relationship between the work an intellectual produces and his or her life in terms that are not simply biographical? What can we know about how and from what sources intellectual projects arise? How can we hope to understand the meanings of intellectual works and trajectories sociologically without completely jettisoning the experiential level of that production? What can we know about how intellectual influence works? When we construct intellectual histories and thereby try to make some sense of who goes where, what are the criteria we should use? What ultimately are the things we need to account for in understanding intellectual production and the meaning of ideas and intellectual work? These are some of the questions I will address, and a serviceable theory of the intellectual *habitus,* intellectual experience and identity, and intellectual production, empirically derived and tested in this particular site of twentieth-century France, is what I hope to work toward in the pages that follow.

Both Durkheimian sociology and French poststructuralist thought have received considerable attention in the French- and English-speaking academic worlds over the past fifteen to twenty years. Significant literatures now exist on the histories of both, though connections between the two are only infrequently and unsystematically explored. Historical work on the Durkheimian school frequently finds its sources in nineteenth-century French neo-Kantianism and traces its influence through contemporary forms of functionalism and sociological positivism. The work on the possible meanings and usages of poststructuralism has brought with it a concern for establishing the genealogy of this peculiar branch of literary and social theory. Various theses connect it to the broader anti-humanist and structuralist movements that originated in linguistics, to the peculiar French reading of Nietzsche by the literary avant-garde, or to the anti-Marxist left intellectual radicalism associated with the political and cultural upheaval of May 1968.

Notwithstanding the considerable amount of attention paid to these questions, only rarely have sociological tools been brought to bear on them. What were the actual sociological conditions of the intellectual and political worlds in which these thinkers were formed and matured? What intellectual networks did they participate in, and what institutions did they pass through during their educational and scholarly development? In short, what are the precise factors that produced their intellectual selves? Most of the existing efforts content themselves with textual readings of the Durkheimian and poststructural sources, while real intellectual networks and sociologies are largely ignored, and they privilege lines of descent claimed by the poststructuralist authors themselves—a shaky analytical strategy.

I attempt to attend both to the textual level and to a more careful historical and micro-sociology of intellectual influence within which to frame it. The core of my argument is as follows: the work and lives of the key representatives of poststructuralist thought (Michel Foucault, Gilles Deleuze, Jacques Derrida, and Jean Baudrillard) constitute an effort to retheorize and reinvigorate the venerable concept of the sacred. This claim raises the question of the sources from which they derive this theoretical concern. I believe the central source can in fact be located in Durkheimianism, an intellectual predecessor that is generally considered something of an antithesis to poststructuralism. While this intellectual connection *has* been recognized by some other writers, at least in part simply because some of the poststructuralists mention the Durkheimians explicitly in their own work, they have not attempted to demonstrate in empirical terms just how this connection between the purportedly positivist Durkheimian school and the skeptical, anti-positivist poststructuralists was constructed through real intellectual networks and intellectual *habitus*. Indeed, the problem seems at first glance daunting, if not impossible: How, in an argument about intellectual trajectory and personality, can we possibly get from the ascetic, *soi-disant* scientist Durkheim to the libidinous transgressor Foucault?

Empirical and sociological substantiation of the link between Durkheimian thought and the poststructuralists will require not only a close examination of the poststructuralists, but also (and first) an excavation of the work and lives of the several Durkheimian thinkers who, in their collective intellectual activity, most directly influenced the poststructuralists. These are the members of the small sub-group of contributors to Durkheim's journal *L'Année sociologique* who were most centrally concerned with the sociology of religion: Durkheim himself, Marcel Mauss, Henri Hubert, and Robert Hertz. These thinkers were dedicated to simultaneously examining the role of the intellectual in society and acting in the world themselves as intellectuals, with an emphasis on the necessity of remaking the sacred in the secular modern world, and their particular methods of resolving the tension between theoretical work and engaged lives served as powerful and empirically demonstrable influences on the later generation of poststructuralists. In the reconstruction of their intellectual project, I borrow conceptual tools from Weber's sociology of religion to formulate the notion of *mystic Durkheimianism*, which is distinguished from *ascetic Durkheimianism* along a number of axes that demonstrate particular orientations to problematics or dynamics that were central areas of contention for intellectuals at the time (and which remained so, although with substantive thematic shifts, for the poststructuralists as well). These problematics were: 1) the appropriate political role of the intellectual, if any; 2) the parameters and limits of scientific knowledge of human experience and action; and 3) the appropriate moral institutions and theories to replace the institution that had previously provided the moral center for French society, the Roman Catholic Church, and with which to most effectively organize society.

In formulating a specific set of orientations to these key problems and working them out both in their intellectual and personal lives, the mystic Durkheimians prove to be an important historical and theoretical link from early sociological thought to poststructuralism.

The Modern Intellectual and the Sacred in France: Doing Sacredness Otherwise

As I am making a case for a relationship between a certain kind of intellectual (and a certain kind of intellectual *project*) and the concept of the sacred, one might reasonably expect at least a brief discussion of the general question of precisely what constitutes: 1) an intellectual; and 2) the sacred.

Ron Eyerman is certainly correct when he notes that many works attempting to define intellectuals "begin by stating how difficult the task is" (1994: 1), and this book takes its place in that venerable tradition. The term is used in myriad ways, and, while some writers invoke it in a generic way to refer to all those in all times and places who have lived and worked primarily in the realm of ideas, there are specificities of the French historical and social context that make a tighter definition possible and even necessary. Here, there are some reasonable starting points, but even these call for caution in application. Raymond Aron's distinction of two poles of activity, effectiveness/culture and imitation/creation, permits a location of intellectuals toward the cultural and creative poles, but what of engineers or members of a research team doing normal science, for example? Rémy Rieffel invokes Debray's distinction between a high and low intelligentsia in order to delineate and justify a study of intellectuals that concentrates only on those who have access to a large public (Rieffel 1993: 17).

The very term *intellectuel* has a distinct social history. It is linked to the appearance of that particular type of social actor that first emerged in *fin-de-siècle* Paris, in response to the concerted effort by the French military establishment and cultural Right to make Captain Alfred Dreyfus a national scapegoat, and that found archetypal expression in the famed "*J'accuse*" letter of Émile Zola. This critical historical episode in the emergence of the modern French intellectual is discussed at some length in this book's third chapter, but for now it is perhaps sufficient to note that the definition of the *intellectuels*, what made them different from earlier historical examples of writers, philosophers, and cultural producers, has much to do with their explicit use of academic and intellectual capital in the service of political and social struggles (Charle 1990). It is arguably here that we see the birth of an idea of the essence of the intellectual that has become almost an issue of common sense acquiescence in much literature on intellectuals—that is, *the intellectual as centrally defined by his or her relation to the political sphere.* The *intellectuel* is not merely a man or woman of ideas, but one who endeavors explicitly to put his or her ideas to work in the service of some political or social project, who conceives of him or herself as fundamentally the kind of actor with a privileged capacity to speak authoritatively to compelling political and social issues of the day.

Of course, thinkers who endeavored to put their ideas into the service of political and social causes or powers existed prior to this relatively late juncture in history. Thomas Molnar accepts in its essentials this definition of the intellectual, but he argues for its point of origin as the early fourteenth rather than the late nineteenth century, since this is the period during which the long-standing intellectual and political unity of the Christian faith was disrupted by the medieval struggle of papacy and empire, and thinkers subsequently began to mobilize themselves and their ideas on behalf of one or the other (Molnar 1961: 9–10).

Whatever the historical point of its emergence, though, this definition of the intellectual as a thinker who puts his or her thought explicitly at the service of some political or social agenda or goal and who understands his or her cultural production as intimately tied or at least amenable to intervention in the sphere of power in society has attained a wide acceptance in sociological circles, and it has lent itself particularly well to the analyses of Marxist and Marxist-inspired writers who see the intellectual's role and activity as fundamentally entwined in the conflict of social classes and political factions. The history of Marxist theorizing about the intellectual is rich and complicated, from Marx's own criticisms of the "philosophers [who] have only interpreted the world" when the task at hand was to change it, to Lenin's formulation of the intellectual as revolutionary vanguard burdened by history with the task of bringing the masses to consciousness and revolution, Gramsci's subtle recasting of this Leninist program with the notion of vanguard "organic intellectuals" themselves drawn from the masses and thus more capable of working out the practical problems of the masses with the tools of critical theory, and Alvin Gouldner's cautious evaluation of the New Class of technicians and professional intellectuals as a "universal class in embryo" (Marx 1972: 145; Lenin 1966: 72–77; Gramsci 1971: 323–77; Gouldner 1979: 85).

In this perspective one also finds privileged what we should recognize as a more or less purely *macro*-sociology of intellectuals, in which the important factors for consideration concern the place and function in the overall social structure played by intellectuals as a class. The *micro*-sociology of intellectuals and the study of the intellectual experience of meaning in intellectual production are largely ignored by Marxist thinkers and those centrally inspired by them in their study of intellectuals.

As a sociologist, one can scarcely discount this perspective on the study of the intellectual, as it reveals fundamental aspects of the inevitable implication of ideas in social and political conflict and struggle. Nonetheless, there is significant oversimplification in such definitions, arising from the unjustified privileging, to use Weberian terms, of a certain kind of interests and positions (material) over other (ideal) interests and positions. It is certainly true that concerns about political power, whether as a conservative seeking to maintain order or a radical seeking to subvert it, and strategies for achieving personal success in the intellectual or other worlds are frequently parts of an intellectual's self-positioning, but what becomes, in such a perspective, of "ethical convictions ... personal beliefs ... [and] passionate reactions" on the part of intellectuals (Rieffel 1993: 14)? Can those be made sense of solely in the framework of political struggle? Arguably, a model for understanding intellectual production that aims more broadly than the Marxist model does would offer an advantage in understanding intellectual production and meaning more fully.

There are clear indications of how we might construct a broader perspective on intellectual orientation present in many of the more complex efforts to define the intellectual. One recent such effort classifies intellectuals as "that social category which performs the task of making conscious and visible *the fundamental notions of a society*" (Eyerman 1994: 6; emphasis added). Let us think more carefully about what is indicated here. The fundamental notions of a society, in the language of most classical sociological theory, had a profound connection to and reliance on myth and religion. Indeed, in historical terms, the connection between intellectual activity and religious functions is strikingly clear. In archaic societies, sorcerers and shamans were the social location of many of these "fundamental notions," most importantly those concerning the relationship between the visible and invisible worlds. In the great agrarian empires of antiquity, priests occupied this position. In the Western Middle Ages, the clerics created a new institution, the university, to propagate and expand the intellectual production that was nearly universally recognized as their proper charge. One can see clearly the genealogical relationship between the priestly classes and the modern intellectual in, e.g., the fact that the French still use the term "clerics" to refer to intellectuals, viz., Julien Benda's *La Trahison des clercs*.

While it is true that the Renaissance and later the Enlightenment enabled some Western intellectuals to take a certain critical distance from the church in redefining their role as leading the struggle against superstition, in doing so they also inevitably engaged in a certain kind of remythification that reaffirmed their ties to the medieval clerics and the archaic sorcerer-priests. This remythification took different forms: e.g., the quasi-deification of reason, Romantic myths of man in nature, and the nationalist myth (Morin 1991: 59–61). A fair amount of classical sociological theory, including the work of Comte, Durkheim, Weber, and Simmel, was centered on the dilemma of a modern world in which the old fundamental notions of sacrality and ritual seemed to be giving way, with no clear replacements in sight, and much of this work noted the central importance of the intellectuals in both the existence and the possible resolutions of this critical problem.

Thus can we begin to postulate the complex intertwining of these two notions, the intellectual and the sacred: "[T]he intelligentsia pursues an original role inherited from that of the sorcerers and great priests but which, at the same time, is born of the critique of sorcery and of religious culture" (Morin 1975: 109). Here are historical and sociological clues as to how we might productively think about the intellectual as centrally connected to the sacred, even in a secular modernity in which many intellectuals seem most dutifully engaged in the demystification and destruction of that notion.

Probably the best known attempt by a sociologist to frame the intellectual's identity in such terms of relation to the sacred comes from Edward Shils. In his discussion of the intellectual and his relation to political power, he notes that the bulk of the individuals in any given society orient themselves largely, if not completely, to the "directly gratifying ends of particular actions, the exigencies of situations, considerations of individual and familial advantage, concrete moral maxims, [and] concrete prescriptions and prohibitions"; in short, they have only intermittent or perhaps almost no need for contact with "ultimate values, be they cognitive, moral, or aesthetic" (Shils 1972: 3). Intellectuals, on the other hand, are defined by their uncommon need for "frequent communion with symbols that are more general than the immediate concrete situations of everyday life and remote in their reference in both time and space"; they are internally oriented toward a transcendent realm of value and experience, and they feel compelled to explore this orientation externally "in oral and written discourse, in poetic and plastic expression, in historical reminiscence or writing, in ritual performance and acts of worship" (ibid.).

This realm toward which intellectuals orient themselves Shils calls the sacred, which is broadly consistent with the Durkheimian conception of the sacred as defined centrally by its opposition to the profane, or that which is mundane, quotidian, not separated from the everyday and vulgar by a particular atmosphere of reverence and potency. He is clear though that his argument encompasses apparently secular as well as overtly religious intellectuals, as "science and philosophy (for example, and we might include here the nineteenth-century offspring of these two parents—namely, social science), even when they are not religious in a conventional sense, are as concerned with the sacred as religion itself" (Shils 1972: 16). Similarly, Marxists and other similarly oriented intellectuals who attack the traditional notions of the sacred and orient themselves toward the revolutionary project of the proletariat or some other seemingly secular object or goal can be understood as within the parameters of this definition as well.

Shils's definition is intriguing for a number of reasons. Insofar as it aspires to be a universal description of intellectuals, it attempts to offer some possibility of examining intellectuals cross-culturally and across time periods without completely losing the ability to make comparisons along shared criteria and without hopelessly becoming lost in a radically historicist, relativist dilemma that can make difficult any discussion of the commonalities of different intellectual trajectories. If there is some unifying thread in intellectual activity and orientation, however loose, then one can perhaps escape to a degree from the often paralyzing suspicion evinced by the intellectual historian for any attempt to, for example, speak seriously and rigorously of a comparison of the Sophists of Periclean Athens and the Parisian poststructuralists of the 1960s and 1970s.

It also suggests, by mapping out an evolutionary history of the intellectual's project orientations, the points at which the modern secular intellectual and his or her contemporary, the modern religious intellectual, might be productively examined as descendants from a common lineage. In any event, this much ought to be fairly evident once one takes more than a cursory look at the real, lived histories of some exemplary twentieth-century intellectuals, for example, Heidegger or Wittgenstein, and notices the significant overlap of intellectual and religious interests and motivations, but too often this method of reading the trajectory of intellectuals is discredited out of hand by those convinced before the fact that the intellectual's goal and the religious seeker's goal must have little or nothing in common.

The case for the universality of the definition is ultimately unconvincing for numerous reasons that need not be laid out here. Yet, examination of the particular historical and social space we are interested in demonstrates how Shils's definition might apply at least in some particular circumstances. In the specific context of the world of French intellectuals, as André Bélanger (1997) has pointed out in his intriguing study of the French intellectual tradition and its tremendous influence by the broader Catholic tradition of the country, the profoundly French model of the intellectual as legitimate articulator of principles of objectively correct ethics and politics *vis-à-vis* a public that takes the role of the laity in relation to the intellectual priesthood and that, unlike the public in Protestant countries, readily and consistently acquiesces on such matters, stems from the deeply hierarchical and priestly character of French Catholicism. Thus, even seemingly clearly secular French intellectuals, and even if they personally emerge from diverse religious traditions, such as Durkheim himself (Jewish by birth) and Sartre (Protestant), among others, can still be considered fundamentally Catholic intellectuals in this sense, as they share certain profound characteristics with the Catholic priesthood in their methods of discourse and in their relationship to their public.

The potential utility of some variant of this model for the French intellectual world is also suggested by Allan Stoekl's (1992) study of the intellectual in twentieth-century France. Stoekl suggests that the modern French intellectual can be best understood as caught between two oppositional categories (which he derives from Roland Barthes), the writer and the author. The first is concerned with representation and communication via argumentation of a rational tenor, while the second is engaged in "the not necessarily rational force of writing or language itself" (Stoekl 1992: 7). In these two forms, which encompass and exceed more institutionally-centered efforts to categorize the different types of French intellectual such as Kauppi's (1996: 27) "savant" (university pole) and "littérateur" (literary pole), the French intellectual has taken up the seemingly contradictory political tasks of acting both as representative and theoretician of the state and as critical dissident, and the stylistic and political conflict in these two models of intellectual identity is at the heart of the French situation. Durkheim, according to Stoekl's argument, occupies a foundational place in this narrative, as he was the first modern French intellectual to clearly pose the opposition in its essential form, which is in fact concerned with the intellectual's relation to the sacred. In Durkheim's treatment of the totem as at once "(re)instituting act and … representation" (Stoekl 1992: 8), that is, as both rational and pre-rational expression of the social bond, he is laying down the terms of the task of the twentieth-century French intellectuals who followed him: namely, to reconcile the two within oneself, and within the terms of the category of the sacred.

In short, Shils's definition of the intellectual and his or her orientation toward the sacred entails a real reconceptualization of interpretive and sociological work on intellectuals. Again, I do not intend to go so far as to follow that definition in its universal application; we can remain skeptical as to whether or not *all* intellectuals can be adequately understood in these terms, despite the attraction of such a definition. Yet there are compelling factors in the particular historical and sociological intellectual space that is the focus of this study which make this model of some fairly obvious utility, even given the clear historical connection in the French context between intellectual activity and political activity. It should be clear enough that ultimately the sort of definition of the intellectual that takes as its central focus the merely political or social positions and effects that are the outcomes of a certain practical application of ideas cannot adequately account for the interior motivations toward meaning and existential self-conception and construction that are the necessary precondition for, e.g., subsequent engagement, or refusal of such engagement, *qua* intellectual in the Dreyfus Affair or the movement of May '68. Conceptualizing and studying the intellectual as most fundamentally a political actor, whose ideological positions are to be discerned and then mapped with respect to the ideological positions of others in order to obtain the real meaning of his or her thought and life, or as a faceless representative of a particular social space without particular inclinations toward the construction of meaning in the world, is too reductionist for the researcher interested in the most profound sources of the motivation to become an intellectual and to construct an intellectual life, identity, and *oeuvre*. Ultimately, if everything is reduced here to the level of political or social struggle, we limit ourselves to forever talking about a limited subset of the outcomes of a primary set of orientations and interrogations, rather than about those primary factors themselves. Coincidentally, such a reduction makes it impossible to consider historically the emergence of that particular tradition of suspicion of political and other authority that is characteristic of a significant proportion of modern intellectuals, albeit in varied forms (Shils 1972: 17), as the reductive move naturalizes something, i.e., the overt politicization of the intellectuals, that is in reality a profoundly historical phenomenon. In addition, it is not clear that these primordial orientations and interrogations to which Shils points always and necessarily work themselves out in the realm of political and social positioning. They may instead be manifest in empirical outcomes, in the work or in action, that are much less difficult to place in the web of political or social power struggles.

Yet I will have to be nuanced in my application of Shils's model even within the French intellectual scene. If *all* French intellectuals are taken to be concerned centrally and to the same degree with the sacred, much of the significance of what is unveiled here is significantly muted. For we can locate a particular thread in the French intellectual tradition that treats the sacred in a much more concentrated, focused, and central way than is discernible in much of the rest of that tradition, which indeed makes the construction of a new conception of the sacred in modernity and of an intellectual program for engaging with it the centerpiece of the intellectual project.

As noted previously, little has been said of any possible poststructuralist infatuation with the notion of the sacred or any related notions until relatively recently, when discussions of postmodern theology began to spring up, and even these are still generally far from arguing that poststructuralism constitutes an attempt to reinvigorate an intellectual experience of the sacred. Even in the case of the Durkheimians, where a significant and explicit investment was made in the explicit study of the sacred and its pursuit historically and cross-culturally, few commentators take seriously the idea that the Durkheimians themselves are engaged in "intellectual action ... [that] contains and continues the deeper religious attitude" to place oneself into contact with the "the ultimate ground of thought and experience" (Shils 1972: 16). But my argument is that there is contained within that Durkheimian effort to rigorously investigate the sacred as a foundational feature in the social life and forms of meaning of all societies not only a sociology of religion, nor even solely a sociology of knowledge geared to fathoming the primary categories of human perception and conceptualization; there is also an investigation of the piece of the human world which is itself of primary interest to intellectuals, and, as such, this effort is a process of inquiry into the nature and evolution of the intellectual and the intellectual life, and its orientation constitutes an intellectual *habitus* passed on in some specific historical and sociological ways to the poststructuralist thinkers.

What follows in the succeeding chapters is an examination of the work and lives of the poststructuralists and the Durkheimian sociology of religion group as something that is theoretically richer and more reflexive and existentially charged than traditional interpreters and biographers have generally acknowledged. Where commentators have tended to focus on narratives of the Durkheimians' efforts in their academic work to make sociology scientific, and in their personal lives to participate in a political project geared toward the creation of democratic and rational socialism, and of the poststructuralists' criticisms of foundationalist schools of thought and their personal investment in radical left political projects of various kinds, I argue that if interpretations of their intellectual project are too narrowly and exclusively posited, in the end they miss a key element of the meaning of those projects. In short, they fail to recognize that the poststructuralist and Durkheimian projects are fundamentally concerned with the nature, historical development, and cultural peculiarities of the intellectual life itself and its consequences and meanings for the rest of society, and this concern, manifested strikingly in both the works and lives of these thinkers, is a crucial lens through which we should view the specific details of their thought and action. A significant element of both of these projects involves an investigation of the situation of intellectuals and especially of the ways in which intellectuals commune with the sacred, and this study will demonstrate where that is going on in those projects, both explicitly and implicitly. I follow Shils's definition as far as it will reasonably take us, and therefore I read significant other elements of the intellectual projects of the poststructuralists and the Durkheimian religion cluster as ultimately more fully comprehensible only within the framework of an engagement with the sacred, and therefore with the very question of the nature of the intellectual life. What will emerge in the following chapters is a picture of the Durkheimians and the poststructuralists as "secularized cleric[s]" (Bélanger 1997: 83).

A Note on the Sociology of Intellectual Micro-societies

It is implicit in the above that it makes sense to talk about the small group of Durkheimians and poststructuralist thinkers named as distinct and coherent social groups, with some significant degree of mutual influence and interconnection and with an identity that allows us to distinguish them from other intellectuals and intellectual groups in their vicinity. But how can such a definition be defended, given the obvious fact that both groups clearly were in contact with and influenced by a wide variety of other intellectuals? What allows us to recognize these particular groupings as conceptual objects of examination that cohere and stand as legitimate?

Let me emphasize again that the central difference between this work and other recent works that have discussed some connections between Durkheimian thought and the birth of poststructuralism (e.g., Richman 2002; Stoekl 1992) has to do with methodology. Those works limit themselves to methods of literary criticism, though they do occasionally make use of certain elements of historical and social argument, however fleetingly and unsystematically. This is a study in the sociology of intellectual knowledge production and influence. The crux of my argument has to do with the connection between two groups of intellectuals in terms of macro- and micro-sociological factors: Through the media of specific institutional means and through other micro-social networks, a particular kind of Durkheimian project is communicated to a later generation of thinkers and taken up in a form recognizable as Durkheimian, despite obfuscation of this fact extending from certain other factors in the macro-intellectual environment in which the two forms of thought emerge. Therefore, it is of great importance that I demonstrate the reasonableness of talking about the Durkheimians and the poststructuralists examined here as discrete social units, rather than as unrelated individual atoms.

The case is close to self-evident for the Durkheimians. There is overwhelming evidence of the intellectual collaboration of Durkheim, Mauss, Hubert, and Hertz. These latter three men, and especially Mauss and Hubert, were Durkheim's closest collaborators and confidants in the *Année* project and in his broader intellectual, political, and private life. Mauss (1872–1950) was his nephew, the son of Durkheim's sister Rosine, and his closest intellectual colleague during the years from the establishment of the *Année* to his death. He became, upon Durkheim's death, the acknowledged inheritor and successor to the Durkheimian legacy without debate or challenge from others on the team, taking possession of the unpublished manuscripts and lectures of his uncle[1] in order to control their gradual dissemination to the intellectual world and assuming Durkheim's position as general editor of the *Année* in its ill-fated second series in 1925. Hubert (1872–1927), who was one of Mauss's closest friends and his long-term intellectual collaborator, was introduced to Durkheim and the *Année* through his relationship to Mauss, but developed a significant unmediated relationship to Durkheim, which stemmed from a combination of shared intellectual and political projects and a mutual concern for the moral direction of Mauss. Finally, Hertz (1883–1915), who was separated in age from Mauss and Hubert by almost ten years, was the student and close intellectual collaborator of both Durkheim and Mauss and was recognized by both as one of the most important young contributors to the *Année;* Durkheim would write in a biographical notice at Hertz's death in 1915 that he felt this blow "more painfully than anyone" as Hertz "had been [his] student and he remained [his] friend" (Durkheim 1975a: 439).

Philippe Besnard's authoritative account of the relationships among members of the *Année* team indicates more schematically the strength of the ties connecting Durkheim, Mauss, Hubert, and Hertz. In his network map of the Durkheimian team (Besnard 1983), the trio of Durkheim, Mauss, and Hubert make up the central cluster at the heart of the team; the only other team member to whom Durkheim had anything approaching such close ties is Paul Fauconnet, who was however separated from Mauss, Hubert, and Hertz by his areas of research and writing (largely in political organization and sociology). Hertz, although rightly characterized as only in the second rank of importance as an *Année* contributor, is recognized as ranking behind only Mauss and Fauconnet in terms of the degree of strength of his affiliation to Durkheim. This map of the network supports my claim for the central importance of the cluster examined here, if only from the standpoint of the role the group played in the production of work for and direction of the *Année.*

Beyond formal network maps of intellectual collaboration, we know from the voluminous correspondence among these four that their interconnection was not simply professional but personal. Mauss and Durkheim were members of the same family who often convened for family holidays together; Hubert was Mauss's closest friend, while Hertz was one of the most beloved students of the older men. In subsequent chapters, I make significant use of the correspondence among the group members to demonstrate nuances in their intellectual positions and identities.

What of the poststructuralist group, Foucault, Deleuze, Derrida, and Baudrillard? Its cohesiveness is perhaps not so obvious at first glance as it is for the Durkheimians, who worked closely together on the same journal for an extended period of time and authored numerous collective studies, but the evidence is still considerable. Foucault and Deleuze were exceptionally close intellectual companions beginning in the early 1960s until sometime in the mid 1970s, frequently commenting in writing on one another's work, working together on political and social issues, and socializing at the homes of friends. The two worked together at the University of Paris campus at Vincennes in the early 1970s, Deleuze arriving in 1969 explicitly as a result of Foucault's efforts. Their interconnections, however, go back even before this period of close collaboration, as both studied with Georges Canguilhem, the renowned historian of science who left lasting impressions on the intellectual perspectives of both. Foucault and Derrida shared an intellectual history as well, as both were *normaliens,* or graduates of the École Normale Supérieure, and they each commented (if sometimes critically) upon the work of the other; though close in age, Derrida also actually attended courses as a student given by Foucault at the École Normale. The two also shared some of the same "networks of sociability" (Rieffel 1993) with Deleuze; all three, for example, were affiliated during the 1960s and 1970s with the journal *Critique,* a fact explored in detail in Chapter 10.

Baudrillard is in some ways the relative outlier in this group, as perhaps Hertz is among the Durkheimians. His institutional history is significantly different than the experiences of the other three; he was never at any of the institutions at which they spent their intellectual careers (École des Hautes Études en Sciences Sociales, University of Paris Vincennes, Collège de France). He taught sociology (beginning as Henri Lefebvre's assistant) at the University of Paris Nanterre campus, which became best known for giving birth to the student movement that eventually ignited the events of May 1968, from 1966 to 1987. The fact that he was the only one of the four in this group who was not, in institutional terms, a philosopher (he taught in a department of sociology at Nanterre) meant he was somewhat excluded from some of the prestigious circles they inhabited in a French intellectual world where sociology was still seen as an inferior discipline. He had no deep association with the journal *Critique,* which joined the other three, though he did publish one piece with the journal during the period of the involvement of the other three (Baudrillard 1975). His early intellectual career was associated to a certain institutional degree with the anti-structuralist Marxism of Lefebvre, but his real intellectual mentor was Roland Barthes. Though not a sociologist, Barthes was influential among those in the social sciences who were becoming interested in semiotics during Baudrillard's early years as a scholar. He was a frequent attendee at important sociological conferences of the 1950s and 1960s (e.g., the 1956 conference on "La Crise de la sociologie," which also was attended by important French sociologists such as Georges Balandier, François Bourricaud, Michel Crozier, Jean Duvignaud, Lefebvre, Alain

Touraine, and Edgar Morin), and he taught courses on the sociology of signs (Rieffel 1993: 68). Baudrillard's work in the 1960s and early 1970s was heavily influenced by Barthes. In his own words, "Roland Barthes is someone to whom I felt very close, such a similarity of positions that a number of things he did I might have done myself" (Baudrillard 1993c: 203–04).

Here we find one of the central facts linking him to shared social worlds with the others, as Barthes clearly played a powerful, personal role in the early constitution of what would later become known as the structuralist movement. He knew Foucault extremely well; in fact, the two gay men were, according to some sources, occasional lovers until around 1960 and remained close friends afterwards. Barthes was also closely associated with the *Tel Quel* group, which also included Foucault and Derrida in its circle of intimate associates. I argue in Chapter 6 that Barthes can be considered a "master of ceremonies" in Arpad Szakolczai's terminology for the poststructuralist group. That Baudrillard knew the work of Deleuze, Derrida, and Foucault is obviously seen in his published responses to some of that work (e.g., Baudrillard 1977). He was also closely associated with Félix Guattari, who was a friend and collaborator of Deleuze from the late 1960s until the end of his life (L'Yvonnet 2004: 15–16). But it will become clearer just how much he shares with the other three when I have more fully explored the nature of the intellectual micro-societies they inhabited and the intellectual trajectories into which those micro-societies were oriented, a task undertaken in later chapters.

Before turning to that task, in the next chapter I set forth in more detail the theoretical principles underpinning this book. The structure of the remaining chapters adheres to a logic that I outline here to combat confusion as vigorously as possible. My method recognizes two sites in which the question of the intellectual's role in modern society is taken up by both of the intellectual micro-societies under examination here: in their intellectual work, and in the practice of their lives as social and political actors. A sociological interrogation of either of these two sites must certainly begin with an exploration of the general social and historical space in which their work and lives unfolded, with the goal of better understanding how their manner of taking up this question was affected by the general social field in which they found themselves. As the Durkheimians come first chronologically and provide the template for the poststructuralists, I start with them. In undertaking a sociology of Durkheimian knowledge production, I need to produce both a macro-sociological picture of the institutional field within which the Durkheimian work emerges (Chapter 3) and a micro-sociological picture of the more intimate, closer networks in which it is embedded (Chapter 4).

Once both of these elements are in place for the Durkheimians, I sub-sequently do the same for the poststructuralists (Chapters 5 and 6). This then provides the necessary grounding in sociological detail to show precisely how the Durkheimians and the poststructuralists made use of the notion of the sacred in their lived engagement in identity and politics (Chapters 7 and 11, respectively) and in their scholarly work (Chapters 8, 9, and 12). The remaining chapter in the book (Chapter 10) outlines how two institutions, the inter-war Collège de Sociologie and the journal *Critique,* provided embodied and interactional ways in which particular ways of thinking about and living the connection to the sacred could be transmitted from Durkheim's generation to that of the poststructuralists.

Notes

1. He would also, upon the deaths of Hertz and Hubert, collect their unpublished manuscripts and notes and assume responsibility for completing and then publishing substantial segments of this work. Further, he used their notes on various subjects (e.g., Hubert on the history of Celtic civilization, Hertz on sin and expiation) as a foundation for courses he gave at the École Pratique des Hautes Études and at the Collège de France.

2 Intellectual Production and Interpretation
The Intellectual Habitus

What can sociological work tell us about the meaning of intellectual work? This is the question at the heart of this book. I need to establish the basic theoretical and methodological principles with which to fill my toolkit for the task ahead. Fortunately, much of the hard thinking has already been done by others; my task here is simply to indicate what is being borrowed from whom and how it is being bent, sharpened, or otherwise altered it to fit my needs.

Intellectual Production *à la* Bourdieu

Pierre Bourdieu's theoretical framework for the study of intellectual production is presented in *The Field of Cultural Production* (1993). Unsurprisingly, his two most basic theoretical concepts, field and *habitus,* play key roles in his understanding of intellectual work. Some rehash of basics is justified at this point. The field is a historical and social grid in which actors interact according to field-specific laws, using field-specific varieties of social, economic, and cultural capital to compete with others for prestige and dominance. Fields are only relatively autonomous, as other fields can and do affect what happens in any given field, but the internal dynamics of any given field are the key to understanding behavior within it. All fields are characterized by a binary division between dominant and dominated elements within them. As intellectuals are among the dominant social classes, the intellectual field is located in the dominant end of what

Bourdieu refers to as the field of class relations. However, within the field of dominant social classes (the field of power), they occupy a dominated position *vis-à-vis* economic and political dominant groups. Thus, the field of cultural production makes up the *dominated* fraction of the field of power, which is itself *dominant* within the larger sphere of class relations (Bourdieu 1993: 38). This unique position means that there are two antagonistic principles of hierarchization, or modes in which competition is carried out and prestige earned, at work in the field of cultural production: a heteronomous principle that derives from economic and political capital and ranks works according to their market and political clout, and an autonomous principle that derives from cultural capital and ranks works according to internal, intellectual criteria (Bourdieu 1993: 40).

The existence of these two principles and their variable effects on different kinds of intellectual production enable us to better understand those different kinds of production. Some production within the cultural field is oriented primarily to markets external to that field, i.e., to audiences consisting of those who are not themselves cultural producers, while other cultural products are directed primarily toward audiences consisting of cultural producers or intellectuals. Although these different varieties of production can emerge from both university and extra-university intellectuals, the affiliation with an educational institution is one of the characteristics that serves generally to distinguish intellectual production along this line. Intellectual production by university teachers and researchers is generally oriented toward audiences of other such producers, although again, even within the field of university intellectual producers, we can find this same binary of the two principles of hierarchization at work. Indeed, Bourdieu speaks of a homology of the various fields in which one can trace certain kinds of opposition (that between producers for other producers and producers for external audiences, or that between holders of specifically cultural capital and holders of social and political capital) across all fields and see the same oppositions appear in a wide number of fields and sub-fields (Bourdieu 1984: 59).

Even before we look at the category of *habitus,* we might ask where and how this model of fields would situate Durkheimian and poststructuralist thought. Bourdieu did not direct his attention to the university milieu inhabited by the Durkheimians, but others utilizing his theoretical framework have. Jean-Louis Fabiani (1988) explains the institutional affiliations and orientations of the philosophers of the Third Republic by determining the alchemy by which specific class, geographic, familial, and educational capitals translated themselves, within the logic of the field, into certain positions. The struggle within the field is ultimately reducible in his analysis to a confrontation between philosophers of a spiritualist orientation and those of a positivistic bent. The former tend to hold an idea of philosophy as a singular and rather esoteric activity comprehensible only to those with a particular gift best described as aesthetic and who tend to come from families of the Parisian business class, while the latter reject the esoteric view of the discipline held by the spiritualists and tend to come from the provinces and the middle bourgeoisie (Fabiani 1988: 91–97). The distinction Fabiani delineates is traceable to two traditions in French philosophy, those of the descendants of Maine de Biran and Auguste Comte respectively, and he acknowledges that it maps easily onto the two dominant, constantly struggling forms of French philosophy indicated by Michel Foucault, namely, the philosophy of experience, meaning, and the subject, and the philosophy of knowledge, rationality, and the concept (Fabiani 1988: 160).

Fabiani groups the Durkheimians with the positivist philosophers, who are ranked along the autonomous principle of hierarchization. Their opponents within the field, the spiritualists, wield an inherited social capital and address an audience that extends beyond the reaches of the university and the sphere of other cultural producers. In a later effort to add complexity to this opposition, Fabiani has acknowledged two differentiable positivist philosophical positions in the Third Republic, one of which is that of the Durkheimians, who are true to the social origins of positivists (i.e., provincial sons of intellectuals), while the other is represented by the movement around Xavier Léon and the *Revue de métaphysique et de morale* and, though also positivist, shares the Parisian bourgeois origins of the spiritualists (Fabiani 1993).

The usefulness of such a mapping of the philosophical activity of the Third Republic is readily apparent. Fabiani closely links intellectual production within the philosophical sphere to transformations in the French university in the mid and late nineteenth century, showing how the increase in teaching posts resulting from the expansion of the university system led to an increased professionalization of the philosophical field that had previously been dominated by individuals situated outside the university. This professionalization demonstrated itself in the realm of publication as well, as nearly all the important academic philosophical journals in France appear during this period. He also endeavors to demonstrate how developments in the philosophical curriculum in the *lycées* and universities seemed to influence changes in the relative importance of philosophical sub-fields as reflected in thesis topics and books published. More specifically, he notes a marked increase in work in the realm of social and civic morality that is certainly linked to the direction of secular reforms of the university being carried out during the period (Fabiani 1988: 50–55).

However, the problematic side of this work becomes clearer when the categories of philosophical orientation are examined in more detail. Fabiani provides no real explication of the content of these categories. They are linked to particular social conditions of origin and institutional spaces with very little attention to the actual empirical manner in which spiritualism or positivism is manifested in the work and intellectual project itself. One can scarcely deny that there may be some representatives of the philosophical space for which such a demonstration is too obvious even to necessitate formal demonstration, but for the majority of producers active in the field this is not the case. Their lived enactment of a philosophical project in their work and position-taking in the field is more complicated and inconsistent.

Fabiani is clear about his view of the relation between the social conditions of emergence of an intellectual project and the shape of that project: "… theoretical choices and projects of individual careers should be related to transindividual dispositions produced by the inculcation of a homogeneous scholastic contents … and by a common experience of the social world which engenders identical perceptive schemas" (Fabiani 1988: 77). In other words, the shared experience of a social world and an institutional trajectory in which "objectified philosophy" is imparted to students is the framework to which we should turn in order to make sense of what seem individual choices on the part of the producers. Fabiani is arguing that the philosophical insistence of the period on the utter freedom of choice of the philosopher with respect to his work direction is precisely one of those characteristics that comes not from the individual but rather from the institutional inculcation of this disciplinary myth in the minds of all those so socialized. But is this kind of reductionism justified? If we reject it, are we then forced to argue for individualist explanations for particular intellectual projects and production as the only available alternative?

Before responding to these questions, let us consider additional Bourdieusian efforts to map the scene of Durkheimian sociology. Christophe Charle, in his attempt to use Bourdieu's model to understand the socialist movement at the École Normale Supérieure at the *fin-de-siècle*, is more nuanced than Fabiani. This group of socialist intellectuals (a number of whom, including Hubert and Hertz, were members of the *Année* team) is classifiable, given their intellectual and political position *vis-à-vis* their contemporaries, as avant-garde in both political and cultural terms insofar as its socialism stems from an elitist sense of political and cultural separation from the rest of French society (Charle 1994: 138–39). Charle adeptly shows how the bulk of the socialist students at the ENS are of comparatively disadvantaged socio-economic origin and reads their socialism as an effort to create a space of solidarity and integration within an institution in which they feel relatively ill at ease due to their comparative lack of the relevant capital needed for fuller integration. The destinies of these socialist intellectuals were split along the axis of intellectual work/politics, with some leaving the university and a research career for full-time militant political work while others retired from socialist politics in order to fully dedicate themselves to their research, and a third group attempted to keep a hand in both worlds (Charle 1994: 151–52). The proclivity of any given individual to choose a path from among these three options is neatly described by Bourdieu's notion of the role played by cultural capital in integrating or alienating individuals from institutional spaces. Those individuals who came from backgrounds that adequately prepared them for adjustment to the university world generally opted for a distancing from socialist politics and a full integration into that world for which they were so well suited, while those who chose the third, indecisive option generally had non-intellectual and relatively disadvantaged backgrounds that did not permit them to become fully acclimated to the institutional life of the university and that likewise made them comparatively less susceptible to total immersions in politics based on idealistic notions of the masses more typically seen in those from higher socioeconomic positions.

The problems that emerge from Charle's picture, however, are the same ones I noted in Fabiani. The categories posed are clear, and some individuals do easily fit in one or another of them, but there are complexities of trajectory that are difficult to reconcile with this analytical neatness. Hertz and Hubert, the two Durkheimian sociologists of religion included in his sample, should both be situated, according to the argument, in the third, indecisive category, but Hubert's socialist engagement, intense during his ENS years and the period of Latin Quarter agitation around the Dreyfus Affair, waned considerably subsequently and was essentially non-existent by the end of World War I. As I will show in Chapter 7, Hubert's socialism even at its most intense was an intellectualist, idealist socialism, while Hertz's was embodied and anti-intellectualist, and this distinction reveals important differences in their separate intellectual and personal projects. There exists abundant textual evidence, both published and unpublished, of the specificities of the manner in which the socialism of Hubert, Mauss, and Hertz was integrated into a larger intellectual and personal project that serves to complicate the clear categorizations of Charle. Like Fabiani, he classifies these various intellectual trajectories without a consideration of the most relevant traces of the projects, i.e., the works and other details of intellectual life in which those trajectories are most clearly described.

Elsewhere (1990), Charle has attempted to use Bourdieu's theory in understanding a broader sub-section of intellectual activity in the Third Republic concerning the positions taken by those intellectuals who intervened in the Dreyfus Affair. Political positions on the case of Dreyfus are strongly correlated with a number of sociological variables expressing, in Charle's view, an objective state of crisis in the intellectual field. Among university teachers and researchers, Dreyfusards are younger, more likely to occupy dominated positions in the university hierarchy and to be affiliated with disciplines in the social and physical sciences, and more Protestant or Jewish than anti-Dreyfusards, who are older, affiliated with more dominant educational institutions and traditional disciplines, and disproportionately Catholic. Among literary intellectuals, the same divisions according to age and institutional consecration apply and, additionally, we find Dreyfusards disproportionately grouped among the avant-garde literary genres, while those who oppose them are more often to be found in traditional genres (Charle 1990: 193–212). In this work, much like in Bourdieu's analysis of the post-1968 French intellectual scene, the underlying principle of the Bourdieusian sociology of intellectual production is on clear display. Here it becomes obvious that the focus of the method is to attempt to explain the *political* position-taking of the intellectual class, be it *vis-à-vis* the highly charged Dreyfus Affair or the equally electric events of May 1968 in France.

What then of Bourdieusian efforts to understand and situate the poststructuralists? Bourdieu and Louis Pinto have contributed a number of works on this theme that have the same promise and the same limits already observed in the work on the Durkheimians. Pinto's two books (1986, 1995) on the philosophical field in which poststructuralism emerged echo Fabiani's argument in a number of ways. Pinto finds the field of French philosophy in the 1960s characterized by the opposition of two polar positions: a "scholarly, orthodox pole" faces a "worldly, prophetic or avant-garde pole" (Pinto 1986: 63, 173). The two positions are sketched out with reference to two empirical representatives, Ferdinand Alquié and Jacques Derrida, who had nearly identical educational histories, but whose careers differed by their professional rank, the institutions in which they taught, and the publishers who distributed their work (Pinto 1986: 173–74). Unlike Fabiani, Pinto has little to say about the social origins of these two philosophical types, but in other ways Fabiani's spiritualists are much like Pinto's prophets: anti-scientific, rooted in a humanities/literary tradition, and directed toward an audience largely outside the specialist audience of other academics. Fabiani's positivists and Pinto's orthodox are likewise parallel in many ways: Both are rooted in a culture of specialization and scientificity. A significant difference, owing to shifts in the overall intellectual institutional field since the Third Republic, has to do with the fact that the orthodox philosophers, unlike the positivists of the earlier period, occupy prominent positions in the most prestigious Parisian intellectual institutions. Earlier, the positivists were the upstarts attempting to crack the institutional walls, but the general tenor of philosophy had changed significantly enough between the two periods to make the desire to be more scientific normative (Pinto 1986: 109).

Structuralism would explicitly call on this narrative in attacking the orthodoxy, claiming to be the "true scientific method" in philosophy and the human sciences, while poststructuralism would distance itself radically from this part of its structuralist heritage. However, for Pinto, both structuralism and poststructuralism are to be found in the ranks of the prophetic philosophers in that they seek to move philosophy outside the traditional academic channels and audiences and, in their frequent choice of literary topics, both align philosophy with a literary tradition. Some of the difficulty with Pinto's categories begins to emerge here, and he indirectly points to it himself when he has a difficult time classifying Michel Foucault in his system. Foucault can be located, depending on what period of his work one considers, in either the camp of those dedicated to philosophy as a wing of scientific culture (the Foucault of the work on psychology and medicine) or the camp of the literary philosophical avant-garde (the Foucault of the work on Raymond Roussel or Magritte) (Pinto 1986: 92–102; 1995: 134).

Bourdieu's major work taking up the poststructuralist movement is his book-length study of Heidegger (Bourdieu 1988). Here, in an indirect way, he launches the most serious of criticisms against those in the French poststructuralist movement who had taken up Heidegger's work in an effort to construct a leftist philosophical program to challenge the establishment. While those partisans of the German philosopher had claimed that his engagement with Nazism was detachable from the core of his philosophical writing, Bourdieu's close reading of Heidegger's central terminology endeavors to show that fascism is deeply implicated in that very terminology. Heidegger's *habitus* is reconstructed, beginning with an examination of the purported post-Weimar disposition toward nature and mysticism and proceeding through an investigation of Heidegger's origins in the provincial, anti-intellectual petite bourgeoisie. Finally, the terminology of Heidegger's philosophical oeuvre is "revealed" to be fundamentally tied to a fascist politics. "Alienation" for Heidegger is considered only in its ontological context, rejecting what Bourdieu sees as the far more central question of economic alienation, and "care" is defined in such a way as to bolster a reactionary, anti-mass politics that sees the "mob" as frivolous, incapable of caring for themselves, and dependent on others for their care (Bourdieu 1988: 68–85).

Again, the argument here regarding French poststructuralism is indirect. Nowhere does Bourdieu actually discuss in his theoretical terms the conditions and positions of the poststructuralists directly, but the entire book is framed as a kind of warning to and dismissal of those among Bourdieu's intellectual contemporaries who were interested in Heidegger as a solution to philosophical and political problems. Elsewhere, Bourdieu (2004: 17) discusses in biographical terms his antagonism to the "belief in the omnipotence of rhetorical invention" and the model of "professorial aristocratism" embodied chiefly in his generation by French followers of Heidegger.

One point shines brightly in all of these Bourdieusian efforts to sociologically frame the Durkheimians and the poststructuralists. Although these authors acknowledge repeatedly that an immense amount of information goes into occupying any position in the cultural field and thereby also into the process of fully explaining it (see, e.g., Bourdieu 1993: 32), the explanation from this model seemingly always reduces to a mapping of the *political* position of the participant in the cultural field. Indeed, for Charle, and more generally for Bourdieu, the crux of activity in the cultural sphere is no different than what is central to activity in other spheres: The goal of all actors and all actions is everywhere and always to destroy opponents and to become the dominant force within the field from which position one can then set the definitions as to what is and is not worthy of attention within the field. It may not seem unreasonable to follow Charle in seeking to trace Dreyfusard and anti-Dreyfusard political positions to class origins, religious affiliation and institutional situation and status and then to understand the political struggle over the fate of Dreyfus in terms of more general struggles for power within the cultural and other fields between "two Frances ... the optimism of the democratic wave breaking through all caste barriers of the left 'intellectual'... against the pessimism of the besieged fortress of the 'elite' menaced by the mob or of the nation corrupted by foreign minorities of the 'intellectuals' of the right" (Charle 1990: 225–26). However, a problem arises when works and projects are made to submit to this political logic of war against opponents, and the aspect of intellectual self-construction and identity that is part and parcel of their status *vis-à-vis* the historically evolving notion of the sacred disappears completely. It may well be that there are players in the cultural field whose actions are completely determinable as political calculations designed to maximize their power in the field and to destroy foes, but it seems overly simple to make this a functional imperative for cultural producers in general and to reduce *all* intellectual activity in this way. From the Bourdieusian perspective, one can perhaps understand much regarding the relationship of the cultural field to other, larger social fields, and even between obviously competing and oppositional sub-fields within the cultural field, but what of the nuances of much more local networks of collaborators and colleagues working on projects that are not so clearly about attaining the dominant position in the field? What of the works that emerge from projects that are explicitly or implicitly reflexive attempts to understand or construct the self?

The *Habitus* Reconstituted in an Experientialist Framework

Despite the preceding criticisms, I do not intend to simply reject Bourdieu's genetic structuralist approach to intellectual production. With appropriate modification, it can greatly aid in the understanding of intellectual production. Let us go back to the concept of the *habitus*. Bourdieu defines it as the "durably installed generative principle of regulated improvisations ... a practical sense which reactivates the sense objectified in institutions ... inscribed in bodies by identical histories" (Bourdieu 1990[1980]: 57). It acts as a set of predispositions to action on the part of individuals socialized in objectively identical social conditions that make inevitable certain trajectories for those actors when properly combined with the specific institutional structures whose logic is encoded in them. The concept permits the sociologist to escape completely from the language of the individual and to read what is in more conventional accounts described in the vague language of individual will or whim as fundamentally social. But there is a certain predisposition of the category itself to a sociological determinism that tends toward a reduction of cultural production to a reified calculus in which structure creates *habitus*, which determines practices, which in turn reproduce the same structures. Although Bourdieu rejects such a reading of his theory, the bulk of his empirical work on intellectual production frankly tends in this determinist direction.

I propose a modified definition of *habitus* that avoids this determinism yet does not thereby detach the concept from its anti-individualist logic. I want to retain the notion of a fundamentally relationally-generated set of predispositions but avoid mapping it uncritically onto a static macrosocial grid. We simply cannot be so quick to presume from the categories of conventional sociology, e.g., social class or ethnicity, that individuals who share membership in one or more of these categories therefore share the same objective *habitus*. Talking about a "working class *habitus*" is inevitably a deformation of reality. This is not to deny that such a category may indeed tell us something real about shared characteristics across some group of individuals. But we can and should deny that talking about such a category means all we need do is classify particular individuals in the relevant class in order to know everything meaningful about their *habitus*. The concept of *habitus* must be complicated by an understanding that the formative experiences of individuals, while always deeply social, are never *objectively identical*. So, Bourdieu is doubtless correct when he argues that university institutions attempt to produce and recruit students with a specific *habitus* (Bourdieu 1984: 56–57), but it must be added that they likely *never* fully succeed in this task, as the *habitus* of specific individuals is informed by social networks and experiences beyond those of that institution alone.

While attempting to integrate Marxist sociological principles dialectically into existentialist analysis, Jean-Paul Sartre vehemently rejected the kind of "lazy Marxism" that would, for example, reduce the poet Paul Valéry to an abstract cipher for the socio-economic class from which he sprang. His theory, he argued, offers a way "to find mediations that allow the concrete individual—the particular life, the real and dated conflict, the person—to emerge from the background of the *general* contradictions of productive forces and relations of production" (Sartre 1968[1960]: 55–57). In the same way, I want to attempt to make use of Bourdieu's categories more concretely than he himself does. Just as Valéry is the product of relational, social forces and fortuities that elude simple macro-attention to his membership in the social class of the petite bourgeoisie (e.g., his formative experience within his family, his educational and early intellectual encounters, his relations to teachers and colleagues, etc.), so too are the Durkheimians and the poststructuralists the products of social networks and histories that are too complicated to allow them to be reduced to cookie-cutter petit bourgeois products of the École Normale Supérieure. Histories, while always social, are also distinct enough to merit closer attention to the details that contribute to significant differences in such predispositions, especially in such cases when the product being examined (intellectual work) is *defined* by nuance and subtle distinction from the start.

Nick Crossley (2001) has injected some of this nuance into the notion of the *habitus* by suggesting the need to augment it with Merleau-Ponty's idea of habits. These are embodied, learned skills that are acquired not intellectually but by doing something. Some habits are learned by imitation of others (e.g., brushing one's teeth as a child), others arise through "innovative and creative praxes" or combine imitation and innovation (e.g., the specific way one has to push, turn, and wriggle a key to make the sticky lock on the front door open). Ultimately, though, all action becomes part of an embodied individual's being by becoming habituated. We constantly learn new habits and our individual corporeal schema is constantly changing, albeit slightly and slowly. Crossley calls this situation a "moving equilibrium" (2001: 137). In this view, though most of the habits individuals have will be shared among other members of the groups to which they belong, an individual's corporeal schema or bodily *habitus* is never completely identical to that of any other individual because their experiences are not exactly the same. If thus for bodies, so too for ideas and intellectual projects.

Phil Smith has still more recently (2004) proposed another writer with whom we might enlist to enrich Bourdieu's notion of *habitus:* Marcel Proust. He notes that, although it deals with characters who are only partially or compositely nonfictional, Proust's work is widely recognized as constituting "a systematic phenomenology of human action and mental life as well as an implicit cosmology of class in so far as this influences behavior" (2004: 108). While much of the work of a structural picture of Parisian class society that we find in Bourdieu can also be located in Proust's *Remembrance of Things Past*, we also find in the latter a much more nuanced effort to grapple with the contingent elements of identity construction and maintenance. The self as sexualized and motivated by desire intersects with the self formed by class relations, and "[u]nanticipated encounters with people and objects" move selves in directions that cannot be very well tracked by purely structural models (P. Smith 2004: 110). The end result in Proust's account is a self that is multiple, even chaotic and contradictory, which must be reconstructed with great analytical care and sophistication.

The fact that Smith invokes *a novelist* as an exemplar of the analysis of *habitus* is not itself an entirely innovative move. Bourdieu himself wrote a number of essays on Gustave Flaubert in which he treats the novelist as a forefather in the same sociological tradition to which he belongs. Much of French realist fiction of the mid to late nineteenth century saw itself as a competitor of sorts with the emerging discipline of sociology for the right to speak authoritatively about social life and identity in modernity (Riley 2006). Smith's suggestion that we should understand the tasks of the sociologist of knowledge and the novelist as unitary because they both must come to grips with the inescapability of narrative, dramatic genre and style in understanding the meaning of a life (i.e., meanings require narratives) marks his intervention here as innovative. The cultural sociological framework within which he is working offers some powerful tools for understanding intellectual life-works in terms of cultural narratives. I will have more to say about this a bit later on in this chapter.

Questions about Texts: What Counts as "the Intellectual Work"?

Where ought one look to find evidence of the points of generation, innovation, and change in an intellectual project? The question is far from
straightforward, as possible responses are to a significant degree influenced by the *a priori* notion of just what constitutes an intellectual project
that a researcher brings to the analysis at its outset. One can define as
irrelevant or unimportant before the fact a certain genre of document
or site of examination due to an overly rigid adherence to a given model
of interpretation. Any attempt to get at the sociological conditions of the
emergence of a project must be vigilant with respect to such predeter-
minations of focus. If one is interested in understanding the emergence
of thought as a process that is deeply imbedded in the existential conditions of the life that produces it, one is faced precisely with the questions of defining what is and what is not "part of the work" that are raised
in dramatic fashion by Foucault in his celebrated essay on authorship
(Foucault 1977: 118–19). Dominick LaCapra provides a useful response
to this problem of evaluating the role texts play in an intellectual project.
He discusses the difference in status we tend to attribute to, on the one
hand, *works* (e.g., *The Phenomenology of Mind*) and, on the other, *documents*
(e.g., a tax roll or a will). The difference maps directly to Austin's performative and constative speech acts. Respectively, the one brings about a
change in situational context, while the other describes and is measured
by its correspondence to facts. We tend to presume the differences are
fundamental, but LaCapra argues convincingly that both document and
work contain documentary and work-like textual components that call
for a careful deciphering of the two in each kind of text. This is generally
in keeping with Sartre's approach to reading intellectual projects, and
LaCapra elsewhere refers explicitly to Sartre's method in examining the
life projects of Baudelaire, Genet, and Flaubert as examples of this need
for attention to the complex intertwining of work and document in the
construction of the meaning of an intellectual life. In the case of Genet,
Sartre is concerned with texts of work-like or documentary quality in their
"existential function for Genet's personal development" (LaCapra 1978:
181). Thus, it is clear that one cannot simply bracket off one or the other
of the two kinds of texts before the fact, as it is their mutual relationship
to the life and work that is important.

   It might perhaps be objected that this is all well and good for an exceptional sort of creative intellectual like Genet, but that different standards ought to apply to scientific intellectuals. Surely, such a critic might
note, it is at least clear that normal science, in Kuhnian terms, need not be
studied in this manner. But the point about the deeply existential nature

of any intellectual project is certainly not limited to those like the individuals examined by Sartre. Moreover, the poststructuralist group and the Durkheimian group must be seen as deeply existentially concerned individuals whose projects, while obviously not reducible to purely personal concerns, are nonetheless inevitably tied to them. Therefore, we need a more holistic approach to deciding which textual evidence constitutes relevant evidence concerning their life and works than that suggested by some analysts (see e.g., Schmaus 1994).

Correspondences and Experiences in Intellectual Production

The reconstruction of the real networks in which intellectuals work obviously necessitates the consultation of texts beyond the realm of the published, prepared-for-public-consumption work. Correspondence and other non-published sources offer insights into the lived development of ideas and position-takings. In the case of the Durkheimians, who were engaged in a highly collective endeavor and did much work and thinking through correspondence, this methodological tool is only that much more essential to constructing the meaning of their intellectual project. These sources offer the researcher insight into a thinker's work that is unavailable in published work (Blum 1992: 3). They are a powerful contribution to a sociological theory of intellectual production insofar as they can bridge the gap between the intimacies of the thought process itself, which, absent documentation and empirical verification, is too easily relegated to internal and individualist processes, and the primordial sociality and dialogical quality of intellectual production.

    Correspondences are not, however, all alike. In his study of the correspondence between Henri Lefebvre and Norbert Guterman, Michel Trebitsch defines two types of intellectual correspondence, each of which enables reconstruction of intellectual production and explication of intellectual projects that is impossible from published sources. The first he names "network correspondence" (*correspondance-réseau*), which is that among a group of mutually-affiliated intellectuals, often organized around a central figure, who share some common objective or official project. This type is often semi-official in character and is generally "less interesting in its contents than in its function" (Racine and Trebitsch 1992: 70–84). It provides insights into the sociological emergence and operation of intellectual networks and their structure, organizational hierarchy and durability. It may often consist of the quasi-official correspondence among the members of a scholarly journal or a department that deals with institutional and formal organizational questions and issues. Some of the correspondence between Durkheim and the lesser members of the *Année* team and that among those lesser figures (e.g., Célestin Bouglé, Paul Lapie and Dominique Parodi) fits this definition (Besnard 1983: 40–70), as does the correspondence among members of the *Critique* editorial group (which included Foucault and Derrida) dedicated to the mundane business of assigning reviewing chores.

The second type of correspondence Trebitsch defines is "laboratory correspondence" (*correspondance-laboratoire*). Here, the interest lies not simply at the organizational level, but at the substantive level of ideas. As in the case of the correspondence between Lefebvre and Guterman, this type is characterized by a close intellectual friendship between intellectuals who share common preoccupations of an aesthetic and/or ideological nature and who utilize their correspondence as a sort of laboratory for the testing of concepts and subjects, and in which the correspondent is viewed as a sounding board for the very process of intellectual production. However useful network correspondence is for understanding the formal organization of intellectual networks, it is in this second type that we are more likely to see the emergence of the ideas themselves and of their relation to the lives and engagements of the thinkers involved. Clear examples of this kind of correspondence abound in the existing correspondence among the central members of the Durkheimian group. For example, the voluminous correspondence of Mauss and Hubert, and especially that of the period from 1896 until the war, during the period when their collective work was proceeding at its most feverish pace, is almost an ideal type of this kind of correspondence. In these letters, one finds not only the organizational language of the *Année sociologique* hierarchy, but a concentrated treatment of themes in the work, a mutual working-through of various problems and dilemmas faced in their common projects and the development of an intellectual and personal camaraderie that shows the ways in which the intellectual project is related to personal and existential concerns. I will make ample use of this kind of correspondence in the interpretive work presented in later chapters.

There is a third type of correspondence, not present in Trebitsch's model, that we might add to this typology of intellectual correspondence, a type we can call "experience correspondence" (*correspondance-expérience* or *correspondance-existentielle*). This type is significantly more difficult in some ways to identify, as it is neither purely theoretical and scholarly, nor purely devoted to description of the practical exigencies of everyday intellectual communication. We can think of this third type of correspondence as a primary textual site wherein the connection is most apparent between the intellectual project (the abstract scientific, philosophical, or artistic inquiry) and the personal, existential project (the lived and anxious engagement by the individual in the attempt to construct meaning in the face of death and chaos). Here, one finds the clearest evidence of the evolution and the playing out of a *life-work* in Arpad Szakolczai's (1998) terms. Intellectual theories and work are not held apart from lived experience but can be shown to intersect. Indeed, one can see here the application of the one in the other, and the interplay works in both directions. Examples among the Durkheimian group can be found in the letters of Hertz and Mauss from the front during the war, or in Durkheim's letters to Mauss on the latter's commitment to the career of scholar or on the effect upon them of the deaths of various *Année* members in the war, or in the Mauss-Hubert letters in which the two discuss their own callings to the intellectual priesthood and their anxieties in the face of such decisions. In all these examples, one can retrieve insights into the actual level of meaning of the work in the life of the individual involved, i.e., the sense of the work in practical terms for the individual's own struggle for meaning and order. Such writing can be motivated by particular extreme experiences, as is the case with the letters of Hertz and Mauss from the front, that throw the individual into situations from which he or she displays in a more brilliant light the existential import of the ideas that he or she normally engages with more distance and reflection. Journal or other writing to self that is directed to this kind of reflection on the life-work intersection can also be placed in this category.

We face practical archival limitations in consulting this kind of text. For the poststructuralists, we do not often have access to this kind of unpublished, private information yet, as they are so recently deceased that the archival collections are yet incomplete and unavailable to researchers, or family members have made explicit decisions not to turn over such correspondences to archives. Nonetheless, there are numerous other informal textual sites such as interviews and documentary films[1] to which I will turn attention in establishing an overall picture of the work that accounts for as many elements as possible of their intellectual formation and position-takings.

Sites of Intellectual Production: Intellectual Interaction Rituals

So the question of which documents we ought to look to for evidence of the nature of intellectual production is complex. So too is that of which empirical sites of intellectual production we should consider. For Bourdieu and others influenced by his thought, the central collective entity influencing intellectual production is the cultural field generally and its subdivisions, i.e., the dominated and dominant poles within the field.

Terry Clark (1973) examined the Durkheimians through a consideration of the smaller, more local group he called the *cluster*. More recently, Randall Collins (1998; 2004) has gone still further in constructing a theory of the local situation as the starting point for the understanding of intellectual production. Borrowing the notion of *interaction rituals* from Erving Goffman (1982), he argues that the fundamental moment of intellectual production takes place in these local situations in which the following three ingredients are present: 1) a group of at least two people is physically assembled; 2) they focus attention on the same object or action, and each becomes aware that the other is maintaining this focus; and 3) they share a common mood or emotion (Collins 1998: 22).

These situations in which the symbols of a community are generated and engaged with are the intellectual equivalent to the religious rituals that are the source of meaning-production for religious groups. Intellectuals, Collins argues, create and internalize the symbols necessary for their individual and group identity in local, ritualistic activity that yet, because of the peculiarly universalistic and transcendental nature of their claims, links them to a network that exceeds that physically present at any one given interaction ritual. The ideal empirical sites in which intellectual interaction rituals take place are events such as the public lecture or formal debate, as it is here that intellectuals pursue the sacred object, "truth," through the concrete ritual activities of argument and "serious talk" (Collins 1998: 25–26). It is only in such concerted periods of sustained discussion and argument that symbols of a sufficiently complex and abstract level can be generated, manipulated, and internalized.

This notion of the interaction ritual has a significant amount of utility in the sociological exploration of intellectual production. Moreover, Collins's indication that an intellectual's trajectory can be fruitfully investigated as an *interaction ritual chain*, i.e., as a specific historical sequence of these interaction rituals over time and space, points us in the direction of a thoroughly sociological approach to understanding intellectual production that still provides some safeguards against the kind of reductionism into which Bourdieu falls. These interaction ritual chains would be at once thoroughly social and yet by definition not fully structurally determined. There is, however, a significant difficulty in Collins's definition of the intellectual interaction ritual that limits its capacity to thoroughly examine intellectual production, at least that which is the product of reflexive and innovative intellectuals. To define the central moment of intellectual ritual interaction as that of the public talk, lecture, conference, etc. is an excessively narrow reading of the symbolic and generative process in intellectual production. Of course this is an important and powerfully social site of the process, but it is far from clear that it is the *central* site in which intellectual production is generated. Collins is eager to separate this, which he sees as representative of the "serious talk" of intellectual existence, from "mundane, non-intellectual thoughts" and activities in which intellectuals engage, but how can we determine in an *a priori* fashion that the important work only really gets done in the sites of public ritual?

We can perhaps draw a telling parallel here with the religious life of the believer. No one would argue that the sites and experiences of public ritualistic display and collective acts of worship should be discounted from a study of the religious experience, but could one argue that the elements of the religious experience of the believer that take place outside those sites are non-religious? In fact, do not moments of extreme importance for this experience (conversion experiences, for example, or mystical experiences of particular intensity) often take place outside those sites of public ritual? Likewise, we must endeavor to find the elements of the intellectual experience that are not fully present in those public rituals if our goal is a complex understanding of intellectual production, and particularly so when the intellectuals under investigation are the kind of reflexive intellectuals whose projects cannot neatly be separated from their lives and everyday experiences. It is perhaps not unimportant that it is a byword in intellectual circles that, *contra* Collins, the bulk of what happens in public conferences and debates and the like among professional intellectuals is at least as much about explicit politicking and socializing as it is about concept generation and development, if not more so (Berger 1963: 11).

Perhaps there are intellectuals whose key moments of intellectual development and identification can be directly traced to such public rituals, but surely there are many who would on the contrary claim that the chief moments of their own conceptual generation and penetration by communal symbols came in other, less public but still social sites and networks. If the public rituals Collins describes can be defined, still adhering to his Goffmanian framework, as the *front-stage* of intellectual interaction rituals, we must include elements of the *back-stage* of that same ritual process in order to more fully understand the knowledge and projects generated. Questions of what is front-stage and what is back-stage become more complex when the intellectuals involved approach their work with something other than a purely professional attitude. The kinds of projects described by Szakolczai (1998) or by Pierre Hadot in his work on Stoic philosophers (1981), which can be translated only as a holistic life, a total praxis weaving together front-stage and back-stage, render problematic the sort of strict analytical delineation we find in Collins. Finally, Collins's insistence on front-stage interactions as the key elements in intellectual production merely reinforces his reliance on a conflict model for interpreting action in this sphere. Like Bourdieu, he is so convinced that intellectual production must be primarily motivated by conflict ("Intellectual life is first of all conflict and disagreement" (Collins 1998: 1)) that, though he may well be right in the main, he thoroughly overlooks how cooperation works in intellectual production.

An excellent example of the kind of alternative sites to which one must be prepared to look to understand intellectual production sociologically is provided by the recent attention of sociologists and intellectual historians to the role played by the café and the brasserie as site of intellectual production and network-building in French culture. It is well-known that "the golden triangle" of brasseries (Le Balzar, Le Soufflot, and Le Champo) have played an essential role as an intellectual site for the manifestation of sociability in Simmelian terms (Rieffel 1993: 36).

Whether one is examining the existentialist/*Les Temps modernes* group around Sartre and de Beauvoir at the Café de Flore, the surrealists at the Café le Cyrano, the role played by the Pont-Royal as the preferred café of the Gallimard editorial team, or the Twickenham as the general headquarters for the editorial team at Grasset around Bernard-Henri Lévy, it is clear that here we have an important local site of intellectual production that eludes the attention of the Bourdieusians as well as those like Collins who are more attentive to the local but still too focused on the public, professional sites of intellectual frequentation (Racine and Trebisch 1992; Rieffel 1993). Though cafés do not make up an important site of intellectual production for the groups I am studying, there are numerous other non-public, non-professional sites that do, e.g., the political meeting and the family home (where Durkheim often invited Mauss and sometimes Hubert to work together). In the case of the poststructuralists, there are other examples of such typically French sites for intellectual interaction, including "La Roulotte," which was the name given the apartment of Yves Montand and Simone Signoret in the 1960s and 1970s at which groups of their intellectual friends (including Foucault and Deleuze) gathered for socialization, conversation and political strategizing. Other examples here are the apartment of Paule Thévenin, which was frequently the site of "private" reunions of the *Tel Quel* group, which included Derrida and Foucault, and indeed the apartment of Foucault himself (Rieffel 1993: 48, 51, 54).

The Narrative of Intellectual Production

Arpad Szakolczai's work provides us with some of the keys to understanding the simultaneously intellectual and existential nature of some kinds of intellectual projects. He points us to the notion of the *life-work* as a project that is both research problem as documented in intellectual work *and* lived engagement with existential questions that extend from and are inseparable from the research problem. He too understands the process of the intellectual project as centered around ritualistic production and internalization of symbols, even if his understanding is rather more embodied than that of Collins. The key concept he uses to understand how intellectuals engage these ritualistic processes is that of the *experience*, which Szakolczai defines in the sense of its Latin etymology as "trial, proof, experiment, peril, danger and testing" (Szakolczai 1998: 22). Experiences which are undergone by intellectuals are of various types (e.g., childhood experiences, reading experiences, reflexive experiences), but all share the fundamental status of rites of passage, i.e., moments of lived reality in which an individual moves through a liminal phase of transformation with the aid of a social network of *masters of ceremonies* that entails at its conclusion a change in the individual's mode of being (1998: 23–33). Masters of ceremonies can be encountered face-to-face or they can be met in textual form, but in either case they are met during the formative years of an intellectual's career and play a crucial role in the negotiation of specific intellectual initiations, such as the entry into particular institutional positions. In borrowing the analytical tools that Victor Turner formulated as a response to the structural functionalist stranglehold on the discipline of anthropology, Szakolczai likewise offers the sociology of knowledge production a powerful means to respond to reductionist structuralist methods. This notion of experience as a sort of modern rite of passage offers us still another useful tool with which to read intellectual production. Indeed, it provides a careful way to discuss sociologically the production of intellectual knowledge and projects in a manner that is attentive to both existential micro-situations and to structural factors.

In talking about rites of passage and ceremonies, we are in the realm of narratives. The symbolic and interpretive strain in anthropology from which Szakolczai borrows takes human culture as fundamentally about the business of story-telling. He is interested primarily in certain kinds of stories that Turner labels *social dramas*, which involve a process by which an individual or sub-group breaks away from a group, experiences crisis, locates a remedy, and reassesses his or her position *vis-à-vis* the original social groups (V. Turner 1980). Another, more systematic effort in the sociology of knowledge that has explored with great care the role of narrative in culture is that of Jeffrey Alexander and the Yale Strong Program in Cultural Sociology that he founded, along with his student and colleague Philip Smith. Borrowing from the work of Clifford Geertz, Alexander takes up as his own Geertz's notion of "thick description" in order to build a cultural theory capable of rendering culture as actual actors do, i.e., as narratives in which action is sensible precisely because of the place it occupies in the narrative. Culture is in this sense textual, and, again following Geertz, can be reproduced as a text. However, Alexander goes beyond Geertz in arguing that a basic set of oppositions is present in all or virtually all cultural narratives. These oppositions are in fact those fundamentally religious ones having to do with sacredness and profaneness to which the Durkheimians dedicated so much attention in their own work. These foundational narrative elements are the tools that enable Alexander to avoid the hermeneutical relativism of Geertz and instead suggest a narrative theory that is both hermeneutical and structuralist. Alexander and Smith borrow further from various contemporary narrative and genre theories to point to a number of basic narrative genres (e.g., tragedy, irony, the morality play) that can be studied across societies.

Alexander's work provides still more nuanced conceptual language and tools for an understanding of intellectual production and life-works. Intellectuals are no different than any other cultural actors: They too need narratives, and they get their narratives from the same sources mined by others. The cultural sociology of intellectuals must be about the reconstruction of the narratives that make up their life-works. It will escape no one's attention that, in mining Alexander's cultural theory for my own work, I propose using a program for the study of cultural production derived in significant part from Durkheim in order to study Durkheim himself. This should be read as an indication that the work of Durkheim, like the work of any great theorist of the social world, must necessarily be applicable to an understanding of the life of the theorist himself as well as the lives of everyone else in society.

Note

1. There exist at least two films about Derrida (*D'ailleurs Derrida* (2000) and *Derrida* (2002)), one about Baudrillard (*Mots de passe* (1999)), and one about/with Deleuze (*L'Abécédaire de Gilles Deleuze* (1996)).

3 The Scene of Durkheimian Sociology

A View of the Parisian Intellectual Field at the Turn of the Nineteenth Century

We can date the period during which the core activity of the Durkheimians takes place roughly from 1896 to 1914. The first date is the year of the founding of the *Année* and Durkheim's first meeting with Hubert through his nephew. The latter date marks the outbreak of World War I, and both Hertz and Durkheim died during the war, while Hubert had little more than half a decade to live following its conclusion. The period of the greatest influence of the Durkheimians, at least in terms of their presence and power in the university and publishing worlds and in political organization and activity, maps roughly onto this period, which is nearly identical to the lifespan of the first edition of the *Année* (1898 to 1913).

The landscape into which the work of the Durkheimian sociologists of religion must be situated is at once cultural and political, and I will reconstitute key elements of both the cultural and political worlds in which they participated, while noting that the two frequently intersected. The period of the French Third Republic (1870 to 1940), and even the much smaller period set out above as the central period of formation and activity of the Durkheimian religion cluster, is overflowing with historical significance for French politics and culture generally and for the French intellectual specifically. In Chapter One, I suggested that three broad problematics emerged to confront the French intellectual in the Third Republic, resulting from the larger political, social, and cultural shifting brought by the rise of the Republic itself. These involved debates over:

1) the proper political role of the intellectual; 2) the proper intellectual means for understanding human action and especially the proper place of the new social sciences in this sphere; and 3) the formulation of a secular morality and moral pedagogy to replace the rapidly declining moral authority of the Roman Catholic Church, an institution that actively opposed the new Republic.

These problematics demanded responses on the part of intellectuals as part of both their scholarly work and their personal efforts to construct modern identities as intellectuals and citizens. My examination of the French intellectual field of the period is centered within the parameters of these three problematics, and I focus on them through the lenses of three events. These specific events, or areas of dispute, are more or less clearly defined in terms of time and space to the period under examination, and they demonstrate with great clarity the efforts by our group to respond to the exigencies of the intellectual situation and to situate themselves *vis-à-vis* other positions in the field. The three events, each of which is tied to at least one of the problematics, are: 1) the Dreyfus Affair; 2) the establishment of sociology as a legitimate competitor of the traditionally dominant academic discipline, i.e., philosophy, and the frequently antagonistic relations of the two; and 3) the debates over educational and pedagogical reform in the Third Republic.

As the activity of the Durkheimians is most obviously bounded, first, by the French academic world of the university and *lycée* systems; second, by the professional intellectual institutions that were formally outside the university system but that participated significantly nonetheless in French cultural life; and, third, by the institutions of scholarly publications, I begin my examination of the three key events with the last one listed above.

The Educational Reform Movement in France in the Third Republic

The end of the nineteenth century is, as Christophe Charle (1983: 77) notes, "a privileged epoch for an attempt at a social history of the university field" because it is a period during which the number of university professors and posts increased dramatically while important changes took place in the shape of the university career, the professorial ideal, and the field of disciplines. The causes of the reform movement were complex. Some of the changes originated from within the ranks of the teaching profession itself. Teachers at secondary and higher educational levels began, even prior to the fall of the Empire, to call for professionalization of the educational system due to dissatisfaction with their comparative lack of social status and low salaries, the lack of coherence in the structure and hierarchy of teaching posts and promotional tracks, and a desire to emulate the organizational structure of the German educational system (Weisz 1983: 55–69; Karady 1983). In 1868, the minister of public instruction, Victor Duruy, commissioned a large-scale statistical study of the French system of higher education. He championed the German university as a model for imitation by the French, sending French scholars to Germany to study the neighboring system in close detail, and he was responsible for the creation in 1868 of the École Pratique des Hautes Études, an institution for specialized post-graduate study that mirrored important aspects of the coveted German research institute (Weisz 1983: 60–62). Duruy provided an important ministerial focal point for a more general sentiment among those in the teaching profession that reform was necessary.

Other evidence during the Second Empire of the push toward reform came at the level of French secondary education, in the *lycées*. The centralized state-administered *lycée* system, which was considered "the masterpiece of French pedagogical structures" (Prost 1968: 21), had traditionally been heavily weighted toward a classical curriculum of Latin and Greek. In 1863, Duruy introduced a special program in the *lycées*, the *enseignement secondaire spécial*, which was destined to be the first significant move in a deluge of anti-classical educational reforms to follow in the early years of the Republic. This program, intended by Duruy and his allies as a practical mechanism for funneling into industry the secondary students who were deemed incapable of the classical curriculum, replaced the classical curriculum with the study of applied sciences, French, and a modern foreign language (Ringer 1992: 114–15). Later changes in curriculum, motivated much more explicitly by an anti-classical and modernist pedagogical orientation, would build on this program in a concerted effort to fundamentally remake the system of secondary education.

The coming of the Third Republic pushed educational reform ahead with a renewed urgency, as it now became explicitly linked to political agendas as well as to the professional interests of the class of teachers. There was much evidence of a general fear of national inferiority in light of the overwhelming performance of the German educational system and the obvious dividends it paid in scientific research, technological advance, and military power. This was linked to the suspicion that such inferiority was an indication of a general cultural decline, so the malaise in the educational system had to be treated by renewed ideological and pedagogical efforts toward social unity and order. Weisz (1983) has noted the frequently prophetic tone taken by reformers as they linked the problems in French society to failings of the educational system and predicted disaster if adequate changes were not made. Some reform-minded teachers and politicians invoked a notion of the German university as a kind of intellectual marketplace, arguing from liberal grounds for a corresponding reform of the French university, while others argued that German universities maintained a corporate solidarity that furthered the interests of its members far more effectively than the state-centered, overly bureaucratic French system.

In 1878, a group of twenty-four eminent scholars in the letters and sciences formed the Société de l'Enseignement Supérieur to mobilize support for reform both inside and outside the university that was to be based on the German model by increasing emphasis on research and publication and on the teaching of research as a pedagogical method in place of the traditional rhetorical performances in public lectures. It is important to reiterate here that the reform movement, before the early years of the Third Republic, was limited to members of the professoriate and only became a broader movement once the debate around professionalization was linked to broader social and political debates. The Société, which included such central participants in the French academic scene as Ernest Lavisse, Fustel de Coulanges, Paul Janet, Gabriel Monod, Louis Pasteur, Ernest Renan, and Hippolyte Taine, published a journal, the *Revue internationale de l'enseignement,* that presented and defended the reform cause as well as the German model and actively reached outside the intellectual community to the political realm for support and funding. By 1880, it numbered over 500 members and was among the most effective means by which the reform movement was enlarged and organized within the academic ranks and subsequently spread to the political sector (Weisz 1983: 64–69).

Education, Morality, and the Self

Predictably, once the reform debate moved outside the parameters of the professionalization debate within the professoriate, it took on some of the tones of larger political and cultural disputes. Some important Republican political figures supported reform because they believed higher education could be harnessed to some of the more important political goals of the new regime, i.e., social integration and the construction of a secular moral ideology. In line with the dominant political ideology of the early years of the Republic, which was the solidarism of Léon Bourgeois and the Radical Party (Hayward 1961), the reform advocates in the political classes saw a need for educational change as part of the larger social task of constructing a social democracy that would avoid the Scylla and Charybdis of extremist collectivism (on both the right and the left) and liberal economic individualism of an asocial variety. There was therefore room for agreement with the professoriate on the call for increased research and professionalization, which could be linked to the explicit political goals of solidarism: the establishment of a secular social order generated from scientific determination of the "ineluctable laws of natural determinism which could alone command the free consent of rational beings and at the same time provide an impregnable, objective foundation for ethics" (Hayward 1961: 25). The solidarist Republican politicians sought to enlist the reform movement to the extent possible in their own project, which was itself inspired by the positivist, anti-clerical and social reformist French Revolutionary tradition. This marriage of political and professional goals in the reform movement contributed to making educational debates at the *fin-de-siècle* one of the most explosive cultural powder kegs in the history of the Third Republic.

It is in the context of the Republican effort to establish a *morale laïque* at least partially through educational reform that we can best understand the place of the Durkheimians in the educational debates. Attempts to construct a secular morality were a frequent element of French intellectual life during the nineteenth century (Weill 1925; Charlton 1963; Stock-Morton 1988), but they take on a social and cultural import at the turn of the century that is unmatched in other periods. The very term *morale laïque* is an invention of the Third Republic, intended specifically to refer to the ethical precepts and system taught in the public school system (Stock-Morton 1988: 1). All those who proposed some variation of a secular morality were, though opposed to one another on a range of other issues, united in one common undertaking: the displacement of the ethical and moral authority of the Roman Catholic Church and its largely Jesuit pedagogical institutions. The reform movement in the universities has been described as fundamentally motivated by this struggle "to tear the soul of French youth away from the Jesuits" (Debray 1981[1979]: 43). Of course this meant that intellectuals and political figures who supported the role of the Church as purveyor of morality and ethics were opposed to the efforts of the reformers, and the antagonism between Catholic *intégrisme* and Republican secularism on this issue is a defining division of French cultural and social life of the period. However, the two opposing forces were hardly monolithically composed; significant nuances are discernible in both groups, and it is at times even difficult to draw the line at all.

One of the chief divisions existing among those in favor of the educational institution of a secular ethics concerned differences regarding the nature of society and of the human agent. The French had long nurtured a strong tradition in secular moral theory derived from Kantian moral philosophy. This tradition was based on the idea that the source of morality resided in the individual's innate knowledge of good and evil and his feeling of obligation to conform to the good, which makes itself known in the human conscience as the goal of absolute justice. In the work of the philosophers Victor Cousin and Charles Renouvier, the *morale laïque* exists pre-socially in human beings as an individual psychological fact rooted in the radical moral freedom of the individual (Stock-Morton 1988: 33–40, 55–59). Neo-Kantian secular moral theory tended to adapt existing religiously-based moral notions such as the ideas of God and the immortal soul to its own moral philosophy, instead of utterly rejecting religious categories in favor of wholly secular replacements. Cousin, for example, described secular moral philosophy as something of a distillation of Christian moral theory, an elaboration of the same basic truth that "does not destroy faith [but] enlightens and nurtures it and raises it gently from the half-light of symbols to the full light of pure thought" (Janet 1895: 251).

Opposing this radically individualist and spiritualist secular moral theory was another tradition rooted in a more social, collectivist conception of the foundation of moral law and much more concerned with separating secular moral theory from religious morality on important metaphysical questions. This tradition took its name from the journal *Morale indépendante*, which was created in 1865 by two disciples of Pierre-Joseph Proudhon. Drawing its inspiration from Proudhon's moral theory, which was based on the reciprocity of respect among persons rather than on the individual's innately felt duty to the absolute moral law, the journal dedicated itself to the construction of a secular moral theory and an educational platform from which to expound and teach it that would radically separate itself from that of the Church and of religious discourse generally (Stock-Morton 1988: 69–72).

In 1866, the Ligue de l'enseignement, an organization devoted to the popular dissemination of the idea of a *morale indépendente,* was born and it began establishing libraries, giving public courses and petitioning the government for appropriate changes in the public educational system. True to its roots in Proudhonian philosophy, the Ligue demonstrated from its beginnings a strong political stance in favor of socialism, workers' rights, and a vehement anti-clericalism. Although the excesses of the Commune in 1871 terrified enough of the French bourgeoisie to create something of a reaction against the radical collectivist moral philosophy of the Ligue and other such groups, and thereby to stifle to a considerable degree its influence at the level of the government and institutions, this second tradition in French secular morality continued to exercise an important influence during the Third Republic through its tremendous support among the more radical elements of the anti-clerical and socialist left.

The Durkheimians, and especially Durkheim himself, were clearly on the side of the educational reform movement during the period under investigation, but locating them precisely on this issue of *morale laïque* is a rather complicated task. Durkheim was an important participant in the debates over reform, especially after his arrival in Paris at the Sorbonne in 1902. Some even speculated that the very reason he was called up to that central post to replace Ferdinand Buisson in a chair in Science of Education had much more to do with his sympathy with the reformers and with the project for a secular ethics than with the actual substance of his work (see, e.g., Halévy 1979: 208–9). Even while still at Bordeaux, Durkheim had, with his colleague Octave Hamelin, formed a pro-reform group of professors and students known as La Jeunesse Laïque. The group had a decidedly socialist political bent and held regular meetings at which platforms were formulated and position papers presented on questions of the teaching and dissemination of secular morality in French society (Lukes 1973: 358). Once he had moved to the position at the Sorbonne, his course on pedagogy and education became a focal point for the debate around the reform movement.

The year of Durkheim's arrival in Paris also witnessed the enactment of several key reforms in the university system that still further emphasized his stature in the reform debates. In 1902, the *enseignement secondaire spécial*, which had initially been conceived as subordinate to the classical secondary curriculum, was formally given equal status in the secondary system. This led to calls for changes in the organization of pedagogical study and to the incorporation of the École Normale Supérieure, the institution traditionally charged with the education of secondary and university professors, into the University of Paris in 1903 (Isambert-Jamati 1971). The logical outgrowth of these various moves toward regularization of pedagogical education for those seeking to become secondary and university professors was the move to require all such students in the Parisian university system to attend a core course on the history of pedagogy in France. Who better to deliver such a course than Durkheim? Thus, from the first year of his assumption of the Sorbonne chair, Durkheim's course (first, on moral education; then, in 1904, on pedagogical evolution in France) was the only required course for all *agrégation* candidates in the Parisian system. This provided him a tremendous influence, especially given the results of yet another important shift in the educational system that saw a significant increase of the percentage of *lycée* teachers holding the *agrégation*, and therefore made for a much closer flow of ideas from

the university level to the secondary educational system and on throughout French society (Weisz 1983: 276).

Determining his precise position regarding the various competing
versions of *morale laïque* is still less than straightforward because, though
Durkheim was identified by some contemporaries with the solidarists and
by others with the more radical secular-left moralists, his position was not
reducible to either. This can be noted in perhaps its most developed form
in the lecture course on pedagogy and morality he gave at the Sorbonne.
Here, Durkheim distances himself from both Kantian individualist moral
theory and the radical anti-clerical and anti-religious language of the proponents of *la morale indépendente*. The moral role of the secular school is
central, he argued, and its task is to constitute "a morally unified milieu
that ... acts upon the entire nature [of the student]" (Durkheim 1969:
39), and in this it remains essentially the same as the religious school that
precedes it. As Christian education acts fundamentally to instill "a certain
attitude of the soul ... a certain *habitus* of our moral being," so the secular
moral education Durkheim proposed must "constitute in the student an
interior and profound state, a sort of polarity of the soul that will orient him in a defined direction not only for his infancy, but for his life"
(Durkheim 1969: 37–38). The schema of education thus has not changed.
Indeed, the domain of morality even in the secular school remains "a *sacred* domain ... that raises [everything it includes] above our empirical
individuality, that gives it a sort of transcendent reality" (Durkheim 1963:
8; emphasis added). It is out of the question to create a secular morality by acting negatively, by simply removing every extra-secular notion
and forbidding any recourse to religious notions, as the proponents of
la morale indépendente would have it. Equally, Durkheim's conception of
the elements of morality makes clear his opposition to an uncomplicated
Kantian individualist standpoint. The first two of these elements, the spirit
of discipline and the sense of attachment to a group, are clearly social in
nature, and the third, the autonomy of the will, achieves its true autonomous character only through its voluntary acquiescence in external, i.e.,
social, constraint (Durkheim 1963: 98–100).

Durkheim's conception of secular morality borrowed heavily from the
religious categories it sought to replace, and in a manner that is telling
of his view of religion generally. He championed what he called a secular
cult of the abstract individual person who would be recognized always in a
Kantian sense as an end and not a means, and he even postulated this abstract person as the new sacred object of the secular age. But, against the
individualist moralists, Durkheim was clear in a 1906 essay on moral facts
that the only stable ground of moral action is not the individual but a *sui
generis* collective being which was society itself. This establishment of the

individual as primary moral fact rests upon a communitarian structure; in the neo-Kantian language of Durkheim's professor of philosophy at the École Normale, Émile Boutroux, it was a "republic of persons" that would become the new object of moral education (W. Miller 1996: 9).

The most noteworthy element of Durkheim's vision of *morale laïque* is the great degree to which it was predicated on a basis of compulsion, discipline, and faith. While the 1906 essay seeks a distinction from Kant's notion of morality based solely on duty by adding desirability as a fundamental characteristic of moral acts, Durkheim provides nothing more than social compulsion and discipline as the basis of such desirability: "We shall maintain that it is impossible to desire a morality other than that endorsed by the condition of society at a given time" (Durkheim 1953: 38). Morality thus stands firmly on a foundation of obligation (W. Miller 1996: 221). In this light, we can better understand Durkheim's great regard for Rousseau, which stemmed in large degree from the latter's case for an *authoritarian* educational process. Both men believed that moral authority, while ultimately based upon reasonable principles, could achieve unanimous assent only under conditions of disciplinary pedagogy. Thus, Durkheim's moral position, which attempted in some ways to straddle the conflicting discourses of liberal and communitarian moral theory and, for precisely this reason, achieved at least in appearance a certain nuance that made his position attractive to those seeking compromise, sought to resolve the conflict between the two but in the final analysis leaned heavily in the direction of the latter.

The presence of the Durkheimians, and especially of Durkheim himself, in this debate over morality is best testified to by the vehemence of the attacks they received from those who saw them as a force of moral disintegration. Some such attacks came from Catholic writers, concerned fundamentally with the religious question (Stock-Morton 1988: 139–43). Others indicate the complexity of the interconnections between questions of morality and politics, on the one hand, and questions of knowledge and the role of the intellectual in society on the other. Chief among these was the attack on the Nouvelle Sorbonne mounted by Agathon. "Nouvelle Sorbonne" was a term of disapprobation invented by Henri Massis and Alfred de Tarde, two journalists who adopted the pseudonym Agathon and in August 1910 launched an attack on the institution in the form of several articles in popular Paris newspapers including *L'Écho de Paris, Paris-Journal,* and *L'Éclair.* They saw the Sorbonne as having undergone profound and disastrous changes under the direction of a cabal of moral relativist, secular, and anti-patriotic intellectuals that included Durkheim. Massis and Tarde denounced the disintegration of moral education championed by the Sorbonne group, but not from a religious position. Rather, their argument was that the Sorbonne, in championing an educational model based upon the reduction of the importance of classics and the rapid growth of specialization, especially in new "pseudo-scientific" realms like sociology, was denying the particular cultural genius of the French spirit (Bompaire-Evesque 1988: 13–14). The emphasis on anti-classical and specialist education at the Nouvelle Sorbonne, Agathon argued, was a result of the unhealthy influence of German cultural trends and a deformation of the specific "French genius that consists of order, clarity and taste" (Bompaire-Evesque 1988: 113). The new education championed by Durkheim, which was based on research groups and scholarly bureaucrats adept at compiling "bibliographies of bibliographies" and inevitably sacrificed the individual to the mass, struck Agathon as a moral scandal (Lepenies 1988[1985]: 50–52). In seeking to borrow from the language of the natural sciences to analyze the human condition in the humanities and newly-created social sciences, these disciplines were committing a serious moral offense against the free individual (Ringer 1992: 239).

Another side of the opposition to the moral program of the Nouvelle Sorbonne came from the Action Française (E. Weber 1962). Politically, the Action Française was far to the right of Agathon, and its criticisms of the Nouvelle Sorbonne were flatly situated in an anti-Republican, anti-democratic, and monarchist nationalism. In the view of Pierre Laserre and Charles Maurras, the group's leader, the central flaws in the Sorbonnard program stemmed from the abandonment of the classical curricula, but it was not the loss of individualism that they feared as its result. Rather, it was the historical and religious stock of French national identity, the joint product of Catholic religious and Roman political institutions, which Laserre and Maurras, saw as the chief casualty of the new pedagogical ideal. What was to be feared from the Sorbonne was the ideological preference of the isolated and rootless individual over the firmly rooted Catholic Frenchman in constant contact with his deceased ancestors through moral (religious) and political (monarchical) heritage (Bompaire-Evesque 1988: 124–25). Thus, Durkheim and company, seen by Agathon as dangerously radical *collectivists*, were for the Action Française dangerously radical *individualists*.

The Debate on the Scientific Study of Humankind: Sociology vs. Philosophy

In addition to the political and cultural struggle over the definitions of morality and the moral agent, there were seemingly more academic but still popular struggles being played out over issues of science and the study of man that profoundly shaped the institutional context of the emergence of Durkheimianism. In fact, these debates over the possibility of scientific knowledge of humankind were quite intertwined with the moral questions of duty and ethics. If this period of the Third Republic is not literally the moment of the birth of the social sciences, it is certainly the moment of the beginning of their institutionalization; we can perhaps talk about this crucial period, in the same terms used by Laurent Mucchielli (1998), as that of the discovery of the social and its possibilities for explanation of human action. The discovery was, however, one marked by numerous interdisciplinary negotiations and struggles over precisely what this discovery meant. The primary challenge to the nascent discipline of sociology on the proper scientific understanding of human nature and action came from the venerable queen of the disciplines, philosophy.

French sociology counted as one of its most important intellectual ancestors the philosophical positivism of the early and mid nineteenth century that was propounded by Saint-Simon and his disciple, Auguste Comte. Owing both to this source of influence and the overwhelming institutional and cultural power of the discourse of philosophy in French intellectual life, sociology was engaged with philosophy in a struggle over the rights to important problems of human meaning and action from the very first. Several contemporary analysts of French intellectual culture have emphasized the traditionally suspicious and aggressive attitude of institutional philosophy toward the emergent discipline of sociology (e.g., Bourdieu 1984; Pinto 1986; Fabiani 1988), and there is a large measure of truth in this perspective during the *fin-de-siècle*. The key point in understanding their relationship sociologically is their relative institutional power at the time. Philosophy was represented in chairs and curricula throughout the French educational system from the *lycée* level, where, since the start of the nineteenth century, an eight-hour philosophy course had held primary place in the classical secondary curriculum (Ringer 1992: 248), to the university and the *grandes écoles*. Sociology, on the other hand, was restricted during this period to extra-university "écoles d'érudition" which granted no degree, such as the École Pratique des Hautes Études, the Collège de France (Karady 1976: 281), and private research and educational foundations (T. Clark 1973: 111–16).

Philosophy's thorough entrenchment in the university was itself a recent development in its own evolution, as it was only with the same educational reforms that took place in the early years of the Third Republic, which effectively brought into being the French university intellectual, that the "philosophe universitaire" became the norm, instead of the philosopher who made his career outside the university. Fabiani (1988: 28) notes that perhaps the three most important philosophers of the mid nineteenth century, each representative of a powerful contending philosophical orientation (i.e., Comte the positivist, Maine de Biran the spiritualist, and Renouvier the neo-Kantian), were all extra-university figures. At this same time, philosophical production skyrocketed, aided by the need for philosophical instruction manuals and "popular works" in addition to increased scholarly activity associated with university presses and reviews (Fabiani 1988: 24–25). The two most important modern philosophical journals, *Revue philosophique* and *Revue de métaphysique et de morale*, emerged during this period. The former was the first non-sectarian journal established specifically for the publication of specialized university philosophical research, while the latter quickly became the center of philosophical activity during the period, directly engaging some of the central questions taken up by the sociologists and even counting some of the *Année* members, including Durkheim himself, among its contributors (Fabiani 1988: 32; Prochasson 1993a).

There were several lines of opposition among university philosophers during the period, the most important of which was perhaps that between positivists and spiritualists, although neo-Kantian criticism constituted a significant alternative theoretical orientation to both of these and was adhered to by many philosophers, including those working in the Renouvier lineage (Mucchielli 1998: 91). The spiritualist type, owing to the combination of his native cultural capital and the traditionally idealist orientation of the discipline, occupied the dominant position in the philosophical field and a goodly portion of its legitimacy came from its authority outside of academic institutions. The spiritualist program for the anthropological study of humankind put it directly at odds with sociology on a number of levels. Its very conception of the possibility of knowledge about humans, and especially its radically individualist understanding of knowledge creation and intellectual work, militated against a socially contextualized understanding of the conditions of knowledge and a social model of intellectual work like that presented by Durkheimian sociology. Spiritualist philosophy, epitomized in the epoch by Henri Bergson and his many disciples and followers, took as given the impossibility of ultimately objective and scientific foundations for human knowledge. In Bergson's work, the central theoretical concept is that of the *élan vital*, the irrational, unpredictable vitalist life force that is elemental in all processes in the universe. Bergson's thought thus became celebrated in circles most thoroughly opposed to mechanism and rationalism, including elements in the occult revival and in the Catholic intellectual renewal in the early years of the twentieth century (Grogin 1988). He held a high profile chair in modern philosophy at the Collège de France and, despite his own relative lack of organizational and institution-building skills, a kind of movement had arisen around him.

Numerous commentators on the philosophical field of the period place Durkheim/Durkheimianism and Bergson/Bergsonianism at opposing poles, whatever those poles happen to be, given the particular analysis. For some (T. Clark 1973; Grogin 1988), the Latin Quarter during this period is classifiable along the axis of Cartesianism and spontaneity. According to this schema, Durkheimianism is Cartesian, while Bergsonianism is spontaneist. Others consider the intellectual field by examining smaller sub-fields. Christophe Charle (1990), for example, looks only at the position-takings occasioned by the Dreyfus Affair and devises a more complex map of intellectual positions. In this different schema, we find Durkheim and Bergson and their disciples again neatly divided, the former model Dreyfusards according to Charle's criteria, and the latter almost equally model anti-Dreyfusards.

Though these delineations pointed to by Clark, Charle, Fabiani, and others have a good deal of merit, it is also clear when we look more closely at lives and works of relevant figures that things are somewhat less tidy in at least a few important respects. The status of the two patriarchal figures of Bergson and Durkheim during the period examined and the nature of the field in which they were situated, i.e., its susceptibility to the influence of generally known master thinkers rather than to little known hyper-specialists, makes it highly likely that members of each camp would have had ample opportunity to be familiar with the work being done in the other. Bergson especially had achieved a very considerable reputation by this time that would continue to increase with his election to the Académie française in 1914, his receipt of a Nobel Prize in literature in 1928, and his attainment of the highest rank in the Légion d'honneur in 1930. It was in fact almost impossible to completely escape the influence of Bergsonianism in the Parisian intellectual scene during this time, as he had become arguably the dominant philosophical and intellectual presence in the France of the pre- and inter-war years. But we can be quite more specific than this with respect to some important Durkheimians, as they had gone considerably further in their reading of Bergson than the formal acquaintance necessitated by required course readings or general intellectual culture. Some allies of Durkheim were strongly attracted to Bergson's thought, and some for significant periods of time. Maurice Halbwachs, for example, attended both the *lycée* Henri IV and the École Normale during parts of Bergson's tenure at the same two institutions and was deeply marked by his thought, most obviously in his own work on collective memory.

The most profound point of contact between the Durkheimians and Bergsonian thought took place within the group we are considering in this book, which makes sense on a purely substantive level as both they

and Bergson were centrally concerned with religion. Mauss, though sometimes capable of mimicking Durkheim's polemical disdain for Bergson
and his disciples,[1] nonetheless cites him approvingly as a contributor of
important psychological data in an essay on the rapport between sociology
and psychology (Mauss 1950: 294, 307). This essay shows that Mauss held
a more nuanced position on the connection between the two disciplines
than that we find in Durkheim. In both his unfinished doctoral thesis on
prayer and in a little known but fascinating conference paper on the common genesis of Hindu and Western mysticism, he argues for an understanding of the contemporary trajectory of religion toward increasingly
interior, mystical experience that is essentially indistinguishable from
the position of Bergson, though of course Bergson explicitly attaches a
personal affirmation to this observation that is absent in Mauss's analysis
(Mauss 1968a: 361–62; 1968b: 556–60).

Hubert's interaction with Bergsonian thought takes place primarily in
a 1905 essay on the nature of religious time. This theme had been the subject of one of Hubert's courses at the École Pratique des Hautes Études
and, for this and other reasons, it is almost certainly primarily the work of
Hubert himself rather than a collaborative effort with Mauss, as was more
usually the case with important sociological works from this period that
bore his name.[2] The task he sets for himself here is, in sociological terms,
the exploration of the ways in which time as experienced during religious
rites is structured by the same system of collective representations that
provide the general framework for other realms of experience in a given
society. This was a typically Durkheimian argument on epistemology of
the sort most explicitly set forth in the 1903 essay on collective representations co-written with Mauss, and at the surface level Hubert gives little
indication that he wishes to move too far from the limited sociological examination of the social rules that govern, with a kind of "legislative rigidity," the experience of religious time and into a discussion of the nature
of that experience itself (Hubert and Mauss 1929: 190). He is nonetheless
led by his discussion to a number of interesting conclusions that contribute to the foundations of a sociology of knowledge strikingly imprinted
with Bergsonian traces.

The central problem, argues Hubert, is to determine how societies
resolve, through the creation and maintenance of collective representations, the contradictions and tensions between the objective, quantitative
time in which religious rites are carried out and the transcendent, qualita-
tive, infinite nature of the sacred. He is thus involved in an exploration
of the problem of the sociological construction of the very categories by
which the world is apprehended by individuals, concentrating on a specific experience of time that, by its complex nature, promises to show us

something fundamental about the construction and character of these categories of understanding. Religious time, whether depicted in myth or actually experienced in ritual and religious festival, is not experienced as objective time. Religious facts are experienced not as taking place before, after, or at the same time as other events or facts, but rather as part of another stream of time that Hubert calls "un temps-milieu" (Hubert and Mauss 1929: 194). Time here cannot be objectively measured in discrete and chronological units that appear to us by the standards of an objective calendar or clock as equal in length, for they are not experienced as such. Religious calendars, e.g., the Aztec *tonalamatl*, are not intended to *measure* time so much as to provide a necessary rhythm to rites and mythic reenactments that might be completely separate from the rhythm of objective time (Hubert and Mauss 1929: 195). Hubert distinguishes five central properties of this religious time, each of which points to the opposition between this kind of time and mathematical, objective time (Hubert and Mauss 1929: 235). It is not by mere coincidence that he sounds Bergsonian here, as he explicitly cites him as his source:

> Our investigation touches here on philosophical analyses in which the representation of duration in the individual consciousness has recently been the object of study ... M. Bergson has concluded that the notion of time is not only that of a quantity, but that it is also qualitative ... he replaces, as generative elements of the representation of time, the notions of magnitude, position, and succession with that of an active tension by which, on the one hand, the harmony of independent durations of different rhythms is realized in the consciousness and, on the other, the images on the different levels of this same consciousness are distributed and circulated. (Hubert and Mauss 1929: 210)

Hubert, in his understanding of how the categories of understanding (which include the experience of time) work, agrees with Bergson that the crucial element is the constructed, creative nature of that experience. Even when he moves away from Bergson's analysis, he retains its central thrust and merely attempts to move the focus from the *individual* construction of the experience of (religious) time to a *social* construction: "It must be that the associations that define the qualities of time, as well as the terms that compose them, have a sacred character ... this notion of the sacred ... cannot form in the mind of the individual as such; it results from *subjective experiences of the collectivity*" (Hubert and Mauss 1929: 220; emphasis added).

Hertz's Bergsonian connection is even more substantial. We know that it was while he was at the ENS that he became acquainted with and attracted to the work of Durkheim (Parkin 1996: 2–3), who was by then teaching in Paris at the Sorbonne, but it is rather surprising to learn that it was during this same period that he attended the course of Bergson at the Collège de France. More than this, Hertz wrote excitedly several times to Alice Bauer, his future wife and close intellectual companion, about Bergson's ideas, calling him an "inventor" whose "subtle and bold" thought was engaged in the exploration of problems Hertz saw as "the most pointed and pressing of the day."[3] He makes affirmative reference to Bergson's thought in other discussions with her, most tellingly in letters written during a short stay in Germany in the fall of 1902. Here, he describes trips to art museums and concert halls in a language saturated in the avant-garde modernist conceptions borrowed from the vitalist philosophical discourses of the day, most centrally those of Bergson and Nietzsche. In one particularly compelling passage, he speaks of music's power to reveal humankind's inner profundities and, in purely Bergsonian terminology, talks of musical experience as far more directly linked to the essence of human consciousness than is mere rational discourse:

> Music has revealed … that what can be expressed in words is merely … consciousness refracted through the requirements of action or social life, and consequently deformed, but that the essence of our life is the spontaneous … Music alone … reproduces the continuous and complex outflow of the interior life … Bergson … is in a sense the psychologist of music.[4]

Later, while at the front during the war, he writes to her of reading a Bergson speech in which the latter equated French and German civilizations with his own philosophical categories of life and matter, respectively, in order to argue for the moral vibrancy of the former and the static brutality of the latter. Hertz saw this argument as inaccurate in that it failed to admit an element of spiritual and moral *élan vital* to be found even in the basically unjust German cause. It is interesting, though, that even in disagreeing with Bergson's interpretation of events here, Hertz does not so much reject his categories as utilize them himself in a more nuanced fashion. He had written a previous letter to her, five days prior to this one, in which he acknowledges that "there is all the same some truth" in Bergson's analysis, and readily accepts Bergsonian terminology in doing so: "Let's not forget that already after Frederick the Great the admirable machine of the Prussian state had lost its soul. This seems to me to be the misfortune that weighs on the German troops" (Hertz 2002: 147). This earlier reading of German mechanical brutality and French spiritual spontaneity, which is so obviously indebted to a Bergsonian framework of understanding, rings rather clearly elsewhere in many of Hertz's discussions from the front of the two sides and their relative merits and demerits. In a letter written during the previous September, for example, he sounds almost euphorically Bergsonian: "We [i.e., the French] will be victorious and this victory will be that of spirit over mass, of generous impulse ["élan"] over brutal discipline" (Hertz 2002: 55).

As the preceding short analysis shows, there was a complicated engagement with the thought of Bergson on the part of the three younger Durkheimians. This small demonstration of the attachment of the Durkheimian project to elements of Bergson's philosophy, which is proffered by some as the polar opposite of Durkheimianism, shows some of the complexity of the intellectual field in which Durkheimianism emerged. It also points toward some of the significant distinctions and variations to be found within the Durkheimian project itself that will be explored in their full importance in succeeding chapters.

The rise of the social sciences, and especially of Durkheimian sociology, contributed to a situation within philosophy that was seen by many as a crisis. The one item nearly the entire philosophical field could agree upon was that the path to legitimacy for sociology, both institutionally (in the form of chairs and research groups in universities) and scientifically (in the form of reviews and influence in the intellectual community at large), entailed encroachment on the traditionally privileged hunting grounds of philosophy (Karady 1979: 50). Philosophy had also suffered at the curricular level as a result of the changes brought about by the new secondary options agreed upon in 1902, which emerged from the work of the Ribot Commission of 1899, as only two of the four *baccalauréat* sequences in the new system retained the philosophy requirement, and the social sciences took on greater significance (Ringer 1992: 250).

A large percentage of the *Année* collaborators were *agrégés* in philosophy (Besnard 1983: 34–35), and they often competed for chairs and positions with others similarly trained who had remained more firmly within the disciplinary boundaries of philosophy. Durkheim's overall intellectual project, even if one did not consider it as primarily an endeavor to establish a new discipline *outside* of philosophy that would attempt to usurp the latter's core themes, could be seen as an independent and innovative effort to solve traditional philosophical problems such as those of the categories of understanding and the whole/parts distinction *from within* philosophy. This made him a dangerous challenger to philosophical rivals (Nielsen 1999). The Durkheimians maintained relatively warm relations with Xavier Léon and the regular contributors to *Revue de métaphysique et de morale,* owing to their shared commitment to a rationalist engagement of moral questions and perhaps also to a shared educational trajectory (Fabiani 1993: 180), and Durkheim was careful, especially early on, to clarify to philosophy and the classics that his view of the moral and educational revolution to be carried out did not entail their elimination (Karady 1979: 53–54). Still, philosophical worries about the imperialism of Durkheimian sociology were hardly unfounded. The combination of the crisis of philosophy and the emergence of the social sciences, with their important political allies among the Republicans, made it easy to see the Durkheimian enterprise as a whole as "one of the major attempts … to resolve the crisis of university philosophy by transforming its spiritual substance as much as its thematic material, thereby authorizing the progressive replacement of a personnel trained in spiritualism by new professors of a scientistic and positivist … obedience, among whom the sociologists would assume a choice position" (Karady 1979: 55).

With this sketch of the debates around morality and education and the disciplinary struggle of philosophy and sociology, we can more easily see how the Durkheimians were uniquely and favorably situated in responding to the problematics facing intellectuals in this period. First of all, in the Durkheimian group, as has been demonstrated at length by Clark, Karady, and others (T. Clark 1973: 181–90; Besnard 1983: 71–89), Durkheim fulfilled the role of the consummate cluster leader. He was a tremendously effective intellectual power-broker who thoroughly understood the ins and outs of the French university system and how to effectively engage in intellectual and ideological combat within it. In many of the polemical disputes with other disciplines on this issue, Durkheim organized responses that were devastatingly effective. The fact that several of the leading opponents of the Durkheimians, such as Gabriel Tarde and Charles Seignobos (Charle 1998: 150–52), were isolated individuals who failed to create a team and actively promote its institutionalization through the creation of teaching and research posts often produced devastating results in the academic game of polemical attack and response in which sheer manpower is an important factor in the ability to respond to critics and mount offensives of one's own.

Beyond this seemingly personalist explanation for Durkheimian success, though, is the fact that, with respect both to the scientific knowledge question and the moral dilemma posed by secularization, the Durkheimians offered responses that avoided dangerous extremes far better than some of their opponents, and in this way they captured the interest and alliance of important figures and movements in the administrative and governmental Republican and Solidarist efforts. Of absolutely crucial importance here was Durkheim's relationship with Louis Liard, who, first as director of higher education and later vice-rector of the University of Paris, exercised a profound administrative and political effect on the Third Republic. The constant support of such a powerful ally was of immeasurable aid to the Durkheimian cause; indeed, Durkheim probably owed his initial appointment in Bordeaux to Liard's influence and assistance (Durkheim 1998: 53; Besnard 1983: 75). On the moral issue, Durkheim attempted to find a way between the rigorous pro-religionists and the radical secularists, finding a language that was secular without lapsing into radical anti-clericalism. On the scientific question, he presented a case for a socially-rooted methodology for understanding man that avoided the increasingly disparaged racialist discourses of some of his sociological and ethnological competitors (T. Clark 1973; Mucchielli 1998). The Durkheimian position also managed, at least in the treatment of the moral issue, to avoid attacking individualist positions too radically, and they thereby subtly evaded classification alongside the radical collectivists. This combination of factors provided the Durkheimians, at least for a brief period of time prior to the war, with a unique capability to speak influentially to a range of views and positions on these key debates.

Notes

1. In a letter from 1905 to Hubert in which he expresses dissatisfaction with Hubert's essay on religious time ("Here I do not find a true satisfaction with your work, perhaps simply because I have not had any input into it"), Mauss points specifically to what he sees as the inappropriateness of Hubert's use of "the psychological nonsense of Bergson" regarding time (unpublished letter contained in the Fonds Hubert-Mauss in the archives of the Collège de France, FHM henceforth).
2. François-André Isambert (1979: 187) points out the complexity of determining the respective contributions of Mauss and Hubert to their work, both their collaborative work and the work bearing only one of their two names but that nonetheless arose from the close intellectual relationship they shared for so many years. With respect to this essay, however, he alludes to comments by Mauss on the work in the *Année* in which he provides a critique and explicitly refers to "il" (Hubert), instead of "nous," as the author.
3. Hertz to Alice Bauer. n.d., Fonds Robert Hertz (hereafter FRH). Laboratoire d'Anthropologie Sociale, Collège de France, Paris.
4. Hertz to Alice Bauer, n.d., FRH. The phrase "the psychologist of music" was originally "the psychologist of emotion," but Hertz crossed out the latter.

4   Écoles, Masters, and The Dreyfus Affair

Institutions and Networks that Shaped the Durkheimians and the Political Affair that Positioned Them

The macro-level overview of the social and cultural landscape in the previous chapter is a start to understanding the emergence of the Durkheimian intellectual, but just that. An adequate interpretation of the *habitus* requires a micro-level investigation of its origins as well. This chapter will use some of the theoretical tools outlined in Chapter 2 to focus on the specific educational institutions and environments that shaped the Durkheimian group. It will also pursue Szakolczai's suggestion regarding the place of "masters of ceremonies" in the lives of the Durkheimians. Finally, it will explore the complex ways in which Durkheimian intellectual identity was focused by the signal event of their time that raised the question of the intellectual's role in the broader social world, the Dreyfus Affair.

The two central institutions in the lives of the Durkheimians in their formation as students are the École Normale Supérieure and the École Pratique des Hautes Études. Durkheim was a student at the École Normale from 1879 to 1882. Mauss, who at the suggestion of his *normalien* uncle did not attend the École Normale, pursued graduate work at the École Pratique des Hautes Études from 1895 to 1897 and later taught at the same institution from 1900 until retirement in 1939, save for a period of five years during World War I (1914 to 1919). Hubert was a *normalien* from 1892 to 1895, a student at the École Pratique from 1895 to 1897, and a lecturer there from 1901 until his death in 1927 (with the same five-year interruption due to the war). Hertz was also a graduate of the École Normale, having attended from 1901 to 1904, and a lecturer at the École Pratique from 1908 to 1912. Thus, three of the four were *normaliens* and three of four (but not the same three) were affiliated with the École Pratique's Fifth Section in Religious Sciences. But in what precise ways did these institutions affect the trajectories of Durkheim, Mauss, Hubert, and Hertz? To answer this question, I need to explore those institutions historically and sociologically in a bit more depth.

The École Normale Supérieure was founded in 1795 by the National Convention in the early years after the Revolution, and it was designed to educate teachers as part of a national plan to disseminate the ideas of the Revolution throughout the French population (R. Smith 1982: 5). As such, it was part of the French system of *grandes écoles*, which also included the École Polytechnique, the École Nationale d'Administration, the École Royale Militaire, the École Navale, the École des Ponts et Chaussées and the École des Mines, among many others. This system was created to provide a specialized training and career path for functionaries, technicians and administrators necessary for the organization and workings of the French state. It was separate from and generally more prestigious than the university system, which only became unified during the years of the Third Republic. The basic purpose of the *grandes écoles* was to provide a training ground for specialists needed by the state, and through the end of the nineteenth century the logic of this system was to create a new *grande école* each time a new kind of important specialist/bureaucrat was recognized (Weisz 1983: 20).

Although in many ways privileged materially and symbolically in comparison to students in the university system, students at the École Normale competed with them for the degrees of *agrégation* and doctorate necessary for higher-level teaching, as the École Normale had no degree or diploma of its own. In this, it was unique among *grandes écoles*. By the beginning of the Third Republic, the superior position of the École Normale in the academic hierarchy of the training of scholars and teachers was well established. More, the ENS experience had become something akin to the experience of a Goffmanian total institution (Rubenstein 1990: 7), at least insofar as it fostered a strong, elitist identification with the institution and something of a broad *Weltanshauung* encompassing social and political positions. Some of this is due to the fact that, until the reforms of 1903, all *normaliens* were required to reside in ENS dormitories and, at least until the early 1890s when the directorship of the school was held by the relatively permissive Georges Perrot and Paul Dupuy, daily schedules and even freedom to leave the campus grounds were highly restricted (R. Smith 1982: 80). Another central element of the collective identity of the *normaliens* was a special vocabulary of neologisms and slang terms invented by the students and used often as a code for denigrating those who were not *normaliens* or were otherwise not considered part of the intellectual elite (Rubenstein 1990: 90–91). Further, in its form and its emphasis on a culture of rhetorical skills and linguistic polish, the ENS retained in formally secular form the Jesuit pedagogical model of the Catholic colleges (Bélanger 1997: 158–60). Attendance at Mass remained compulsory until 1881 (R. Smith 1982: 80).

The social background of *normaliens* tended to be heavily urban with a particularly high representation of the Parisian middle classes. The wealthy most often had more lucrative future career possibilities than becoming *lycée* or university teachers, and so they went elsewhere, while truly lower-class students lacked the classical culture and the financial means necessary to succeed at the *concours* of entry and then through the three years of intense preparation for the *agrégation* (R. Smith 1982: 43, 55). While the politics of *normaliens* had, from the very first, tended toward the democratic Republican left (or the Radical Party, in strict party terms), a significant shift occurred in the general political atmosphere of the ENS in the 1890s. This had to do with the rise of a significant, if still minoritarian, socialist element among *normaliens*. Christophe Charle has demonstrated how this movement began as an avant-garde, both within the ENS and in the larger French society, consisting early on of vastly more students in letters than of those in sciences. This minority would grow considerably during the course of the Dreyfus Affair, falling off after 1904, and regaining force later during the inter-war period as part of the prelude to the rise of the Popular Front (Charle 1994: 137–39).

The emergence of this socialist movement at the École Normale, coupled with the progressive liberalization of the tremendously strict regime at the École during roughly the same period, was highly significant in its effects on the younger Durkheimians. Durkheim, however, completed his ENS training prior to the emergence of *normalien* socialism and the majority of the reforms, i.e., during a period when the strict ascetic structure of the ENS was largely intact and the focus for students in letters (where philosophy was located) was still rigidly classical. This ascetic orientation was personified in the director of the ENS during most of Durkheim's time there, the historian Numa-Denys Fustel de Coulanges.

Durkheim's Master of Ceremonies: Fustel de Coulanges

Fustel had been a professor at the ENS from 1870 to 1880, taking over the directorship in the latter year and holding it until 1883, when he retired from his duties to recommit himself full-time to historical research. Best known among scholars, in his own day and in ours, for his *La Cité antique* (1864), in which he examined the "cult, law and institutions of Greece and Rome," and for the often heated polemics that persisted around his interventions into the history of France, Fustel was perhaps the most respected historian of his day and a recognized progenitor of the scientific (i.e., social) historians of the late nineteenth and early twentieth centuries (Heran 1989: 369–70). His influence on Durkheim is amply documented. In 1892, three years after Fustel's death, Durkheim dedicated his Latin thesis on Montesquieu to "the memory of Fustel de Coulanges." In his preface to the first volume of the *Année sociologique*, Durkheim invokes Fustel, albeit in a partially critical manner, in his argument that the *Année* is designed, not merely as a source for sociologists, but also as a means to "bring sociology closer to certain special sciences ["it is above all history we are thinking of in speaking thus"] that keep themselves too distanced from it, to their own detriment and to our own" (Durkheim 1898: ii). But the more impressive argument for Durkheim's intellectual influence by Fustel is the startling similarity in the central arguments of *Les Formes élémentaires* and *La Cité antique*. In both, one finds a case for the primary role of religious practice and ideas in constructing the civic life and legal and political institutions that superficially might seem unattached to religion. The argument advanced in *La Cité antique* showed how very ancient Indo-European religious beliefs concerning the worship of the souls of the dead, the common historical heritage of Greece and Rome, powerfully affected nearly every aspect of daily civil life, especially the family, morality, private property, and law. Christopher Prendergast (1983–84) suggests that Durkheim's 1895 break from his earlier intellectual orientation and subsequent concentration on the fundamental role of religion is in fact not an effect of his encounter with the work of William Robertson Smith, but rather a rediscovery of Fustel's framework (see also Lukes 1973: 60–65; Jones 1993). François Heran (1989: 369–76) has demonstrated the ways in which the two authors were attacked by humanist, anti-structural critics in the same language and illustrated the fact that even the argumentative styles of the two books are fundamentally the same, especially with respect to the search for and method of proving original or elementary forms of the phenomenon under investigation.

Beyond the specifics of Fustel's thesis on the religious origins of legal and political institutions, though, his influence on Durkheim is visible in a more general manner. His approach to scholarly life was marked by a tremendous ascetic devotion, very much like that later displayed by Durkheim, which I will discuss in detail in Chapter 7. Though his commentary is sparse on his early development and childhood, it appears he

was marked, as Durkheim was, by an early crisis in and loss of a theretofore
fervent religious faith (Catholicism, in Fustel's case), and the scholarly
life and study became for him a kind of substitute religion (Tourneur-
Aumont 1931: 8). He was widely reputed at the École Normale to be at
least as fervent an adherent to this new faith as he had been as a child to
the old one. One former student recounted the profound "moral influence" he had over students, giving off "a sort of austere radiance that imparted intellectual asceticism as much as historical skill" (Lukes 1973: 59).
He was, as Durkheim would be later, a staunch defender of his discipline's
specifically scientific capabilities, and he struggled his whole life against
fellow historians who viewed their discipline essentially as a literary genre.
His anti-aestheticism went so far as to lead him to downplay his admirers'
praise of his sophisticated prose style, even to reject such praise as "for a
scholar ... so many insults" (Tourneur-Aumont 1931: 148). As history was
for Fustel "the science of social facts," classical literary talent was beside
the point (Tourneur-Aumont 1931: 166–88).

For a generation of students at the École Normale and elsewhere in
Paris, Fustel also publicly represented a position on the scholar's political
role from which Durkheim borrowed significantly. His work on the history
of France necessarily involved him in intellectual and popular polemic
about the contemporary political status of the country, national identity
and other such troublesome topics. Fustel, by all accounts a political liberal, clearly had positions on these and other political issues, but, as a
scholar, preferred to speak to them publicly only through the authority of
his scientific work. Like Durkheim, he recognized the inevitably political
significance of intellectual work engaged, as theirs was, with questions of
morality and religion, but understood the scientific and scholarly calling
as forbidding overt interventions into the political arena, save in certain
very drastic situations. Nonetheless, in both thinkers one finds clear evidence of reverence not only for liberal political freedoms but also for a
morality built around concepts of duty and obligation and for the family
as perhaps the most crucially important and powerful institution, calling
for complete social support and unrelenting antagonism to all change
that served to put it in jeopardy (Tourneur-Aumont 1931: 18–19, 202–4).

The Master of Ceremonies for Mauss,
Hubert, and Hertz: Lucien Herr

If the École Normale can be represented during the 1870s and 1880s by
the austere, apolitical personage of Fustel, by the time the younger religion cluster members Hubert and Hertz arrived there, the situation had

changed considerably. In addition to the progressive loosening of institutional strictures, which included a lightening of restrictions regarding
daily schedules and the gradual admittance of programs in modern languages and other non-classical and progressive subjects, the atmosphere
had also changed in the sense of the men and ideas responsible for the
administration and operation of the École Normale. When Fustel left the
directorship in 1883, he was replaced by Georges Perrot, a much less im-
posing intellectual character, to be sure, and also a less authoritarian and
austere presence. Perrot's attitude toward *normalien* education was more
civic, even narrowly political, than Fustel's. Instead of the overwhelming
emphasis on detached scientific method in study and research, Perrot
brought a staunchly republican and civic ideal to the École Normale. The
republican ideal had been the dominant political sentiment among *normaliens* since its very foundation, but a further emphasis on this aspect of
the École Normale experience made itself apparent under Perrot.

This was perhaps clearest in the personalities of the teaching faculty
during Perrot's tenure, who in fact exercised much of the power over
students and the overall École atmosphere under Perrot, as the latter preferred delegating much of this responsibility to them (R. Smith 1982: 60).
Among these figures we can count Gabriel Monod, who would be the
first of the academic intellectuals to call for a retrial for Captain Dreyfus
in 1897; Joseph Bédier, who, like his friend Ernest Lavisse (a historian at
the École Normale until 1880), became a powerful propagandist for the
French cause during World War I; Gustave Lanson, who toward the end
of the century became, along with Lavisse and others, one of the central participants in the republican and secular revolution at the Nouvelle
Sorbonne; and Charles Andler, another champion of the connection between the Republic and the new anti-classical pedagogy and curriculum
and a central actor in socialist and Dreyfusard politics. In effect, one can
argue that the former god of detached and ascetic science, personified
by Fustel, had been replaced by one personified by another personage at
the École Normale who exercised an enormous influence over students
during his tenure there: Lucien Herr.

In the mythical cult of Herr that was created even during his lifetime
and further developed after his death, it is sometimes difficult to separate
hyperbole from the actual facts. Born in 1864 in the same Alsace-Lorraine
region that produced Durkheim and Mauss, and himself a *normalien* and
agrégé in philosophy, Herr made his mark intellectually and politically as a
radical very early on in his career. As a *normalien*, he demonstrated an interest in German philosophy (Hegel and Nietzsche in particular), but despite his universally acknowledged brilliance, he was barely passed at the
agrégation, as conservative ENS professors saw in his interests too much of

a departure from the established course of French philosophical scholarship. Discouraged by this crushing "semi-failure" (Andler 1977: 48) brought about by his radical intellectual stance, Herr turned away from a university teaching career and chose instead to become the ENS librarian in 1887. This was a stunning move for a promising scholar, as such a position was generally something occupied for only a few years at a time by ENS students finishing their theses and carried no institutional prestige at all. But Herr saw it as a way to maintain a purer contact with the intellectual calling than that permitted by the strictures of the existing faculty ideology. His vision of this calling, which was deeply informed by Hegelian idealism, framed scholarship as a key element in the endeavor of consciousness to become truly self-conscious and thereby to achieve the sacred endpoint of the dialectical resolution of oppositions. This endpoint, which Hegel inserted in the spot where earlier theologies had placed God, consisted of Spirit contemplating itself in a state of total knowledge. Charles Andler, who was his closest friend, characterized Herr as a sort of "secular mystic" (Andler 1977: 41) in his orientation to his intellectual and political work. Herr spent long portions of time throughout his life working on a grand thesis on Hegel's thought, a work that unfortunately, like a number of other such vast undertakings, he never saw to completion due to political and occupational constraints on his time. His socialism and his general intellectual orientation retained this deeply Hegelian and quasi-religious overtone throughout his life. One might perhaps see in this orientation something of a transformation of the very devoted Catholic faith to which he had held at least until his years as a *lycéen* at Louis Le Grand in Paris.

As ENS librarian, Herr exercised an influence that is beyond easy calculation over several generations of *normaliens*. As the man responsible for building up the ENS library from a classical to a modern research library (Mauss 1997: 741), Herr had more frequent contact with many students than did their professors, especially in the period after 1903 when the École Normale's separate faculty had been reassigned to the Sorbonne and the Collège de France as part of the reunification of the ENS with the University of Paris. Given his immense knowledge in vastly different fields, his influence was not limited to any one variety of student and he was able to act as a *de facto* research advisor for almost all of them. *Normaliens* spoke of his role in determining their research questions and of his ability to recommend the most recent literature in an amazingly wide array of fields. Herr also played an important role in directing young *normaliens* to the thought and work of Durkheim, and was the recruiting agent for several of the post-1900 *normaliens* who joined the team, including Hertz, Antoine Bianconi, Maxime David, Jean Reynier, and Georges Gelly. He was a fervent supporter of Durkheim and Durkheimians at the institutional level, championing Durkheim's cause several times in the latter's unsuccessful bids to the Collège de France and aiding him in his successful attempt to obtain the chair at the Sorbonne in 1902 (Mauss 1997: 742).

Linked to this intellectual influence, and better viewed as a sub-category of it than as something entirely distinct, was Herr's political role at the ENS. The political drift at the end of the century at the ENS was, as we have already seen, substantially leftward. Herr was an impassioned partisan who saw socialism as a Hegelian perfecting of social arrangements to be brought about by the same process that would lead thought to perfect itself through sustained self-criticism and reflection. His massive influence on socialist thought and practice in French intellectual circles during this period is broadly acknowledged. Both Jean Jaurès and Léon Blum, perhaps the two most influential socialist political products of the ENS, were moved to adopt a socialist politics by Herr's persuasion and passion. Herr was also among the first to rally to the defense of Captain Dreyfus, and he was crucial to the converting of many key players, including Jaurès, to the Dreyfusard cause (Andler 1977: 148). His role as an agitator at the ENS during the height of the Dreyfus Affair (roughly from summer 1897 to the retrial of Captain Dreyfus in autumn 1899) is in fact one of the central ways in which he affected the Durkheimian religion cluster. He began organizing petitions and demonstrations in support of a retrial from his post in the library, and many members of the Durkheimian group including Hubert and Mauss joined with him in this effort. Beyond this, he was the main shareholder in the Société nouvelle de librarie et d'édition, a socialist publishing enterprise headed by Charles Péguy that Herr had salvaged from the bankruptcy that resulted from Péguy's lack of bookkeeping ability, and he brought many students and colleagues (including Mauss, Hubert, and Hertz) into this group as well. This group published *Notes critiques,* a kind of hybrid social science/socialist review to which many Durkheimians contributed (Mergy 1998; Durkheim 1998: 254), and a number of other intellectual socialist tracts and pamphlets of the period.

The Second Master of Ceremonies for Mauss, Hubert, and Hertz: Sylvain Lévi

If the ENS was the first and most important institutional influence in the formation of the Durkheimian religion cluster, then the École Pratique des Hautes Études was clearly the second. This institution, created in 1868 as a sort of graduate school to the Sorbonne, awarded no diplomas but enabled specialists in particular fields to pursue advanced study with expert faculty in close seminar interaction. There were initially four sections in mathematics, physics and chemistry, natural history and physiology, and historical and philological sciences, with a fifth planned section in economic sciences. However, in January 1886, following a stream of changes set in motion by the rise of the Third Republic that included the *de facto* suppression in 1885 of the Facultés de Théologie Catholique (which had long been responsible for the university treatment of religious topics from an unambiguously Catholic position), the fifth section was rededicated to "sciences religieuses" and opened in the very buildings that had formerly housed the Paris Faculté de Théologie (Poulat and Poulat 1966: 27–28).

This Fifth Section at the EPHE would become famous, or infamous, depending on the position of the commentator, as the center of the new religious sciences in France. Though the first chair in "histoire des religions" had already been awarded at the Collège de France a few years earlier in 1880 to Albert Réville (Poulat and Poulat 1966: 26), the Fifth Section quickly became known within and outside the university world as the central location of scholarly historical inquiry into religion that was not officially restricted by any religious creed. Catholic critics bemoaned the fact that Christianity was relegated to the status of one religion among many studied by the seventy-five students and eleven *directeurs d'études* who were there at the founding in 1886. But the fervor of the denunciation from the extreme right and ultra-orthodox religious exaggerated beyond reason the real tenor of the Fifth Section, which, while rigorously scholarly and institutionally secular, could hardly be considered antireligious or even irreligious. The dominant face of the early EPHE was in fact still very much *croyant*, though, instead of the Catholicism of the former Faculty of Theology, it was liberal Protestantism in the persons of men such as Albert and Jean Réville, Maurice Vernes, and Auguste Sabatier that made up the main spiritual orientation of the faculty (Fournier 1994: 91–92).

The central influence on the Durkheimian religion cluster at the EPHE was the Indologist Sylvain Lévi, who joined the faculty there in 1887. Lévi was an expert in Sanskrit and Indian religions and held, simultaneously with his appointment at the EPHE, a chair at the Collège de France to which he had been elected at the tender age of 31. He was universally considered one of the premier historians of religion of the period. His influence is most clearly discernible on Mauss, but he taught Hubert and Hertz as well and was a friend and a colleague to all three, playing a major role in passing along to them "the painstaking procedures of textual analysis and some of the vast substantive knowledge that went into the *Année sociologique*" (T. Clark 1973: 47). The depth and complexity of his influence on the younger Durkheimians and especially Mauss requires considerably more excavation of their personal trajectories to fully unpack, so I reserve that discussion for Chapter 7, where I explore the question of religious identity in the Durkheimians.

The Durkheimian connection to the EPHE provided them access as students to expert discourses on religious history and ethnology that greatly contributed to their ability later, as scholars and teachers themselves, to speak to even the most specialist audiences, while still maintaining a dialogue with more popular and political circles. In sum, the experiences of the Durkheimian religion cluster at the École Normale Supérieure and the École Pratique des Hautes Études, the two institutional locations central to their formation, not only provided them with the necessary intellectual and cultural capital to become important participants in the key intellectual and cultural debates of the period; these experiences also shaped in important ways their sensibilities to the key problematics I have outlined and opened them to particular responses to those issues.

The Dreyfus Affair and the Political Role of the Intellectual: Durkheim's Ingenuity in Defining the Intellectual's Proper Politics

Over the course of this and the preceding chapter, I have explored the situation of the Durkheimian group with respect to two of the key problematics that intellectuals in the Third Republic faced, i.e., the question of secular morality and that of the possibility of scientific knowledge about man. The third dilemma facing intellectuals, which was related intimately to the other two, had to do with establishing the modern *political* role of the intellectual. The Dreyfus Affair provided the focal point of the third problematic in this period.

It is not without significance that the very term *intellectuel* first enters the popular imagination and vocabulary in France during this period. Christophe Charle (1990) has argued that the "intellectuels" as a social group emerged from an internal crisis of the elite social classes that was brought on by contradictions between, on the one hand, the rhetoric of a Republic that valorized meritocracy and the influence of culture and its producers, and, on the other, the actual distribution of power within the ruling classes that revealed only too clearly the lack of power possessed by those intellectual and cultural groups (the *dominated* fraction of the *dominant* class, in the terminology of Bourdieu) *vis-à-vis* the political and economic elites. The unique character of this class of "intellectuels" that emerged here has to do with its manner of intervention in the social world in order to take part in the struggle for power. They were radically separated into warring sub-groups according to the content of their interventions, but all sub-groups shared a method of action founded on collective identity and action, often in the form of petitions or other means destined to unleash scandal and cause public uproar. This new mode of collective action put the accent on the symbolic power of their intellectual status in the form of university diplomas and titles, membership in intellectual societies and associations, etc. (Charle 1990: 7–9). The new "intellectuel" is a cultural producer, just like those of earlier periods, but what distinguishes the former is the fact that, in Sartre's words, "he gets involved in what does not concern him," namely, the struggle for social and political power and "bring[s] with him, by way of assets, the fame he has acquired in another domain" (Juillard and Winock 1996: 11–12).

The Dreyfus Affair provided the scene for the emergence of this new kind of intellectual acting politically *qua* intellectual because of the vast complexity of fervent cultural and political debates intertwined at its core. Dreyfusard and anti-Dreyfusard intellectuals aligned themselves on the Affair according to their positions not merely with respect to the guilt or innocence of Captain Dreyfus, but also according to their positions on French racial/national identity and anti-Semitism, the authority and moral role of traditional institutions such as the Army and the Catholic Church, and the political feasibility in France of democratic and Republican institutions. Thus, Dreyfusards in the university (and the Durkheimians were generally on this side, though with some interesting complications that I take up later) tended toward secular defense of the Republic and progressive democracy or socialism, along with a certain confidence in the power of objective reason to solve problems not only of a scientific but also of a political nature (Charle 1990: 205–6). Meanwhile, their anti-Dreyfusard antagonists defended the necessity of traditional moral and political structures, usually in the form of a defense of the Church, the Army, and even restoration of the Monarchy, against the feebleness and instability of purely human reason.

All three of the problematics I have recognized as structuring the intellectual field during the middle years of the Third Republic were given their weight by the seeming collapse of the capacity of the domain of religion to respond to all three as part of a monolithic knowledge system. Some intellectuals sought the most advantageous manner of providing new answers to the questions from intellectual and political positions that would distance them from the old religious means of addressing the questions while still allowing them to tap into some of the discursive power that those old means still wielded. This would enable them to avoid alienating the most secular factions in French society by appearing too religious, while at the same time allowing them a certain insider understanding of and sympathy to the foundational religious importance and origin of these questions. We can perhaps not unfairly talk about such responses as *quasi-religious* in their makeup. In the public struggle for defining the acceptable terms within which one could address these difficult dilemmas, and in the private struggle for self-definition and personal meaning, some sought a ground that would enable them to pull off a difficult intellectual stunt: to respond at one and the same time in a secular *and* a religious way to problems that were made so serious (as virtually everyone, even the most vehement critics of the Catholic Church, recognized) precisely by secularization and the retreat of religion.

The Durkheimians were uniquely situated to take up these problematics, both for reasons of institutional location and formation and by virtue of the existential facts of their lives and the content of their own interventions. We can see this uniqueness especially in the complex way Durkheim, in responding to the Dreyfus Affair's posing of the question of the political role of the intellectual, skirted this treacherous ground between secular and religious thought and, in fact, *tied the three problematics together with the language of the sacred.*

We can best see the contours of Durkheim's navigation of this difficult ground by looking to the writings in which he most explicitly takes up the topic of the intellectual, though they might seem at first glance marginal to his scholarly work. In fact, the dilemmas Durkheim addressed there, though they clearly encompassed several broad cultural and political issues, were directly tied up in the emergence of the modern intellectual in the Third Republic. Far and away the most important of these texts in Durkheim's bibliography was written in 1898 and addresses the topic of the intellectual as political actor; in so doing, it alludes to several points of connection among the specific reasons he gives for the political rallying of the intellectuals to the cause of Captain Dreyfus, the role of the sacred in society, and the intellectual's task of constructing life and work as such around certain guiding principles.

The occasion of this article, titled "L'Individualisme et les intellectuels," was the debate raised by Ferdinand Brunetière's attack on the *intellectuels* in the wake of Zola's *J'accuse* letter and the petition of support for Zola's pro-Dreyfus position that was submitted by a number of intellectual figures to the Chamber of Deputies (Lukes 1973: 335). Durkheim saw this as an ideal opportunity to respond to the charge that the defenders of Dreyfus were motivated by a political foundation in radical individualism, even anarchism, and by an understanding of the intellectual project as fundamentally in opposition to the traditional order of society and to the sense of respect for what Maurice Barrès called "necessities ... anterior and perhaps foreign to the reason of the individual" (Barrès 1925: 45). Brunetière, Barrès, and others were, despite their sneering use of the term *intellectuel,* not attacking the intellectual as one who thinks, writes, and teaches as vocation from some crudely anti-intellectual position. Rather, they were criticizing what they saw as a radically new and dangerous conception of the intellectual role in society that they believed had rejected what I described earlier as the primary defining characteristic of the intellectual project, namely, *the pursuit of the sacred.* For Brunetière, Barrès, and their compatriots, the sacred, in its manifestation as the traditions and institutions of pre-Third Republic France, was under full-scale attack by those who had rejected the idea that intellectuals were called to explicate and defend the necessity of the sacred and who were instead raising themselves "to the rank of super-men" and, armed with their increasingly narrow specialist knowledge and mouthing misleading slogans about the unlimited powers of science and reason, were deigning to intervene in public affairs on which they had no legitimate right to speak (Lukes 1973: 335).

Durkheim's reply to the anti-Dreyfusard attack on the *intellectuels* sheds considerable light on his position on other dilemmas of the Third Republic having to do with secular education, anti-clericalism, and anti-Semitism. But it does even more than this. Here, Durkheim does not simply respond in a political discourse to a political challenge. Rather, his language is both political and, in the broadest sense, moral and even religious. He defines and defends the role of the intellectual not merely in terms of the part he or she is to play in particular affairs of the political arena, such as the one surrounding Captain Dreyfus, or even in larger social debates such as the one surrounding the inroads made by secular education against the Church during the Republic, but in terms of the very worldview and ethic that is to inform the intellectual's action and work. That ethic must be fundamentally *oriented toward the sacred.* So, in responding to Brunetière's criticisms of the anarchy that will inevitably come from the individualism purportedly at the root of the contemporary intellectual worldview, Durkheim distinguishes the ethic that is behind the pro-Dreyfus movement from the narrow, egoistic utilitarianism that he identifies as the fruit of the ideas of Herbert Spencer and liberal economists. *This* individualism, Durkheim argues, is too often taken by adversaries as the *only* variety of individualism (Durkheim 1970: 262). His individualism descends from a different and more complex intellectual heritage, having roots in such disparate sources as Rousseau, Kant, French spiritualism, and the writers of the Declaration of the Rights of Man. Instead of privileging the concrete individual operating from his or her concrete interests, it points to the privileged status of the human person *in abstracto.* This object becomes something infinitely more powerful than the merely utilitarian self-interest that is characteristic of the variety of individualism Durkheim agrees deserves to be harshly criticized. It takes on the character of a "touchstone" that provides the ground from which to distinguish good from evil. It "is considered *sacred* [and] has something of that transcendent majesty that Churches throughout time have attributed to their Gods" (Durkheim 1970: 264; emphasis added). Thus, an individualism of the sort Durkheim describes makes up "a *religion* in which man is at once believer and God" (Durkheim 1970: 265; emphasis added).

The sources to which Durkheim makes reference in locating the origins of this individualism might lead one to decide that what he is speaking of here is basically the abstract political philosophy of the "Rights of Man" that emerged from the Revolution, and that, at best, it is neither a particularly radical conceptual innovation, nor an unlikely or incongruous philosophical stance for one of Durkheim's political inclinations to take. It would be entirely in keeping with an analysis to which he had adhered since the appearance of his first major work, *De la division du travail social*, in 1893. These narrow political elements of its resonance are not, however, what primarily concern me here. What is of interest is the way in which Durkheim suggests that this is not merely the way in which intellectuals (or other social groups) think about politics. It is also a key to their own self-conception and their personal and collective project *as intellectuals*. After all, political rights and liberty, he argues, are only a means to the sacred end, not the end itself, and such liberty is dangerous when not clearly attached to that proper end (Durkheim 1970: 276). The worship of the abstract individual, as Durkheim defends it, will have as a general societal consequence the reconstruction of a state of moral unity. All have the responsibility to respond to this sacred object, but the task of the intellectuals is made several degrees more profound and more difficult by their particularly privileged position with respect to this object. Durkheim argues that this cult of the individual, of the abstracted and generalized human person and his or her "divine" nature, has become the modern manifestation of the sacred, worthy of a kind and depth of respect best approximated by religious metaphors (Durkheim 1970: 272). For the general populace, this respect begins and ends with a relatively dogmatic acceptance of the sacredness of the worshipped object, but intellectuals have as their task precisely the close examination and study of the same object. It is, after all, only the intellectuals, like Durkheim himself, who are properly situated to report on the radical changes in the nature of the sacred that have come with the modern world, or to remind us, in response to the charges of cultural conservatives, that in fact their alternative to Durkheim's proposed morality, namely Christian morality, is actually its genetic forebear and shares nearly all its most important elements (Durkheim 1970: 272–73). Only the intellectuals have a relationship with the sacred realm that involves them not merely in worshipping it, but also in telling us *why* we do so, and in *defending the necessity of doing so*. This shift, then, from previous modes of interaction with the sacred to this new mode is even more profoundly resonant for the intellectual because, although all will be directed to this discipline of the new morality, it is the intellectual who will both indicate the new sacred object and live in closest proximity to it given the nature of his or her work.

Understanding the full importance of this text in Durkheim's thought necessitates still more contextualization. The moment at which it appears is an important one in Durkheim's career. By this point (early 1898), he had completed the first three of the four major works of his lifetime (*Le Suicide* was the last of those three in 1897) and was finishing the publication of the first volume of the *Année sociologique,* which appeared in February of that year. Though he was still in Bordeaux, it was clear that his reputation was growing and he was already being viewed in the university world as a likely candidate for a post in Paris when the right circumstances coalesced. Perhaps most significantly for our purposes, though, is the fact that he was at this moment fully launching himself into the phase in his work that he himself characterized as the definitive direction in which he would move for the rest of his life, a direction that entailed a radical shift from his early work. This was the reorientation of his work to a focus on religion as the central category for sociological analysis.

According to Durkheim, this shift occurred in 1895 and was initiated by something we can only call a "reading experience," in the terms of Arpad Szakolczai (1998), in its purest form: the encounter with the work of William Robertson Smith on totemism and religion in primitive society. He is startlingly clear about the shift he felt this triggered in his own thought, claiming in a letter to the *Revue Néo-scholastique* that this reading helped him for the first time to understand the "essential role played by religion in social life" (Deploige 1912: 402). It was, he says, the point at which he understood that "[r]eligion contains ... all the elements that ... have given rise to the various manifestations of collective life" (Durkheim 1899: iv–v). Moreover, we can mark the year of his retrospective acknowledgement of his shift, 1898, as the year in which Durkheim was working on projects that must be classified as among his first substantial pieces of research on the theme of religion. Early in the year he wrote an essay on "Représentations individuelles et représentations collectives" that rehearsed the argument more fully sketched out later concerning the fundamentally social nature of the most basic representations of human consciousness, which he argued are religious in origin. We also know from correspondence that he participated heavily during that same year in the research and editing, if not the primary writing, of Mauss and Hubert's major work on sacrifice that appeared in the second volume of the *Année* in early 1899 (Durkheim 1998: 143–46, 173–75).

But the real connection between life and work that occurred for Durkheim in this period has to do more specifically with the Dreyfus Affair and the ways in which it provided a ground for intellectual interventions of an original variety into the political sphere through the use of the same definition of the sacred he provided in the response to Brunetière. We find Durkheim at this moment at a level of active political engagement that surpasses any other period of his life except perhaps that of World War I. In addition to his written interventions into the political debate over the role of the intellectuals, he was actively involved in public political rallies related to the defense of Dreyfus. He was also one of the most important members of the Ligue pour la Défense des Droits de l'Homme. His correspondence of the period, especially that with Hubert, who was deeply involved in the Dreyfusard activity in Paris, is filled with his concern for these matters. This is striking given his reputation in many accounts as a proponent of the intellectual as detached researcher who should not meddle in political power struggles for fear of compromising the scientific accuracy of his research. Why this frenzied intervention into the realm of the political at this particular juncture?

It is possible to trace, from the collision of Durkheimian thought with the combination of the "religious turn" indicated above and the complex cultural moment of the Dreyfus Affair, a kind of foundational experience that then informs the rest of Durkheim's work. For it was here that several key elements of deep concern to Durkheim, already present in a less focused way in earlier work, began to coalesce into a coherent and sustained effort to elaborate the role of the intellectuals in contemporary society through an investigation and reconstruction of the various means through which they act upon society. We know that Durkheim, from the very beginning, saw his vocation as that of something of a "secular priest" (Filloux 1977: 9) and that he believed the role into which he was moving had a very wide-ranging importance and power to influence the social world. The Dreyfus Affair was an exceptional case that demonstrated how Durkheim's conception of the intellectual's role in society subsumed the political question, the scientific question, and the moral question into the language of the sacred. Durkheim linked his recognition of the religious origins of the categories of thought (through the "reading experience" of Robertson Smith) to the task of the educator or the intellectual (which were already concerns in his courses and writings on education), and this is the individual who most intimately wields the tools of thought and who finds himself occupying the place in modern society vacated by the priest. This leads him to a powerful realization of the intellectual's relationship to the sacred that is put into operation by the radical event of the Dreyfus Affair, an event to which Durkheim reacted precisely as though it were one of the religious experiences of collective effervescence, (LaCapra 1972: 76), and especially so for intellectuals, that he would discuss in such detail in his last and most important work.

In this light, his statements on the deep affinities between religious thought and modern scientific activity in *Les Formes élémentaires* take on an even more radical cast. In exploring the social origins of religious representations and thus redefining the sacred object of religious activity, Durkheim is in fact exploring the social origins of scientific representations as well and redefining the sacred object toward which modern intellectual activity is to orient itself. More, as I have already suggested, Durkheim's substantial body of work on educational philosophy and pedagogical evolution and his long-term concerns with morality likewise take on a significance for the definition of the role of the modern intellectual that are in danger of being overlooked if we do not recognize the importance of the texts and experiences of the crucial year of 1898. In this light, we can understand the entire body of that material as a prescription both for the personal project of the intellectual and for the specific manner in which he is to substitute himself for the priestly figure and thereby direct the shaping of the collective conscience through pedagogical policy. In his lectures on pedagogical evolution in France, for example, we find a clear argument for the religious origins of pedagogical theory and the subsequent pseudo-priestly role of the instructor in the "formation of minds" through the "pedagogical faith." Durkheim's vision of the intellectual emerges here in startling terms, at once prophetic and priestly (Durkheim 1969).

In this mapping of the important cultural and political struggles of the middle Third Republic and their manifestations in various institutional settings inhabited by the Durkheimians, I have tried to put into relief the manner in which their unique position within this institutional and social matrix permitted them to rethink the intellectual's role through the possibility of a set of responses to the relevant questions that achieved a creativity and a complexity unmatched by most other participants in this network. The examination of Durkheim's fusion of the intellectual question into the reformulation of the experience of the sacred is the prelude to a fresh analysis of the Durkheimian treatment of the sacred in their scholarly work, which will come in later chapters.

Thus far, I have mapped out the ways in which broad cultural and political crises of the Third Republic informed the Durkheimians' way of thinking about the intellectual's role. In the next chapter, I look more closely at the ways in which similar cultural and political structural factors affected the context within which their descendants, the poststructuralists, did *their* thinking about the intellectual and the sacred.

5 The Scene of Poststructuralism

A View of the Parisian Intellectual Field from the End of WWII to the 1960s

As we leap half a century forward from the previous chapters, much obviously changes in terms of historical detail. But with respect to the broad set of problematics that defined the emergence of the *intellectuels* in the Third Republic, there is significant structural continuity between the two periods. Indeed, the same three intellectual problematics that I described facing the Durkheimians over the last two chapters can be recognized in the field in which the poststructuralists emerged. The problematic concerning the political role of intellectuals is informed in this second period by the dominance of Marxist notions of the engaged intellectual. This question is clearly a central concern of the dominant intellectual of the period, Sartre, and his model of intellectual engagement is the focus of the debate that emerges in 1960s France around the question of the political responsibilities of intellectuals.

The second problematic, that of the legitimate forms and expressions of intellectual knowledge, here features the relatively newly minted body of work labeled "structuralism" that emerged from linguistics and the social sciences and challenged the traditional university system and disciplines rooted in classicism, which had survived to a large degree intact after the assaults of the Third Republic modernists. By the late 1960s, the embrace of systematicity and scientism in structuralism is challenged from within by the thinkers now commonly labeled "poststructuralist."

Finally, the problematic of the creation of a new educational and broader social morality is present in the struggle between the old forms rooted in colonial, bureaucratic, and Gaullist France and more recent anti-colonial, anti-Gaullist, and anti-bureaucratic visions of moral identity. The educational structures move toward liberalization during this period, as this moral sentiment spreads itself into a wide swath of French culture and politics. One event figures centrally in the playing out of debates in all three of these problematics in this period: the revolt of May 1968. It is a flashpoint in which we see illuminated the contending sides on all three problematics: the Gaullist and Marxist intellectuals versus the *gauchistes;* the philosophical traditionalists and the apolitical structuralists versus the politicized poststructuralists; and the educational traditionalists at the Sorbonne versus the modernists and anarchists at the new educational institutions that had been created in the period. Let us turn then to a sketch of the intellectual field our poststructuralist group inhabited.

The Opiate of the Intellectuals?: The Power of Marxist Communism in Post-War Intellectual France

Any discussion of the French intellectual scene from the end of World War II through the 1960s must concentrate a good deal of attention on the very considerable role played by Marxism. French intellectuals in sympathy with Marxism had existed since at least the Soviet revolution of 1917, and intellectual "compagnons de route" such as André Gide had been visible symbols of the influence of Marxist communism since the early 1930s (Winock 1997: 278, 281, 358). But the heavy influence of Marxist thought on the French intellectual field of this period can be more fully accounted for by a complex of social and historical specificities of the French scene in the wake of World War II.

First, there was the undeniably important role played by French communists in the Resistance and the overwhelmingly Manichean worldview that dominated intellectual politics in the wake of the war. According to this worldview, one was either clearly a member of the Resistance or, by default, a collaborator, and the two political groups with the clearest claim to Resistance membership were the Communists and the Gaullists. The symbolism invoked by the Communists in regard to the Resistance was powerfully linked to the martyrs in the party; it called itself "the party of the 75,000 shot" in reference to those who lost their lives during the Occupation (Winock 1997: 514). Tony Judt (1998) has gone so far as to argue that the exigencies of the Occupation and the Resistance themselves created a set of binaries that were less than easy to escape. According to him, a number of "overlapping tropes" came to dominate French intellectual discourse in the post-war years: 1) violence; 2) the sexual; 3) treason; 4) collaboration; 5) resistance; and 6) the enemy (Judt 1992: 49–

54). One can see these quite clearly at work in the establishment of the Comité d'épuration de l'édition, which was formed just after the war by a Communist National Writers Committee that had emerged during the Occupation. This group, which included Jean-Paul Sartre and Simone De Beauvoir, took as its task the identification and punishment of intellectuals who collaborated with the Nazis during the War and Occupation (Drake 2002: 13). The context within which the group did its work cannot be overemphasized; this was a period in which nearly 11,000 French citizens were executed without trial (Judt 1992: 58). Although many writers and editors would be found guilty of collaboration by the committee and sentenced to various lengthy prison terms, the condemnation to death and execution of Robert Brasillach, a *normalien* and editor-in-chief of the anti-Semitic newspaper *Je Suis Partout*, which was one of the central journalistic faces of Vichy France, became a symbolically foundational moment in post-war French intellectual culture. Here, the struggle with fascism and anti-Semitism melds neatly into basic French conceptions of the cultural importance of the intellectual and the political responsibility with which he was charged. The result is a model of intellectual politics in which political position-taking is of the most dreadful seriousness imaginable and the only foolproof way to demonstrate the purity of one's politics is to identify with the Resistance and the political group that came to be most identified with it, the PCF. Liberal perspectives on speech rights simply made no sense in this context, as intellectual work was seen not as speech, but as action, and intellectual collaborators were not infrequently dealt with more harshly than industrial and economic collaborators (Drake 2002: 20–21).

In the wake of the war, the Communists quickly separated themselves from their political competitors in the struggle for the hearts and minds of the intellectual classes. Even the Gaullist claim to have avoided the pollution of "fascist treason" would be quickly challenged in the early post-war period by the Communists and their fellow travelers, notably Sartre. In 1947, De Gaulle launched the Rassemblement du peuple français (RPF) as a political movement in part dedicated to constitutional reform that would empower the executive branch. Sartre's journal *Les Temps modernes* immediately denounced the move as representing a "danger of dictatorship" and compared the RPF to Jacques Doriot's fascist Parti Populaire Français. Simone De Beauvoir compared the RPF's proposed factory committees to the fascist labor movements of the pre-war period that had been created explicitly to compete with communist labor unions (Drake 2002: 53).

How did the PCF and Marxist communism attract the support of French intellectuals? The Party, while from the first demonstrating a suspicion of intellectuals as a class, nonetheless recognized the practical importance of intellectual support early on and wooed them by promoting the work of those who demonstrated proper communist orthodoxy in directly material ways, e.g., by reviewing them in its journals (Drake 2002: 39–40, 43). But beyond individual interest in the promotion of their work to Party membership, there were a number of political realizations brought home by the Occupation that shifted many intellectuals toward an increased openness to Marxism. These included the recognition that France was no longer a great power and no longer seemed to be the possessor of the one true revolutionary tradition (the seeming success of the Soviet Union providing the evidence here), that nationalist universalist political discourses seemed to have the best chance to be politically effective, and that the masses were both a potential threat to and ally of the intellectuals who could be most effectively tamed by the French Communist Party (Khilnani 1993: 45). Moreover, the universalist and scientific pretensions of Marxist thought appealed greatly to the two "pillars" of French intellectual practice post-1789: abstract principles of truth and justice, and the universality of reason (Hazareesingh 1991: 55). More concretely and historically, four other factors made Marxist/Communist adhesion attractive to intellectuals: 1) the high prestige of Stalin and the Soviet regime in the wake of the Red Army's victory over the Nazis; 2) the significant Communist role in the Resistance; 3) the alleviation of intellectual isolation that was afforded by affiliation with the world-historical project of the workers; and 4) the certainties "about life and the future" offered by Marxism, parallel to those "that Christian fundamentalists find in the Bible" (Drake 2002: 41).

The third point speaks to an intriguing element in the French intellectual character of the period. This might well be termed the *fetishization* of the working class by French Marxist intellectuals. Raymond Aron (1955) spoke of this as the myth of the proletariat, and it is indisputable that a significant portion of the French intellectual classes in this period pointed to the condition of the working class as something deserving of particular admiration and even imitation (Hazareesingh 1991: 85). Sometimes, this identification took the form of a kind of intellectual self-loathing and self-sacrifice in the historical mission of the working class. Sartre's famous line about not letting down the workers at Billancourt was echoed by many others. Paul Éluard, for example, rigorously criticized Socialist Realism but avoided doing so before the workers because he believed "we mustn't upset those who are struggling" (Judt 1992: 208, 212).

The various discourses of Marxism/Communism to which intellectuals were attracted worked well beyond the ranks of orthodox PCF intellectuals. Even if it is clearly true that there were intellectuals aligned in the early post-war era not only on the PCF/USSR side and on the side of the Gaullist opposition (most notably Aron and Malraux), but also in a "neutralist" position that equally opposed both communism and radical anti-communism, there were very broad intellectual principles in Marxist thought that had a wide appeal even among French intellectuals who could not be neatly defined as Marxists (Drake 2002: 51). Far and away the most dominating intellectual figure of the period, Jean-Paul Sartre provides a useful example here, so I briefly sketch some of the history of his intersection with Marxist thought throughout the period between the end of World War II and 1968.

The Sartrean Example: Intellectual Fellow Traveling in the Post-War Period and the Touchstone of the Engaged Intellectual

So great was Sartre's influence during the post-war period that intellectuals were obliged to position themselves with respect to him, even if they utterly opposed him. Much has been written on the successes of existentialism as a philosophical and political model, indicating the place of Sartre's journal *Les Temps Modernes,* and his individual characteristics as a kind of polymath intellectual (philosopher, novelist, and political writer with a purported Resistance record as well) who was uniquely placed to dominate the French scene. Within a year of the end of the war, he had written two widely read novels on intellectual engagement and launched his journal, which had an original editorial committee of himself, Simone de Beauvoir, Maurice Merleau-Ponty, Raymond Aron, Michel Leiris, and Jean Paulhan (Drake 2002: 24). It quickly achieved intellectual hegemony because it was the one post-war journal that most effectively encapsulated the spirit of engagement and the spirit of personal freedom, offering "a philosophy of 'commitment' whose watchword is 'sympathize, but don't join'" (Boschetti 1988[1985]: 79).

That phrase perfectly summarizes the Sartrean position on intellectual politics. In the early postwar period, he was clearly unaligned with the PCF, having refused to subordinate what he took as the necessary freedom of the intellectual function to rigid and collectivist party discipline, and *Les Temps modernes* was formally unaffiliated with the Communists. In fact, Sartre's philosophical perspective was vigorously attacked by the PCF and Marxist intellectuals as hopelessly bourgeois, based on a concept of individual freedom that was seen by the most militant communist intellectuals and party members as simply incompatible with the Marxist vision of the collective will of the working class and the undeniable sweep of the historical dialectic toward a post-bourgeois world in which Sartre's liberal freedoms would be swept away. Existentialism was even connected to fascism by orthodox PCF intellectuals through its relationship to the thought of Heidegger (Drake 2002: 28). Despite the vigorous attack on existentialist philosophy mounted by the PCF, Sartre frequently expressed sympathy for the Party and Marxist political principles more generally. Ultimately, he came to understand that the political goals of the Communists were in line with his own, as both sought to further the interests of the anticapitalist revolutionary working classes (Drake 2002: 52, 56–57). Sartre, Merleau-Ponty and other key intellectuals of the period who were not PCF members briefly affiliated themselves with the RDR (Rassemblement Démocratique Révolutionnaire), a non-communist revolutionary leftist political movement, during the late 1940s as a formal way of expressing political sympathies with Marxist principles while avoiding commitment to the PCF, and Sartre left the movement in late 1949 when the RDR embraced anti-communism (Drake 2002: 60–62). Sartre moved in the early 1950s to a much clearer position of fellow traveler of the PCF in the wake of a Communist demonstration in 1952 that was brutally repressed by the police; he wrote "Les Communistes et la paix" as evidence of his movement to the side of the PCF (Drake 2002: 79).

This close position of alliance lasted only until the Soviet invasion of Hungary in 1956, when he again established some ideological distance from the PCF. Nonetheless, Sartre and other fellow traveler intellectuals continued to engage in some of the discursive and argumentative strategies central to the Communist position. Of central importance here was the strategy of largely uncritical support for Soviet and Eastern European communist states which took the form of a certain negativism. A double standard of evaluation was consistently applied for capitalist and socialist countries, as the former were seen as representatives of unadulterated evil when they failed, while the latter were seen as perhaps yet unrealized but well-intended when they did. Political identities were expressed not as "pro-Stalin, pro-labor camp, pro-communism" but rather as "anti-Truman, anti-colonialism, anti-liberalism" (Judt 1992: 178). When serious and documented criticisms of the Soviet labor camps started to emerge, some Marxist and *marxisant* intellectuals pointed to the "concentration camp" of the working class area of Montreuil near Paris as evidence of "capitalist labor camps" (Judt 1992: 175). Soviet atrocities were made relative by arguing that the Russian civil war and World War II (which were to be blamed squarely on capitalism) had killed far more people (M. Christofferson 2003: 70). When Sartre and *Les Temps modernes* did on occasion speak about Soviet authoritarianism, for example, in an October 1947 radio broadcast "Tribune des Temps Modernes," they always noted that the USSR was forced into this position by the imperialist powers (Drake 2002: 58). As late as 1950, an editorial in *Les Temps modernes* authored by Sartre and Merleau-Ponty on the Soviet camps downplayed their singularity by comparing them to the French colonies (M. Christofferson 2003: 68–69).

Although numerous controversies of the late 1940s had some effect on the power of communist ideology for the intellectuals, it was not until the Rousset Affair of 1949–50 that the PCF suffered considerable damage to its reputation among the intellectuals. David Rousset, a founder of the RDR, called in 1949 for a "commission of enquiry into the Soviet camps" (Drake 2002: 67). He was attacked by the Communist review *Les Lettres françaises* as an agent of the capitalist powers deliberately lying about the nature of the camps. Rousset sued the review and won the case. Numerous intellectuals spoke and wrote publicly in support of Rousset and against the communists. *Esprit* and *Les Temps modernes* took on the issue of the camps during the time of the Rousset trial, and some of the differences among formerly ideologically united intellectual comrades on the left that would later turn into major fault lines began to emerge here. It was only a few years later that Sartre's major breaks with Merleau-Ponty and Camus would take place.

The event however that most clearly led to the full unraveling of intellectual support for the PCF, but not (immediately) for the Marxist narrative of the engaged intellectual, was the war in Algeria. Though the debacle of the Soviet handling of the situation in Hungary in 1956 had major repercussions in terms of intellectual alienation from the Party and its front organizations (M. Christofferson 2003: 39), the tremendous social costs exacted by the independence struggle in Algeria and the connected events in France between 1954 and 1962 significantly prepared the way for the crisis of 1968 in exacerbating the tension in French society between the radical left and the political mainstream. The Algerian War years were witness to a progressive movement leftward on the part of large segments of the intelligentsia, as they sought to incorporate the discourses of counter-imperialism and Third World liberation into the language and action of the engaged intellectual. The PCF, meanwhile, demonstrated itself incapable, especially at the outset of the war, of making sense of the Algerian conflict outside of a framework of cut-and-dried Stalinism. The Party supported the Mollet government, voting "special powers" for the prosecution of the war in 1956, and only came to a position of strong opposition to the war with the emergence of OAS terrorism in France (M. Christofferson 2003: 39–40). Ideological reasons for this position-taking are not difficult to come by; Algerian nationalism seemed inspired at root by Islam and this certainly would make it difficult for the explicitly atheist hard-line Marxist to see the FLN as political allies. Indeed, many secularist French intellectuals outside the PCF felt the same way (Rioux and Sirinelli 1991: 15). More broadly, though, the central ideological axis of

Communist thought, i.e., the binary opposition of proletariat and bourgeoisie, broke down in the face of Algeria. Not only the party, but also the working class that they championed, evidenced conservatism on the question of colonialism (M. Christofferson 2003: 43). A new binary, Third World revolutionary and imperialist power, became the operative maker of meaning on the French intellectual left, although this took time. Both Sartre and Aron were seen as heretics in their respective camps for being among the first major French thinkers to take an explicitly anti-colonial stance (Rioux and Sirinelli 1991: 119), but in the hurly-burly of the war experience, much of the French intellectual left would come to follow them by 1962.

The post-war ideological meaning matrix collapsed under the weight of the war and a new set of narratives about how to be an engaged leftist intellectual emerged. These new narratives rejected the statism of both the PCF and the Gaullists, and the universalism of the French left Republican project was also targeted by this new intellectual generation that had seen only too clearly how discourses about "the rights of man" did not preclude the carrying out of atrocities on peoples considered beyond the pale of the Republic. The Algerian War shifted the discourse about the politics of the intellectual to the left, to the detriment ultimately of the Communists and to the benefit of new *gauchiste* groups and ideologies that emerged after the war. In Chapters 6 and 11, I will take up in micro-sociological detail the ways in which the shift away from Communism and toward *gauchisme* (and ultimately to a still more radical turn toward issues of spirituality and mysticism) on the French intellectual left of the 1960s influenced the emerging poststructuralist conception of intellectual political identity. Other macro-sociological factors that set the stage for post-structuralist identity-formation require examination here first.

Philosophy Confronted by the Social Sciences II: Structuralism and the Emerging Space in the Fifth Republic of the Consecrated Heretics

Three of our four poststructuralists were, like the bulk of the Durkheimian sociologists of religion, *agrégés* in philosophy, and the fourth, Baudrillard, who never passed the *agrégation*, interacted significantly with the philosophical field in France throughout his life, notwithstanding the facts that he sat for the *agrégation* in German and was formally situated for the entirety of his academic career in a sociology department. We must therefore carefully consider the nature of the philosophical field in France during their formative and productive years, especially in its relationship to the social sciences, which remained charged with conflict and cultural import throughout this period.

Broadly, the period of the intellectual formation of the poststructuralists stretches from the early post-World War II years through the early 1960s. The dominance of university neo-Kantianism in French philosophical circles, which was championed and personified first by Renouvier, then Brunschvicg and which had won out in the philosophical struggle during the Third Republic over both the positivists and the Bergsonian spiritualists (although the latter school remained more influential on non-academic intellectuals and in the broader public than neo-Kantianism (Schrift 2006: 12)), had begun to wane by the 1930s. It was replaced in the generation that included Sartre, Merleau-Ponty and their cohort by the "three H's"—Hegel, Husserl, and Heidegger (Descombes 1980[1979]: 3–7). Although they had a strong opponent in another Husserlian-influenced philosophical position that found expression in the "formalism, intuitionism, and … theory of science" of Gaston Bachelard, Jean Cavaillès, Georges Canguilhem, and Alexandre Koyré (Schrift 2006: 36), phenomenology and existentialism eventually emerged in this period as the dominant French philosophical school, personified by Sartre, Maurice Merleau-Ponty, and Gabriel Marcel. By the end of World War II and through roughly the early 1960s, the dominant philosophical and intellectual position was that of a "syncretic humanism" derived from the thought of the three H's. Perhaps its most representative single text was Sartre's *Critique of Dialectical Reason,* which, in its reconciling of Marxist and phenomenological traditions, presented a distinctly optimistic and even utopian vision for humankind that was centered in a "strong confidence in revolutionary social progress, to be achieved by human agents freed from the alienating chains of mercantile society and imbued with a sense of moral responsibility and political commitment" (Pavel 1992: 3).

However, by the mid-50s or early-60s, the subsequent intellectual generation had set its sights on an attack of syncretic humanism and its chief exponents. Some have characterized the period following the dominance of the "three H's" as that of the rise of the "masters of suspicion"—Marx, Nietzsche, and Freud. Vincent Descombes (1980[1979]: 12) argues that Sartre's generation can be distinguished from that of Foucault by the differing position of Hegel in the *Zeitgeist* of the two generations. In the earlier period, "the only way to reconcile the contradictory demands of modernity was to advance an interpretation of Hegel," while by the 1960s, Hegel had been utterly rejected and relegated to the philosophical scrapheap, or at least turned on his head in some radical way approximating Marx's own method of moving beyond the author of the *Phenomenology*. Dialectical thought in the Hegelian mode is the very condition for philosophy for the Sartre generation, while the *critique* of the dialectic achieves the status of a general rule for the philosophers who follow in the generation after him.

There is something quite interesting buried in this brief history of the philosophical influences of the poststructuralist generation that I want to explore. We know that reading Nietzsche, the prime source of anti-dialectical, anti-Hegelian thought in this generation, was not yet something that frequently took place in established educational institutions; indeed, as we saw in the previous chapter, even a figure as revered as Lucien Herr was essentially denied a position on a university faculty in large part because of his interest in Nietzsche. Foucault notes more than once the fact of Nietzsche's extra-institutional status (see e.g., Foucault 1991[1981]: 44). Others who have considered the question at length agree with him that up through at least the early post-World War II period, that is, when the poststructuralists were of school age, Nietzsche was very rarely considered seriously or taught by university philosophers (Le Rider 1999: 193). In fact, virtually the sole Parisian academic philosopher of any standing during the period of the intellectual formation of the poststructuralist group who engaged Nietzsche seriously was Jean Wahl, a professor at the Sorbonne closely associated with Georges Bataille and Roger Caillois (Le Rider 1999: 183).

If the poststructuralists and others in their generation were reading Nietzsche, and we know they were, then they were not doing it as part of their formal educational training. They were instead directing themselves *outside* of the academic world for intellectual resources to subsequently put to use *inside* that world in the interests of invigorating it. This was but one key example of a broader phenomenon during this period. We might go so far as to speak of a general sense of opposition to scholarly culture in the wake of World War II and the Occupation that is present through a wide swath of educated French society. This *Zeitgeist* consisted of "nothing less than the ambition to transform the accepted notions of what culture was, of what education was, and of what it meant to live a cultured and scholarly life" (Rigby 1994: 245). In some ways, the entire discipline of philosophy, especially in its university manifestation, began to be seen as too austerely removed from the real events of the times. In a French intellectual world that had long enthroned the Queen of the Disciplines and that had established very little in the way of alternative intellectual institutions for the social sciences that might have counter-balanced this lack of engagement on the part of philosophy, this meant that philosophy herself would see some significant transformative efforts during this period. Many of the leading philosophical figures of the emerging post-Sartrean generation (including Foucault, Deleuze, and Derrida) would move in at least some of their work in directions that forced traditional philosophical discourses into the terrains of the social sciences, even if they still formally spoke as representatives of the discipline of philosophy.

The French intellectual world of the late 1940s through the early 1960s was a world in which philosophy largely retained its leading role in the university but with some significant changes underway. The centers of academic tradition, the Sorbonne and the ENS, maintained a consecrated place due to their histories and, in the case of the ENS, the ability to grant the *agrégation*. These institutions were characterized by a focus on classical knowledge, with philosophy the focal discipline around which all else revolved. The human/social sciences were deemphasized there, to put the matter lightly. It was not until the startlingly late date of 1958 that a degree in sociology was finally created in the university system and the massive symbolic gesture was made at the Sorbonne to change the name of the Faculté des Lettres to the Faculté des Lettres et des Sciences Humaines (Drouard 1982: 74). The fate of the social sciences, seemingly on the rise at the end of the nineteenth century and with the support of a popular political ideology of secular Republicanism, had radically shifted after Durkheim's death. Ever since the days of Duruy's reforms of the nineteenth century that included its creation, the École Pratique des Hautes Études had been one of the sites of struggle over the role and future of the social and human sciences in France. Duruy himself had desired the creation of an EPHE section on economic sciences, but the project died on the vine in 1869 at the fall of his ministry. Earlier, in September 1868, he had expressed the difficulty of broaching the topic of establishing institutional centers for the study of the social and economic in the highly politicized French academic world: "I was allowed to create [the EPHE] without a word of opposition because it only concerned chemistry and natural history; if I had pronounced the name of that economic science of which you speak so well, I would have stirred up violent attacks" (Mazon 1988: 22–23).

Although Duruy's efforts had come to naught, other efforts were made in subsequent years to circumvent the structural problem facing the French social sciences of securing intellectual and financial approval for such an institution from the French state (Mazon 1988: 29). However, they also quickly ran into political difficulties. In 1929, the old EPHE veteran Marcel Mauss presented a proposal to the Laura Spelman Rockefeller Foundation for a comprehensive institution dedicated centrally to research and teaching in the social sciences. In his proposal, he explicitly stipulated that economics and the mere gathering of economic data regarding production and consumption should not be the centerpiece of the institution. Rather, it should be specialized in research in all social scientific disciplines and integrated physically by the creation of "a central building ... work cubicles ... a research library" for the scholars of the institution (Mazon 1988: 46). Mauss's proposal was received by the Rockefeller Foundation at the same time as another that was drawn up by Charles Rist, a professor of law in the Paris law faculty. The two proposals conceived of the social sciences in radically different ways. Rist thought the emphasis should be on quantitative data on contemporary economic and social life, and he explicitly rejected "the purely speculative and theoretical" (Mazon 1988: 44). In political terms, Rist's proposal was precisely the kind of thing likely to appeal to a funding source such as the Rockefeller Foundation, whose interests in the social sciences reverted ultimately in the view of Pierre Bourdieu to a desire for the production of effective mechanisms of social control and the combating of the socialist menace (Mazon 1988: i). Mauss's vision was viewed with profound suspicion, as was his leftist political disposition. Stunningly, the Rockefeller Foundation even asked Rist's opinion of Mauss's competing proposal and basically accepted the former's exceedingly negative portrayal of Mauss as "essentially a politician who has produced nothing himself" (Mazon 1988: 47). Rist's proposal was funded lavishly in 1931, leading to the creation of the Institut scientifique de recherches économiques et sociales. Mauss's ambitious proposal was rejected. Sociology, it seemed at this point, was vanquished to the periphery of the French academic world, perhaps forever.

French Durkheimianism Post-Durkheim (1917–1945) and the Question of Disciplines and Knowledge in the Sixth Section of the EPHE

But how had this situation come to pass, after what had seemed in the early years of the twentieth century like the impending triumph of Durkheimian sociology in the Parisian institutional complex? We need first to look at the fortunes and influence of orthodox, academic Durkheimianism in intellectual circles after Durkheim's death in 1917. Here, the essential and startling fact is the degree to which Durkheim failed, despite his obvious skills and resources as the leader of an intellectual movement, to successfully institutionalize Durkheimianism. The efforts by Durkheim and some other members of the *Année* team to solidify his brand of sociology at the institutional level were considerable, especially in the years following Durkheim's appointment to the position at the Sorbonne. The dividends were impressive in the short run, but the Durkheimian presence in the university in the years following the conclusion of World War I fell off dramatically. The reasons for this were several, but perhaps the most obvious and important was the fact of the war itself. The Durkheimians suffered crushing losses of many key figures in their movement (Besnard 1983: 34–35; Mauss 1969: 473–99; T. Clark 1973: 209).

Another factor is basically personalist in nature, but sociological in implication. Terry Clark argues convincingly for the efficacy of the patron/cluster model of power-building in the French academic world, and the death of Durkheim meant the loss of one of the more effective patrons in this game for the *Année* team. Durkheim was a gifted organizer of collective work with a thorough commitment to a vision of progressive scientific discovery and a facility as the central node in a hierarchical group structure that superbly fitted the rigidly hierarchical French academic world (T. Clark 1973: 184–86). The loss of the great patron Durkheim meant not only the inability to continue the collective labor of the *Année*, but also the absence of an effective figurehead and leader for the entire movement within the French university.

There were also larger shifts in the context of Parisian intellectual life between the two wars that made reception of orthodox Durkheimianism increasingly indifferent, if not hostile. Clark (1973: 199) speaks of a general shift in the Latin Quarter climate after 1905 from Cartesianism to spontaneism that hindered the reproduction and further expansion of Durkheimian thought. It seems clear that some kind of significant shift regarding receptivity to orthodox Durkheimian sociology, and still more generally, to sociology *tout court,* did indeed take place at some point in the decades just prior to and just after the end of the Great War. However, the reasons for such a shift are complex and hard to pinpoint neatly. Despite the thinning of Durkheimian ranks in academic chairs and related administrative positions, there were still a few well-placed and senior Durkheimians in important and influential posts after the war; Bouglé and Fauconnet were at the Sorbonne and Halbwachs at the university in Strasbourg (Heilbron 1985: 204–5). Yet there were no new recruits to the Durkheimian cause in its former institutional locations. While Durkheim's early recruits had virtually all been *agrégés* in philosophy and history, these two disciplinary sources of Durkheimian recruitment dried up completely. The traditional disciplinary suspiciousness of social science that was powerfully characteristic of most university philosophy in the French system, which had seemed momentarily to be changing with the growth in prestige of Durkheimian sociology, reemerged in the inter-war period with a vengeance. The failure to create a program of studies yielding a higher degree in sociology meant that no new carriers of the banner could be produced in this manner either.

But if the institutional situation for sociology was dark in the inter-war period, World War II nearly killed it altogether. One can even speak of "radical decapitation" of the Durkheimian lineage during the decade surrounding the end of the war in 1945, as within that ten-year period, Bouglé, Mauss, Fauconnet, and Halbwachs died, leaving the school with no centrally placed players in the French academic world (Mazon 1988: 71). During the war years, many younger French social scientists (e.g., Georges Gurvitch, Lévi-Strauss, Jacques Soustelle) left France for the United States and the New School for Social Research in New York City, where a French language École Libre des Hautes Études was created in 1942 and served as a gathering place for many of the French social thinkers who could find no institutional home in their own country (Mazon 1988: 72).

It was only in the late 1940s that an institution for the social sciences that eventually (by the start of the 1960s) would come to substantially challenge the position of philosophy for hegemony in the French intellectual Zeitgeist was finally created in Paris. As in the case of Rist's Institut, this came only with funding from a non-French source, the same Rockefeller Foundation. Pierre Auger, the director of French higher education, and Charles Morazé, *agrégé* in history with professional connections to the *Annales* historians Lucien Febvre and Fernand Braudel, contacted Rockefeller officials immediately after the war and established a preliminary list of disciplinary directors for a projected Sixth Section to the École Pratique in April 1947 (Mazon 1988: 87). Funding was obtained and the Sixth Section officially opened its doors in the fall of 1948. The first program included a number of figures who would later be seen as the progenitors of structuralism in France (Febvre, Braudel, Lévi-Strauss) as well as some other significant names from the ranks of the social sciences (Caillois, Henri Lefebvre, Gurvitch). Braudel was quickly named the head of the new section and he ably directed it through the dangerous ideological waters of those early years (Mazon 1988: 126–29). Between 1958 and 1965, he brought in a stunning array of talent: Alain Touraine, Roland Barthes, Cornélius Castoriadis, Jacques Derrida, and Pierre Bourdieu, among others. The reputation of the Sixth Section as an institutional home for structuralism was broadly understood within a decade of its creation (Healy 1995: 50; Rieffel 1993: 428). It was formally emancipated from the EPHE in 1975 and renamed the École des Hautes Etudes en Sciences Sociales (EHESS).

Driven internally by a discourse of modernization of the knowledge of the human world, the Sixth Section moved increasingly from its earliest years in a direction that fundamentally challenged the still-reigning syncretic humanism of Sartre and his allies. The unmodified term "structuralism" is too basic for making sense of what was going on in the Sixth Section, as there were at least three different kinds of structuralist thought emerging during this period: 1) *moderate* structuralism, which characterized "those rationalist theorists [such as Tzvetan Todorov] who were attracted to the results of recent linguistics, but refrained from borrowing its concepts and methods *stricto sensu*"; 2) *scientistic* structuralism which borrowed more extensively and indiscriminately from structural linguistics (e.g., Lévi-Strauss and Greimas); and 3) the most important category for this study, *speculative* structuralism, which "unit[ed] the philosophical and ideological branches of the movement" and counted among its central members Foucault, Derrida, the later Barthes, and Baudrillard (Pavel 1992: 4–5). Despite significant differences among the three, they were united in their opposition to syncretic humanism by their significant borrowing from linguistics and a deeply critical stance toward humanism, subjectivity, and truth.

The spirit of the EPHE is neatly encapsulated by Bourdieu (1984) in his analysis of the Barthes/Picard affair of the mid-1960s and the manner in which it demonstrated the opposed intellectual character of the EPHE and the Sorbonne. In 1965, Raymond Picard, a distinguished Sorbonne professor of French literature, wrote *Nouvelle critique ou nouvelle imposture*, an attack on Barthes's *Sur Racine* and *Essais critiques* in which he argued that the "new criticism" in the structuralist vein was nothing more than swaggering bombast, long on politicized jargon but empty of any real substantive contribution to the understanding of literature. Merely engaging Barthes publicly was a radical move for the Sorbonne scholars, who, as Élisabeth Roudinesco describes, generally "never wanted to speak of modern literature, nor of linguistics, and still less of psychoanalysis" (Derrida and Roudinesco 2001: 23). The tenor of Picard's response, however, was scathingly critical. Barthes responded with *Critique et verité*, which endeavored to show how traditional scholarship's reliance on notions of objective literary standards is actually a refusal to acknowledge its own ideologically-derived presuppositions. One might at first glance believe that Bourdieu is overly dramatic in dubbing this exchange "the Dreyfus Affair of the literary world" (1984: 152), yet it does have some points of similarity with the battles in the Third Republic over the Nouvelle Sorbonne. In that earlier cultural war, as I recounted earlier, it was the New *Sorbonnards* who represented the new disciplines, the approach of science, and the political left, while the traditional literary Sorbonne and the extra-university literary world represented reaction, individualist creation and the political right. In the Barthes/Picard affair, on the other hand, Picard and the Sorbonne represent the side of reaction and tradition, while Barthes and the EPHE are the functional equivalent in this space of the New *Sorbonnard* challenge to the status quo with a new and purportedly scientific language.

But things are also somewhat more complicated in the later struggle, and indeed these complexities are significant. *Both* Picard and Barthes invoke the language of scientific clarity in their discourses, the one calling on a science of literary critical principle carefully tested over time, the other a science of criticism informed by the new social scientific and structuralist methods that enable linking of literary texts to the social. Barthes even claimed for himself the conservative mantle of "true guardian of national values," insofar as he was seeking to make France's literary past relevant in the present (Barthes 1981: 46–47). His position is further complicated by the fact that he also invokes, partially as a result of the openness of the EPHE culture to what Bourdieu calls "journalistic criteria and values," some of the same *literary* themes of creativity that were the stock of the traditionalist enemies of the Nouvelle Sorbonne (Bourdieu 1984: 148, 155). This does not however too much obscure the basic fact of the two positions: Barthes (and by extension the EPHE, and especially the Sixth Section) remains the critic of traditional academic technique and custom, the harbinger of new and radical intellectual tools, and Picard (and by extension the Sorbonne) is the defender of the scholarly status quo. This opposition is absolutely central for understanding the developments in French educational institutions during and after the May 1968 period, which I will discuss later in this chapter.

How then did the EPHE manage not only to compete with but even to overtake the Sorbonne and the university system in terms of the prestige and influence of its central ideas and thinkers by the mid-1960s, and how did these factors affect the intellectual framework within which the poststructuralist group constructed positions *vis-à-vis* the question of disciplinary alliance and knowledge? The answer likely begins with the same structural peculiarities of the French academic world that help explain why it took so much longer for the social sciences to find an institutional anchor there than was the case in, for instance, Germany. A number of studies of the rise of structuralism and the specific institutions in which it reigned during the period under discussion here have pointed to some key institutional facts: 1) the centralization of the French academic world, which contributed to dual tendencies to fuse disparate intellectual disciplines and genres and to make it easier for fashionable new ideas (especially those, like structuralism, that propose a centralized mode of knowledge) to attain a broader success than they do in less centralized institutional settings; 2) the overarching purpose of the modern French university system from the days of its creation under Napoléon, that is, its primary activity of training future teachers and other professionals and the consequent secondary role assigned to research in those universities, which in turn contributed to 3) the centrality of a very specific kind of intellectual market which has been theoretically elaborated by Raymond Boudon and which entails the production of scholarly work that is aimed at and susceptible to the judgment not only of other scholars but of an interested non-academic public as well (Parodi 2004: 195–96, 198; Pavel 1992: 134).

This last point deserves elaboration. Boudon's framework for intellectual markets is tripartite. At one end, there are intellectual markets that consist of production solely for other intellectual producers, and here strictly institutional intellectual criteria for judgment are applied to works. At the other, there are markets in which intellectual production is geared to the widest possible diffusion into the mass public, and hence the criteria for judgment shift toward pluralism and the lack of intellectual rigor. In the middle, we find a kind of intellectual market that is split between other intellectual producers and a limited segment of the mass public that is relatively educated and interested in intellectual matters but still largely incapable of evaluating works strictly on objective intellectual grounds, and thus in this model there is an inevitable movement away from intellectual rigor, not as pronounced as in the second market situation but still significant. The French situation is remarkably oriented toward that intermediate, split intellectual market. Intellectual success thus depends not simply on acclaim by intellectual colleagues, but also on the splash a work can make among the interested, non-scholarly public. Parodi describes the path to consecration on the part of Lévi-Strauss as a representative example of this system at work. Early failures to accede to a position at the Sorbonne and the Collège de France, in appeals solely to other intellectual producers, were followed in 1955 by the publication of *Tristes tropiques,* which achieved a wide success among the reading French public and made Lévi-Strauss a household name among that public. The wave of this success in the intermediate, mixed market carried Lévi-Strauss quickly to and then beyond the institutional positions he had been unable to achieve purely by his efforts in the scholarly marketplace (Parodi 2004: 202–3).

It is certainly the case that mass media institutions such as the press and television played a key role in the presentation and translation of structuralist work to the educated mass public. The example of the tremendous media campaign around the publication of Foucault's *Les Mots et les choses* in 1966 has been frequently noted as one of the earliest moments in which the power of these mass media in promoting intellectual work was demonstrated. The massive campaign in the weekly *Le Nouvel observateur* (which included a laudatory review article by Foucault's close friend, Deleuze) and *L'Express*'s coronation of the "genius" behind a new "philosophical revolution" (complete with a three-quarter page photo of said genius) were aptly summarized by Jean-Paul Aron as representing something new in French cultural production and consumption: "We are at that turning point at the end of history where the advertising bombardment ... of signifiers, signs of nothing, begins to assault what was until now the vaguely protected landscape of culture" (Aron 1984: 272).

Beyond the simple fact of increasing the institutional viability of the social sciences in a French academic world that still recognized philosophy as its sole queen, discussion of the effect of the EPHE Sixth Section/ EHESS must include questions of its general intellectual and political atmosphere. There was a striking liberalism, in both political and institutional terms, about the Sixth Section in comparison to the university system that contributed to a sense of freedom from traditional restraints of professional criteria in recruitment of professors. As the EHESS was conceived as an institution that would teach students how to do research by introducing them to the active research of the professors rather than through established courses, a substantial amount of liberty existed in terms of the requirements for instructors. This meant unorthodox researchers in underappreciated disciplines, and even those who were non-French and engaged in non-French research projects, could here find an institutional position. The contrast with the pedagogical conservativism of the university system could hardly have been greater. In addition to the differences in qualifications and origins of many of the professors, the EHESS differed also from the university system in the micro-sociological factor of pedagogical style. The importance of the seminar as pedagogical site was emphasized. This meant a valorization of a kind of collective work that consisted of bringing together small groups of 15 or 20 to undertake an "apprenticeship" in research at the feet of a "master revered for his knowledge and erudition" (Rieffel 1993: 429–30). In this, the example of earlier EPHE instructors like Sylvain Lévi lived on. A classic example from the 1930s was the Hegel course of Alexandre Kojève. Another celebrated example was Barthes's 1962 seminar, which wound up consisting of nearly a hundred students gathered together in a kind of neo-tribal utopian micro-society (Rieffel 1993: 431).

This model of instruction contrasted radically with the regime in place at the Sorbonne, where things had changed little since Durkheim's day. There, the professor spoke from on high to a sea of silent listeners. Instead of fresh research in each new seminar, many professors repeated the same lectures over and over again, and distance between faculty and students was the rule (Colquhoun 1986: 5; Rieffel 1993: 445).

Nanterre, Vincennes, and the Avant-Gardization of the Universities: The Revolution in the Fifth Republic in Morality and Education

The issue of radical shifts in pedagogical style extended beyond the EHESS and encompassed far more in its meaning than narrow questions of pedagogy. In fact, it was a central part of a broader movement during the 1960s and 1970s to radically question the basic means of producing moral citizens in the French nation. As such, it is crucial to situate this discussion in a context that ultimately extends beyond the educational institutions themselves and endeavors to capture the larger social and cultural revolution that took place in France from roughly the mid-1960s through the mid-1980s.[1] Just as the university reforms of the Third Republic need to be framed within the broader secularization process that weakened the role of the Church in French moral culture, the reforms of the 1960s have to be understood in the stream of more powerful and general currents that sought to weaken the post-war dominance of ascetic and bureaucratized institutions (notably, the French state itself and the institutions that had replaced the Church for many, the Gaullist and Communist Parties) in the interest of a moral and cultural ethic of direct democracy.

In purely demographic and economic terms, France in 1946 was a decimated nation. The population would only really recover from the massive losses of the two wars and begin to experience growth in the mid 1960s (Mendras 1994: 14). But by this time, the stage would be set for massive changes in French society that should be considered, as Henri Mendras indicates, as a second French revolution just as profound as the first. In economic terms, the changes were obvious: the massive movement of French workers away from agricultural and small household business occupations; the emergence of consumption industries as the dominant economic force, replacing the base industries that had driven the French economy up through the mid 1960s; the decrease in the average work week that began in 1965 (1994: 15–16, 20–21). But a revolution in cultural terms was also taking place here. The end of the Algerian War in 1962 meant for the first time since 1939 that French political values could be considered and debated outside of the framework of the immediate crisis of war (1994: 15). This meant a number of things, but most centrally that political position-takings of a variety that had been disallowed by the pragmatics of a nation at war were now on the playing field. Broad cultural changes associated with economic growth also began to emerge. A shift took place from the post-war austerity and asceticism necessary for the rebuilding of a demolished economy to more bluntly hedonistic values. Nudity in magazines and films were no longer taboo, and the commonly accepted if informal rules of decency in fashion came under attack by a sexual culture of self-expression and identity. The cultural category of youth officially emerged in 1962 with the birth of the teen magazine *Salut les copains,* and by decade's end many young people would be echoing pop singer Antoine's challenge to his mother: "My mother told me 'Antoine, get your hair cut,' and I responded 'If you like, Mom, in twenty years'" (Prost 1992: 119–20). The Vatican II reforms of the mid 1960s further liberalized the ethic of an already weakened Catholic Church, and young people in the 1960s began to turn away from that traditional moral source of French culture in greater numbers than ever before. As Mendras puts it, "The millenarian invocation of the Our Father: 'Give us this day our daily bread,' scarcely speaks any longer to the well-nourished Occidental world" (1994: 16–17, 403–4, 411–12).

It was within the framework of this broad shift in French moral culture that transformations took place in the realm of school culture and pedagogy as well. I alluded to some of this already in the previous section in the discussion of how the arrogantly aristocratic discipline of philosophy began to change in response to the more democratic challenge of the social sciences, but the movement encompassed more than changes in the orientation of specific disciplines and reached fundamental elements of how schools should go about the business of teaching any subject and what the relationships of students to teachers ought to be. "Éducation á la française" up until the beginning of this second French revolution had been essentially based in disciplinary training of various sorts: physical restraint in the earliest years of schooling and in the home as well, in order to produce a well-mannered, upright, and generally silent student (Mendras 1994: 167–68). The reforms brought to the French university by the Faure Law of November 1968, which had their clearest realization in the creation of the experimental campus at Vincennes in 1969, are in some specific ways a criticism of that national pedagogical culture. The Faure Law, named for the education minister who was its principal author, was the first real attempt to address the massive problem of the post-World War II French university system. The Fouchet reforms of 1966, which had created the three-cycle system in higher education, had been guided by the traditional university culture and politics and had resulted in making more acute the problems of hierarchical clumsiness and student bottlenecks (Passeron 1986: 376–77; Tuilier 1994: 526). The latter problem was becoming potentially catastrophic as the decade progressed. From 1960 to 1967, the student population grew by more than 40,000 students per year, or roughly 10 to 15 percent yearly, and the two years before the May events saw even greater spikes of nearly 50,000 in 1967 and nearly 80,000 in 1968 (Prost 1992: 122–23). Faure's intention was greater than to create a law about university organizational politics. It was a project for transforming French society that he saw as necessary to address a university crisis that was in his view only one facet of a much larger youth and social crisis. The goal was to create effective citizens (Musselin 2001: 55). In this sense, the Faure Law can be compared to the Third Republic reforms of the university system at the end of the nineteenth century that were discussed earlier, as both were explicitly seen as parts of a society-wide set of transformations. Yet the Faure Law differed from those earlier reforms. It made clear that the conduct of the university system could no longer rest solely in the hands of professors, but had to extend to a democratic process involving all its constituent members, including students (Musselin 2001: 57–58). This meant making the government of a university system more like the government of a society, which meant "privileging the universe of public speaking and deliberation over that of action" (Musselin 2001: 61).

The various cultural and political conflicts at the heart of the French university system were especially evident on two campuses of the University of Paris, one northwest of the city at Nanterre and another southeast at Vincennes (the latter was moved northward to St. Denis in 1979). Both campuses had attracted an impressive array of intellectual heretics, both consecrated and otherwise. In addition though to their direct role in providing an institutional space, formally inside the Parisian university system, for a number of the poststructuralist thinkers in our group, they also indicated a number of broader shifts in French intellectual and moral culture that are of interest to us.

Nanterre and Vincennes were peripheral, both geographically and philosophically, to the French university system at their creation. The University of Paris X at Nanterre is located about five kilometers from central Paris. It became a full-fledged university only in 1970 when the faculty of letters that was hastily created there in 1964 with the intention of providing some relief to the overflow of students at the Paris campuses, and especially at the Sorbonne, merged with the law school that had been created in 1968 (CNE 2005: 3). Nanterre quickly became known as a gathering place for radical students and faculty. Some of this had to do with the physical facts of the campus. The classrooms and student residences were piled on top of one another, making public/private distinctions difficult to preserve. The surrounding environment was inhospitable, consisting mostly of slum housing inhabited by poor and immigrant residents. The Latin Quarter and the student community and culture it contained were a long 30-minute RER ride away (Feenberg and Freedman 2001: 4). As a result, many Nanterre students of the epoch felt that they were living in a "student ghetto" (Le Goff 2006[1998]: 46).

Nanterre's uniqueness did not stop at the physical, however. The spirit of contestation was heightened by the presence of radical faculty in a number of the newer social science disciplines, which almost automatically attracted students interested in social critique and action (Tuilier 1994: 529). The Nanterre campus was deliberately constructed as a flagship in the Paris system for both the newly-resurgent social sciences and

the anti-authoritarian, progressive pedagogical philosophy that was dominant at the EHESS. The proportion of faculty at Nanterre in the human
and social sciences was higher than in any other Parisian institution of
higher learning (Reader and Wadia 1993: 91). Sociology had only recently
returned to the university system. Prior to 1955, it was taught at only four
universities in all of France (the Sorbonne, Bordeaux, Strasbourg, and
Toulouse), and it had been mostly relegated to research institutions outside the university system. But in the 1955 to 1968 period, "[t]he number
of students taking sociology, the popularity of the social sciences and the
decline of the humanities all helped the rise of sociology in the faculties"
(Colquhoun 1986: 7). The sociology department at Nanterre was headed
by Henri Lefebvre, a renegade, anti-PCF Marxist who had come from
Strasbourg where his work had been a central influence for the emerging Situationist student movement there (Le Goff 2006[1998]: 46), and
included also Alain Touraine and Georges Lapassade, two others known
for their intellectual and political radicalism. With the arrival of younger
sociologists such as René Lourau and Jean Baudrillard, the department's
reputation as a hotbed for political and intellectual ferment, extreme
even on a campus that in its entirety was considered "the culture medium
of extremism," was made early (Lemire 1998: 18). Although its overall
intellectual orientation was not structuralist (Delannoi 1989: 32), its position *vis-à-vis* the traditional cultural politics of the university and of democracy more generally was basically in line with the critical position that
was represented by the structuralist movement. It was this department
that produced from among its students one of the most important of the
leaders of the May 1968 movement, Daniel Cohn-Bendit. The general atmosphere on the campus throughout this period was summed up, albeit a
bit hyperbolically, by Paul Ricoeur, appointed faculty doyen there in 1969,
who was promptly greeted in his new position by a passing student *via* an
act of "coronation" with a garbage can lid (Le Goff 2006[1998]: 161–62):
"[A]t any moment a murder could be committed" (Rémond 1979: 114).

The campus at Vincennes, which opened in January 1969, was explicitly conceived as an experimental university, "the incarnation of modernity and the avant-garde and therefore the bastion of anti-academicism,"
a kind of deliberate "anti-Sorbonne" (Rieffel 1993: 439; Dosse 1992: 169).
At the very core of the processes by which the new Vincennes campus was
put together was a radical opposition to deeply rooted French traditions.
Instead of the Vincennes faculty being assembled by the existing faculties
at other Paris universities, as had, for example, been the case at Nanterre
(the faculty of which was designated by the Sorbonne faculty), a central
committee of twenty-four members was organized with the responsibility
to name the faculty at Vincennes themselves. The practical selection of the

members of this core committee, and subsequently the selection of members of the faculty by the committee members, was carried out in a radically anti-institutional and improvisational manner that relied heavily on personal and frequently ideological alliances. The committee expressed an interest in bringing in "new talent" at Vincennes, young researchers without much previous teaching experience but who would have a positive attitude toward the events of May 1968 and what they represented institutionally for the university (Souilé 1998: 49). As a Vincennes faculty member who served for several months in 1970 as university president put it, " a certain idea of democracy" had invested this university project from the very beginning, and it was not mere representative democracy that was the target. The idea was, on the contrary, to "live concretely … total democracy" (Beaud 1971: 48).

Among the committee members charged with the creation of the original faculty were Roland Barthes, Georges Canguilhem, and Jacques Derrida. Their personal relationships with Foucault and knowledge of his work and reputation were sufficient to lead them to select him as head of the all-important Vincennes philosophy department. Foucault then selected a number of thinkers very close to his own intellectual framework, including his close friend Gilles Deleuze and Michel Sèrres. When Deleuze actually took up the position two years later, he brought along with him his friend, Jean-François Lyotard, who had been at Nanterre since 1966. Foucault also brought in a collection of young former ENS students of Althusser and other militants of various stripes such as Alain Badiou, Jacques Rancière, François Regnault, Judith Miller, Henri Weber, and Etienne Balibar (Souilé 1998: 50–51). The overall tenor of the philosophy department and the entire campus was dominated by a "*gauchiste* effervescence," multidisciplinarity, and structuralism. The university even created a department of psychoanalysis (an idea that originated with Derrida) that was headed by Jacques Lacan's "first lieutenant" Serge Leclaire (Dosse 1992: 171, 176).

The ideological tilt of the new faculty was quickly attacked by conservatives and other critics. One televised special on Vincennes called the Vincennes faculty "confessionnelle," i.e., literally, "denominational" or ideologically aligned (Beaud 1971: 18). It certainly was the case that much of the coursework offered in Foucault's philosophy department during the early years at Vincennes departed significantly from the traditional curriculum and the history of canonical philosophy preferred in the established institutions. Many of the courses indicated a central concern with Marxist and *gauchiste* themes, and many others not so directly politically radical still dealt with thematics far outside the traditional realm of philosophy, for example, Foucault's course on "The Discourse of Sexuality," or Deleuze's on "Logic and Desire" (Soulié 1998: 51–52). The Vincennes faculty defended the alternative substance of many of the courses in philosophy and elsewhere as a much needed effort to "teach things that differed from the contents of programs that were old, ossified, or, under the appearance of neutrality, resolutely conservative" (Beaud 1971: 15).

It was not only in the substance of particular courses offered or in faculty political attitudes that Vincennes marked a difference from the mainstream university. Interdisciplinarity was seen as a central element in its uniqueness. Although the faculty initially organized itself into disciplines out of sheer facility, the movement toward the fusion of disciplines and perspectives began early. The basic course unit of the UV (Unité de valeur) began to take on a radically multidisciplinary aspect (Beaud 1971: 26–27). The new campus explicitly attempted to pedagogically attack the traditional structures in place at the Sorbonne and elsewhere in the established French academic world. Huge lectures in which professors spoke to silent throngs were to be rejected in favor of small, informal seminars. Professors and students used the informal *tu* instead of *vous* in their classroom conversations (Rieffel 1993: 440). The professor was not understood as "the holder of knowledge (correct or incorrect, contested or uncontested) that one had to record, file away, and deliver in a sufficient state of preservation the day of the exam; and he [was] no longer (or nearly so) the judge, the censor, the 'cop' on whom success or failure depend[ed]" (Beaud 1971: 15–6). Instead, the student and the professor were part of a collective entity working together in the pursuit of knowledge, where each party criticizes the other and thereby enables a mutual progression. Students were freed to attend classes as auditors whenever they liked, which over time increasingly and perhaps inevitably helped contribute to a variety of administrative and organizational chaos (Dosse 1992: 172).

In purely demographic terms as well, Vincennes differed radically from all the other existing Paris campuses in that it attracted a large percentage of non-traditional students. One in two Vincennes students worked full-time outside of school (the figure was 1 in 20 in other University of Paris campuses); the average age of Vincennes students was 27; and foreign students represented more than one-third of the student body (the figure was 10 percent in the French university system generally) (Debauvais 1976: 9). Article 23 of Faure's reform of the higher education law stated clearly that universities could receive as students those who were already engaged in professional life, whether or not they held "university degrees," so long as they could pass entry examinations of their aptitude, which usually consisted merely of an individual interview with faculty, and Vincennes applied this radical article very seriously (Beaud

1971: 33–34). There were some 8,000 Vincennes students in the opening year who did not hold the baccalaureate, roughly one-third of the whole student population, and the percentage had grown to nearly half by 1971 (Beaud 1971: 34). These non-traditional students came from all walks of working life, from diverse parts of the country, and from abroad, and they had a wide variety of reasons for pursuing higher education. Whether prevented from pursuit of higher education by individual circumstances (illness, family responsibilities) or broader social structures (class origins), Vincennes provided the sole site in France where "the real, urgent, massive social need" to receive these students found a response (Beaud 1971: 34–35). The conflict between those who defended the movement of radical change in the university culture and those who instead saw the Faure Law as having endangered the system with a "mass of the unfit and the unserious" was a central feature of the French cultural atmosphere during this period (Passeron 1986: 377).

The macro-details of the intellectual field I have just described set the table for poststructuralist intellectual position-taking. The legacy of the Sartrian engaged intellectual, the return to the French academic scene of the social sciences in the guise of structuralism, the shifts in the French educational system, and the ways in which those shifts were connected to broader debates about how to morally shape French citizens provided a context in which intellectual identity formation took place. Following Bourdieu, one can postulate a logic at work in this field that would tend to privilege a certain kind of *habitus* and its modes of intervening. In the next chapter, I look in closer detail at the specific institutional trajectories of the poststructuralists and at the masters of ceremonies who most shaped their *habitus*, before turning to the role played by the event of May 1968 in the development of their intellectual project.

Notes

1. The bulk of the discussion to follow on this topic is drawn from Mendras's *La Seconde revolution française, 1965–1984*, which has become something of a modern classic in the French social sciences.

6   Écoles, Masters, and May 1968

Institutions and Networks that Shaped the Poststructuralists, and the Political Affair that Positioned Them

The institutional trajectories of the poststructuralists, like those of the Durkheimians, pass through a number of the same institutions and intersect with a few key figures who shaped their *habitus* profoundly. Central here are the École Normale, the Sorbonne, the École Pratique, and three intellectual figures associated with each institution: Louis Althusser, Georges Canguilhem, and Roland Barthes, respectively.

The École Normale played a key role in the intellectual formation of several of the poststructuralists, as it did for Durkheim, Hubert, and Hertz. Foucault, who arrived there in 1946, and Derrida, who came in 1952, were *normaliens,* and Derrida was Althusser's assistant at the ENS early in his teaching career and later taught philosophy himself there from 1965 to 1984. For both, the effect of the ENS on their careers and persons extended even into the years before they arrived at rue d'Ulm, for both underwent several years of preparatory classes and study designed specifically for the highly competitive entrance exam to the ENS. Most twentieth century *normaliens* have undergone this post-baccalaureate educational experience, which generally consists of two years of study, known in academic argot as "*hypokhâgne*" and "*khâgne.*" The traditionally closed, socially reproductive nature of the *grandes écoles* system in France is reflected in a notable trend in these pre-ENS preparatory courses: students who undertake them in Paris, and with former *normaliens* as instructors, have a much greater probability of gaining entrance than students who take such courses in the provinces with instructors who have themselves not passed the ENS entrance exam. Foucault began preparatory study in Poitiers, largely because his family feared sending him in 1943 to occupied Paris alone (Macey 1993: 13), but quickly moved to Paris when the war ended and began *khâgne* at the celebrated *lycée* Henri IV, where Derrida spent three years doing preparatory study for the ENS entrance exam. Such intense competition and the inevitable failures that accompany it (both Foucault and Derrida failed the entrance exam at least once prior to achieving success, and both also failed the *agrégation* once before passing) also had the frequent effect of marking the experience of *khâgne* and Normale with intense pressure and subsequent psychological suffering. Both Foucault and Derrida had experiences of significant depression and psychic unhappiness while undergoing this process, which Pierre Bourdieu has well described as internment in a Goffmanian total institution (Foucault 2001a: 18; Derrida 1995 [1992]: 343; Bourdieu 2004: 119).

The École Normale in the late 1940s and early 1950s, while still clearly a culturally traditional institution in many ways, had begun to show the influence of the broader political shifts in post-World War II France. While, as I noted earlier, socialist perspectives had begun to emerge at the ENS in the last years of the nineteenth century, this period saw still greater radicalization of *normalien* politics. In the wake of the war, Marxist political perspectives invaded the rue d'Ulm, and a notable minority of *normaliens* joined the Communist Party. While Khilnani (1993: 90) says 15 percent of *normaliens* were PCF members by the end of the 1940s, the historian Emmanuel Le Roy Ladurie, a 1949 graduate, has claimed that the figure was actually likely closer to one-fourth during this period. Ladurie goes on to sketch the political tenor of the ENS in more embodied and empirical terms by noting the treatment accorded to the only Gaullist *normalien* he remembered from the period: "That rare bird … We decorated him with the title 'fascist,' which this liberal of the center right scarcely deserved. When he went up a stairway, it was the 'rise of fascism'" (Peyrefitte 1998: 73). This new perspective at the ENS was symbolically made clearest perhaps by the occasion of the annual ENS ball in 1959, when, in the wake of the creation of the Fifth Republic, the newly-appointed President De Gaulle was publicly snubbed by *normaliens* on ideological grounds. The explanation of one *normalien* likely summarized the situation for many: "One does not shake the hand of a dictator" (Dufay and Dufort 1993: 205). The influence of Marxist thought at the ENS however was broader than the ranks of official Party members. French intellectual Marxist communism was not an undifferentiated phenomenon, and while there were some living stereotypes of robotic Stalinist/PCF lockstep among the intellectual classes, many others maintained more distance from the French Communists and the Stalinist line while continuing to identify themselves with Marxism and communism (Hazareesingh 1991: 102, 126). Beyond the PCF *normaliens,* one could find also anti-Stalinist Marxists who advocated for a more open Communist Party from the left of the Stalinists. Notable here was a group named "the Saint-Germain-des-Près Marxists" by other *normaliens,* including Paul Veyne, Jean-Claude Passeron, and Gérard Genette, and headed by none other than Michel Foucault (Dufay and Dufort 1993: 191).

This new kind of politicized atmosphere was one of the central characteristics of the ENS during the period Foucault and Derrida were there. It was personified, and with some intriguing complexities, by the renowned *caïman* (*normalien* slang for ENS professor) with whom both had a lifelong relationship: Louis Althusser.

The Communist/Catholic Master of Ceremonies: Althusser

In certain respects, the role played by Lucien Herr at the ENS during the time spent there by Hubert and Hertz at the turn of the nineteenth century was played from the late 1940s until 1980 by Louis Althusser. The influential Marxist philosopher, himself a *normalien,* came to the École Normale as a lecturer in 1949 and remained there until he murdered his wife and was consequently institutionalized in 1980. Although the full contours of his structuralist Marxist theoretical *oeuvre* would not come into existence until more than a decade after his first year as an ENS lecturer, he was a member of the PCF from 1948, and he clearly had a significant intellectual and political influence on *normaliens* due to his "availability and the courteous readiness with which he offered advice to anyone who strayed into his … office" (Macey 1993: 24). With a host of shared intellectual and political interests, Foucault and Althusser quickly became close friends at the ENS. Each had written a *diplôme d'études supérieures* on Hegel (Althusser under the direction of Gaston Bachelard, and Foucault for Jean Hyppolite), and both had a significant interest in epistemological questions. They also were apparently drawn together by a shared "struggle against madness," as Eribon (1994: 320) puts it, owing to their mutual bouts with depression and fears of mental illness. Foucault joined the PCF for a brief period in 1950, apparently at least partially at the urging of Althusser, and in 1953 he presented to the group of communist ENS students a paper on materialist psychopathology at Althusser's request (Macey 1993: 37; Foucault 2001a: 21). Althusser consistently and proudly claimed Foucault as "his student" in terms clearly highlighting his own purported influence on the younger philosopher. In writing, for example, to a friend about Foucault's book on madness, he emphasized the close relationship of mentor and student and called the work "stupefying, stunning, inspired, a muddle and yet a light" (Althusser 1998: 211, 215). Even when Althusser disagreed with Foucault's work or with his ever-changing political stance *vis-à-vis* Marxism, their deep friendship was the most basic theme to which he returned (Althusser 1998: 698). Foucault was one of the regular visitors Althusser received, first in the hospital and then at his home, after the murder of his wife in 1980.

A final point of connection between Althusser and Foucault is in the tragic personage of Jacques Martin. This enigmatic student of Althusser and friend of Foucault met both at the École Normale and became identified by both, according to the accounts of mutual friends and correspondence, as a kind of impoverished and mythical "philosopher *sans oeuvre*" with whom both felt a strong bond owing to his deeply personal way of living the philosophical life as well as the bouts with emotional depression that ended in his suicide in 1963. Althusser apparently initially became interested in Marx at least partially at the suggestion of Martin and dedicated his *For Marx* to his student, who was by then already dead (Eribon 1994: 321). Martin failed the *agrégation* and his scholarly output was limited to translations of some German texts; at his death, he was apparently working on a translation of a work of some importance for the three men, Herman Hesse's *The Glass Bead Game*, which is a fictional account of a philosophical and spiritual order reminiscent of the École Normale (Moulier-Boutang 1992: 449–60). For both Althusser and Foucault, Martin represented the "ghost of failure," a fearful image of what might befall them too if they were unsuccessful in walking the tightrope between genius and insanity (Macey 1993: 26). The peculiar way in which his life became a kind of template for the rigorous philosophical/spiritual project, dedication to the pursuit of knowledge even at the risk and eventual suffering of insanity and death, tells us some important things about the perspective on the intellectual life held by Althusser and Foucault.

Derrida was even closer than Foucault to Althusser, as he was his colleague for two decades at the ENS, having been recruited to the position by Althusser (Derrida 2002: 150). The two became friends literally on the day in 1952 when Derrida arrived at the ENS as a student and Althusser in time came to regard him as one of the great thinkers of his era, speaking of him in his autobiography as "a towering figure" and a "giant of a philosopher" (Mallet and Michaud 2004: 602; Althusser 1993 [1992]: 178, 182). They shared the profound personal characteristic of birth in French Algeria (Derrida in El-Biar in 1930; Althusser in Birmandreis twelve years earlier), a point that is of no small importance, especially as their friendship began just a few years before the start of the Algerian war. In at least one interview, Derrida painted their relationship in terms that were limited to personal affection and more or less excluded questions of intellectual influence and exchange (Derrida 2002: 147–48). He also pointed in this interview to the political atmosphere at the ENS in strikingly negative terms and noted the curious fact that he and Althusser had spent twenty years teaching together at the same institution, as close friends, without ever really broaching certain political questions having to do with Marxism and communism (Derrida 2002: 156–58, 164). Unlike Foucault, Derrida never joined the PCF and he speculated that this fact in some ways distanced him from Althusser.

Yet elsewhere he hints at more of a possible intellectual connection in their two projects. He acknowledged a correspondence with Althusser on his Husserl book (in 1962) and on Althusser's book on Montesquieu a few years earlier, from 1959 to 1960 (2002: 150). His engagement with Husserl interested Althusser, Derrida noted, because the Marxist philosopher was attracted to the idea of a possible connection between Husserl's transcendental idealism and his own rereading of Marx; Derrida has noted he was "not far from thinking that himself" (Derrida and Roudinsco 2001: 170).[1] He referred to his book on Marx, written just a few years after Althusser's death, as a kind of "homage" to his old friend, a reading not at all difficult to justify given the fact that Derrida there classifies the whole of his own project as "this attempted radicalization of Marxism called deconstruction" (Derrida and Roudinesco 2001: 169; Derrida 1994[1993]: 92). He also acknowledged that what the strange internal "intellectual sociology … of that *normalien* milieu" may have framed as differences were in fact intimately connected political positions (Derrida 2002: 158; Derrida and Roudinesco 2001: 132, 138). Like Foucault, Derrida was one of the regular visitors Althusser received during the ten-year period after the murder of his wife. The text he read at Althusser's funeral enigmatically but powerfully spoke to the influence of his mentor and to the "fathomless … multiplicity" of Althusser's person (Derrida 1993: 242–43).

But if these two members of our poststructuralist group were personally close to Althusser,[2] in what specific terms can we talk about the latter's *influence* on them? I can suggest a further parallel with Lucien Herr that involves Althusser's complex relationship to religion and spirituality. In the years before World War II and his time as a prisoner of war, Althusser was a Royalist and a Catholic, indeed, even a leading figure in the Catholic youth movement. His relationship to Catholicism has been the subject of intense scholarly interest. Some have suggested that, in fact, he never fully repudiated the faith (Khilnani 1993: 85). Ultimately, we do not really know as much as we would like about Althusser's move from Catholicism to Marxism, but we do know something of the fervency of his youthful Catholicism because there exist a number of notebooks he kept during his time in *khâgne* at Lyon from 1936 to 1937 that provide excellent testimony to the fact. Here, the young Althusser writes vividly of his spiritual life, of religious retreats, and of his communion and confessions. He sketches Christian iconography (the crucifixion, the Virgin, Mary Magdalene) and composes prayers, some quite eloquent. His deep Catholicism (he calls it a "beautiful marvel ... a completely totalitarian religion" in which it is "a true relief to put one's trust" [3]) fairly leaps from nearly every page of these intimate journals. The notebooks also attest to the close personal relationship Althusser established here with Jean Guitton, the renowned Catholic philosopher, and to the way in which his youthful thinking on a vocation as a professor of philosophy was influenced by Althusser's perception of Guitton's Catholic faith. In a passage from the journal dated March 1937, he describes how he sees a career in philosophy relating to his religious faith:

> [Guitton] is truly very attentive to me. Perhaps he takes such care of me thinking that my vocation might be the same as his own. He recently disclosed to me that he believed I was destined for philosophy ... I understand quite well that at the bottom of any Christian vocation there is a crucial question, that of Christianity ... I think I can predict that philosophy is perhaps rather the best possible source of faith because it obliges a man to think of religion, to put everything into question again in order to better penetrate, and because the highest faith is that one thinks while living it ... I am also quite well aware of all that philosophy ... can cause a man to lose. It requires a formidable asceticism which calls for the close examination not only of the body but also of the mind.[4]

Long after his embrace of Marxism, Althusser maintained an intimate relationship with Guitton. Jacques Lautman (2000: 38) describes Althusser encouraging his students to attend Guitton's lectures in 1955, when the PCF had accused the Catholic philosopher of collaboration and endeavored to enforce a boycott by party members of his courses.

But still more of Althusser's Catholic attachment remained after his move to Marxism and the production of the books that brought him intellectual fame as a structuralist Marxist. He remained supportive of leftist Catholic efforts to engage the working class and it was rumored that he paid regular, secret visits to a community of nuns who lived near the École Normale (Althusser 1993: xv). Althusser continued to think of the possibility of a rapprochement between Marxism and the Catholic Church long after he had publicly left the Church, even, according to Élisabeth Roudinesco, seeking on several occasions an audience with the Pope in order to "unite, in a fusionary act, the two guardian figures of his history"

(2005: 208–9). These efforts to make philosophy and religion compatible in Althusser's project are evident too in his relationship with Stanislas Breton, a Catholic philosopher and theologian who had a very close friendship with Althusser dating from the mid 1960s and extending to Althusser's death. He was also a priest who was affiliated with the Passionists, a Catholic order founded in the early 1700s by Saint Paul of the Cross, one of the great Catholic mystics of the eighteenth century. Like Foucault and Derrida, he was a frequent visitor to Althusser after his wife's death and in fact he met Foucault on one memorable occasion while visiting the hospitalized Althusser. In a letter sent simultaneously to Breton and Foucault in July 1982, Althusser proposed a collaborative work by the three of them dealing with themes of Christian morality and male friendship that they had apparently discussed at some length at their meeting. He describes the event as "an extraordinary exchange of ideas and of experiences that I will never forget" (Eribon 1994: 346). The proposed collaborative work, which Althusser foresaw as "without precedent" never came to fruition, and we do not know how Foucault responded to the invitation, if at all. But it surely does suggest something important regarding Althusser's enduring position on the discourse between philosophy and religion. It is unlikely that this point could have been missed by anyone as closely connected to him as Derrida and Foucault were.

The Sorbonne's "Philosopher-Terrorist": Georges Canguilhem

The two non-*normalien* poststructuralists, Deleuze and Baudrillard, did not share the experiences of Foucault and Derrida at the ENS, but their institutional trajectories did overlap with those of the other two in other ways. They both entered the *lycée* Henri IV (Deleuze for *khâgne* in 1945, Baudrillard for *hypokhâgne* in 1948) for preparatory study, but both left after one year and turned away from the gilded, elite path of the *grandes écoles* and toward the university system, and specifically toward the Sorbonne. During the early post-war period, when they were there, conditions at the Sorbonne were reflective of a situation of institutional maladjustment that would only grow in the following decades. Problems of overcrowding and the general failure of "an elitist and maladjusted concept of the university," which would become a full-blown crisis by 1968, were already quite in evidence (Tuilier 1994: 512). Although more democratic than the *grandes écoles*, the system of which the Sorbonne was the heart was still massively troubled by issues of exclusion and class reproduction. Students from the working class were at this point still non-existent, and even students from petit bourgeois or other "*cadres subalternes*" who could be found

among those sitting in Sorbonne lecture halls experienced a radical disjuncture between the traditional educational culture they were assumed
to know and value, on the one hand, and the preparation they had received and the intellectual concerns they brought from their specific
class perspectives, on the other. The disjuncture between that traditional
Sorbonne culture of narrow positivism, which was the unintended legacy
of the Nouvelle Sorbonne of the Third Republic, and the epistemology
of new disciplines and perspectives (e.g., psychoanalysis, Marxism, existentialism) further emphasized the failure of the institution to adapt
to change (Tuilier 1994: 508–9). Certainly things would become much
more acute by the 1960s, but students passing through the Sorbonne
even twenty years earlier could not have failed to experience much of the
same alienation.

There was a legendary philosopher at the Sorbonne whose influence
on several of the poststructuralists bears close examination: Georges Canguilhem. He directed Foucault's doctoral thesis in 1961 and Deleuze's
thesis for the *Diplôme d'Études Supérieures* in 1947, and Derrida served as
his assistant at the Sorbonne in his first substantial teaching position after
passing the *agrégation* (Foucault 2001a: 29; Deleuze 2002: 24; Mallet and
Michaud 2004: 602). Foucault first met him as one of the examiners at
his second attempt at passing the ENS entrance exam in 1946 (Macey
1993: 18). After Foucault became a well-known and controversial thinker,
the two engaged in a long dialogue on the concept of the normal; the
student responded to the teacher's magisterial first work in his own first
book, which was the thesis on madness he wrote under Canguilhem, and
the teacher then modified his own original argument in response and
acknowledgement (Roudinesco 1998: 39–40). The full extent of his effect
as a mentor on an entire generation of young students who encountered
him, and especially on the members of our poststructuralist group for
whom he served as a mentor and master of ceremonies requires more
careful excavation of the details of his work and life.

Canguilhem's unique position in the field of philosophy was due in
part to the fact that he also had an education in medicine and therefore conceived of issues in the history of biology from the simultaneous
perspective of a medical doctor and a professional philosopher (Debru
2004: 17). His work radically criticized positivist and mechanist thinking
about scientific knowledge, whether in the work of Comte, Descartes, or
Claude Bernard, from a position deeply influenced by Bergsonian vitalism (Debru 2004: 18; Braunstein 2000). *The Normal and the Pathological*
presented a perspective on the history of the life sciences that highlighted
the weaknesses of deployments of the concept "life" that failed to place
at the center of its definition the opposition between the two terms in

the book's title. As Foucault recognized, Canguilhem brought a crucial understanding to the history of science and knowledge:

> [T]here are in the knowledge of life phenomena which keep it at a distance from all knowledge which can be referred to the physico-chemical domains; it is that life could find the principle of its development only in the interrogation of *pathological* phenomena. It was impossible to constitute a science of the living without taking into account, as essential to its object, *the possibility of sickness, death, monstrosity, anomaly and error* ... at the limit, life—from this comes its radical character—is that which is capable of error ... one must accept that *error is the root of human thought and its history.* (Foucault 2001b: 1591, 1593–94; emphasis added)

It might be noted too that there is a strong similarity between this language and that of Nietzsche in his discussion of the origin of truth and falsity in science (Foucault 2001b: 1255).

But the explicit content of Canguilhem's work in the history of science was only part of his reputation and influence. His character as a legendary teacher is attested to by many. His impatience with intellectual frivolity and foolishness sometimes expressed itself in a brusqueness that doubtless had much to do with his rural peasant origins in the far southern reaches of France; he was "classic and severe" (Roudinesco 1998: 12), "feared for his temper, a tone of voice that was half-rustic, half-Charlus" (Aron 1984: 9).[5] But he was not simply feared; he was also "admired ... imitated, loved" by students (Roudinesco 1998: 37) His generosity to students and intellectual interlocutors was without bounds and expressed itself even in a pedagogical classroom style that could sometimes appear authoritarian. In this, he was the veritable incarnation of the spirit of resistance that intimately mixed authority and generosity in the unique manner characteristic of his provincial origins (Debru 2004: 15; Alibert 1928: 3). Bourdieu spoke of him and of Jules Vuellemin in telling terms as "true 'exemplary prophets' in Weber's sense" (1987: 14).

The hands-on practicality of his intellectual work was reflected in the distinctly anti-Parisian and rural bearing he brought from his youth in the village of Castelnaudary in Languedoc-Roussillon. This peasant *habitus* was evident not only in the obvious form of his accent (Roudinesco 1998: 15), but also in the frequently militant manner in which he opposed what he saw as foolish or illogical in the French intellectual world. As a young student disciple of the radically pacifist philosopher Alain at the École Normale in the 1920s, he found himself in serious trouble several times because of his public mocking of the French army. He was accused by the ministry of war of "revolutionary propaganda" and later intentionally got himself demoted during his mandatory military service (Roudinesco 1998: 17). His pugnacity and combativeness translated themselves, with the rise of the Nazi threat, into heroic and dangerous involvement in the French Resistance. He left his university post on the coming to power of Pétain, an act of refusal of Vichy collaboration that he classified in his typical manner: "I did not pass the *agrégation* in philosophy in order to teach Work, Family, Country" (Roudinesco 1998: 24). He became involved in the resistance network as a *maquis* or guerrilla fighter and he put his medical skills to good use caring for wounded resistance fighters (Roudinesco 1998: 25–26).

This activity might seem a contradiction if, starting from Foucault's distinction of the two major poles in French philosophy, i.e., the philosophy of the subject and the philosophy of the concept, discussed in Chapter 2, we recognize Canguilhem as belonging in the latter category. How is it that a philosopher in the apparently more speculative of the two groups becomes a legendary figure in the Resistance, while so many other philosophers in the apparently more activist affiliation were rather less militant in the event? It is, in Foucault's words, "as if the question of the foundation of rationality could not be disassociated from the interrogation of the social conditions of its existence" (2001b: 1584). Canguilhem himself provides the answer in his own tribute to his close friend, Jean Cavaillès. Cavaillès was also a philosopher and professor at the Sorbonne, and also a Resistant, although one who was apprehended by the Gestapo in August 1943 after having escaped from his Vichy captors and executed in January 1944 at the age of 40.

In his description of the philosophical project of his friend and its intimate connection to his violent resistance to Nazi authoritarianism, Canguilhem also engages in autobiographical reflection. What is the relationship between thought and action? It is that action is the inevitable consequence of, indeed the *effect* of, belief in reason. Reason cannot simply be a series of logical proofs and abstractions; it is embodied and violently responds to attacks, vitalistically and spontaneously. It necessarily becomes a personal politics of resistance insofar as it is taken seriously as a devotion. He notes how Cavaillès provided the response to the question of the efficacy of the intellectual life precisely in his military activity in the Resistance; this constituted "a lesson in action for those who judge incompatible these two notions [of combatant and professor]" (Canguilhem 1976: 33–34).

The "terrorist philosopher" who was Cavaillès is thus not a contradiction. He is the inevitable product of a deep commitment to the reason praised by the philosophers who, generally speaking, are incorrectly led to believe that their commitment to reason forbids their participation in its transgression, i.e., in acts of destruction, sabotage, terrorism, the killing of other human beings:

> One understands that C. was logically a member of the Resistance ... Nazism was unacceptable in that it was the negation ... of universality, in that it sought the end of rational philosophy. The struggle against the unacceptable was thus ineluctable. And by 'struggle' I do not mean merely whispered indignation in the hallways ... [or] the filling of mailboxes with vengeful letters. By 'struggle' I mean armed combat ... Here was an intellectual who ... by a totally free choice became ... a philosopher terrorist." (Canguilhem 1976: 36–37)

This is a profound and tragic reflection on the destiny of the heroic philosopher who was his friend Cavaillès, a man who willingly, even joyously, gave up the intellectual œuvre he would not have the mortal time to complete in exchange for his acts of resistance and rebellion against "the unacceptable." Roudinesco summarizes Canguilhem's interrogation aptly: "What might have been the œuvre of a Marc Bloch, of a Cavaillès, if they had not fallen in combat? But inversely, what would have been Canguilhem's place in French philosophy if he had found death in the scrub grass before even beginning to compose his work?" (Roudinesco 1998: 27). Ultimately, no answer can be given to those questions. The chance outcome of action decided. But that the action be motivated by heroic adherence to the principles of philosophical reason was essential for Canguilhem.

When the events of May 1968 shook the Parisian campuses, Canguilhem was firm in his opposition to the student rebellion and to its scholarly spokesmen, but it is relatively clear that something of the spirit of rebellion and heroism he personified had in fact been communicated to at least a few of his former students who aligned themselves on the side of the revolutionaries.

The "Mother" of Poststructuralism: Roland Barthes

According to one historian of structuralism, if Lacan was the movement's "severe father," Roland Barthes was its "mother figure" (Dosse 1991: 94). He was very close to Foucault, whom he met in December 1955, when he was 40 and Foucault only 29, during the decade stretching from the mid 1950s to the mid 1960s (Eribon 1994: 211). Some have speculated that the two gay men were lovers for at least part of that time, and they frequently spent nights together in cafés and vacationed together (Macey 1993: 82; Calvet 1990: 155). They had an apparent falling out at some point in 1963 or 1964. Foucault's long-term lover Daniel Defert argued that the break happened simply because Foucault had just at that time begun living together with him and pulled himself away from his earlier nightlife in order to better work during the evening when he was most able to do so (Calvet 1990: 172–73). Whatever the reason for the break, the bond between the two remained significant enough that it was Foucault who became Barthes's sponsor for a chair in literary semiology to the Collège de France in 1976, writing a lengthy defense of the position and of Barthes as the ideal candidate (Calvet 1990: 255; Eribon 1994: 219–22). Once Barthes was elected, their friendship was renewed. Foucault visited Barthes several times in the hospital after the latter's accident in 1980 and delivered a moving eulogy in which he spoke passionately of their friendship (Eribon 1994: 231–32).

Though Eribon suggests irony in Foucault's friendship with Barthes, he is also clear that the former explicitly acknowledged the influence of the latter's work on his own perspective, even if Foucault rarely mentioned Barthes explicitly in anything he wrote. In a radio interview for France-Inter in 1975, when Barthes joined the Collège de France, Foucault called him "someone of great importance to me … it was certainly him who most helped us to shake up a certain form of university knowledge which was in fact non-knowledge" (Eribon 1994: 216). It is perhaps even possible to suggest that Barthes had a slight role in establishing Foucault's intellectual reputation early in the latter's career, as he wrote one of the very few positive reviews of the book on madness, for which Foucault remained grateful the rest of his life (Eribon 1994: 215).

Barthes also played a profound, if less personally intimate, role in Baudrillard's evolution. The latter apparently attended Barthes's seminar at the EPHE (where Barthes taught from 1960 to 1976, when he took up the post at the Collège de France) in the early 1960s on "The Sociology of Signs, Symbols and Representations" (Kauppi 1996: 77). This seminar of the early 1960s was by all accounts a very special place. All the elements for the formation and the spiritual training of a corps of Barthes-ians were in play here: Barthes distributed at the start of the seminar a lexicon of "basic terminology," five pages of semiotic and structural terminology, the better to inform attendees of the language expected, along with a "very sociological" bibliography, and tied the seminar into the broad current of the social sciences; the seductive charm and voice of the master are generally remarked by attendees, even to the point of noting that this man "publicly perceived as … a man of texts" was in fact a great orator capable of visibly moving a listening audience; a core group of students attended the seminar year after year. Calvet describes the seminar as a cross between "a royal court, a Fourierist utopia, and a great fraternity" (1990: 192–95, 196). Barthes was also a member of the jury, along with Bourdieu and Lefebvre, for Baudrillard's *thèse de doctorat de troisième cycle* on "The System of Objects" in 1966. Baudrillard's early work on the sign systems of consumer capitalism is obviously and deeply indebted to Barthes, and he was clear in interviews of the "deep affinity" he had for the work of Barthes, whom he placed in his own personal "bestiary" of key influential figures (Baudrillard 2001: 16, 22).

The personality of Barthes emerged from a set of circumstances that clearly positioned him in a minority status with respect to a number of social variables. He was raised, in pressing economic straits much of the time, by a single mother to whom he was extraordinarily devoted for the entirety of his life. Her death in October of 1977 was, by all accounts, a "catastrophe" for Barthes, as her presence in his life was "an essential, irreplaceable element" (Calvet 1990: 271). He also suffered from pulmonary tuberculosis, which began at age 18 and continued to cause him serious difficulty, including long periods of hospitalization, until he was in his early 30s (Calvet 1990: 51, 68, 93–95). He spoke of the illness as something that "at the time, before chemotherapy ... was a veritable way of life ... A person with tuberculosis could seriously envision ... the idea of an entire life at the sanatorium ... [,] a kind of life not without connections to the monastic idea. The savor of a well-ordered life, of the strict constraints of a schedule, as in a monastery" (Barthes 1981: 277–78). The illness struck Barthes in a particularly cruel way in that it made it impossible for him to continue the educational path toward *hypokhâgne* and the École Normale, toward which he had directed himself from early in his life; for the rest of Barthes's life this bitterly affected both his understanding of himself and his relation to the university (Calvet 1990: 55). In an interview late in his life, he discussed his status as an "uncertain subject" *vis-à-vis* the academic establishment in detail, noting that his affiliation with "marginal institutions" (CNRS, the École Pratique, the Collège de France) gave him an "objective marginality" (Barthes 1981: 343).

Barthes' politics were complicated, as undoubtedly was his political influence on students. His own statements of his politics offer an array of fine theoretical nuance and historical specificity. Barthes had been firmly on the political left since early in his life, reading and becoming infatuated with the passionate, literary, and philosophical character of Jaurès as early as 1932 (Calvet 1990: 42–43). He characterized his intellectual work as having a "discrete but obsessed" connection to the political (Barthes 1981: 235). Yet the violence of militant "political discourse," in either its Stalinist or *gauchiste* forms, that depended simply on attaining a certain "decibel level" to be heard, was something to which Barthes was powerfully averse: "[T]o carry out a radical counter-cultural action is simply ... to depend on stereotypes ... I would say that violence itself is an extremely overused code … An attitude of radical cultural destruction seems to me thus thoughtless [and] relatively ineffective" (Barthes 1981: 286, 166).

Against the "spectacularly violent and destructive activities" of the *gauchistes*, he believed there was "a job of deep *subversion* to be done" (Barthes 1981: 164; emphasis added). He often came back to the term "subversion": "For me, it's a clearer word than the word 'revolution.' It means: come from below to cheat things, to divert them, take them elsewhere than the place one expects them" (289–90). Being an intellectual radical for Barthes required "an extreme sensitivity to the ubiquity of power—it is everywhere—and to its endurance—it is perpetual. It never tires … [and] it is plural" (Barthes 1981: 286). The directness of the engagement of tactics of identity on the part of the *gauchistes* seemed to Barthes a clear error. With respect to e.g., the *gauchiste* groups dedicated to work on the question of the repression of homosexuality, a topic obviously of some import to Barthes, his sense was that it was a mistake for homosexuals, once freed from formal social repression, to fall back into a static collective identity (Calvet 1990: 223). A proper left political "sensibility" should not allow itself to be taken hostage by some self-imposed ideological set of rules of purity and rigor; he vehemently criticized on these grounds the critical response he had received from many on the left on the occasion of his (in)famous lunch with Valéry Giscard d'Estaing (Barthes 1981: 288). He once spoke of feeling "divided between my situation in a political space and the aggressive discourse coming from that space" (Barthes 1981: 236).

Despite his particular reaction to the street politics of 1968 and the subsequent years, he certainly did have a politicizing effect on students, different from and perhaps complimentary to that of Althusser. Where the latter's effect in political terms was more overt, a member of the PCF teaching a renewed intellectual Marxism to a generation of young activists and scholars, Barthes's political effect was transmitted in a more diffuse manner. He gave no lessons in how to reorganize the party, cultivate relations with the workers, or reread the master revolutionary theorist, but instead provided a broad theoretical means of politicizing literary texts and techniques. Writing itself could be political for Barthes, and more than political. In an interview with Bernard Henri-Lévy, Barthes responded tellingly to a question regarding the criticism by some on the left of his "sacralisation of writing": "There is always some of the sacred somewhere … So suppose it comes in writing for me. I repeat: it is very difficult to sacralize nothing … I surely sacralize. I sacralize … the pleasure of writing" (Barthes 1981: 296).

Althusser, Canguilhem, and Barthes encountered several of the poststructuralists precisely at moments in their careers that were crucial. In many cases, as just detailed, they were explicitly in the position of supervisors of theses or directors of courses in which the poststructuralists participated as students. Their relationships to the poststructuralists often exceeded the merely professional and ran into the personal, as was the case with the relationships of Lucien Herr and Sylvain Lévi to the Durkheimians. The evidence indicates that their influence on our poststructuralist group was broader and more diffuse than a mere communication of a set of concepts or theoretical orientations to disciplinary problems. It was of the order of a way of being an intellectual and creating personal meaning as such. This way of being an intellectual was saturated in a discourse that mixed the scholarly, the political, and the sacred.

Structures Cannot Descend into the Street and Sartre Cannot Speak for the Masses: How Poststructuralism Won the Contest to Define the Political Intellectual in the Wake of the May 1968 Events

The crisis of May 1968 indicated many things about French society, extending from the structural problems with its educational system to the labor struggle and on to the legacy of the Algerian War and the colonial project to which it had been linked. It was also a critical moment in the death of one kind of intellectual *qua* political actor and the emergence of another, and that is my focus here. As the Dreyfus Affair provided the opportunity for a new kind of intellectual figure (the Durkheimian) to emerge and become, if only very briefly, dominant, so May 1968 presented an opportunity for the uniquely situated poststructuralists. The student revolutionaries largely swept away the Cold War intellectual, even in its fellow traveler mold *à la* Sartre, despite his efforts to engage them. The intellectual as dispenser of wisdom on every conceivable topic from on high could not survive the radically egalitarian effervescence of that May. A new mode of intellectual identity, one that not only respected but revered the populism of the students in the courtyard at the occupied Sorbonne, that refused to speak for others and instead actively sought the voices of the voiceless, and that recognized in the most vivid terms the limits of its own expertise and knowledge, began to coalesce largely around the theoretical frameworks presented by the more radical versions of poststructuralist thought then emerging. And as the Durkheimians had been advantaged in the struggle for dominance during the Dreyfus Affair by the nuanced way in which their position offered a response to all three problematics (political, epistemological, and moral) at once, so the poststructuralists gained ground against their rivals by speaking a language that was recognized as theoretical, political, and quasi-religious at the same time. This language centered on and embraced the category of the radically Other, whether empirically represented in the Algerian, the working class, the criminal, or the madman. I explore this figure in its chief post-1968 incarnations in detail in Chapter 11.

As Pavel (199289: 135–36) has argued, the idea that May 1968 created poststructuralism is one that cannot be effectively defended. Instead, we should see the poststructuralists as having presented modes of political action as intellectuals that proved in the test of that May to be superior, at least in the short run, to other such modes presented by other intellectuals. May 1968 also represents the core event through which we should understand the trajectory taken by Foucault, Derrida, Baudrillard, and Deleuze beginning in the late 1960s. Poststructuralist French thought differed thematically from its structuralist forebear in several key ways: It rejected structuralism's jettisoning of history and the subject and re-embraced those concepts as essential to the philosophical project; it made a stand with difference against identity; and, perhaps most importantly (and in this it offered a powerful criticism both of structuralism and its existentialist opponent), it signaled a return to the philosophical consideration of ethics and religion (Schrift 2006: 56). The accomplishment of the poststructuralists was to distinguish themselves from the Sartrean humanists on the one hand, and the structuralist anti-humanists on the other, without completely losing traction among either the populists on the barricades or the avant-garde intellectuals in the universities and editorial offices. Their triumph was, like that of the Durkheimians at the *fin-de-siècle*, only fleeting; by the mid-70s, their failure to fully ensconce themselves in the universities led to the "institutional dissolution" of the movement (Parodi 2004: 212). Yet the evidence of their effort to rethink the problematics facing them continued to manifest itself in their work throughout their lives.

But let us not proceed too quickly. We do well to begin with some basic sociological facts about the May events and the preexisting situation that made them possible. Whatever else one believes about them, one thing seems indisputable: they signaled a profound problem with a rapidly growing social class in France—the intellectual and professional class. Important segments of this largely youthful class of highly educated, culturally and politically sophisticated upper middle-class individuals were clearly dissatisfied with the current state of French cultural and political society, and not merely the May events but also much of the ensuing decade of the 1970s provided a stage for the demonstration of their discontent and their proposals for change. The very site of origin of the May events is a clear indication of the centrality of these intellectual classes, and especially a specific fraction thereof. The same new kind of academic institution first represented by the École des Hautes Études en Sciences

Sociales, where the anti-bureaucratic "opposition to scholarly culture" noted in the previous chapter was dominant, gave birth to May 1968: It was at the new Nanterre campus of the University of Paris that Daniel Cohn-Bendit (a sociology major) and his fellows forged the March 22 Movement, which contributed significantly to the closing of the Nanterre campus and later to the massive arrests and closing of the Sorbonne on May 3, which in turn sparked the first street fighting that night between students and police and, ultimately, the Night of the Barricades a week later. It is clear that this was not a wholly unique French phenomenon, as other student rebellions of significant import took place during this period, indeed in this same year, in many other parts of Europe and the world. But we must reckon with this event fundamentally as a problem of the role and identity of the social class of intellectuals.

At the center of May 1968 was an opposition between two politico-cultural phenomena: a radical populism that was essentially anarchist in nature and that lurched increasingly quickly throughout the late 1960s and early 1970s toward complete acceptance and celebration of anything considered characteristic of the people, and an intellectual avant-garde that was seeking new understandings of the conditions of life in what was rapidly becoming known as post-industrial society. To a fair degree, this opposition was prominent here because of the fact that the central social group responsible for the instigation of the events of May was that of left-wing students, almost by nature drawn to both populism and the avant-garde at the same time. But there was also a history of this dialectic in the French cultural past. The historical relationship of the most populist political and most avant-garde artistic and intellectual discourses had been largely discordant in France, especially since the end of World War II and the rise to power of the PCF, which systematically attacked avant-garde works and ideas as elitist and useless to the proletariat. The evolution of avant-garde artistic movements was fundamentally crisscrossed by political debates about the accessibility of the movement to the workers, and ultimately many of those who retained a practical connection to radical populist politics necessarily fell away from the avant-garde and into more traditional aesthetic and intellectual positions, while those who remained ardent in their commitment to avant-garde principles eventually dismissed radical politics. The struggle of surrealism with the communist movement in France during the 1920s and 1930s is exemplary here (see Nadeau 1989[1948]: 135–36, 191–92, 221).

The May movement was animated by this same desire to combine aesthetic and political avant-gardes. Trotskyism, Maoism, and various anarchisms found themselves aligned with aesthetic currents inherited from the extreme reaches of the Dadaist movement that had rejected André

Breton's authoritarianism and pursued instead Tristan Tzara's total rejection of preconceived rules as to what constituted artistic expression
and experience. A long line of formerly politically irrecuperable artistic
radicals, from Sade and Jarry to Artaud and Lautréamont, were now mobilized as political figures, spokesmen for a new, nonpartisan (i.e., non-
PCF), libertine, anti-bureaucratic, and anti-statist aesthetic left politics.
Not the structures of the state but the practice of everyday life, with its
bored bourgeois refusal of illicit experience, had to change if politics
were to be remade. This represented a kind of marriage of the figures of
the engaged *intellectuel* and the libertine artist, the creation of a hybrid
intellectual figure consisting of the political head of Sartre surgically sewn
onto the debauched body of Verlaine. As a strategy it was attempted perhaps most directly in this period by the *Tel Quel* group. Throughout the
1960s and 1970s, this journal sought ways to combine the political populism of the Gauche prolétarienne (GP), a Maoist-anarchist movement
which was the leading post-1968 political force on the radical left, with
the modernist avant-garde. Yet ultimately *Tel Quel* did not so much marry
the two, lacking the correct theoretical language for doing so, as simply
move rapidly from pole to pole, first that of literary avant-garde, then that
of populist radicalism, and finally that of a conservative spiritualist mysticism. When *Tel Quel* became *l'Infini* in 1981 (with an entirely new editorial
staff), the move from "Maoist extremism to religious spiritualism" (and
terminologically, the rejection of "*intellectuel*" and embrace of "*ecrivain*")
was complete (Healy 1995: 314; Hourmant 1997: 229).

If *Tel Quel*'s story was comparatively complicated here, those of the
structuralists and the Sartreans were more straightforward. The one remained attached to an abstract avant-garde theoretical position at the
expense of political position-taking in the new populist discourse, while
the other attempted to engage the latter while failing to realize that traditional humanist theoretical positioning was decidedly out of favor in
the bubbling pot that was the Parisian intellectual world of the late 1960s.
The very nature of the near-collapse of the French state at the hands of
a totally unexpected revolt originating not from the factories but from
the universities seemed to put the lie to the foundation of structuralist
thought, i.e., the insignificance of the event and the individual actor in
the face of the large-scale structures and systems that were actually the
relevant actors on the historical stage. This criticism of the objectivist pretensions and the political distance of much of the reigning structuralism
of the period was neatly summed up in the phrase coined as a criticism of
A. J. Greimas and Roland Barthes: "It is clear that structures do not go out
into the street" (Dosse 1992: 140). Two other central structuralist figures,
Lacan and Lévi-Strauss, were strongly opposed to the students during the

May events and it is fairly easy to mark this period as one of decline for their influence in the Parisian sphere. Lévi-Strauss summarized the situation thus: " … structuralism is no longer in fashion. Since May 1968 all objectivity has been repudiated. The position of the youth corresponds to that of Sartre" (Hirsch 1981: 160).

Sartre's vision of the revolutionary potential of the "group-in-fusion" (instead of the static social class) as articulated in *Critique of Dialectical Reason* certainly resonated theoretically and subjectively with the May movement. He was, however, unable to build this into a full theory of revolution on this basis, and this is why he dropped volume two of the *Critique* (M. Christofferson 2003: 46). The reality is that the post-1968 period was a period of decline for Sartre and the *Temps Modernes* group (Boschetti 1988[1985]: 224–41). To be sure, Sartre was taken up as a kind of talismanic figure by some of the leading figures of the 1968 rebellion (and so it was symbolically quite important when he interviewed Cohn-Bendit at the occupied Sorbonne and thereby lent his celebrity to the cause), but this was largely to put him to uses not fully in line with his intellectual and political designs. Sartrean relations with younger radical intellectuals during this period are nicely captured in an account by Simone De Beauvoir of the effort during this period at the *Temps Modernes* to bring in younger thinkers to "fill a lacuna" in the journal. These younger thinkers (e.g., Régis Debray, Nikos Poulantzas, Sylvie Le Bon) were often students of Althusser and intended to use *Les Temps Modernes* to "expose their ideas" instead of adhering to the *Temps Modernes* party line; the attempt to add these younger thinkers was thus abandoned (Brillant 2003: 27). In 1970, the event that encapsulates the Sartrean effort to embrace the legacy of 1968 took place: the move by the government to outlaw *La Cause du Peuple*, the newsletter of the GP, and Sartre's subsequent decision to distribute the paper on the streets in support of the group. Here was the Sartrean New Intellectual looking to find "a new way of being with the masses in refusing a distinctive power, in having the same sovereignty as any member of the masses, but no more" (M. Christofferson 2003: 65, 67). But, ultimately, the New Intellectual was not new enough in that he or she did not sufficiently distance him or herself from the humanism that deeply penetrated Sartre's existentialist Marxism. The image of Sartre and De Beauvoir on the streets selling copies of the GP's newspaper implicitly alluded to the reduction of Sartre, the great thinker of all things, to the status of newspaper boy. While he was in the streets handing out papers, the ideas of others would carry the day in the universities and in the political meetings. The great master thinker was seeing the end of the days of master thinkers, even while *anti-master thinker master thinkers* were emerging in his stead.

It may seem difficult to see the differences between Sartre's New Intellectual and the "specific intellectual" famously proposed by Foucault (1977) and articulated earlier in a published discussion with Deleuze. Both posited the need for intellectuals to refuse to speak for others, but the latter did so more radically and in a way that called into question even the dependence of traditional intellectual discourse on humanist and rationalist epistemologies. The specific intellectual had to "struggle against the forms of power that transform him into its object and instrument in the sphere of 'knowledge,' 'truth,' 'consciousness,' and 'discourse,'" in Foucault's words (Deleuze 2002: 290). Deleuze added a conception that served to radicalize even the intellectual as discrete agent: "[T]he theorizing intellectual has ceased to be a ... representative consciousness. Those who act and who struggle have ceased to be represented ... Who speaks and who acts? It is always a multiplicity ... There is no more representation. There is only action" (2002: 289). I will return to the Foucauldian/Deleuzian formulation of the specific intellectual in Chapter 11.

We come now to the question of precisely in what ways the poststructuralist group responded to the May events. Foucault was not even in France at the time, but he strongly identified with the "spirit of May" and offered a perspective on it that proved compelling. He was in Tunis teaching philosophy in early 1968 when he had an experience that he later described glowingly as fundamental to his understanding of politics. The Tunisian government began a crackdown on the activities of radical students and in March there was a general strike of the student population. The police attacked the university in response and numerous students ended up arrested and facing charges of years in prison. Foucault reacted by allowing the activist students to continue publishing their banned tracts in his flat. Although his already-significant reputation likely prevented any real reprisals, he was threatened by police and even beaten at least once (Eribon 1989: 206). He characterized his experience in the most profound of terms:

> It wasn't May of '68 in France that changed me; it was March of '68 in a third-world country ... what on earth is it that can set off in an individual the desire, the capacity, and the possibility of an absolute sacrifice without our being able to recognize or suspect the slightest ambition or desire for power and profit? This is what I saw in Tunisia. (Foucault 1991[1981]: 136)

After returning to France, he made much of this difference between the real radical experience of Tunisia and the simulation of revolution in the courtyard of the Sorbonne, even purportedly telling a colleague who was with him in Tunis that he would respond to students who criticized him for not being on the barricades in May by telling them, "While you amused yourselves on the barricades in the Latin Quarter, I was engaged in serious business in Tunisia" (Eribon 1989: 215). Though there was certainly some intentional hyperbole in this statement, as Foucault explicitly acknowledged in the same interview in which he lauded the Tunisian experience that "without May of '68, I would never have done the things I'm doing today" (Foucault 1991[1981]: 140), Foucault actually found a way to out-radicalize the radicals in making the Tunisian experience into a critical commentary on the May events in France. The language of "absolute sacrifice" and the allusion to the 1968 spirit as consisting of a "moral force" and the "necessity of myth" made clear a certain effort to invoke quasi-religious terminology.

Baudrillard was at Nanterre in May of 1968. Well before the events of that month, he and other sociology faculty members authored a letter published in *Le Monde* that actively supported Situationist students who were under attack from the university (Brillant 2003: 72). He described his active involvement in the political radicalism that was then endemic at Nanterre by noting that "we participated in the general assemblies and were on the barricades" (Baudrillard 2005: 35). His courses were among those where student radicals gathered to find "places of dialogue where the teacher/ student hierarchy was erased" (Brillant 2003: 159). His language in describing the May events is like Foucault's, i.e., shot through with quasi-mystical or religious allusions. May 1968 was "a kind of pure object or event … an event which it has been impossible to rationalize or exploit, from which nothing has been concluded. It remains indecipherable" (Baudrillard 1990[1987]: 105–6, 114–15). He even read it as a kind of symbolic act of auto-sacrifice of the logic of previously dominant intellectual frameworks for understanding politics and conflict: "When the dominated class … prefers to act as a radical non-class … to act out its own death right away within the explosive structure of capital … then the result is June '48, the Commune, or May '68. The secret of the void lies here … [in] the Latin Quarter on the afternoon of May 3" (Baudrillard 1990[1987]: 58).

Derrida explicitly claimed never to have been a "soixante-huitard" and to have been from the first "on my guard, even worried in the face of a certain cult of spontaneity" (Derrida 1995b: 347). In this same interview, though, he talks of his involvement in demonstrations and his organization of "the first general meeting at the time at the École Normale," and also points to "a seismic jolt" that accompanied May 1968: "[T]hrough the cult of spontaneity and a certain naturalist utopianism, people doubtless became aware of the artificial, artifactual character of institutions" (1995b: 348). In the midst of the May adventure, Derrida participated in some of the most concrete and prolonged efforts to democratize the university. He was a signatory to a long text by Pierre Bourdieu published in *Le Monde* on May 21 wherein an effort was made to "adopt the point of view of those excluded from the scholastic and university systems" and to defend a pedagogical mission that would "transmit to all, by recourse to new pedagogical techniques, that which a handful ... owe to their social milieu" (Brillant 2003: 229). He was also actively involved in the "critical and popular summer schools" that followed the May events in Paris and Strasbourg. Modeled on the "critical university" of West Berlin that had erupted in November 1967 as a part of the student movement there, these attempted to undo the fragmentation of the disciplines and radically change teacher-student relationships (Brillant 2003: 422).

Deleuze was in Lyon in May 1968, working furiously on *The Logic of Sense*, but the events clearly served as a major element in orienting his approach to politics. Indeed, it can fairly be said that May 1968 gave Deleuze a politics, as he was essentially politically uninvolved before this period. He spoke of a "kind of passage into politics" that took place for him as a result of the May events (Deleuze 1990: 230). His formulation of the meaning of May 1968 sounds much like what we have already heard from the others: "May '68 is rather of the order of a pure event, free of all normal and normative causality ... it was a clairvoyant phenomenon, as if a society saw all at once what it contained of the intolerable and saw also the possibility of something else" (Deleuze 2003: 215). In the mid 1970s, when the phenomenon of Nouvelle Philosophie emerged, Deleuze attacked it vigorously as driven solely by "the hatred of '68" and defended the spirit of the May events against conservative attacks (2002: 131).

One event, which slightly precedes the May rebellion, captures effectively the strategic positioning of the poststructuralist group between political radicalism and the structuralist avant-garde. In February 1968, the Marxist journal *Raison* organized a panel on "Les Structures et les hommes" which was to span four days of conferences at the Sorbonne and was intended essentially as an opportunity for Marxist intellectuals to attack the perceived apolitical status of structuralism. To appear and too clearly side with the avant-garde would decrease one's capital in the radical community, whereas there were other dangers in being linked too closely to Marxist discourses. Deleuze, Foucault, and Derrida, all already well-known (while Baudrillard was yet to achieve the recognition that would begin to come to him in the early 1970s), were invited to participate. None attended (Brillant 2003: 46)

The centrality of the Other in the poststructuralist intellectual response to May 1968, which I turn to in Chapter 11, owed much to a political event that also laid the groundwork for the May events, even if this is not as well understood by commentators as it should be: the decolonization of Algeria and the Algerian war of independence. I cannot detour into a nuanced discussion of this massive political and cultural fact of the French scene of the middle twentieth century, but I must at least note a few points of extreme importance for my thesis. As I have already noted in passing, the intellectual left reacted to the Algerian conflict in conflicted ways. The PCF was not supportive of the nationalist movements in either Algeria or Indochina and believed instead that the preferred future for those countries was "national self determination only if the colonials were willing to accept their assimilation into a greater 'fraternal union' with France" (Healy 1995: 111–12). The party also recognized that the French working class was deeply racist and an incorrect position here would deny it power at home (Sorum 1977: 44). No notable intellectuals during the 1950s dared to support Algerian independence until Raymond Aron's *La Tragédie algérienne* in 1957 and the famed Manifesto of the 121, which made a "declaration of the right of insubordination in the Algerian War," did not come until 1960. There was a profound generational division in how French intellectuals dealt with the question of Algeria. Those leftist intellectuals whose political positions developed during the 1920s and 1930s and who aligned themselves in the Dreyfusard tradition supported the idea of a France with an Enlightenment colonialist project at a very fundamental level and had to be faced with much information in the way of French atrocities and the sheer impossibility of a continued French Algeria before they accepted independence. Their sense was that French colonialism was part of a "special mission from God" that involved "bringing progress and enlightenment, in sacrificing itself for the other nations" (Sorum 1977: 23).

If here was French humanism at its most profound, then the generation that brought about the anti-humanist philosophy of structuralism was certainly destined to call at least some of this history into question. And indeed the generations born in the 1920s and 1930s were much less tolerant of that Enlightenment myth (Sirinelli 1990: 223–24). For them, the cultural air was heavy with rejection of the "West is best" ideology and a turn to other ways of engaging the world, as I noted in Chapter 5. Structuralism at its roots could be seen as part of an intellectual critique of Western culture (Dosse 1991: 10). Core structuralist texts like Lévi-Strauss's *The Savage Mind* were an attack not simply on the existentialism of Sartre but on Western models of political engagement (Healy 1995: 71–79). There were also non-structuralist intellectuals who responded to the war in Algeria with a kind of precursor to Edward Said's *Orientalism* argument. Jacques Berque, himself a *pied noir,* forcefully denounced the Enlightenment prejudice against the non-Western Other and Maurice Maschino invoked the concept of the Other to explain the nationalist response to the dehumanization of the colonial project. Such efforts "eventually became one of the most important intellectual developments during the French-Algerian War" (LeSeuer 2001: 216–17). Further contributing to this fascination with Otherness was the significant intellectual activism against the American war in Vietnam in the several years before the May events (M. Christofferson 2003: 50; Brillant 2003: 101–21).

The victors in intellectual political terms in the wake of the Algerian conflict were those who had mingled criticism of the French state with an attack on the universalism of the French colonial project. An embrace of populist politics and theoretical avant-gardism led to a rejection of all forms of thought that hinted at the trope of the totalizing (M. Christofferson 2003: 40). The failures of the French state and the PCF with respect to the conflict in Algeria short-circuited any possibilities for expressing an intellectual politics in nationalist or communist/socialist modes. It was ultimately a *gauchiste* and Other-directed form of intellectual politics that our poststructuralist group adopted. The break of 1968 was in many ways much like the break of 1898 in its repercussions for intellectual politics and positioning. In both cases, stock polar responses were doomed to lose out to responses that were able to tie together seemingly contradictory themes; in 1968, the avant-garde and the populist, and in 1898, the secular and the religious. In 1898, Durkheim constructed an intellectual position that entailed a mobilization of a new sacred category, that of the individual, which would become the political and intellectual focus for the members of his class (the former clerics). In 1968, the poststructuralists did the same with the foreign, working-class, criminal, radical, or insane Other.

Notes

1. There are also several letters in the Fonds Louis Althusser at l'Institut Mémoires de l'Édition Contemporaine (hereafter IMEC) in Caens from Derrida that address intellectual issues. For example, in a letter dated 1 September 1964, Derrida acknowledges receipt of a text, very likely some part of what would become *For Marx*, and comments: "I found the text you sent me excellent. I feel as close as possible to the theoretical anti-humanism you propose with as much force as rigor … I understand quite well nevertheless the necessity of 'ideological' humanism at certain moments, the necessity of ideology in general even in a communist society, etc … We will have to talk about all of this, with Marx's texts at hand … and you'll assign me some reading" (Derrida to Althusser, Fonds Louis Althusser. IMEC).

2. I note in passing that Deleuze too was on very friendly terms with Althusser, although he did not study with him. There are letters from the former to the latter in the Fonds Louis Althusser at IMEC that attest to a warm friendship and intellectual relationship.

3. This is part of an entry dated 14 January 1937. The three notebooks Althusser filled during this year with his daily thoughts on his schoolwork, his plans for the future, his relationships with teachers and other students, and his spiritual experiences and ideas are contained in the Fonds Louis Althusser at IMEC.
4. On the page facing this journal entry is a charming sketch Althusser made of "mon maître, Jean Guitton."
5. The Baron de Charlus is a decadent aristocratic character in Proust's *À la recherche du temps perdu.*

7 Being a Durkheimian Intellectual

We now have something of a macro-sociological image of the two fields in which our two groups of intellectuals put their ideas into play, as well as information on the masters of ceremonies for the two groups and the central political event that positioned both. However, the reconstruction of their *habitus* requires a closer examination of the ways in which the members of the two groups actively viewed and set about the process of constructing identities as intellectuals in the two periods from within more intimate micro-social networks of influences and collaborators and in response to the set of intellectual problematics I have outlined.

What are the relevant data that go into the construction of the intellectual *habitus* of the Durkheimians? Earlier, I cited Philippe Besnard's (1983) network analysis of the *Année sociologique* team to show how central this sub-group was in the overall project. It is of note that all four were centrally concerned with the same object in their work: religious life. Are there any facts that can help us understand, first, *how and why these four key members took up the study of religion in the first place,* and second, *what the personal stakes in that intellectual decision may have been?*

The Sociological Study of Religion as a Personal Choice

Intellectual orientations are intimately linked to personal dispositions. Intellectuals do not choose the topic of a life's work randomly, but on the basis of already given social and experiential facts. Conventional narratives on the history of Durkheimian sociology point to Durkheim's Robertson Smith revelation in 1895 regarding the central importance of religion in social life. They frequently point also to his determination to construct a comprehensive social science with which to untangle the confusing reality of modern society and then claim that subsequent treatment of religion by other members of the *Année* group is fully explained by the objective research needs of the Durkheimian project. This kind of explanation would have it that the specific subject matter of religion here is hardly of central personal importance to those who study it. The decision was purportedly made wholly in response to the imperatives of the discipline and the scientific endeavor.

Although this kind of narrative is clearly too simple to explain the situation fully, we must be careful not to dismiss its explanatory power too quickly. We know after all that Durkheim had a huge influence on the intellectual life of his nephew. He convinced Mauss to avoid the more prestigious path to the École Normale Supérieure and instead to study with his uncle in the relative hinterland of Bordeaux where Durkheim could exercise firmer control over him. After being coached through the *agrégation* by Durkheim, Mauss was heavily influenced by his uncle to take up the study of religion almost exclusively at the École Pratique des Hautes Études. His account of the decision, recorded long after the fact in 1930, emphasized the need expressed both by his uncle and himself to "put his force in the best place to render service to the new-born science and to fill in the most serious holes" (Mauss 1979: 214). But he also alluded in this same account to his "philosophical taste" as part of the decision-making process in selecting the sociology of religion as his specialization over two other competing possibilities, quantitative/demographic sociology and law. We need to remain alert to the inevitable complexity involved in any such far-reaching decision. It is not irrelevant that this account of the decision came so long after the fact, and at least a partial explanation for it can be found in the professional concerns Mauss felt at this point in his career (when he was seen as the successor to Durkheim at the head of the *Année* movement) to maintain integrity and consistency in the mythology of the Durkheimian project. Further, good sociology presumes that a thorough account of an actor's motives cannot be derived from the actor's self-reporting. There was a complex concern in the Third Republic for religion and its role in French society on the part of intellectuals of all personal positions regarding religious faith. The issues I discussed in Chapter 3 affected the members of our group in ways that are difficult to trace. We can be more exact, though, in looking to the effects of relations and factors of a micro-social level, beginning with an effort to situate these men as individuals with histories and ethnic identities, families of origin, and other traces of an indelible marking of position, a lived *habitus* that powerfully informs their action in the world.

Religious Identity and the Durkheimians: The "Jewish Question"

The question of religious identity ought to suggest itself at first glance as among the most important factors in understanding the decision of scholars to study religion. There exist a number of treatments of the role played by Durkheim's ethnic status as a Jew (e.g., Pickering 1993; Strenski 1997), some very insightfully exploring this aspect of his identity and its effect on his intellectual work and political life. We could profitably expand that discussion to include Mauss, also the descendant of Alsatian Ashkenazi Jews from Épinal in the northeastern province of Lorraine (which at Mauss's birth in 1872 was in possession of the Germans), and Hertz, born of Parisian Jews of German origin and thus also Ashkenazi. Hubert, by contrast, was born into a liberal Parisian Catholic family. It is striking to note that *three of the four central contributors to the Durkheimian sociology of religion are of Jewish origin.* Substantively, though, what does this mean, given the fact that none of the three men could in any reasonable way be identified as adults as practicing members of the Jewish faith?

We have a fairly clear idea of the path that Durkheim himself took toward the personal rejection of the Jewish faith into which he was born. The marking of his life trajectory by his Jewishness perhaps began at his naming, as Durkheim's actual first name is not Émile, but David. Both his father, Moïse, and his grandfather, Israël, had been rabbis, and he was himself directed by his father early in life to prepare to follow in the tradition. He was enrolled in rabbinical school as a young man, learned Biblical Hebrew in order to study Jewish religious texts, and gave every indication himself at that age of contentment with this life plan (Fournier 1994: 35). It was only while enrolled at the École Normale that he began to distance himself openly from the faith of his father, finally breaking completely with Judaism sometime during his first year there (Lukes 1973: 44). According to all sources, this event left deep traces in Durkheim, who retained a certain sense of remorse throughout his life for having failed to maintain the family tradition (Fournier 1994: 36). He continued to join the family for traditional religious holidays in Épinal, taking part in the rituals with a general understanding by other family members that he did not share the beliefs to which the festivities were historically attached.

Mauss's case is, at least according to some commentators, nearly identical to that of his uncle. Victor Karady treats the topic brusquely: "It would seem [Mauss] ceased practicing his religion very early, *with no tearing or tension in the family*, which was very strongly dominated by the influence of Durkheim" (Mauss 1968a: xix; emphasis added). Here, the subject becomes a *non*-subject. Fournier (1994) is somewhat more attentive to the complexity and importance of such an event in the course of the life of an individual raised in a highly religious family environment. He discusses the difficulties sometimes created by the admixture of traditional religious family celebrations, which of course occasionally included rather rigorous abstentions, interdictions, and rules of comportment, dress, etc., with two intellectual family members who had, at least in the most obvious ways, separated themselves from the faith (Fournier 1994: 39). He is also careful to indicate the intricacies of the Jewish education Mauss, like Durkheim, received as a youth and at least some aspects of its legacy for his later intellectual life, i.e., the use he would make of his knowledge of Hebrew in some of his historical research for the works on sacrifice and prayer (Fournier 1994: 40). Fournier tells us the Jewish name Mauss received at his Bar-Mitzvah (Israël) and mentions an essay Mauss wrote for the *Revue des études juives* in 1926 in which he discusses, in a footnote, the etymology of that name (1994: 38). Overall, however, the impression one receives from Fournier's account is not entirely unlike that of Karady, i.e., that, ultimately, very early in his life and in some relatively unproblematic and final way, Mauss definitively broke with the deeply imbedded religious beliefs and traditions of his family. From that point, although he continued to attend family religious celebrations and even to participate in them in some minimally acceptable way, he separated himself completely on an emotional and intellectual level from those beliefs and traditions.

But closer inquiry into the intricate ways in which both uncle and nephew were affected by their religious upbringing and the specifics of their respective breaks with the faith provides a somewhat more complex picture. Durkheim himself is reputed to have commented upon his own intellectual life that "it must not be forgotten that I am the son of a rabbi" (Filloux 1977: 35), and there are more than a few ways in which the influence is plainly seen in his attitude toward sociology and the intellectual life in general. While Durkheim chose not to follow his father *literally* as "carrier of the rabbinical discourse," he arguably nonetheless "occupies otherwise" that same place as bearer of a discourse that, in its structure, is quite comparable to the rabbinical discourse inspired by Jewish holy texts (Filloux 1977: 36). In the place of the adulation inspired by the omnipotent God of the Torah, Durkheim's message is one of the adulation inspired by the omnipotent creative power of *society*. Durkheim's reading here follows closely the structure of the rabbinical teaching, which is, according to Filloux, not surprising given his thorough saturation throughout his formative intellectual years in the Torah, the Mishnah and the

Talmud. For Durkheim, "Like God, society is creator, life, happiness, paternity" (Filloux 1977: 36). Filloux goes still further and argues that Durkheim's re-appropriation of the orthodox imagery of Yahweh is not only informed by a transformation of the religious symbolism of orthodoxy, but also by a need to appropriate *the symbolic force of the Father,* both in the sense of God the Father as eternal patriarch and in the sense of Emile Durkheim's actual father, Moïse, himself a patriarchal figure *par excellence.* According to this argument, Durkheim, despite his explicit rejection of the belief system of Judaism, accepted the symbolic language of that faith and remodeled it to fit his new sociological discourse. In so doing, he also took as a central element in his approach to intellectual life the sovereignty of the person of the patriarch that he had absorbed from both the image of Yahweh the Father and his own real father. Filloux argues that this re-appropriation of the father's role in new garb had taken on a political guise early in Durkheim's career and that it later assumed an explicitly religious guise, at least insofar as the object of Durkheim's closest attention becomes religion, at precisely the moment of the death of Durkheim's father in 1896.

Other commentators have contributed further useful insights on this issue. Edward Tiryakian (1978) argues that, inasmuch as the specific work by Robertson Smith that seems to have most affected Durkheim presents early Jewish religious life as a coherent social and symbolic system, Durkheim was moved by his reading of this work to reconsider the connections between orthodox Judaism and this early Judaism and patterned his later religious and moral thought on these frameworks. Louis Greenberg (1976) locates the essence of the influence of the faith of Durkheim's father on the son much earlier than the 1896 experience; he sees it in the austerity and duty-bound asceticism of the home over which Moïse Durkheim presided. Although Durkheim was to react against the narrowness of the professional and ethnic choices of the father, recognizing the ways in which they had restricted his father's options economically and socially, he nonetheless absorbed the overall ascetic framework of the rabbinical tradition in which his father was schooled and modeled his own intellectual and personal life accordingly. Ivan Strenski has raised familiar objections to all of these arguments about the Jewish affinities in Durkheim's intellectual life. According to Strenski, Durkheim, in his efforts to defend the contemporary practitioners of those traditions against anti-Semitic and liberal attackers, developed an understanding of religion that was nearly identical to that of *liberal* Jewish and Catholic theologians of the day and, like them, he wanted to maintain some of the symbolic efficacy of religion divorced utterly from the specific beliefs and rituals to which they were initially attached (Strenski 1997: 150–52).

There are thus good reasons to read the influence on Durkheim's intellectual worldview and trajectory by his Jewish background and experience in a more complex and multi-faceted manner than has generally been suggested. Let me be clear: This is not to suggest that his thought is in some hidden ways essentially Jewish. Rather, one finds in Durkheim a certain sensibility to religious questions that is informed by his immersion in a particular kind of *world-construction apparatus.* As Peter Berger (1969) argues, all individuals, intellectuals or not, face the task of constructing from the chaos of empirical reality an orderly *nomos,* i.e., a symbolically meaningful world, and religious systems and their accompanying theodicies are the primordial way in which this activity is undertaken. It is *not* that Durkheim's thought is *Jewish,* but rather that his way of making sense of the world is deeply informed by his immersion in the Jewish manner of constructing a meaningful world and that we must therefore carefully consider the relationship between the two if we want to get at the core of that thought.

In the case of Mauss, the scenario is in some ways still more complex. We know from his uncle's correspondence of at least one very tense situation that resulted from Mauss's demonstration to his family of his inability to accept their faith as his own. In October 1900, Durkheim discussed with Mauss the surfacing of conflict in the family surrounding his refusal to make "demonstrations of piety" at his mother's request. Mauss apparently had declined to accompany his grandmother to temple, fearing such an act would indicate to others his participation in the Jewish worship that he had left some years before, and this had caused his mother some significant distress. Durkheim offered practical advice to Mauss on how he ought to have proceeded in such a case and was critical of Mauss's excessive attitude yet generally supportive of his position: "Certainly ... [y]ou should refuse to undertake an act of apparent piety, but not to give help to grandmother" (Durkheim 1998: 270–71). There is much other evidence in Mauss's own correspondence that demonstrates the relative persistence of this issue. His mother was a devout practitioner of her faith, as was Mauss's father Gerson, and there is evidence to suggest that they consistently hoped for a re-evaluation of spiritual position on the part of their son and spoke frequently with him about this.[1] Mauss's relationship with his mother Rosine was generally marked by great closeness and perhaps made even more intimate by the fact that she was Durkheim's sister. He was the eldest child in the family and received great attention from the attentive matriarch, who became *de facto* head of the household fairly early when his father died suddenly of heart disease in 1896. Durkheim alludes in another letter to her having asked him to "form" her son, as she perhaps recognized in her brother the new prototype of the patriarch their father Moïse had been and wished to place Marcel in that same position on her side of the family. Despite Mauss's intransigence in the episode recounted above, there were apparently many others in which Rosine Mauss was indeed able to convince Marcel to participate in family religious celebrations, which he and Durkheim routinely attended at the family home. There is also testimony from some close to Mauss that he continued to observe at least some Jewish holidays even as late as the 1940s (Strenski 1997: 194).

But beyond the complexity of Mauss's very close relationship with his devout mother is another and more intellectually central influence that very profoundly affected his understanding of his Jewish heritage and its role in his intellectual and social life. This is his relationship to Sylvain Lévi, the great Indologist who was his teacher of Sanskrit and Indian religion at the École Pratique des Hautes Études and who became one of Mauss's very closest friends over the course of his life, second in closeness perhaps only to Hubert. Lévi was a powerful influence on all the members of the religion cluster, as I briefly noted in Chapter 4, both as teacher/mentor and as a member of the intimate circle of the Durkheimian group, but he exercised the most profound influence on Mauss. Mauss would say of Lévi's *Doctrine du sacrifice dans les Brāhmanas* that it "was made for me," and this work was clearly one of the central inspirations of the work on sacrifice completed by Mauss and Hubert in 1899. Mauss referred to him as his "second uncle," a notable comparative commentary on the extent of Lévi's influence in his life, given what we know of the huge influence his first uncle had over him.

Like Mauss and Durkheim, Lévi was from Alsace-Lorraine. Moreover, Lévi was a devout practitioner of Judaism and remained so his entire life. Lévi's Judaism was not of a typically modernist variety like that, for example, of Salomon Reinach, for whom the ritual and mystery of traditional, orthodox Judaism had been replaced by the language of religious progress in which reason becomes a tool to be used in studying religion and the ameliorative force that chases all the primitive elements from faith. Lévi faithfully observed traditional ritual practices and interdictions. When asked in 1926 for his comments for a volume assembled by the *Cahiers contemporaines* on contemporary intellectual understandings of God, he mounted an unambiguous attack on the modernist program to dissipate the mystery surrounding the question of God and to place humankind at the pinnacle of the universe: "The 'reasonable' minds prohibit the imagination; they drain symbols of their meaning ... This conscious and voluntary mutilation of the domain of thought is a disquieting symptom of our age" (Tonquédec et al. 1926: 145). For Lévi, the spectacle of man as king of the universe was laughable: "Sad king, pitiful on his masquerade throne, plaything of unknown forces that attack and crush him!" (Tonquédec et al. 1926: 145).

One cannot simply point to Lévi's Jewish faith as something that must necessarily have affected his work in such a way as to thereby signify something obviously meaningful regarding his relationship to Judaism to those, like Mauss, who were influenced by that work. But Mauss was not limited to Lévi's published work in extracting meaning from the latter's position on these issues. He also frequented the Lévi home, and Lévi and his wife often visited the Durkheim/Mauss family home as well. This was a relationship that very much exceeded that of professor and student or of two scholars. Mauss noted that the example of Lévi went far beyond his writings to also encompass political and moral life. Lévi had been active in various Jewish philanthropic organizations such as the Alliance Israëlite Universelle and had worked actively during the early and mid 1930s to aid and shelter Jewish and other refugees from the anti-Semitic regime that had just come to power in Germany (Mauss 1969: 542). Further, according to Mauss, he exemplified in his daily life a character so perfectly refined and noble that one had recourse only to religious terminology in naming it. Mauss employed a wide array of superlatives in describing him as "a great man, a sage, a good man, a strong and able man and a saint" (Mauss 1969: 545), but it is perhaps the last that is most intriguing. The word "saint" appears no less than three times in direct reference to Lévi in Mauss's brief obituary of his teacher. In one passage, Mauss, after naming Durkheim, Jaurès, and Lévi as the three men to whom he was the most dedicated during the first and formative part of his life, distinguishes the latter from the others in calling him "the closest to the future Maitreya[2] … the most actively human, which is rare even among the saints, among even the most saintly of the saints" (Mauss 1969: 544–45).

Mauss himself participated in the activities of the Alliance Israëlite Universelle under the influence of Lévi, and he even became the first of the Durkheimians of Jewish descent to begin publicly identifying himself as such during the 1930s (Strenski 1997: 124). Strenski makes clear the connection between Lévi's Indological work and his Judaism, a connection that makes even more interesting the thesis that religious and Jewish motivations influenced Mauss's own intellectual career. Lévi had begun his intellectual career as a scholar of Judaism, but made the shift to Indology early on, recognizing the fact that the study of the history of Indian religion provided a unique way into contemporary religious and political debates. The opposition of Aryan-Indian and Semitic had then been *au courant* for some time in some (especially German) intellectual circles, and it was utilized by some ideologically motivated researchers to demonstrate the superiority of Aryan culture and history and the diametrically opposed nature of Semitic civilization (Strenski 1997: 126).

Lévi's intervention into such debates was a clever attempt to locate an implicit discursive path toward defending Semitic religion and history from these attacks precisely by *undermining* the opposition between Indian-Aryan and Semitic. He denied Aryanist arguments for the purity of the Indian religions, arguing instead that India, like Israel, was a nation open *via* its connection to the sea to cultural infusions from elsewhere. This served simultaneously as a denial of Aryanist implications for the purity of Aryan civilization and the opposed impurity of Semitic civilization. He also tried to demonstrate the deep similarities between Indian and Semitic religion. As part of his defense of orthodox Talmudic Jewish practice and ritual, he compared it favorably to traditional Brahmanical Hinduism as an organic and embodied set of religious practices that, whatever its failings from the perspective of universalist modernists and humanists, was tremendously effective in preserving the essence and cohesion of a community precisely because of its anti-abstract qualities (Strenski 1997: 126–33).

Mauss's encounter with Lévi's Indological work was not the first time that he had brushed this intersection of intellectual work and religious/moral/political motivation. As a young student of philosophy at the University of Bordeaux, he studied the work of Spinoza with Octave Hamelin, a disciple of Renouvier. Of particular interest to Mauss in his reading of Spinoza, judging from pages of notes that are preserved from this period,[3] was the influence on Spinoza by Jewish thinkers. Whereas the conventional French reading of Spinoza had been of a rebel against established Judaism who was during his lifetime excommunicated from and shunned by the Jewish community into which he had been born, Mauss was instead interested as a young student in the things Spinoza had *retained* from his Jewish masters. During this same period of Mauss's reading of Spinoza, we find a considerable effort by others reading him to separate him from the uncomplicated atheistic interpretation of Spinoza that had become the established French reading in the wake of the Revolution and to read him instead as a kind of pantheist, something much closer to Novalis's characterization of him as a "God-intoxicated man" (Jaspers 1964: 16). Mauss even notes in an intellectual self-portrait that, while at Bordeaux, he had selected as one of his two thesis topics "the tight bonds" uniting Spinoza and Léon L'Hébreu,[4] a discovery he claims to have made in 1893; he only dropped the idea four years later when someone else beat him to the punch and published on the topic (Besnard 1983: 145; Fournier 1994: 71). One can only speculate here, as there are no polished treatments of Spinoza in the Maussian œuvre,[5] but such an interest certainly makes sense in light of the complicated relation Mauss had with his own religious birthright, and it contributes further to establishing a connection between his intellectual project generally and a set of very complex personal attitudes towards religious faith and phenomena.

Let us turn to the other younger Durkheimians, Hertz and Hubert. Hertz's father Adolph was a German Jewish immigrant who had spent some time in business in the United States, where he made his fortune and where he probably met his (also Jewish) wife Josephine Strahlheim before coming to France. His experience of his Jewishness differs from that of Durkheim and Mauss in that, according to his son Antoine, neither of his parents were practitioners of the Jewish faith.[6] Although there is no direct evidence to the contrary among the records of Hertz's family life, we might nonetheless raise some questions regarding this assessment of the relationship of the Hertz family to their Jewish heritage, given some other facts. There are, for example, letters from a young Hertz to his sisters, Cécile and Fanny, in which he candidly ponders the nature of his relationship to the Jewish faith, recounting instances of anti-Semitic prejudice he had experienced and his efforts to come to terms with his own conception of his Jewish identity. A more powerful example of Hertz's complicated position regarding his religious identity is revealed in a letter to a British friend on the occasion of the marriage of Hertz's sister Dora. She had opted for a conventional Jewish ceremony, and Hertz's recounting of the situation is revealing:

> [W]e were all deeply moved by the impressive greatness and solemnity of the antique service. I think more and more that if one has to be religious, it is better to take it all in—I mean, no rationalism, no secularization of the divine, no mean adaptation of the grand absurdity of true religion to our petty intellectualist scruples. If I was a Roman Catholic, I would certainly be with Pius X against the modernists. Those people are ashamed of having a religion—they try to beg their pardon from the intellectual people and the freethinkers—they take as humble and "reasonable" an attitude as they can—and they lose what is the essence of religion, the emotional power, without winning intelligibility.[7]

This position of comprehension and even sympathy for religiously orthodox ways of understanding the world seemingly runs counter to both the radically secularist view often attributed to the Durkheimians and Strenski's argument that, while they can perhaps be linked with religious allies in their task to remake the symbolic landscape, this link is with the modernists and not the orthodox. This sensitivity and even attraction to the kind of serious moral and ascetic project that is at the heart of much orthodox religious practice seems to have accompanied Hertz throughout his life and to have constantly intermingled with his secularist and rationalist impulses. His attraction to the moral exuberance of religious community became still more intense during Hertz's stint on the front during World War I. Here, he frequently spoke of his experiences in religious language, speaking of himself as someone who had felt throughout his whole life "the nostalgia of the absent cathedral" and finding in the war something of the effervescent moral unity that had once been commonly held in religious community (Hertz 2002: 219). He expressed admiration for the pious commitment to their task manifested by his Catholic fellow soldiers and found himself in agreement with Maurice Barrès, one of the leaders of the anti-Dreyfusard intellectual faction, in seeing the army as a kind of "great religious order" (Hertz 2002: 175, 240).

As with Durkheim and Mauss, Hertz's sensibility to religious experience and ways of thinking was not in any simple way categorizable as Jewish. In fact, he struggled throughout his life to free himself from certain elements of Jewish identity in order to make clear his allegiance to the national community. His letters from the front, which are full of expressions of sympathy for religious sentiments, are yet also full of Hertz's desire to distance himself from a purely Jewish identity. Earlier in his life, he had explicitly refused to align himself with the Dreyfusard cause, even denouncing Zola's intervention into the affair as "clumsy" and "lamentable" because Hertz sympathized with the nationalist concerns for the weakness of national and military security that were created by the tumult surrounding the affair and felt a responsibility to make clear his allegiance to France in such a crisis.[8] Hertz even attributed his career choice as scholar to his Jewish identity, albeit indirectly as a result of French anti-Semitism. In another letter to Dodd, which dates from Hertz's pre-ENS days, he writes: "If I were not ... a German Jew, I would have, I think, gone into politics ... But you know that anti-Semitism is at its height at this moment."[9] In the obituary he wrote at Hertz's death, Durkheim echoed this notion of Hertz's academic calling, and specifically his interest in religious topics, as originally a political calling that had been re-routed (Durkheim 1975a: 440). His account sounds much like the accepted story of Mauss being led to religious topics by the scientific exigencies revealed to him by Durkheim. Though there is certainly some truth to it, this closer look at Hertz's complex relationship to religious topics makes apparent that the motivation came also from much deeper sources.

Hubert was born into a relatively well-off Catholic family, his father having made his fortune in the hosiery trade before retiring early to dedicate himself to "intellectual distractions" (Fournier 1994: 104). Hubert lost his faith under circumstances about which we know little, but he maintained close relations throughout his entire life with Catholic clergy, theologians, and practicing laymen, many of whom had been his teachers and fellow students at the *lycée* Louis Le Grand. Among these was Albert Houtin, who was close to Hubert's friend and mentor Lucien Herr and the biographer of the controversial Catholic modernist Alfred Loisy. Houtin and Hubert were also colleagues at the Musée Pédagogique after the war. Another close associate was Hubert's teacher at the École Pratique, Louis Duchesne, a celebrated historian of Catholicism and a practicing Catholic who, though modernist in his scholarly work, maintained an alliance with the Catholic orthodoxy in the face of the most virulent modernist assaults on orthodox articles of faith during the *fin-de-siècle* period. Notably, he refused to take his student Loisy's side in his attack on the dogmatism of the Vatican, an attack that brought Loisy's excommunication from the Church (Strenski 1995: 40–44). We know too that Hubert eventually distanced himself from the Dreyfusard movement because of what he viewed as its anti-clericalism (Bourgin 1938: 381–83). His general sentiment of respect for the Catholic faith, and for religious faith generally, is abundantly evident in his published work. He believed that "religions have been our educators and our wet nurses" (Reinach 1927: 178) and saw their disappearance and replacement by new systems of world-construction as a complicated and dangerous, if perhaps historically inevitable, affair.

According to several commentators, Hubert's personal bearing clearly bore the marks of his religious formation. Salomon Reinach, who was Hubert's superior during the latter's long tenure at the Musée Saint-Germain, said of him that "he had perhaps by heredity the Jansenist mark about him" and noted that neither the often raucous student world of the École Normale nor the even more obviously vulgarizing period of his mandatory military service had been successful at extirpating his priest-like reserve and courtesy (Reinach 1927: 178). Mauss commented often to him on his excessive asceticism, and Hubert characterized himself at least once as a "Benedictine."[10]

Durkheimian Varieties of Socialism and Perspectives on the Intellectual as Political Actor

As we have seen, the political dilemmas facing intellectuals at this historical juncture in France were tightly intertwined with cultural debates that were at root often about religion and morality. As the debates over the proper political role of the intellectual were linked in sometimes very intimate ways to the religious dilemma (e.g., what could be the source of an intellectual's legitimacy as a political actor or authority in the absence of religious authority? and, for the intellectuals themselves, in what ways might the political be approached as a kind of civil religion?), the Durkheimians' interventions into these debates were often charged with those religious questions.

In the 1895–1896 academic year, Durkheim dedicated an entire course to the history of socialism and particularly the thought of Saint-Simon. The thesis on the importance of corporative groups for the reinvigoration of modern society advanced in his work on the division of labor and in his lectures on professional ethics has also been widely interpreted as basically socialist, if reformist rather than revolutionary. In the lectures on socialist history, he even treats the rise of contemporary socialist movements as a direct consequence of what for him is perhaps the single greatest political and social tragedy of modernity, i.e., the suppression of the guilds in France after the Revolution. Thus, the very existence of the class struggle is for Durkheim tied to the disappearance of the institution that secured the integrated functioning of class society (Durkheim 1958[1893]: 102–5; Gane 1992: 135–64). Some have claimed that Durkheim subtly advertised his political leanings to his students by entering the lecture hall daily with a copy of *L'Humanité* under his arm (T. Clark 1973: 190). Others have gone so far as to see Durkheim's "original project" as political and socialist, and they have read the scholarly career as the result of an evolutionary movement in that original project (Filloux 1977). Yet, throughout his life, Durkheim never officially joined any political party and limited his explicit political activity to a few key periods and events: the Dreyfus Affair, "a few symbolic gestures of militant patriotism" during the buildup to World War I, and then heavy, active propaganda work during the war (Lacroix 1981: 24).

In fact, there is a significant political role for the intellectual in Durkheim's vision, and, as we saw in Chapter 3, it is closely tied to his moral project and to a more personal quest for meaning. But it clearly envisions a neat separation between the calling of the intellectual and that of the political actor, and Durkheim derived an ideal of moral and political participation by intellectuals that recognized their proper role as that of "advisers [and] educators" (Durkheim 1970: 280). Indeed, the lecture course on socialism is centrally devoted to denying the necessary connection some saw between socialism and sociology and of protecting the scientific integrity of the latter from the former.

Mauss, on the other hand, was an active socialist from at least his days as a student at Bordeaux in the early 1890s, where he met militant students such as Marcel Cachin, who was also studying philosophy with many of Mauss's teachers. Mauss became a member of the local Groupe des étudiants socialistes and, later, of the Marxist Parti Ouvrier Français (Fournier 1994: 60–61). Mauss's radicalism and militant stance increased after his arrival in Paris in 1893. There, he penetrated into the larger and more sophisticated circle of militant socialist youth centered at the École Normale. He made the acquaintance of many of the central young participants in these radical circles of the day, including Charles Péguy and the Milhaud brothers Edgar and Albert, and took part in the activities of a radical student group known as the Ligue démocratique des écoles. His long career of writing for socialist and political journals and tracts got underway during this period as well (Fournier 1994: 73–75). Mauss continued to be very politically active in socialist circles throughout the mid 1920s, followed by a lull leading up to the advent of the Popular Front government in 1932, at which point he briefly resumed a significant level of political activity and writing.[11]

An intriguing component of his political perspective that is present throughout the course of his career tells us something important about the true role of politics in the intellectual and personal project of Mauss. His early socialism is radical, utopian, and geared to direct action; in Bordeaux it is with the P.O.F., a Marxist party, rather than the reformist socialist S.F.I.O. of Durkheim's friend Jean Jaurès, that Mauss allies himself. His early political writings and talks speak in a revolutionary language alien to Durkheim: "Socialist schools ... are unanimous in saying: Bourgeois society should be destroyed ... Action always precedes theory ... Socialist action is, finally, naturally *revolutionary*" (Mauss 1997: 72–82; emphasis in original). In this same early (1899) article, Mauss speaks appreciatively of Marx (Mauss 1997: 74–75). When he arrived later in Paris and made the acquaintance of Lucien Herr, he quickly became a key figure in the orchestration of the debating and street-fighting tactics of engagement with anti-Dreyfusard opponents (Mauss 1997: 740–45; Birnbaum 1972: 142).

A significant portion of the utopianism gradually disappeared from his socialism, in part due to his closer relations with Jaurès, the resolute anti-utopian, and in part due to his increasing ties with English socialist groups, and especially the Fabian Society, who were significantly more pragmatically oriented than their continental counterparts. However, what did not significantly change was what he viewed as the real engine for socialist political action and the proper emphasis of a socialist party agenda. His sympathies were throughout most strongly with the cooperativist movement within the socialist parties, and he saw the transformation of models of exchange within and among those cooperatives as perhaps the key element of a socialist reformation of society. This position was of course informed by Durkheim's brand of guild socialism/corporatism, in which corporate collectivities built around occupational identities would be the major building blocks of society as well as the engines of societal integration and socialization. But it went well beyond Durkheim's vision in a number of ways, not the least of which was that it was at once more geared toward direct intellectual activism and significantly more plebian than that of his uncle (Gane 1992: 139–42). Mauss's vision of the socialist project, and of the intellectual's role in that project, was predicated on a specific notion of how the intellectual was to participate in such a project that, by definition, exceeded the narrow knowledge-producing interests of the intellectual. He had recognized, in his own political work with various cooperativist groups and especially with the Groupe d'Études Socialistes (about which more shortly), the necessity of such a model of intellectual work if it were to prove truly helpful to the socialist political struggle and not devolve into intellectual demagoguery. Participation of the intellectual is direct here, in the hands-on business of formulating strategy and workable answers to questions and problems, but the ultimate task of the intellectual is to efface himself *qua* theorist of abstract doctrines before the pragmatic and empirically-oriented popular consciousness. This understanding of the intellectual's political role was consistent with Mauss's belief that effective socialist political action must achieve a seamless blending of objective, scientific analysis and an "interior impetus" if it is to inspire action emotionally (Fournier 1994: 446).

For Mauss, the intellectual must be motivated not by the desire to rule through his expertise, but by something else that, despite the language of rational political evolution he had inherited from Durkheim, provides a key into Mauss's worldview and his understanding of the task of the modern intellectual. Against both the socialists of violent revolution and those of reason and individual self-interest, Mauss argues that "a purely rational society" is perhaps something unachievable, and the foundation of socialist politics, now and in the future, must be "human charity … love, or, if you prefer, ultimately, devotion." He invokes "the old Greek and Latin concepts of *caritas,* for which the modern 'charity' is such a poor translation," a notion that could not be farther from the pole of objective rationality (Gane 1992: 196). This *caritas,* which has a long tradition in Western thought as the usual Latin translation of the Greek *agapē* (αγάπη) of the New Testament and thus as one of the Christian theological virtues detailed by Paul, entailed a spirit of affection and selfless giving that Mauss explored most famously in his work on gift-giving and exchange. Though the bulk of this study is a treatment of ethnological evidence from primitive and pre-modern societies, the conclusion makes perfectly clear that Mauss intends the analysis to apply to the contemporary world, and specifically to the disappearance of this variety of reciprocal giving and receiving that creates the moral and political ties necessary for peaceful social existence. In this conclusion, he speaks in the language of the political actor: "It is necessary ... that the rich—freely and also forcibly—come again to consider themselves as a kind of paymaster for their fellow citizens ... There must be more good faith ... more generosity in contracts and ... in the sale of necessary commodities. And it will also be necessary to find a means to limit the fruits of speculation and usury" (Mauss 1950: 262).

Though many of the forms of *prestation* and *contre-prestation* that Mauss examines are clearly fueled by self-interest (though not narrow *economic* interest but rather *symbolic* interests of honor and prestige), and though in some forms they are even subtly masked acts of violent combat (Mauss 1950: 188, 269–70), the lesson Mauss draws as to how this system of exchange should resonate politically in contemporary society is resolutely pacifist (see especially Mauss 1950: 278–79). We might well call it, by consequence of his ultimate explication of the deep motivating force behind the impulse to give and receive, quasi-religious. For Mauss explains the obligation to return what is rendered with the Polynesian concept *hau,* which means roughly "spirit of things" and indicates the Polynesian belief that the objects themselves have a spiritual essence or power that compels the exchange. Still more intriguingly, Mauss briefly discusses a variety of exchange that may well be at the root of all exchange, and that in any event clearly establishes a relationship between his analysis of gift-exchange and the analysis of religious sacrifice: "the gift to the gods." He treats it only in passing, citing the lack of a "general study that would be necessary to make evident its importance," but the connection alluded to between sacrifice and gift is nonetheless telling (Mauss 1950: 164). It is instructive to note that Mauss, in an unpublished section of his work on the nation in which he discussed the character of those varieties of socialism to which he himself most closely adhered (i.e., syndicalism, co-operativism, and mutual aid societies), compared their spirit, their sense of sacrifice and violent passions to that of religious movements. In the socialism of Mauss's vision, "it is a matter of ... a kind of religion of man for man" (Mauss 1997: 94).

Like Mauss, Hubert too had an early and powerful attraction to socialist politics. Unlike Mauss, however, he was a *normalien* and met with the single most influential political figure in his life while a young student at the École Normale. This individual was Lucien Herr, whom I discussed in Chapter 3. In the years of the most vehement political turmoil around the Dreyfus Affair, Hubert became an important player in the network of activist students around Herr. He was Durkheim's main connection to this Paris network during the Affair, as Durkheim was still in Bordeaux at this time, and he apparently discussed political matters much more frequently with

Durkheim than he did even with Mauss, who was somewhat less closely tied to Herr, the hub of the entire network. A wealth of letters from Durkheim to Hubert in 1898 and 1899 deals with questions of organization around the Affair and the creation of the Ligue pour la Défense des Droits de l'Homme.[12] Hubert's "veritable cult" for Herr, based upon his appreciation of both his scientific acumen and his moral force, is undoubtedly a significant part of what led him to adopt a socialist position. Moreover, it manifested itself in a great dedication to Herr's work in the ENS library, for beyond his political connections to Herr, Hubert also served as his assistant in the library from 1893 to 1894 (Fournier 1994: 204).

Despite the clear evidence of Hubert's participation in socialist politics at the ENS and afterwards, his activities on the political front are more difficult to trace than those of Mauss because, unlike his friend, he did not leave a long trail of writings that adumbrate specific political positions. He also seemed less conflicted on the issue of separation of intellectual and political work than Mauss, and in that sense was perhaps more like Durkheim himself than Durkheim's nephew. Though Hubert clearly saw the socialist and Dreyfusard projects in a light similar to that of his political mentor Herr, he refused to fully give himself over to the political. He stands out as a nearly perfect example of one of the three profiles of *normalien* socialists Christophe Charle suggests in his analysis of this group from 1867 to 1914, which I discussed in Chapter 2. While some socialist students ("the politicians," per Charle) at the ENS during this period gave up scholarship to directly pursue political careers (e.g., Albert Thomas, Jaurès, Léon Blum), others like Hubert ("the scholars") "remain[ed] theoretical sympathizers … but no longer intervene[d] except in exceptional situations" (Charle 1994: 151).

Charle's third category, "those who refuse to choose" (Charle 1994: 152), recalls Mauss and brings us to Hertz. A consideration of the latter's experience of the political reminds one of Mauss in more than one way, as here the imposition of religious categories on political acts and meanings is still more marked and startling. Hertz may have been the most politically involved of all the Durkheimians. He turned relatively early to socialism largely as a result of his close friendship with several members of the British Fabian Society. Founded in 1884 by Sidney Webb, his wife Beatrice, and the Irish playwright George Bernard Shaw, the Fabians were an innovative group of socialist intellectuals who foresaw the onset of socialist society not through violent revolution, but through the gradual permeation of socialist ideas throughout society that would be effectuated by the steady propaganda and literary work of intellectuals like themselves. Besides Shaw, several other leading controversial literary figures of the Anglo-Saxon world of the period were involved in the Fabian Society for at least some period of time; for example, H. G. Wells had a very tortured but lengthy stay, and G. K. Chesterton was briefly a member.

From this group, Hertz took some of his basic ideas about the socialist project and its relation to the intellectuals. He involved himself energetically in socialist agitation and organization from his days at the ENS, where he too met and was profoundly influenced by Herr, who is one of those most directly responsible for Hertz becoming a Durkheimian.[13] In 1908, he created the Groupe d'Études Socialistes, a think tank designed to enable socialist intellectuals to formulate responses to specific and carefully defined social problems and to offer them as practical policy to the S.F.I.O. The group created a publication project that was dubbed the *Cahiers du Socialiste;* it published and distributed the position papers formulated by members of the group to a general public. Hertz also involved himself heavily in the Universités populaires and the Écoles socialistes that followed them (Prochasson 1993b: 61–66; 1997), as well the cooperativist movement that flourished at the *fin-de-siècle.* He frequently lectured on such subjects as the thought of Saint-Simon and the socialism of the Fabian Society and maintained close relations with important members of the cooperativist movement (Hertz 2002: 209, 212).

If the political commitments of Mauss and Hubert seem to be rooted in a religious vocabulary, in Hertz's case this fact is even more apparent. During his time at the front from early August 1914 until his death in mid April 1915, he frequently spoke of his socialist "faith" in terms that demonstrate a complex re-appropriation of a language usually associated with the religious opponents of scientific socialism:

> As a socialist ... I have always affirmed that the thought of common health alone sufficed to inspire ... the gift of each individual, up to and including the complete sacrifice of self ... without a need of symbolism, or mythological figuration: it's now or never that I must prove my faith ... Until now, I have scarcely suffered from the war ... and all the little pains I have had to bear ... I have "offered" them easily and with a contented heart to my God, as they say in the Christian convents. To ... find oneself in giving oneself, that's the beautiful opportunity this war offers us. (Hertz 2002: 98–99)

He spoke from the front of "nostalgia ... for the ardent and strong communal life, for active and directed service that dissipates all doubts" (Hertz 2002: 219). He also explicitly compared socialists and Catholics in their deeply spiritual understanding of the war and the reasons for fighting it, arguing that only these two groups "understand why they are fighting" (Hertz 2002: 175). These were clearly emotions Hertz had felt for some time, as he had alluded much earlier to the "mysticism" at the root of his socialist passion in a letter to his friend Pierre Roussel: "I have recently entered into contact with the workers (miners) ... yesterday, you could have seen me behind a red flag ... followed by a crowd of workers, real workers, in the night and the mud, in a lugubrious little village (cf. *Germinal*). You'll recognize my mysticism of the 'crowd'" (Riley 1999b: 48).

The Nationalist Intellectual: Durkheimian Variations

Another perspective in which the Durkheimians took on the question of the political role of the intellectual had to do with nationalism. Let us recall that, according to Bourdieusian schemas of the Third Republic intellectual field and particularly with respect to the Dreyfus Affair, those on the Dreyfusard side were typically anti-nationalists critical of the reactionary nationalism of their militarist and anti-Semitic foes. The central criticism leveled against them by the nationalists was that they were unwilling or unable to make a privileged place for the French nation in their political worldview. Some of the more adamant internationalists among the Dreyfusard and socialist ranks such as Jean Jaurès were virulently attacked as enemies of the French nation and, given the contemporary political concerns regarding Germany, possibly even German agents and sympathizers (Azéma and Winock 1976: 202–7).

The start of the Great War significantly changed the atmosphere of the conflict between nationalists and anti- or non-nationalists among French intellectuals, and most of the latter became at least qualified nationalists under the force of events. The members of the Durkheimian religion cluster also rallied to the nationalist cause at the war's outbreak. Durkheim played a crucial role in the intellectual propaganda machine, serving as secretary to the publication committee of a series of propaganda works written by himself and other top-level French intellectual figures that were translated into many languages for dissemination to Allied and non-Allied countries. He wrote two book-length attacks (*Qui a voulu la guerre? Les origines de la guerre d'après les documents diplomatiques* and *L'Allemagne au-dessus de tout: la mentalité allemande de la guerre*) on the German role in instigating the war and subsequently attempting to blame it on the Allies. Later, in 1916, Durkheim contributed several essays to a collection titled *Lettres à tous les Français,* in which he and others presented arguments from military and economic facts designed to help bolster the French public's confidence in an inevitable, if protracted and difficult, French victory.

Yet, despite their clear patriotic position, the general sense of Durkheim's war efforts is thoroughly reasoned and consistent with the several statements he had made on the topic of nationalism and patriotism prior to the war (Llobera 1994). His position was that neither the anti-patriotism of the revolutionary left nor the exclusive nationalism of the extreme right could be defended, and he advocated and practiced instead a kind of *rationalist* patriotism based upon adherence to universalist moral principles such as those of the French Revolution. This form of patriotism could and should co-exist, Durkheim argued, with an idealist internationalism, a patriotism of the universal and the global toward which the present world was moving in evolutionary fashion (Durkheim 1970: 293–300). Utterly absent in this account and in Durkheim's own practice of patriotism, even during the war, is the sort of mystical and non-rational nationalist sentiment and its manifestation in quasi- or explicitly religious forms found, for example, in Péguy or Barrès. Patriotic mythologies, national hero cults, and other such commonplace expressions of the contemporary French patriotic right and left were rejected completely by Durkheim, paralleling the rejection of all non-rational and emotional appeals and expressions in his measured advocacy of socialism.

The other Durkheimians exhibited a variety of patriotic nationalism during the war that can only be classified as enthusiastic, albeit tempered by their considerable attachments to German culture and learning. This position is especially exaggerated in the case of Hertz who had probably spent the most time of the three in Germany and who spoke German fluently from childhood. Both he and Mauss served at the front (Fournier 1994: 373–76; Parkin 1996: 12–13).[14] Hubert too was mobilized in March 1915 as an infantry sergeant, but his physical constitution was judged too weak to permit service at the front and he was assigned to the office of Undersecretary of Artillery in Paris. He soon joined two other Durkheimians, François Simiand and Hubert Bourgin, in the "Thomas network," a small group of socialist intellectuals gathered together as part of his staff by the socialist political figure (and close friend of Jaurès) Albert Thomas, who was a critical participant in the war effort at home, first as State Undersecretary of Artillery and Military Equipment and then as Secretary of Armament in the second Briand cabinet (Fournier 1994: 377–78).

Much as the socialism of these younger members of the religion cluster was immersed in a quasi-religious language, so too they sometimes conceived the French nation in this same symbolism and terminology. Mauss, perhaps the most involved socialist and committed internationalist of the three,[15] remained the most wary of the brand of war nationalism that often became brutally anti-German. He endeavored to neatly separate the "true Germany of thought and of goodness" from the "Germany of force and lies" and, even at his departure for the front, maintained his allegiance with the slain Jaurès, perhaps the most vigorous French opponent of the war: "We want, as Jaurès wanted, men to love one another."[16]

Still, at the front Mauss wrote frequently of the overwhelming sense of collective identity and mission created by the war effort and the reinforcement of national identity as against all other sectarian identities. He alluded often to the "benefits of communal action," the "*esprit de corps*," the "sensation of being elbow-to-elbow" with comrades that, in his post-war evaluation, contributed hugely to the success of syndicalist movements that were able to recreate this sense of camaraderie (Fournier 1994: 374). More personally, he noted his own enthusiasm for this collective experience: "I am doing smashingly well. I was as little suited as possible for an intellectual life and I am enjoying this life that the war makes for me … I ride a horse, I play soldier … *I was made for this and not at all for sociology.*"[17] He notes elsewhere this distinction between the intellectual life and the active, participatory life of the *homme éngagé*, alluding to "this incapacity of the [Third] Republic to produce anything other than intelligent men, this incapacity to produce men of energy."[18]

After the war, Hubert, like Mauss, became more explicitly interested in nationalism as both an intellectual topic of study and as a political question of personal negotiation. As Hubert's areas of specialization included the politically charged topics of primitive and pre-modern European civilizations, and most centrally the history of the Celts and the Germans, he became increasingly involved in intellectual and political debates over the national and ethnic heritage of France. Much like the interventions of Sylvain Lévi into the question of Semitic and Aryan/Indian influence on contemporary European civilization, Hubert's studies of the Celts and the Germans were intellectual and political works at once (Isambert 1983). In *Année* book reviews, he had earlier taken on crude racial myths of Germanic superiority and Aryan inheritance in reductionist "anthroposociological" works such as Georges Vacher de Lapouge's *L'Aryen, son rôle social*, and Hubert's polemical aim in the works on the Celts and Germans was to deny the easy linking of Aryan and German civilizations that was such an important part of much Aryan supremacist and anti-Semitic thought of the period (Strenski 1987: 356–58; Mucchielli 1998: 71–74). But in these works and in the lengthy preface he wrote to his student Stefan Czarnowski's study of the Irish national significance of the myth of Saint Patrick (Czarnowski 1919), Hubert did not stop at such a defensive project of defeating racial mythmaking through the application of historical fact and scientific principle. He delved into one of the key varieties of nationalist mythology that attracted French intellectuals desirous of separating French civilization from Frankish (that is, German) ethnic and cultural stock: He appealed to the myth of *celtisme*, the idea of the fundamentally Celtic heritage of French civilization (Strenski 1987: 362–63; Hubert 1974a: 28–29; 1974b: 295).

Hubert recognized the power of political national myths and apparently rejected the hyper-scientific demythologizing position in order to embrace the mythological power of history in identity-construction. His introduction to Czarnowksi's book was a kind of theoretical treatise on the sociological making and significance of mythical national heroes. The hero, he argues, is a being both human and divine, "superman or demigod ... a kind of divinity" but at the same time "he emanates from the society that claims him as its own" (Czarnowski 1919: viii, xxviii). From this unique dual heritage comes his particularly powerful relevance for the community to which he belongs. The hero is "like the living symbol or emblem of a definite society," just as the totem in Durkheim's analysis, which Hubert invokes (Czarnowski 1919: xxxii–iii). This shows the close connection, he argues, between religious belief and hero mythology. In fact, Hubert shows that "mythology is a part of religion," and that heroic myths, like religion, consist of both beliefs and rites that provide the continuing communal life of the myth (Czarnowski 1919: xxxviii–ix). The power of the hero's presence in the community is manifested in festival celebrations of his or her deeds which distinguish themselves from quotidian rituals of religious practice in their exceptional and non-everyday status. The "ritual of the festival is more complex, more solemn, more important or more special than an everyday ritual," and it enables an experience of collective effervescence that is more powerful, in which "all that is communal and that exceeds consciousness of self becomes exterior [and] takes on substance, life, soul, spirit, personhood" (Czarnowski 1919: lviii–lx). Hubert argues that tragedy and drama more generally are to be found in seed form in these *fêtes* where heroic mythology is re-enacted and experienced by the community (Czarnowski 1919: li–lvii). Thus the basic element of the heroic myth historically moves from explicitly religious roots into an aesthetic, literary framework of expression, where, while still clearly retaining religious elements, it can be mobilized effectively in a secularizing society (Czarnowski 1919: lxix).

Interestingly enough, this theoretical examination of the evolution and role of the hero is reaffirmed in Hubert's evaluation of the elements of Celtic civilization that have been handed down to the French. He finds that this essence has precisely to do with the creation of and deep sympathy for heroic mythology, "a sense for heroic poetry ... in a word *a dramatic conception of fatality* that only properly belongs to the Celts" (Hubert 1974b: 294–95; emphasis added). Hubert's reading of the Celts is of a poetic, heroic, hot-blooded, religiously intense civilization with an attachment to notions of honor that made violence frequent. They are not very adept at long-term political organization but artistically energetic in temperament. Hubert's linking of the Celts to the French is telling in his own evaluation of the heroic, the poetic, and the tragic in French national identity (Hubert 1974b: 243–63, 271).

As was the case with respect to his socialism, Hertz is often the most vivid of the three in the expression of nationalist sentiments. Even after having made the transition politically to socialism and intellectually to the Durkheimian team, he described the army, during the second stint of his own required military service, as a positive moral force, using the extreme right's language of "decadence" to condemn the moral laxity of the very socialist movement of which he was a part: "I am still a socialist ... but I fear I may be flirting with heresy. I am turning into a patriot ... a moralist in any case ... I am persuaded that if France has lost the civilizing initiative in nearly every domain ... it is in sum due to a moral slackening ... that stares one in the face here" (Riley 1999b: 50–51). Later letters Hertz wrote from the front in 1914 and 1915 demonstrate an even firmer conviction that the moral force of the army is at least potentially a powerfully important contributor to the reinvigoration of French society. The language he uses there is unabashedly moral and even religious in tenor, as we have already seen, e.g., in his use of phrases reminiscent of Maurice Barrès.[19] The distance between Hertz and Durkheim on this issue is apparent in the former's comments upon reading the first of the latter's several brochures of propaganda in support of the French war effort: "Durkheim's brochure is sober, vigorous, demonstrative; *but however useful it may be, this doesn't go very far!*" (Hertz 2002: 197, emphasis in original).[20] In other words, calls to patriotism that are limited to merely reasoned arguments about facts cannot hope to generate the energy and effort needed.

Hertz made much of the tremendous creative energy of the almost-mythical provincial French soldiers he encountered at the front. In his view, they were responsible for the emergence of a renewed national moral vigor, which reasserted itself at the very moment of the near total defeat of the first month of the war, a fact that only made it all the more poetic and heroic:

> What is dead is precisely that ... France of before and after 1870 ... and in dying she has discovered the other France, the one that does not die ... The history of France has a Biblical grandeur. The French too are a chosen people—the spouse of a jealous god who strikes her terribly when she separates herself from him and runs after false gods—but who loves her and reestablishes her and covers her in glory as soon as she returns to him. (Hertz 2002: 154)

This fascination with the character of the deeply French soldier from the countryside, and particularly those from the northwest of the country, inspired Hertz to collect their folk sayings and stories concerning country life, wildlife, etc. into a work that in unfinished form would be published as "Contes et dictons recueillis sur le front parmi les poilus de la Mayenne et d'ailleurs" and that constitutes the last piece of intellectual work he contemplated prior to his death.[21]

The Scientific Study of Humankind and the Moral Problem of Secularization: Differences within the Religion Cluster, or the Durkheimians *contra* Durkheim

The previous two sections of this chapter point to some distinctions between Durkheim and the other members of the religion cluster with respect to their responses to the dilemma of the political role of the intellectual, and we make a similar discovery in comparatively examining their positions on the other two problematics as well. As we have seen, the Durkheimians' interaction and disputes with the discipline of philosophy were an important element in the emergence of the Durkheimian position in the intellectual field and a key part of their self-distinction on the question of scientific knowledge of humankind. Durkheim's elaboration of his own position on this issue is perhaps clearest in *Les Règles de la méthode sociologique*. Here, he set out the task of sociology and his own role as its founder in terms that recall the project of Descartes two and a half centuries earlier. Indeed, Durkheim expressly cites Descartes several times in announcing his own foundational enterprise of "question[ing] all ideas ... previously received" and "employ[ing] only scientifically developed concepts, that is, concepts constructed according to the method instituted by himself" (Durkheim 1950[1894]: 31). This modeling of the Cartesian project is also apparent in Durkheim's definition of the sociological enterprise as "rationalist" in the preface to the first edition (Durkheim 1950[1894]: xxxix–xl; Mucchielli and Borlandi 1995: 7–11). The central and most challenging argument in the book concerns the celebrated notion of "social facts" and the necessary treatment of them in sociological research as external, non-mental *things* that constrain human behavior (Durkheim 1950: 1–13). Another controversial element of the method described therein, though, has to do with the aggressive criticism of historical nominalism and philosophical empiricism or realism in favor of a reductionist program of classification of facts according to given social types (Durkheim 1950: 76–81). Besnard (1983: 16–17) has discussed at length the widespread dissatisfaction with Durkheim's argument and the imperialist attitude regarding psychology and psychological methodology among the members of the then-forming *Année* team, especially that of Célestin Bouglé, Dominique Parodi, and Paul Lapie, all important early members of the team. But if Mauss and Hubert raised no objections to Durkheim's methodological imperialism at this point, they certainly did express reservations about it and even endeavored to distance themselves from it to a considerable degree later.

This separation sometimes took a rather convoluted path. The polemical atmosphere of the French university world and the embattled status of the discipline of sociology often made it impossible to demonstrate excessive theoretical nuance and variation within the Durkheimian group. Nonetheless, evidence of such differences is not impossible to find, even prior to Durkheim's death. All three of the other religion cluster members demonstrated an often glaringly clear propensity to what was, for Durkheim, an excessive concern for the historical and empirical at the expense of the theoretical and reductionist. Mauss, for example, cited his introduction as a student to the historical methods of Sylvain Lévi as a key factor in his loss of an earlier propensity to reductionist thinking and, more practically, to his inability to carry out what had appeared initially to him as the easy task of systematizing a few facts into a three-year thesis project on prayer (Mauss 1969: 537). Hubert demonstrated his own enthusiasm for sociological immersion in historical method in his brief attempt to effectuate an explicit joining of forces of the *Année* team and the *Revue de synthèse* group of Henri Berr. The Berr group eventually emerged as a competitor, if a relatively friendly one, to the *Année* project, but in 1897 or 1898 Hubert met Berr, who was only then planning the launch of the *Revue de synthèse,* and was very favorable toward the prospect of a shared agenda between the two groups: "He came to ask for my collaboration on the section on history of religion (in part, naturally). I did not tell him no … I believe that such a review can be a competitor for the *Année* if we're not part of it and an excellent aid to us if we are … Talk to Durkheim about this."[22] Durkheim's response, sent through Mauss, was clear about his own position on the shared ground of history and sociology as equal partners: "I refuse to collaborate with [Berr] … I know what a historical review can be—and also a sociological review; but not a review that is neither one nor the other."[23] Hertz too, in the last work he undertook prior to his ill-fated call to the front during the war, was moving in a direction that was taking him away from the sort of comparativist reductionism evident in Durkheim's work and toward a concentration on monographic, empirical ethnologies with minimal effort toward generalizability and theoretical system-building. His *Saint Besse* and the now lost study on "Légendes et cultes des roches, des monts et des sources" were targets of some dissatisfaction from Durkheim (and even from Mauss and Hubert) due to their deviation from the established Durkheimian orthodoxy (Parkin 1996: 11–12, 189).

All this occurred while Durkheim was still alive. After his death, Mauss continued to move in the same direction he once described in the following rather un-Durkheimian manner: "I am not interested in developing systematic theories" (Mauss 1989: 165). Mauss tended in his post-Durkheim intellectual life to a considerable prudence with respect to the kind of systematic pronouncements for which Durkheim was known (Fournier 1994: 468–69; Dubar 1972) and the culmination of his post-war work in the notion of *l'homme total* is in many ways a brilliant synthesis of the sociological, biological, and psychological perspectives on the human subject that permits each of them a certain autonomy and refuses a reduction to sociological explanation in the last instance (Karsenti 1997: 13). Mauss even turned so far against Durkheim's method after the latter's death as to cast suspicion on the very hallmark and point of definition of Durkheimian sociology that had enabled Durkheim to distinguish it so radically from history: comparison. Mauss wrote antagonistically about "that constant comparison where everything is mixed together and institutions lose their local color and documents their flavor" (1950: 149). He was also considerably more nuanced with respect to another central explanatory mechanism in the Durkheimian toolkit: the deduction of complex forms *via* the examination of "elementary forms" in keeping with evolutionary precepts. In his unfinished thesis on prayer, Mauss distinguished crude evolutionary theory, in which simpler, less complex forms are seen as the evolutionary predecessors of later, more complicated forms (this is the basis of Durkheim's argument regarding both the division of labor and religion), and a preferable variety of genetic explanation in which a relation is noted between two forms but in which "we do not intend in any way to explain the complex by the simple. For the most rudimentary forms are not in any degree more simple than the most developed forms. Their complexity is simply of a different nature" (Mauss 1968a: 396).

The distinctions between Durkheim and his colleagues in the religion cluster with regard to the third problematic regarding the establishment of a secular morality can be seen to some degree in these very differences on the scientific question, as the two questions were intimately intertwined. Though Mauss clearly felt a certain responsibility after Durkheim's death to replace him in his capacity as defender of the sociological moral program and outlook, and though he could even speak in this capacity of sociology as "the principle means of educating society" (Mauss 1969: 245), one can hardly classify his position here as any less complex than on the issue of the scientific knowledge of humankind. Even in presenting a case not unlike Durkheim's for the role of sociology as pedagogical means to moral and political development of students, Mauss qualifies endlessly; sociology "is *not* the way to make men happy ... [it] offers no panacea" (Mauss 1969: 245, emphasis added). As I will show in the next chapter, it is in the very personal conception of pedagogy as lived intellectual practice that we see most clearly the differences between Mauss and Durkheim. Where the latter conceived the new moral spirit as centered upon discipline, the former understood the process by which the moral pedagogy of sociology could be successfully imparted quite differently. Hubert and Hertz are still further away from Durkheim on this issue. Hubert preferred to avoid almost altogether the pedagogical and moral debates in which Durkheim was so embroiled, while Hertz found room to align himself with such anti-Durkheimian, anti-Dreyfusard forces as Maurice Barrès and Henri Bergson on the issue of the moral regeneration of France.

A consideration of the distinctions within the religion cluster in their responses to the question of secular morality that was at the center of the debate over pedagogy makes yet clearer a point at which I have hinted several times in the foregoing: Ultimately the three problematics facing intellectuals in the Third Republic must be understood through the lens of one overarching dilemma. At bottom, questions of the shifting political role of the intellectual, of the ability of the social sciences to understand human action and nature, and of the proper moral orientation and training of members of a rapidly secularizing society were dependent on, or perhaps more accurately *extensions of* the question of religion and of the sacred. The first of these dilemmas has to do with the more fundamental question, "Who has the authority to rule?"; the second with the questions, "How and what do we know?"; and the third with the question, "What are our moral foundations?" Each of these questions became especially pressing in the Third Republic because of the increasing inability of the source that had previously provided neat answers to them all to continue to do so: the Roman Catholic Church. Although secular alternatives could certainly be proposed to fill the gaps left by the Church's retreat in these fundamental problem areas, the facts of the historical and social situation in France made most effective the responses that managed, even in secular form, to retain important elements of the religious language with which the Church had spoken to them.

The particular ways in which the Durkheimian religion cluster responded to these dilemmas was powerfully informed by the social and historical contexts within which they were situated. Likewise, the differences we have seen beginning to emerge between Durkheim himself and the other members of the cluster can also be related to issues of sociological import. If each of the Durkheimians was drawn to questions of religion, the religious contexts of their upbringing and intellectual development were in part responsible for their choice of that path; that is, these contexts created a *habitus* that was predisposed to thinking in certain quasi-religious categories. We have also seen the connection between that immersion in religious worldviews and the cluster's later political position-takings as socialists and nationalists of a certain quasi-religious tenor. When significant distinctions are revealed in their respective responses to the moral question or to that of the intellectual's political identity and his intellectual work, I have shown how different experiences and trajectories within the French educational system (and, especially, profound influence by sometimes very different mentors) help to explain the differences.

Armed with this macro- and micro-sociological data on the identity-formation of the Durkheimians, we are finally ready to turn to a close re-reading of their work on the sacred and religion.

Notes

1. In a letter dated 6 April 1898, for example, his mother writes to him, "If you wanted to make me happy, you would do your best to observe Passover" (FHM).
2. According to Buddhist tradition, this is the next of the most perfect of the Buddhas, currently awaiting his incarnation at some undetermined and distant future time.
3. These unpublished notes are held in the FHM.
4. Léon L'Hébreu (Leon Hebreo), born Leo Judah Abarbanel in Lisbon into a noble Sephardic Jewish family in 1465, was an important figure in Italian neo-Platonic thought of the Renaissance.
5. In correspondence, Durkheim alludes to an article Mauss wrote on Spinoza, as well as non-published work on the philosopher that Mauss completed while at Bordeaux, but none of these texts remain (see Durkheim 1998: 34, 50). Mauss himself alludes to "my article on Spinoza" several times in correspondence to Hubert, adding in one letter from his year in Holland that he intends to ask one of their teachers, Israël Lévi, for an introduction into "the Portuguese Jewish community of Amsterdam" as part of his research for the Spinoza project (n.d. (1897–98), FHM). The only substantive explicit reference to Spinoza I could find in Mauss's major works is in "Une catégorie de l'esprit humain: La Notion de personne, celle de 'moi'," wherein Mauss notes that Spinoza's understanding of the "relation of the individual consciousness with the things of God" is "the most sound of all" because he "set above all the ethical problem" (Mauss 1950: 360).
6. Personal communication from Antoine Hertz (Hertz's son) to author, July 1998.
7. Hertz to Dodd, 2 July 1911, FRH. This letter was written in English.
8. Hertz, who was only 16 when Zola's letter appeared in January 1898, wrote to Dodd a few months later, in April 1898, of the affair: "I consider Zola ... at once

guilty and clumsy ... though I am Jewish—or rather because I am Jewish and because I adhere frenetically to the country that chance gave me, I have been made indignant like all truly impartial Frenchmen by the too-famous letter ... he will be condemned anew, that is certain, and I believe he deserves it (unpublished letter, FRH).

9. Letter to Dodd, 8 December 1897, FRH.
10. Hubert to Mauss, [1897?], FHM.
11. Marcel Fournier has assembled a great number of Mauss's political writings (Mauss 1997), and the sheer volume of this collection attests to Mauss's political activity: It makes up more than 840 pages of text.
12. Besnard (1987) published some seventy of these letters.
13. This fact is attested to by unpublished letters from Hertz to Herr on the subject that are located in Paris in the Archives d'Histoire Contemporaine of the Fondation Nationale des Sciences Politiques.
14. Hertz was actually promoted to second lieutenant on 3 April, just twelve days before his death (Hertz 2002: 253).
15. He projected, but never finished, a large-scale study of nations and nationalism in the years just following the war (1920 to 1921); the fragments for the planned study were published in 1954 in the third series of the *Année sociologique* by Henri Lévy-Bruhl. Here, he compared the modern nation to the primitive clan, and the flag to the totem (Mauss 1969: 593–94).
16. Unpublished letter from Mauss to Hubert, 1914, FHM.
17. Unpublished letters to Rosine Mauss, (one n.d., the second dated 1 January 1915), FHM; emphasis added.
18. Unpublished letter from Mauss to Hubert, 1 October 1918, FHM.
19. Durkheim, who had the opportunity to read Hertz's war correspondence after his death while preparing an obituary, wrote to Mauss incredulously of this and other favorable passages concerning Barrès: "There are [in Hertz's letters to his wife] developments of the idea of the regeneration of France that smell of Barrès. He speaks of Barrès, with reservations, but sometimes with sympathy!" (Durkheim 1998: 495).
20. He is discussing *Qui a voulu la guerre ? Les origines de la guerre d'après les documents diplomatiques.*
21. First published in *Revue des traditions populaires,* 1–2 and 3–4 (1917), the rough text was later reprinted by Mauss in Hertz (1970).
22. Unpublished letter from Hubert to Mauss, n.d. FHM.
23. Excerpt, letter from Durkheim to Mauss, included in unpublished letter from Mauss to Hubert, n.d. FHM.

8 🌀 The Sacred in Durkheimian Thought I

What is the definition of the sacred in the Durkheimian school? The text to which virtually everyone who is interested in responding to this question looks is *Les Formes élémentaires de la vie religieuse* where the term is a key to the definition of religion: "A religion is a solidary system of beliefs and practices relative to sacred things, that is, things that are separated and forbidden, beliefs and practices that unite in a single moral community, called a Church, all those who adhere to them" (Durkheim 1991 [1912]: 108–9). But what exactly *is* this thing, the sacred? What is its importance for the intellectual project of the Durkheimians? And are the members of the religion cluster in agreement in their responses to these questions?

Durkheim attempts to elaborate a definition of religion in *Formes élémentaires* in the process of laying out the principles of religious phenomena, but a problem of ambiguity emerges in his effort to conceptualize the term. The distinction between sacred and profane things, he writes, is the fundamental and universal characteristic of religion. Further, religious phenomena, which can be classed into the two categories of beliefs and rites, are designed to express the nature of sacred things and to bring members of the religious cult into communion with them (Durkheim 1991 [1912]: 92–93). The sacred then must be considered always as a conceptual part of a structural pair with the profane, and must at least in part be defined in light of this relationship. Sacred things "are those that interdictions protect and isolate; profane things, those to which the interdictions apply and which must remain at a distance from the former" (Durkheim 1991 [1912]: 98). He recognized a potential difficulty in leaving the definition at this simple structural level, namely, that if the definition depends only on the opposition between the two categories, it is impossible in any given empirical situation to identify which of two such opposed entities is the sacred and which the profane. One can only note the distinction between the two (Durkheim 1975b: 64). He specified therefore that the sacred has a specific character that consists not only of its superiority over the profane but also of its status as a form of energy. It is like an electrified body or a coiled spring, "the seat of a power" (Durkheim 1975b: 64) that acts upon the profane, whereas the latter has only the capacity to provoke the discharge of that transformative energy. Durkheim argues that this sacred power consists in a twofold effect of dominating and sustaining the religious, serving as an "influence dynamogénique," a source of vitality and confidence (Durkheim 1975b: 27). This explains its perennial and universal power in human society.

But this still does not really get to the root of things. The precise nature, if not the efficacy, of this sacred energy remains unclear and amorphous, and its source is difficult to discern. Durkheim proposes to trace the sacred, which takes on so many complex and diverse forms in modern religious systems, back to more primitive manifestations in the hope of ultimately deciphering its nature and source. This leads him to totemism. After distinguishing a number of different varieties of totemic systems and arguing that clan and not individual totemism lies at the origin of religion, and further showing that this clan totemism recognizes three central classes of sacred objects (representations of the totem, animals or vegetables that are clan namesakes, and clan members themselves, in descending order of sacredness (Durkheim 1991 [1912]: 335–36)) that must share some unifying aspect that makes them sacred, Durkheim is finally in position to unveil what he believes is at once the source and the content of the sacred: "Thus the totem is … at once the symbol of the god and of society[, and thus] is it not the case that the god and the society are one and the same?" (Durkheim 1991 [1912]: 364–65). Society forms and worships itself in sacred objects, which are nothing more than hypostatized collective sentiments and forces. The sacred is the presence of society in the form of representations and ideas of the collectivity, transformed into transcendent or divine language and form but nonetheless representing the immanent force of the social.

This much is widely known by any sociologist who has read or taught Durkheim's final book. But does this answer the question of the nature of the *Durkheimian* (as opposed to Durkheim's) conception of the sacred? To get at this question, let us unpack a few of the problems that emerge in Durkheim's reading. First, there is an important element of the definition of the sacred that emerges in Durkheim's argument but which he gives only a rather restricted role in his elaboration of the notion. He notes that

Robertson Smith indicated this critical element of the nature of sacredness, namely, *its ambiguity*. The sacred is not only the *holy or consecrated*, but can also be the *accursed*, "something devoted to a divinity for destruction, and hence criminal, impious, wicked, infamous" (Pickering 1984: 124). The sociological richness of the concept can be demonstrated by tracing the term to its Latin derivation *sacer*, which contains both of the seemingly contradictory meanings. The French *sacré* likewise can mean both, and is frequently used in both senses (*la musique sacrée*, holy or sacred music, and *un sacré menteur*, a damned or accursed liar), whereas the English "sacred" has in practice lost the second meaning. Thus, Durkheim notes, the sacred, in addition to being opposed in a binary relationship to the profane, is itself comprised of two opposing binary poles: the forces that maintain physical and moral purity and order, life, and health, and those that contribute to impurity, evil, disorder, sacrilege, disease, and death (Durkheim 1991 [1912]: 681–82).

The nature of the relationship between the pure and the impure sacred further complicates the scenario, for the two are in many ways not easily distinguishable. Durkheim points out that a pure sacred object or power frequently becomes impure and vice versa, through a modification of "exterior circumstances." For example, in certain societies, a corpse moves as a result of a specific ritual process from the status of an impure sacred object inspiring dread and the possibility of evil contagion to that of a venerated sacred object that is even ingested by surviving family or clan members as a boon and a protection against evil (Durkheim 1991 [1912]: 684). But are pure and impure sacred two distinct manifestations of a single kind of power that is never present in any empirical site at the same moment, or two seemingly contradictory yet actually complementary, mutually dependent facets of any empirically sacred object or force? Durkheim is not clear on this point. He seems to want at once to separate them empirically, while acknowledging a potential of the one to become the other, and to recognize the acute difficulty of actually making a neat distinction between the reverence associated with the pure sacred and the horror linked to the impure. After all, truly intense experiences of the pure sacred are characterized by some degree of what can be called fear or dread, as a certain reverence can attach itself to the horror we feel in the face of the most intensely impure sacred objects (Durkheim 1991 [1912]: 683–84).[1]

Given this ambiguity in the nature of the sacred, some intriguing dilemmas present themselves in drawing conclusions about the role of the sacred in social life. Durkheim argued that ritual practices can be divided into negative or ascetic rites, which are designed to prevent the mingling of profane and sacred worlds and consist entirely of abstentions and interdictions, and positive rites, which are the actual practices that bring the worshipper into contact with the sacred and are ultimately at the heart of religious ritual since only they contain their reason for existence in themselves (Durkheim 1991 [1912]: 509–11, 551). It is the positive rites, the most important historical example of which is the institution of sacrifice, that provide the setting for the most essential element of religious phenomena. This is the element, according to Durkheim's argument, that must and will continue to exist even as secularization makes its inevitable gains at the expense of traditional religion. But which form of the sacred, pure or impure, is encountered in positive rites? The answer would seem to be straightforward: Must it not be the pure sacred, as this is the life-celebrating and beneficent force? Durkheim certainly suggests that this must be the case. He contents himself here with a claim that is hardly argued at all: "[I]f, most often, it is the case [in religion] that good is superior to evil … it is because reality is not otherwise. For if the relationship between these contradictory forces were reversed, life would be impossible" (Durkheim 1991 [1912]: 700).

I will return to this crucial question of the ambiguity of the sacred shortly. But first I need to consider an issue having to do with Durkheim's definition of the sacred that has a significant effect on his reading of its possible manifestations for the intellectual and, more generally, for the mass of society. As we have already seen, Durkheim understands the social, in its manifestations as collective consciousness and collective representations, to be closely connected to the category of the sacred. The sacred and the profane are rigorously opposed, "like two worlds between which there is nothing in common" (Durkheim 1991 [1912]: 95). We therefore need a category opposed to society and the collective consciousness that will take the place of X in the following statement: Sacred is to profane as society is to X. The immediate answer according to the logic of Durkheim's definition of religion (i.e., it can only exist within a church) might seem to be the individual. But is it acceptable to equate the sacred with society in so total a fashion? In so doing, Durkheim is attempting to constitute what for sociologists must be the foundational category, but is it the case that the sacred can hold everything it must hold as such a foundational category? And what are we to make of the category of the profane if it is reduced to the individual? A logical problem seems to emerge from the mutually antagonistic and complete opposition Durkheim posits between, on the one hand, the sacred and the profane and, on the other, the pure sacred and the impure sacred. If the sacred is nothing more than society as against the individual, is it then the case that one of the two varieties of sacred must by definition be opposed to the social? (Lukes 1973: 27; Parkin 1996: 29).

The Sacred and the Intellectual in Durkheim: How is the Intellectual to Worship?

All of this concerns Durkheim's treatment of the sacred at the formal, abstract level, and in its application to the social body generally. To find his most explicit discussion of the role the sacred plays in the *intellectual's* life, we must turn from the work that is concerned explicitly with religious phenomena and look elsewhere. In addition to the collapse of the sacred into society, we find in Durkheim another such reductive move that helped to ground his ideas on the future of the sacred. This second reduction was to make society the source of morality. The sociological grounding of a moral theory was perhaps the central element in Durkheim's intellectual project (Mauss 1969: 480), though he never succeeded in completing more than an introduction and an outline for his planned *chef d'œuvre* on *La Morale* and published only a few essays in philosophical journals on the topic during his lifetime (Durkheim 1975b: 313–14; 1953). The connection between the sacred and morality is approximated first by closely equating religion and morality. Both, he argued, consist of two correlated components. In religion, religious representations are celebrated through prescribed rites, while in the realm of morality, *morale* provides the ideational substance that *mœurs* endeavor to enact in practice, however imperfectly (Durkheim 1975b: 330). Furthermore, both ultimately derive their power to compel certain beliefs and the rites to accompany them from their utterly social roots. Moral acts are never those acts that have merely individual interests as their ends, and individuals in themselves do not constitute legitimate moral ends; therefore, the only possible object of a morality is a group (Durkheim 1953: 37). Durkheim intended this collective being to play the role in his moral theory that is played by the divinity in Kant's (Durkheim 1953 [1906]: 2).

But morality must be something more than merely the restraining notion of obligation and duty, as it is defined by Kant; it must appear to actors as *desirable* as well. Thus, in defining the basic elements of morality in his posthumously published course in moral education, Durkheim included the freedom of the will of the actor in addition to the spirit of discipline and the attachment to a group (Durkheim 1963). This element of desirability provides the way into the comparison, or, rather, equation of morality and the sacred. For is not the sacred, like morality, both compelling, obligatory in its command, and actively loved and pursued by the religious (Durkheim 1953 [1906]: 36, 48)? The two share this seeming contradiction in their structure. The moral domain, even in its secular form, is "as if surrounded by a mysterious barrier that holds it apart from profanation, just as the religious domain is protected from the reach of the profane. It is a *sacred* domain" (Durkheim 1963: 8; emphasis in original).

From here, Durkheim's position on the role to be played by the sacred in contemporary secular society with respect to the general public becomes clearer. I earlier summarized Durkheim's case for the reconfiguration of the sacred in modern society as the cult of the individual. It was this object of consecration and holy devotion to which the masses were to direct their veneration in the contemporary world, in Durkheim's view, inasmuch as the traditional forms of the sacred could not be expected to retain their efficacy (Durkheim 1991 [1912]: 715–16; 1975b: 169–70), and he spent a considerable amount of time in his lectures on educational practice detailing the particulars of how the ground for this new mode of worship would be prepared in the French educational system. If the true sacred object of religion was the social, and if a secular morality had to teach an adherence to social solidarity as its central objective, there could be no better educational program for the inculcation of this new sacred practice than the teaching of sociology, the discipline Durkheim was attempting to place in the seat once held by philosophy as the queen of the human sciences. In 1900, while still a professor at Bordeaux, Durkheim explicated this notion of the sacred role to be played by the teaching of sociology: "It is necessary to show young persons how ... society lives and acts within him, how it is the best part of [their] nature ... The only discipline capable of rendering these truths evident is sociology" (Durkheim 1976 [1901]: 382–83).

While he was referring to the role of sociology in university education in this excerpt, Durkheim made clear in the same paper that sociology's role as successor to religious morality is not to be limited to the elite who reach the university. "Moral conscience must be the same in all classes and in all spheres of society" and therefore the sociological sacred must be inculcated in the primary and secondary schools as well (Durkheim 1976 [1901]: 385). Durkheim's intent thus was that sociology be substituted in the educational curriculum, at virtually all levels, for the former coursework in religious or philosophical morality. We must remember that Durkheim's first course on moral education at the Sorbonne had been clear about initiating the teaching of sociological morality at the elementary school level, and Paul Fauconnet, who wrote the introduction to the published version of this lecture course, noted the existence of another Durkheim course, dating at least from 1908, on "L'Enseignement de la morale à l'école primaire" (Durkheim 1963: vi).

But if this is the model of the modern sacred for the masses, does Durkheim prescribe the same renovated sacred object and practice for the intellectual? It must be acknowledged that, despite some evidence and much secondary commentary to the contrary, Durkheim viewed the case of the intellectuals as separable from that of the general citizen here. Although the manuscript has been lost, we know Durkheim gave a course on "l'éducation intellectuelle" during the same period of his course on moral education (Besnard 1993: 122), and this suggests something of a distinction between the two that corresponds to an intellectual and a moral function. Is it plausible from this to argue that Durkheim saw an intellectual function that was separable from the moral? No, but I do not need to make any such argument in order to present a case in which Durkheim's proposed project for renewal of the sacred for the intellectual and the scientist is, like that for the masses, thoroughly moral, but differently so. Notwithstanding Durkheim's clearly egalitarian political position and deep commitment to democracy, he was no radical leveler; he recognized natural, innate hierarchies among individuals. An early talk delivered by a 25-year-old Durkheim to the graduating *lycéens* at Sens shows a deeply French reverence for "great men" and lays out, albeit in non-systematic fashion, something of a schema for the relations and reciprocal obligations existing among these "grands hommes" and "les petits" (Durkheim 1975a: 409–17). The main question at hand is whether men of genius, the elect, are a menace to the mediocre, or whether the general health is dependent on this elect? Durkheim rejects the extreme argument, in the person of Ernest Renan, that humanity's goal is solely the great man by arguing that "all individuals, however humble, have the right to aspire to the superior life of the mind" (Durkheim 1975a: 413). But if all have the *right* to so aspire, it remains the case that the great majority will not actually *attain* such heights. Moreover, Durkheim finds the argument for radical leveling and the uselessness of great men advanced by the most extreme democrats "just as false ... [and] perhaps more dangerous" than Renan's Nietzschean position (Durkheim 1975a: 414). On closer examination, the position Durkheim advocates between the two turns out to be significantly closer to the latter than to the former. It amounts to a kind of evolutionist theory of great men as moral, scientific, and spiritual points of superiority that emerge here and there to indicate to the mass, which is characterized by a "satisfied mediocrity," the proper direction for the continued evolution of humankind (Durkheim 1975a: 415).

How are they to do this? They are to provide a demonstration to the masses in their lives, but especially by their dedication to the "superior life" of the mind, that "humanity is not made to endlessly indulge in easy and vulgar pleasures" and to lead the masses to "despise that inferior life, in order to detach humanity from this mortal slumber and to persuade it to march ahead" (Durkheim 1975a: 416). So, clearly, though Durkheim cannot accept the argument of the masses as mere fodder for the surge of the great intellectual toward glory, inasmuch as he understands the two figures in necessary relation to one another, he nonetheless elevates the latter to the status of "benefactors of humanity" (Durkheim 1975a: 417) and assigns the former an inferior status. After explicitly naming several of the more typical categories of the "great man," e.g., the artist, the poet, and the thinker, he closes his address by calling on the young graduates not to blush in according to superior men a just deference, for "there is a certain manner of allowing oneself to be guided that does not at all take away independence" and one must know how to respect "all natural superiority" (Durkheim 1975a: 417).

This argument makes the distinction between at least two kinds of social being, the mundane and the extraordinary, and the distinction is contingent precisely on intellectual production. The intellectuals, or at least some select subset of them, are a recognizably distinct group, and Durkheim sees their role in society as distinct from and superior to that of the mundane. Likewise, they have a unique responsibility *vis-à-vis* the reconfigured sacred. Like the priests of earlier times, they are the revealers of the nature of the sacred to the masses and they are thus required to take on an even more exaggerated attitude of asceticism towards it. As we saw in Chapter 4, this idea emerges also from a careful reading of Durkheim's writing on intellectuals at the time of the Dreyfus Affair. The intellectual is to dedicate himself to the new sacred object, to its progressive study through scientific examination, in an ascetic and renunciatory process not at all unlike that evident in the Jewish rabbinate and the Christian priesthood. And in Durkheim's own life, we find a powerful and precise manifestation of this project. Before turning to those details of Durkheim's personal undertaking of the role of intellectual engaged with the sacred, though, let us turn to the conception of the sacred and the intellectual's relation to it which emerged in the work of Mauss, Hubert, and Hertz.

Mauss, Hubert and Hertz on the Sacred

The first detailed exploration of the topic of the sacred in the work of the younger Durkheimian religion cluster members takes place in the essay on magic co-written in 1904 by Mauss and Hubert. The introduction to this essay makes clear that the issue of the sacred is at the foundation of their concerns here. Indeed, they argue that their intention in taking up the study of magical facts was to explore more fully this notion that had been the explanatory root of their earlier essay on sacrifice but that had been insufficiently elaborated there. In the latter essay, they endeavored as good Durkheimians to trace the ritual act of sacrifice to some common primitive form but determined that this was not possible. What they *had* been able to find at the root of all sacrifice were the elements of sacralization and desacralization, i.e., all sacrificial systems establish "a communication between the sacred world and the profane world through the intermediary of ... something that is destroyed in the course of the ceremony" (Mauss and Hubert 1899: 133). But if they succeeded in linking the rite of sacrifice in its essence to the phenomenon of the sacred, they had been prevented by the boundaries of their object of research from fully exploring the sacred itself. Their move to consider magic, a set of practices and beliefs outside the religious that nonetheless consists of rites designed to produce extraordinary effects in the world, was motivated in part by a desire to test the connection of ritual to the sacred that had been advanced in the essay on sacrifice.

Mauss and Hubert begin with the question of the distinction between magic and religion. The stakes in this question for scholars of religious phenomena during the period were quite significant. Frazer had codified the generally dominant intellectualist perspective of much of the British anthropological school on this question in strictly evolutionary terms, arguing that magic, religion, and science emerged in just that order and that each was less logical than its successor. Magic in this schema is the initial effort by which humankind attempts to derive reliable knowledge of the world and to act on it, but it is fatally flawed by "its total misconception of the nature of the particular laws that govern [a] sequence [of events determined by law]" (Frazer 1960: 57). Religion is its simultaneously more sophisticated but more radically false successor (due to its imputation of "elasticity or variability" to natural events, which both magic and science deny), and science is the evolutionary final product of this historical development (Frazer 1960: 59).

Mauss wrote several reviews of the various editions of Frazer's book for the *Année*, as well as numerous other reviews of other works by Frazer, including a lengthy 1913 treatment of Frazer's *Totemism and Exogamy* that closely examined the problem of magic's relation to religion. On one basic point, Durkheim and Mauss (and our other religion cluster members as well)[2] are in accord with respect to Frazer: They do not accept the chronological distinction of a "purely magical age" followed by and neatly separated from an "age of religion" (Mauss 1913: 77). For the Durkheimians, it was unacceptable to speak of magical practices as utterly denuded of any supernatural or mystical content. Magic and religion find themselves frequently in a curiously intermingled relation in empirical cases, as many rituals and beliefs partake of elements of both. The Durkheimians also denied the foundational status of magic as the historical progenitor of religion (Durkheim 1991 [1912]: 607, 609).

But if there was little disagreement concerning the Durkheimian opposition to Frazer's view on this matter, there was yet significant dissension internally among the Durkheimians here. This difference on the distinction between magic and religion was the intellectual ground upon which the younger Durkheimians elaborated notions of the sacred that also differed in important ways from that of Durkheim. For Durkheim, while magic historically and in specific empirical examples intermingled with properly religious belief and ritual and, insofar as that was the case, was therefore of interest to the sociologist, it was nonetheless cleanly distinguishable from religion in one fundamental aspect: The former has no church, while the latter does always and everywhere it exists (Durkheim 1991 [1912]: 103–4). This means that magic is at bottom an individual rather than collective phenomenon. Even in those cases where groups of magicians ally themselves in loose "societies," there is no "moral community" created by a common faith which, as his later equation of the sacred with the social displays clearly, is the very engine for the efficacy of the beliefs and rites shared in that community (Durkheim 1991 [1912]: 106). Religious ideas and practices have power because of their immersion in a moral community. Magic rites, on the contrary, evidently do not derive any power from such sources, and "the magician in no way needs, in order to practice his art, to unite himself to his colleagues" (Durkheim 1991 [1912]: 105).

The evident result of this evaluation of magic's relation to religion is the relegation of the former to the devalued half of the Durkheimian sacred/profane binary, and Durkheim was explicit in linking magic to the profane and to its corollary negative category, the individual (Durkheim 1991 [1912]: 102). But how can magic be so full of religious elements and in profane opposition to the sacred objects of religion at one and the same time? Hubert and Mauss had explicitly addressed this idea that magic was somehow to be equated with the purely individual or the profane. On the first matter, they had taken up the point Durkheim raised, that magic's independence from a community of faith is a ground for its distinction from religion, and recognized the contradiction. If religion derives its efficacy from the social itself, then what explains magic's efficacy? As Mauss and Hubert put it, "we are in the presence of a dilemma: either magic is collective, or the notion of the sacred is individual" (1904: 3). Their conclusion from the facts presented in their study is that magic *is* collective and that it differs only rather superficially from religion in this regard.

Although it is true that it can be called an institution only in a weak sense, it is nonetheless a deeply social phenomenon. This is clear in an examination of the way in which "magical judgments" are carried out (Mauss and Hubert 1904: 125). The fact that belief in magic is so clearly tied to *a priori* reasoning is for Mauss and Hubert the firmest evidence that it must be rooted in something beyond individual judgment and experiment, i.e., in a pre-formed consensus about what constitutes legitimate belief and knowledge that can only come from either a natural human mental structure (which is disproved by the fact that only some groups of people believe in the efficacy of magical knowledge) or from the social.

Furthermore, magic is not merely profane in its conscious and explicit inversion of religious rites. Mauss and Hubert draw explicitly on this pure/impure sacred distinction in order to map religion and magic to these categories, with some qualification and recognition that the great mass of empirical facts fall somewhere in between the two. Religion thus becomes exemplified in rite by the institution of sacrifice, which is centrally identified with the pure sacred and the beneficent powers, while the characteristic ritual act of magic is the evil spell, which is exemplary of the impure sacred and the powers productive of disorder (Mauss and Hubert 1904: 17). Although this classificatory schema is less neat in reality than this suggests (and Mauss and Hubert recognize the complexity in pointing to the mixed pure/impure sacred quality of sacrifice), this effort to classify religion and magic along a different pole than that of the sacred and the profane is of central importance.

Although Mauss and Hubert do not follow Durkheim in radically separating magic from the collective energy of the social, they do recognize that there is perhaps something distinguishable from the sacred that serves as the power supply of magical rites. Moreover, the theoretical thrust of their innovation here is to undermine the finality and the foundational quality of the category of the sacred in Durkheimian thought, for they believed they had stumbled upon a category that included the sacred as a sub-category and that applied therefore not only to the realm of magic but to that of religion as well and, in substance if not precisely in form, even to basic notions of power and force in science. This category proved difficult for them to define neatly, as it comprises a range of experience in many ways alien to the consciousness of the modern West, where an energy that can be embodied in entities and that is at once material and spiritual is conceived as inseparable from the "mysterious milieu" in which it acts (Mauss and Hubert 1904: 107). It is at once a force, a being, an action, a state, and a quality of things or events (Mauss and Hubert 1904: 111–12, 118). They use the Melanesian term *mana* to name this concept, but they argue for its universality in pre-modern societies, finding parallel concepts in many other sites. The Iroquois *orenda*, the Algonquin *manitou*, the *naual* among Mexican and Central American Indians, and the *arungquiltha* of the Arunta in Australia all fulfill the same function and describe the same variety of fourth-dimensional space/force wherein and through which magical action occurs. Even the notion of *brahman* in Vedic India and those of *physis* and *dynamis* in ancient Greece are of the same parentage, even if they have lost some elements of the truly primitive *mana* category. But *mana* is more than just an explanation for the belief in magic; it is also something of a near perfect example of a type of human thought that is clearly linked to the sociological fact of collective experience and existence, as opposed to Kantian categories that are given *a priori* to the human understanding. The proof of this is the fact that this category has been diminished greatly, even eliminated utterly except in vestigial forms, by the "progress of civilization," i.e., with the increase in efficacy of logical and scientific categories of force and action. *Mana* originates as an elemental, foundational category for understanding force in the world, prior even to the sacred/profane dichotomy; in fact, "*the sacred is a species of which mana is the genus*" (Mauss and Hubert 1904: 120; emphasis added). As such, it takes on a tremendous importance in the effort to understand the process by which categories of understanding emerge and the ways in which the social interacts with them.

This recognition of *mana* as a more basic category than the sacred is acknowledged by Mauss as an important and lasting point of difference with Durkheim's thought. In a brief intellectual autobiographical statement, Mauss noted:

> We [Hubert and Mauss] detected at its [i.e., magic's] foundation, as at the foundation of religion, a vast common notion that we called … *mana*. This idea is perhaps more general than that of the sacred. Since then, Durkheim has tried to deduct it logically from the notion of the sacred. *We were never sure he was right, and I continue still to speak of the magico-religious base.* (Mauss 1979: 218; emphasis added)

The later work of Mauss and Hubert bears this out. The position taken on magic and *mana* in the 1904 essay is reiterated in an essay written in 1906 (later reprinted in 1909 as the preface to their volume of *Mélanges d'histoire des religions*) which bore the title "Introduction à l'analyse de quelques phénomènes religieux." They are again explicit in insisting on the social character of magical belief and practice: "Magical rites and representations have the same social character as sacrifice and … they depend on a notion that is identical or analogous to that of the sacred [i.e., that of *mana*]" (Mauss 1968a: 19). They acknowledge in this essay the adoption of their understanding of *mana* by many of the chief figures in contemporary anthropology, citing "supplementary evidence" for their theory provided by Sidney Hartland and Frazer as a confirmation of their results (Mauss 1968a: 21).

Hubert takes a very similar position on his own in his introduction to the French translation of Chantepie de la Saussaye's *Manuel d'histoire des religions*, written in the same year as the essay on magic. He presents a qualified but vigorous criticism of Durkheim's theory of religion and the sacred, aiming at Durkheim's concentration on religious facts attached to a church and to the pure sacred exclusively. Though he was at this point one of the most important contributors to the *Année* team, he evinces hesitation in assessing the merits of the sociological approach set forth by Durkheim for the study of religion. The historian Hubert hoped the sociological excesses would be answered by "meticulous and precise investigations" designed to "inform us about the fleeting indices of social facts, which are very difficult to observe because they take place in large part in the unconscious where they are translated into the consciousness in terms that distort them in order to render them intelligible to the individual reason" (Hubert 1904: xiii–iv). Aiming more specifically at the argument over the magic/religion divide, Hubert criticizes the Durkheimian emphasis on "the formation of doctrines and churches." He sees this as a reduction of "the total history of the religious life," which must include religious practice in societies without established churches or fixed systems of belief (Hubert 1904: xxii). Hubert was quite concerned that the history of religion not be reduced to the history of "church religions," e.g., Christianity, Buddhism, and Islam, to the exclusion of "religions of the people," e.g., Roman, Greek and Assyrian religion (Hubert 1904: xxxi). He also uses a telling comparison in indicating the mutual participation of magic and religion in a greater whole for which the social study of religious phenomena must account: "[I]t is the case that magic forms with religion a more general class wherein they sometimes oppose one another, as for example crime and law oppose one another" (Hubert 1904: xxiv). Durkheim had famously discussed the sociological necessity of crime, demonstrating its importance for an understanding of the phenomenon of normal societies and moral action but stopping short of considering it an equal participant in a "more general class" with legal, moral action. Hubert's intent here is to emphasize the sociological illegitimacy of favoring religion over magic, or the pure over the impure sacred, simply because of an *a priori* moral project. Hubert is still more explicit that the notion of the sacred "appears under two different aspects, depending on whether we consider it in magic or in religion." In the latter case, the sacred takes on the face of interdictions and taboos; in the former, it is "willful sacrilege" (Hubert 1904: xlvi–vii).

The later solo work of Mauss too was in many ways an elaboration of these early insights that distinguished the Hubert-Mauss model from that of Durkheim. This can be seen most clearly in Mauss's work on the gift. In his endeavor to establish the social fact of reciprocal gift-giving as a "total social fact," i.e., as a phenomenon that reveals the dense intertwining of social realms as diverse as the juridical, economic, religious, and aesthetic and even "in certain cases involve[s] the totality of society and its institutions," Mauss borrows the Maori term *hau* ("spirit of things") to define the power gift objects have to compel people to "give, receive, render" (Mauss 1950: 204, 205, 274). Mauss uses the notion of *hau* here in much the same way the notion of *mana* had been used in the earlier essay on magic. He quotes a Maori sage to demonstrate the nature of the spiritual power inherent in the given object itself that provides a "moral and religious reason" for the imperative to give, receive and render the same (Mauss 1950: 153, 160–61).[3] Mauss refuses to reduce either the motive behind the obligation to give and receive gifts or the power behind magical efficacy and belief to some social necessity for order, be it logical or moral (in Lévi-Strauss's criticism of Mauss on this point, it is primarily the former being presumed; in Durkheim's theory of the sacred, it is the latter). In both cases, Mauss's intention is explicitly *inclusive*; he refuses to consider as fundamental to the explanation of religious phenomena a concept that includes only those ideas and practices that are at bottom moral or logically essential to the productive order of the social system and that exclude ideas and practices that elude those moral categories and can even be destructive of social order. This inclusive approach is necessary in the case of magic, in order to account for its deliberately *anti*-moral elements and, in the case of gift-giving, in order to account for *agonistic* gift-giving, such as that exemplified in the Kwakiutl *potlatch* (Mauss 1950: 269–70).

Hertz's discussion of the sacred also reveals different emphases and concerns than those we find in Durkheim. The essays he published in 1907 on the collective representation of death and in 1909 on the preference for the right hand as a manifestation of the larger phenomenon of religious polarity are the main works in an œuvre that was radically abbreviated by his early death. These studies were thematically intended as preludes to a larger work: the study of sin and expiation that would have been his doctoral thesis had he lived to finish it (Mauss 1925: 24). In this work, for which Hertz finished only a draft of an introduction and a rough outline of subsequent chapters (Parkin 1996: 125–26), he intended to comparatively examine the religious practices by which states of moral impurity are determined, punished, and absolved. His argument was that the foundational notions of sin and of expiation are not peculiar to the

Judeo-Christian tradition, as is commonly believed, but that they exist in all and even the most primitive societies (Hertz 1994: 108). An understanding of these practices is absolutely imperative for an understanding of the moral structures inherent in any given religious system. In examining the practices of sin and expiation as social institutions, he hoped to shed light on the social nature of ideas of good and evil, i.e., of the ways in which individuals and groups are morally formed so as to adhere to the given moral structures of their societies through processes involving punishment of acts of transgression and complex rites designed to reintegrate those guilty of transgression and those otherwise beyond the pale of the moral community (e.g., the dead).

In the light of his unfinished thesis, a fuller understanding of his interest in death and the right/left polarity explored in the two earlier studies is made possible. Far from being merely a physical, biological phenomenon affecting single individuals, death is a unique moment for the observation of the powerful set of social mechanisms by which good and evil, healthy and sick, and sacred and profane are distinguished and by which the distinctions are reinforced and reproduced through ritual acts. Let us recall that Hertz's title ("Contribution à une étude sur la représentation collective de la mort") explicitly indicates that it is death as a "collective representation" that interests him. It is something that derives from the social life of the community and that is symbolic and shared, and he used this notion to complicate the misunderstanding of death as a wholly biological phenomenon existing outside the symbolic. In primitive societies,[4] the newly dead actually occupy, for a period of time and under conditions that vary from society to society, a liminal space between the visible community of the living and the invisible one of the dead that demonstrates the construction and operation of this collective representation (Hertz 1970 [1928]: 83). The symbolic work that must be done has to do with the recognition of the dangerous pollution of the social body brought about by the death of one of its members and its subsequent correction, or purification, through ritual acts and interdictions.

The dead individual is initially violently rejected from the society of the living, often along with members of his family and other close associations. The horror of the dead body has its origin here, in the fear of a social body faced with the recognition of its own mortality through the loss of one of its members, rather than in any innate disgust for the physical object of the corpse itself. It is true that Hertz finds that the deceased is treated (along with his close family members) as impure, even potentially malevolent, during the period in which the putrefaction and decay of the corpse takes place, but this is due to the nature of the collective representation of death as a liminal space through which an individual passes, at grave danger to himself and to the society from which he departs, from one stable community to another. The fact that this period between physical death and the final resolution in ritual ceremony and disposal of the remains of the corpse corresponds to a social process of recognizing social disintegration and effecting social reintegration is demonstrated by the lack of such a period for deaths of individuals with no social self, but only a physical one, such as newborns or those so elderly or infirm as to have ceased participating in communal ceremonial traditions (Hertz 1970 [1928]: 79–81). After this period of ritual interdiction and ostracism, and as a result of complex rites of reintegration and purification, the surviving relations of the deceased are eventually accepted back into the living community and the deceased is made a full member of the "mythical society of souls that every society constructs for itself from its own image" (Hertz 1970 [1928]: 73). The ceremony that institutes this reparation and reaffirmation of the two societies is joyous and marked by every effort to rid participants of the stain of pollution so that they can safely rejoin profane society; the event can be quite involved and call for a saving of resources over an extended period in order to extravagantly consume them in a brief and intense feast (Hertz 1970 [1928]: 50–69). He also notes that this joyous healing celebration sometimes calls for a human sacrifice, for which prisoners of war and slaves are most often designated; the male relatives of the deceased generally act as the executors of the sacrifice, in as much as they stand to benefit significantly from its results (1970 [1928]: 52). The most important fact to retain from this investigation of death, in Hertz's estimation, is that an individual death resounds socially as an aggression against the sacred body social that is understood as caused by an impure, evil force and that must therefore be treated almost as an illness.

Similarly, in "La Prééminence de la main droite," the polarity of right and left is read by Hertz as a signifier of this omnipresent and universal necessity felt by a society to protect itself from infection and decay, to preserve purity, and to restore it in cases of pollution through specified and complicated rites of punishment and expiation. Here again Hertz rejects as too simple biological attempts to explain a nearly universal sanctification of the right hand and a concomitant devaluation, even demonization of the left. Although there might be some slight biological disposition toward asymmetry, this cannot explain the overwhelming prevalence of this preference in almost all known societies (1970 [1928]: 85). Hertz's case here is strikingly abrupt, if not brazen. He invokes the omnipresence of the religious polarity sacred/profane in primitive societies, citing, among others, Durkheim and Mauss, and then proceeds to map the right/left opposition on to it along with numerous other such oppositions, e.g., inside/outside, male/female, truth/falsity, life/death, good/evil, and self/other (Hertz 1970 [1928]: 90–93). He then provides numerous examples from ethnographic data gathered among various primitive societies and in the modern West as well to demonstrate the impure, polluting aspect of the left hand and the sanctifying, purifying aspect of the right (Hertz 1970 [1928]: 98–106). As in the case of death, it is a complicated set of social and *moral* distinctions and forms of classification that is at work in organizing the world in a particular way and in molding human behavior accordingly.

It is striking that, in each of these major works, Hertz's focus is upon aspects of the sacred that clearly fit into the impure class, or upon the process by which things move from impure to pure sacred, e.g., the changing status of the dead during funereal rites. Mauss spoke of Hertz's lifelong obsession as a sociologist with "the dark side of humanity: crime and sin, punishment and pardon" (Hertz 1994: 17, 39). Clearly, in this intellectual interest in the aspects of the sacred that Durkheim left relatively unexamined, Hertz was closer to Mauss and Hubert than to the founder of the *Année* team. The three of them were much more focused than was Durkheim on what Jeffrey Alexander (2003) has called "the cultural sociology of evil." It is this attention to the problem of evil in the social that ultimately separates the two treatments of the sacred and the social.

The Sacred as Intellectual and Personal/Existential Concern: Mauss, Hubert, and Hertz *contra* Durkheim on the Intellectual Approach to the Sacred

Throughout the foregoing chapters, I have emphasized the importance of the internal consistency of Durkheim's intellectual, political, and moral projects. In addressing each of the three fundamental dilemmas faced by intellectuals in the period of the Third Republic, Durkheim sought a unified response on scientific, moral, and political grounds. Further, he was able to construct personal meaning and find a personal sacred realm or object in the scientific project of sociology and the production of the *Année* itself. The perceived unity and coherence of this project is one of the features that gives the entire project for the remaking of the sacred some of the same prophetic force and certainty possessed by prophetic biblical literature such as the New Testament book of *Revelation* (Tiryakian 1981). For the other members of the religion cluster, however, the situation was strikingly different. Mauss, Hubert, and Hertz were unable fully to share the Durkheimian response to the moral and scientific dilemmas, and their responses to the question of the political role of the intellectual also differed from Durkheim's. It should come as no surprise then that their personal, lived experiences of the sacred and the paths they mapped out for identity as modern intellectuals were substantially different from Durkheim's as well. They were marked by a certain skepticism and an appreciation for the tragic, and for those elements that cannot only integrate but *disintegrate* society as well.

On the important question of the distinction between the elite and the masses, which Durkheim resolved by an adherence to the naturalness of the distinction and distinct roles for the two classes in their pursuit of the sacred, the younger Durkheimians demonstrate more complication and hesitation. The socialist activism of the younger Durkheimians had been in large measure an attempt to respond to this distinction; it was at least in part an effort to deny the separation of the elite (i.e., the intellectual classes) and the masses through a political ideology that strongly emphasized practical equality of all socialists and the necessity of creating forms of liaison between socialist intellectuals and normal workers. Their attempt to construct a nationalist identity, especially in the context of the war, was also an effort to affirm the erasure of the distinction elite/mass and to deny separate paths to the sacred for the two. This is especially clear in the letters of Hertz and Mauss from the front, in which the two of them reach almost ecstatic levels of rejection of the distinct identity of the intellectual in the desire to merge into a general collective will and French national identity. The very real doubts entertained by both Mauss and Hertz as to whether they could devote themselves fully to academic careers are further evidence of the complexity of their consideration of this problem. At the explicitly scholarly and theoretical level as well, we find an effort by the younger members of the religion cluster to avoid a too-easy acceptance of the elite/masses distinction regarding the sacred project. This is most clear in the comparative amount of attention devoted by all three, and especially Hubert and Hertz, to folk religion and their rejection of the Durkheimian understanding of religion as having to do only or even mainly with church religion.

We can go still further along this line of separation between Durkheim and the others by examining a few more details of the former's model for the intellectual's project and its relation to a specific moral project. Durkheim sees the specifically *restrictive* moral parameters of the prescribed pursuit of the sacred for both great and small men, i.e., those involving the deliverance of the individual from states of normlessness or anomie and into secured ritual frameworks, as paramount. Thus, there is a relative privileging of models for both the intellectual's and the masses' project that conforms to Durkheim's intellectual focus on the pure sacred, and a rejection of models that elude this conformity and veer toward the impure or transgressive sacred. Durkheim's theory and practice of the individual's pursuit of the sacred centers on a basically renunciatory, ascetic understanding of the sacred, while that of the other religion cluster members is significantly more concerned with an aesthetic and transgressive element in the sacred that carries them in different intellectual and personal directions. Durkheim's radical reduction of the sacred to the social and to the morally restrictive, coupled with the clear distinction between elites and the masses, meant an emphasis on the intellectual's project as that of a priestly, monastic figure who was dedicated to renunciatory practice designed to furnish him with the necessary arms against anomie. In Durkheim's own clearest moment of personal anomie, which Besnard (1982) argues was brought about in 1896 by the conjunction of the deaths of his father and his brother-in-law (Mauss's father) and the moment of profound rethinking of his entire career trajectory brought on by his appointment to a much-anticipated chair in *science sociale* at Bordeaux, his solution to his "intellectual and moral disarray" was typically ascetic. It was the increased personal austerity brought on by the launching into preparation for the *Année* in early 1897 and a renewed sense of his overall, systematic research plan that enabled him to "say his goodbyes to anomie" (Besnard 1982: 51–52).

For Mauss and the others, however, the model of intellectual self-construction is somewhat different. As we have seen, there is an attention in their work to figures and situations that brush the transgressive and elude moral regulation: outsider figures such as the magician, the tragic hero, the martyr, and the mystic. This intellectual attention to such outsiders, particularly on the part of Mauss and Hertz, extended to their own lived efforts to make identities for themselves, as we will see in the next chapter.

How do we begin then to address the problem of the relation of the differing intellectual treatments of the sacred by the members of the religion cluster to their own lived experiences as intellectuals in search of personal and social meaning? Arpad Szakolczai has argued that the emergence of sociology constituted not simply a new method for an objectifying understanding of the facts of the social world but also a new form of personal practice by which, in seeking to understand the central dilemmas facing contemporary humankind, intellectuals in search of new meaning structures in their own lives could pursue such projects. He has explicitly labeled the Durkheimian project in this regard as "reflexive anthropological sociology," which he compares (insofar as it has similar goals, both scientific and personal) and contrasts (insofar as he sees them as distinct methodological approaches) to "reflexive historical sociology," a kind of project represented by individuals like Weber and Foucault (Szakolczai 1998: 13; 2000). The Durkheimian interest in the sacred, in this view, is not simply a scientific interest in a specific phenomenon, as the very fact of their interest is indicative of the concept's centrality to the times in which they live. Their attraction to this topic is dually motivated by a desire to understand the role of this notion in general social life *and* to explore its possible relevance in their own personal attempts to construct meaningful lives.

Given the facts of the historical, social, and personal situations of the younger members of the religion cluster, we might profitably use categories taken from discussions of existentialism to better understand them and their approach to the sacred. This is not to attempt a defense of the claim that these younger Durkheimians are in some sense philosophical existentialists, but instead to argue the more complicated notion that the Durkheimian sociologists of religion were, in their situations as particular kinds of social beings (intellectuals with an attraction to religious subjects), at a particular historical and social moment (the moment in French history when secularizing forces were attaining perhaps their greatest influence over French culture and society), confronted by necessity with certain kinds of dilemmas that we can usefully classify as essentially the same dilemmas that gave birth to existentialism. In his study of the relationship between Durkheimian thought and existentialism, Edward Tiryakian defined existential thought as the response to the scientific, technological, political, and moral emergence of the bourgeois society, created by the French and Industrial Revolutions, that consists of a "reaction against a society in which the machine is the tyrant of the worker and the selfless crowd is the dictator of the individual's actions [that deems] it necessary to put into focus man's quest for meaning" (Tiryakian 1962: 77). It is evident that these concerns are precisely the same ones that motivated the initial wave of European sociological concern with radical modern changes in community, authority, status and the sacred and the rise of alienation, the five "unit-ideas" of the sociological discipline (Nisbet 1966). William Barrett's definition of the concerns of existentialism makes still more apparent how much the members of the religion cluster shared, in the way of thematic material, with existentialism. He classes "anxiety, death, the conflict between the bogus and the genuine self, the faceless man of the masses, the experience of the death of God" as the chief existentialist themes (Barrett 1962: 9).

We can perhaps fruitfully think in generational terms to make sense of the differences between, on the one hand, Durkheim's optimistic intellectual positivism and personal stability in his pursuit of personal meaning and, on the other, the less certain, more pessimistic intellectual programs and uncertain personal responses to dilemmas of identity and calling that are evident in Mauss, Hubert, and Hertz. Difficult as it is to make precise statements about the historical appearance of something so general as a sense of "cultural malaise," it is probable that the generation of Mauss, Hubert, and Hertz (those born post-1870) would have most keenly experienced the cultural and political crises of the *fin-de-siècle* during their early years of intellectual maturity. This generation's youthful experience encompassed the crushing tide of international chaos that culminated in the Great War, in which many of this generation would lose their lives in search of the risky experience of lived engagement and personal meaning that could not be found in the empty, bourgeois world of stagnant pre-war Europe. The experience of the Great War itself, which all three of the younger religion cluster members shared more directly than Durkheim, was a powerful *generational* experience that instilled in them a sense of the tragic that had been covered over, if not completely forgotten in previous generations, as Marcel Déat noted eloquently:

> To discover the fact of death in all its simplicity, this was to recover that ancient peasant wisdom that was only sleeping within us. It was not to construct a materialism against a spiritualism. *It was rather, as the existentialists have sometimes done since, to reintegrate death into existence, to remove from it every trace of paradox and scandal. Moreover, in our combat experience, we had recovered and reconquered that existential plenitude to which we had vainly aspired in our feverish intellectual quests.* (Lindenberg 1990: 167–68)

This generation was the first to viscerally experience the failure of both the traditional religious solutions to problems of meaning and self-mastery *and* the rationalistic and scientific replacements offered by the first generation of critics of the religious traditions (which included Durkheim himself). Cultural historians and literary critics most often prefer to classify the onset of existentialist angst and the rise of the figure that Colin Wilson (1957: 67) so aptly named "the outsider" as a phenomenon of the post-World War I period, and clearly, in Déat's words and in the accounts the religion cluster members give of their war experience, this event was crucial in shaping their worldview. But its roots stretch in this generation back before the war, to their interest in non-Western thought and religion, as manifested here in the younger Durkheimians' mastery of Vedic and Near Eastern texts and philosophies, and in certain tragic philosophical writers and themes in the Western tradition. Indeed, there are some clues in the reading experiences of the younger members of the religion cluster in discovering these tragic themes that shed considerable light on their projects. I turn to these in the next chapter.

Notes

1. Interestingly, Durkheim provides as an example of an ambiguous sacred phenomenon pork for "certain Semitic peoples," which is forbidden but in which case it is not clear *why* it is so, that is, if it is pure or impure sacred. We know that Durkheim suffered terribly on the first occasions on which he ate pork after formally renouncing the dietary habits enforced by orthodox Judaism. See his remarks on this topic in his review of Guyau's *L'Irreligion de l'avenir*, where he writes, "The Christian who, for the first time, takes his meals normally on Good Friday, the Jew who, for the first time, eats pork, both experience a remorse that is impossible to distinguish from moral remorse" (1975b: 161).

2. Hertz, for example, wrote a review of *The Golden Bough* in 1912 for the *Revue de l'histoire des religions* in which he takes the same position as Mauss in his *Année* reviews, rigorously criticizing the neat distinction between magic and religion in terms of history and content. Hertz also provided an intriguing explanation for what he believed might be an important part of Frazer's motivation in adhering to such a theory in a letter to his friend Pierre Roussel in 1905: "[Frazer] is fundamentally, passionately irreligious—and anti-Christian. *It is certainly one of the driving forces of his research* (for example, his obstinacy in trying to demonstrate that there is a primary stage of magic before religion—this is to annoy the reverend ministers who believe in the Original Revelation)" (Riley 1999b: 46; emphasis added).

3. Mauss cites Hertz, as the latter had collected a large amount of information concerning the *hau* for his unfinished thesis on sin and expiation and Mauss had come into possession of his notes and papers at the death of Durkheim in 1917. Durkheim had received them from Hertz's wife in 1915 on Hertz's death (see Mauss 1950: 159).

4. Hertz distinguishes this mode of treating death in primitive society and our modern, overly psychological and medical mode, in which death is an instantaneous and merely physical event, and the liminal period, if it exists at all, is significantly reduced (1970 [1928]: 2). His implication though is that however different our understanding and treatment of these matters might seem, at root our own processes of thought and collective representation are profoundly shaped by their origins; thus, this complex sequence of social recognition of contamination and subsequent expiation makes up a "permanent social necessity" (1970 [1928]: 71).

9   The Sacred in Durkheimian Thought II

Ascetic and Mystic Durkheimianisms

In endeavoring to explain the fact that the Durkheimian religion cluster primarily wrote about primitive societies while other important members of the Durkheimian team, e.g., Maurice Halbwachs and François Simiand, concentrated on Western society, W. Paul Vogt argues that the religion cluster studied primitives in part because they had an attitude of "despair" regarding the modern world. They perceived something troubling about the contemporary situation in the West and attempted to use primitive societies as a means for pointing to what had been lost in the move to modernity (Vogt 1976: 43). According to this account, the religion cluster believed that the modern condition contained tragic flaws that resulted in moral confusion and loss of meaning. This is a significant observation, though we must amend it by distinguishing Durkheim, who recognized the crisis but suggested clear and seemingly sure solutions to it, from Mauss, Hubert, and Hertz, whose responses to the crisis can be better understood as *tragic*. I use this term not in its popular and wholly negative sense, but in the sense that derives from the literary genre of tragedy. Rollo May summarizes this definition in a compelling discussion of the tragic aspect of sexuality as the "realization that love brings *both joy and destruction*" (1969: 110; emphasis added). The tragic sensibility is present in Nietzsche's myth of the eternal return of the same, in which one totally affirms life in embracing the eternal reliving of even what seem its greatest sufferings and evils, rejecting, or transcending, both pessimism and optimism (Nietzsche 1974[1887]: 273–74). The tragic is the complex sentiment of "gay melancholy," the deep expression of reconciled suffering and joy found, for example, in Beethoven's last quartets (Sullivan 1960: 148–64).

The clearest example of the encounter of the religion cluster with this kind of tragic thought is Nietzsche's influence on Hertz. From the summary of Hertz's treatment of the sacred in the previous chapter, it is not difficult at the outset to see points of contact between his route of inquiry into what are at bottom *moral* questions and the route taken by Nietzsche. In perhaps his most rigorously argued work, *On the Genealogy of Morals,* Nietzsche sets for himself the same task that is at the foundation of Hertz's inquiry into the primitive roots of the mechanisms of sin and expiation. Here, it is the very origin of our modern notions of good and evil, just the notions Hertz seeks to explore, that Nietzsche pursues. He makes clear that, while his intent is to provide a "critique," such an enterprise must be empirical and historical in addition to philosophical. The questions he poses are compelling: "Under what conditions did man devise these value judgments good and evil? and what value do they themselves possess? ... Are they a sign of ... the degeneration of life? Or is there revealed in them ... the plenitude, force and will of life, its courage, certainty, future?" (Nietzsche 1969: 17). His entire project with respect to morality lends itself easily to sociological categories of inquiry. Nietzsche argues that a dangerous misrecognition of what is harmful and what is beneficial to the social body emerges as a consequence of a particular cultural (i.e., Christian) worldview and the practices that accompany it. This worldview and these practices are themselves founded on a particular way of organizing the world according to a set of moral categories. Nietzsche thus sets out to investigate the origins of these categories, in order to better demonstrate why they exercise the negative effects they do in modernity. Historical and social explanations for the emergence of practices and institutions of guilt, punishment, and asceticism follow, and the end result is an attempt at a kind of therapeutic historical sociology.

Hertz recognizes Nietzsche as an interlocutor of importance on questions of morality in the introduction to his thesis. In laying out the contemporary intellectual debate over the nature of sin and expiation, he cites the opposition of Christian thinkers, who accept the metaphysical reality of sin and the spiritual efficacy of expiation, and newly emergent critical voices that treat these notions as mere delusions. The representative of the latter he chooses is none other than Nietzsche, whose position is summarized as a radical rejection of the reality of sin and an interpretation of the very notion as itself a kind of moral sickness, stemming mostly from the will to domination of priests (Hertz 1994: 59). Having set the stage in illustrating this interpretive conflict between the partisans of faith and those of reason, Hertz suggests he will construct a third position that will dialectically reconcile the two.

But Hertz oversimplifies Nietzsche's position,[1] and an attentive reading of the text demonstrates how close on essentials the two of them actually are on this issue. The thrust of Hertz's "middle way" between orthodoxy and rationalism was to remain skeptical as to the truth-value of the metaphysical grounds from which the religious explained sin and expiation while yet recognizing the crucial importance of such facts as social phenomena. For, he argues, these institutions of sin and expiation serve, under a religious mask, to integrate and reintegrate "the great mass of men" into the collectivity and to provide for them an explanation and justification of moral order and their need to submit to it (1994: 78–80).[2] The utility, and even necessity, of such practices, properly understood in social terms, is thus defended by Hertz from a position that is neither simply Christian nor anti-Christian. Similarly, Nietzsche sees and appreciates the sociological importance of religious belief and practice. He argued that, by relying on revelation and tradition as its foundations and thereby causing "the way of life recognized as correct (that is *demonstrated* by a tremendous amount of finely-sifted experience)" to be accepted so fundamentally as to root itself in the social "unconscious," religious law is a "precondition for any kind of … perfection in the art of living" (Nietzsche 1990a: 189; emphasis in original). If he criticizes the specifically Christian method of fulfillment of this function, it is not because he rejects the metaphysical masking of ultimately social realities but only because "'holy' ends are lacking" in Christianity. Unlike the Code of Manu to which he affirmatively refers, Christian morality, in its egalitarianism, disrupts the deep, conventional nature of society, which is frankly hierarchical and reserves different experiences of hygiene, mastery, and perfection for different varieties of men (Nietzsche 1990a: 187, 189). Elsewhere (1990b[1886]: 86–87), however, Nietzsche even includes Christianity in his sociological appreciation of the legitimating functions of religious morality. In short, his position is far more complex than those who would read him as a purely rationalist demythologizer purport.

The Niezschean influence on Hertz was still more profound than this brief discussion in his thesis might suggest. He maintained a vivid interest in the German thinker throughout his adult intellectual life. This may perhaps be partially explained by his several sojourns in Germany and his interest in and study of the German language (see e.g., Hertz 2002: 172), but something else remains that is inexplicable in such terms. Hertz considered Nietzsche one of those thinkers to whom we should turn "to shake us up," a thinker who "impassions us, troubles us and stimulates our intelligence,"[3] and he often refers to reading him for precisely these reasons, but this may seem nothing too out of the ordinary for an inquisitive French intellectual during a period when certain varieties of German philosophical thought were becoming more widely available in France. What is intriguing is the way that Hertz makes use of Nietzschean conceptual categories and modes of analysis even when he is not explicitly referring to Nietzsche. Indeed, we can perhaps talk of Hertz's *life* as in many respects deeply Nietzschean.

Hertz's understanding and experience of the Great War provides crucial insight into his worldview and into the way in which he lived his philosophical ideas. To say the least, he was an enthusiastic soldier. He was swept up into the state of almost euphoric effervescence that allowed many to speak of the war as a sort of necessary great trial that would determine the moral, political, and spiritual future of Europe, and he often spoke in grateful tones of his satisfaction at the opportunity to participate in such an event. Durkheim presented a version of this effervescence in Hertz during the action that cost him his life which coincides wholly with Durkheim's own personal understanding of moral purity and selfless service to ideas greater than the individual: "In advance, the officers knew that they were marching to their deaths … The calm of Hertz did not contradict itself for one instant … he walked smiling among his men, encouraged them … His thought like his will went out only toward the great and the pure" (Durkheim 1975a: 444–45). But can we safely say that this seeming certainty of purpose and vision in Hertz can adequately be summarized as Durkheim does, or does Durkheim's account perhaps tell us more about *Durkheim* than about Hertz's understanding of the war and his own role in it as intellectual and soldier? The evidence reveals something more troubled and problematic in Hertz's lived experience of the war that perhaps stemmed precisely from the fact that he was not so completely convinced of the consistency of the Durkheimian project in its intellectual, political, and personal facets as was Durkheim himself, or, at least, that he saw this project as complicated by a number of other intellectual and personal concerns (Isambert 1983: 166; Parkin 1996: 14).

Mingled with the selfless moral motivation Durkheim describes is another thread that invokes a language more typical of late Romantic or early expressionist, perhaps even early existentialist, philosophical voices. We hear the anguished struggle of an individual groping his way to self-realization, searching desperately for a way outside the mundane lived experience of the excessively rational, secure, self-assured scholar and into some radically different space that Hertz cannot explicitly name. He is often ecstatic in describing the rarefied experience afforded by the danger of life at the front; it is a purifying simplicity of purpose and will that emerges in this situation of potential personal catastrophe. Hertz is, one might say, even rendered capable of joy in the face of objective horror and death: "You cannot imagine the beautiful music I am hearing at this moment—the grave and terrible symphony that envelops me. From everywhere towards the north, the cannons sound … *We are living in the most joyous excitation*" (Hertz 2002: 53–54; emphasis added). Hertz describes the existential state of the individual at the front, using his fellow soldiers as ethnographic studies of a sort, but clearly meaning to refer also to the deep changes in his own state of being. He points out repeatedly the bracing effect of the rude life in the country, this "marvelous school of acute observation, of endurance, of tenacious pursuit," while noting also a telling mythic parallel to the lived experience of the war in his current reading material: "I am reading Sophocles' *Antigone* … . *The present war is helping me to better understand tragedy and ancient tragedy, always new, helps me to grasp the horror and the quasi-divine sublimity of the events that we are living*" (Hertz 2002: 69; emphasis added).

It is worth recalling here the intense interest in the tragic and in the idea of living and philosophizing in the open air as the epitome of health that are commonly associated with Nietzsche. The shared interest of Hertz and Nietzsche in the use of the Greeks for contemporary moral and other questions goes further than this, though, as it seems clear that at least once Hertz seriously considered turning back to intensive study of classical Greek texts in order to philologically pursue the issues of moral injunction and ritual that he examined in his essay on death (Riley 1999: 51–53). Hertz's descriptions of soldierly heroism are absolutely soaked in the language of Greek tragedy:

> [W]e must work to fulfill our small and obscure role in this great drama in which the principal character … is fate, the old acquaintance of the tragic Greeks. Blind forces lead us … but the man who is truly a man continues to march straight in the tempest … and when brutal destiny brings him to the ground, he yet dominates it through his serenity.
> (Hertz 2002: 139)

At the front, he recalls Napoleon, one of the figures Nietzsche often invoked in his complicated discourse on the emergence of the heroic, in discussing his own participation in an "epic" that he elsewhere likened to the heroic narrative of the Old Testament. Here, France is seen by Hertz as another chosen people, and we cannot help but hear something in Hertz's discussion of France's heroic vigor of Nietzsche's (1990a) discussion of the ancient Israelite sense of their own health and power in their worship of the warrior god Yahweh. This is a vision of a people defined in struggle and by their vigorous capacity to rise to the occasion of great difficulty, all the while remaining so utterly self-assured as to define the very project of justice and of truth as the concern of their own personal, national god (Hertz 2002: 201, 235–38).

This fascination with the epic is accompanied in Hertz's thoughts by the recognition of a fundamental motor for this action that, again, parallels Nietzsche. Hertz writes frequently of an almost mystical belief that victory can essentially be *willed* by the French, i.e., that success will be determined less by crude material considerations of firepower and troop strength than by the purity of *will* of the victor. This is a question for him both of a collective conviction in the superiority of their cause and of an individual will, purified by the magnitude of the consequences and self-transformative in the extreme, allowing in its ascendance the pursuit of heroic self-realization even unto certain death. To be sure, Hertz struggles between this notion of will, personally confident and cheerfully optimistic, and a more clearly self-sacrificial understanding of duty, which is tinged with a bleak resignation in the face of the ultimate task to be accomplished. So he can speak of both the "long sequence of obscure and painful sacrifices" (Hertz 2002: 57) that is the necessary lot of the troops and of a more jubilant and transcendent "confidence" that makes it clear to him that "the victor will be the one who has the most obstinate faith in his cause and in himself" (Hertz 2002: 66). It is with this latter confidence that he can celebrate without contradiction both the terrible music of cannon fire raining down on the Germans and the Dionysian revelry of the simple country soldiers in his regiment (see e.g., Hertz 2002: 206–9).

In his war correspondence, Hertz frequently invokes an archetypal German professor[4] who menaces Europe, a bookish and stagnant figure, representing for Hertz all the negative aspects of a culture of over-specialization, disembodied and despiritualized learning, and the destruction of a holistic blending of intellectual reason and the passionate will. In his "dreams of the future," he sees "a Europe emancipated" from this "horrible archetype" (Hertz 2002: 192). Hertz points to the necessity not to reduce this to an issue of mere national identity, precisely because there are German thinkers who represent for Hertz the ideal of the heroic and vital warrior-philosopher, among whom we must count "Nietzsche—of whom I think often and whom I cannot associate with our enemies, whom he despised as much as he possibly could" (Hertz 2002: 192). This was an echo of a message repeated several times in his correspondence from the front, in which he was clear that, whatever propaganda might be spread by anti-German intellectuals, he would "not consent to … hate everything German—and to abhor Wagner, Nietzsche, etc., under the pretext of this war. Why seek to denigrate, to abase our enemy, who, as Nietzsche says somewhere, is our partner, our comrade of war?" (Hertz 2002: 127).

In short, allusions to Nietzschean themes of will, to the complex discourse of sacrifice and transcendence, and to a certain poetic and aesthetic sense of life seemingly atypical of a Durkheimian sociologist can be found throughout Hertz's adult life. If we find something of a separation of Hertz's professional, academic demeanor as a Durkheimian scholar and his lived and private engagement with the thought of Nietzsche, this is perhaps attributable to the compulsion he would have felt, as a participant in the respectable university world and as a colleague of the very representative in the Third Republic of the serious *Sorbonnard,* Durkheim, to be careful of appearing too influenced by a thinker taken up mostly during this pre-World War I period in France by "profane," *avant-garde* and often literary figures outside the university (Pinto 1995: 22, 29–32). Nonetheless, the fact that Hertz *was* clearly intrigued by this shadowy thinker, that he took him seriously and did not reject him in favor of his respectable philosophical enemy Kant, as did most other academic readers, is striking.

I have already discussed Hubert's intense interest in the tragic hero, in the mythological and religious origins of literature, and in the tragic civilization of the Celts as the precursor to the French, but there remain a few unanswered questions as to the *origins* of this orientation in Hubert. I can suggest with some confidence that it was the profound influence of Lucien Herr that may well have been at the root of some of Hubert's inclinations here. He was almost certainly one of the most important of the influences on Hubert's interest in Celtic civilization and mythology. Though an autodidact in Celtic languages, Herr was by the late 1880s a serious scholar of the subject (Andler (1977[1932]: 74–76). He was also a serious Nietzsche scholar; Andler even suggested that his own voluminous work on Nietzsche should properly be considered a collaborative project with Herr. The example of Herr's "jerky and discontinuous" life, the great scholar without "a plotted career" and forever an institutional outsider, would have been a vivid summary for Hubert and his other close associates of the same sort of intellectual tragedy represented by the life of Nietzsche (Andler 1977[1932]: 227–28). Hubert too was torn in several seemingly incompatible intellectual directions, attempting to pursue interests in archaeology and ancient history along with his more specifically sociological work with the *Année*. The tensions between his wider intellectual ambitions and the requirements of the *Année* were a cause of significant friction between him and Durkheim during several periods of the *Année*'s first series (Besnard 1987: 526–27). Like Mauss, he was forced to work in several different institutions at once (the École Pratique des Hautes Études, the École du Louvre and the Musée de Saint-Germain) in order to adequately pursue his polyglot interests. His personal life also bears much evidence of the tragic, from the early death in 1924 of his wife during the birth of their second son (Fournier 1994: 542) to his heroic struggle against the illness that eventually caused his demise in 1927 (at the age of 55) to try to finish his studies of Celtic and Germanic civilizations.[5] His note to Henri Berr regarding this project, less than two years before his death, is informative of his general disposition: "I am at work. I progress slowly but surely ... I am gradually climbing up the hill ... in very adverse circumstances ... But it seems an evil fortune dogs me, and I do not know what it still has in store for me" (Hubert 1974a: ix).

One of the more informed commentators on Mauss's work, Victor Karady, has said of his overall perspective: "It is an optimistic philosophy of history" (Mauss 1968a: xl). But there is nonetheless an unmistakable concern for the tragic and transgressive side of the sacred in the works on sacrifice and on magic. Beyond this, we can discern in Mauss a more complex personal sentiment with respect to the intellectual's existential position. One element of this emerges in Mauss's sympathies for the thought of Spinoza, which I discussed in Chapter 7. It is not difficult to see the similar existential situations of Mauss and Spinoza: Both were Jews separated from their community of faith by their own loss of that faith, and yet still moved sufficiently by religious questions to make inquiry into them their life-work. As we have evidence of Mauss's interest in Spinoza's Jewishness, he cannot have failed to note this similarity in their experiences. Moreover, he can hardly have missed the tragic elements in the life and work of this solitary man who was hated and feared by both the Jewish community of his birth and the Calvinist, Orangeist enemies of the republicanism he supported in Holland; whose good friends the DeWitt brothers were massacred by a mob that more than once threatened Spinoza's own life; who himself died at the age of 45 of pulmonary disease brought on by the modest trade he had taken up instead of a career in philosophy; and whose entire œuvre was yet an expression of the possibility of overcoming the horrors of life in joyful contemplation of his pantheistic God. Some commentators have explicitly linked Spinoza and Nietzsche in this regard (see e.g., Deleuze 1988[1962]), and Nietzsche himself recognized in Spinoza a kinsman of rare closeness (Kaufmann 1956: 119). It is a great pity that none of Mauss's work on Spinoza remains, but even in this absence we can note the similarities in the two approaches to the intellectual task, especially in the resolutely anti-utopian stream in their thought and in their efforts to resist both vulgar rationalism and irrational dogmatic faith in seeking a middle way to knowledge (Jaspers 1964: 34).

The tragic sentiment in the younger cluster members also played itself out in their profound interest in aesthetics and the artistic. Edward Tiryakian (1979) makes a solid case for the Durkheimian kinship with the French avant-garde of the *fin-de-siècle*. He suggests that the Durkheimians, like the avant-garde artists, were searching for a renovated sacred object: "[T]he pursuit of the Durkheimian school is parallel to that of Proust, in the sense that the implicit or tacit dimension of the *Année* is constituted by *the sociological quest for the Holy Grail*" (1979: 112; emphasis added). We can add some empirical details to Tiryakian's tableau. Hubert held a position at the Musée de Saint-Germain, where he was responsible for, among other things, the organization of several permanent exhibits. Many of his colleagues indicated as a central element of his disposition "his taste for museums, for forms, for art" (Lantier 1928: 289; Reinach 1927). He was himself a painter of some ability and a knowledgeable collector of art, especially of works from the Far East (Fournier 1994: 105–6; Reinach 1927). In addition, he was one of the main contributors to the small *Année* section on art. Mauss demonstrated an intense interest in several of the more radical modernist artistic and musical movements, including cubism (he wrote a short "Homage à Picasso" for *Documents* in 1930) and jazz. He was also a passionate partisan of the music of Wagner (Fournier 1994: 616). Hertz also had profound aesthetic interests, ranging from poetry to painting to music. I have already noted how his interest in Bergson reflected aesthetic considerations to a remarkable degree, and his comments on and references to painting and literature in his correspondence are voluminous.[6]

These aesthetic concerns are rather far removed from Durkheim's well-known position on this matter. As many who knew him noted, he seemed to have no personal interest whatsoever in the realm of the artistic. This was consistent with his intellectual position on the matter, which viewed artistic sensibility as something any healthy society had to limit. We can even see in Durkheim's construction of the definition of *anomie* a negative evaluation of what is arguably a widespread artistic and tragic characteristic: what Baudelaire (1995: 147) called "the taste for the infinite," and what Durkheim, tellingly, read as "the *disease* [or evil] of the infinite." The artistically-motivated personality's limitless taste for aesthetic and sensual stimulation was for Durkheim a dangerous, socially destructive force generated by the absence of proper social moral regulation (Durkheim 1951[1897]: 241–76). Although Durkheim argued that there was a place for activity in society that exceeded proper moral limitations, as even crime could be understood as contributing to social evolution (Durkheim 1950[1894]: 70–72), his position can scarcely be characterized in the same tragic terms that I have tried to show are at the foundation of the thought of the other religion cluster members. For Durkheim, the normal and the pathological are neatly separable into opposed and very normatively charged categories. The other three Durkheimians demonstrate more difficulty accepting such clear distinctions.

The Ascetic and the Mystic: Two Durkheimian *Habitus,* Two Trajectories in the Durkheimian Pursuit of the Sacred

The manner in which the Durkheimians thought about their intellectual calling was of a piece with their efforts toward an understanding of the sacred. Since Weber's discussion of the role of the calling in the modern secular world as substitute for the traditional form of religious devotion to the sacred (see Goldman 1988), it has been recognized that this mode of personal meaning-construction has broader applicability in the Western world, and not solely for intellectuals. In the case of the calling of intellectuals, though, there are some interesting peculiarities, and some such peculiarities of the Durkheimian calling will emerge in the course of this discussion. My argument in a nutshell is that the Durkheimian religion cluster contains two kinds of Durkheimian calling that involve two ways of pursuing the sacred, and that two clearly differentiable Durkheimian *habitus* produce them.

How can we characterize these differing conceptions of the intellectual and his relation to the sacred? Some hints can be found in a classificatory system of models of personal self-construction and moral mastery presented in a series of lectures given by four celebrated French scholars at the École Normale de la Seine in 1920. Emile Bréhier, Henri Delacroix, Dominique Parodi, and Célestin Bouglé (the last two of whom were *Année* collaborators) presented, in discussions that had as their express intention to "demonstrate to *normaliens* the traits the moral ideal has taken on in the different ages of our civilization" (Bouglé et al. 1921: vi), four archetypal figures corresponding to different historical periods and presenting distinct approaches to moral selfhood. They are, in chronological order of appearance:

1. the "sage of antiquity," who sees human motivations as harmonious with the natural world and understands the task of moral man as the making of his own life into a work of art;
2. the Christian, who understands human nature as basically corrupt and in need of supernatural intervention and extreme ascetic practice for redemption;
3. "the honest man," the man of the Renaissance who manages the unlikely reconciliation of the first two archetypes through an understanding of human reason as at once divine and natural; and
4. the modern citizen, who is essentially the Durkheimian sociologist who recognizes the social itself as the source and object of his moral attachment and altruism. (Bouglé et al. 1921)

Though it is not possible to neatly fit our Durkheimians into any one of these categories, we certainly notice certain affinities of each for one or more categories. Durkheim's ascetic, anti-aesthetic project and emphasis on the constraining and restrictive aspect of the sacred bears comparison to the Christian moral ideal in this respect; in fact, his perspective contains elements of each of the last three archetypes, only failing to find resonance completely with the first. In opposition to this, we find that the first archetype, the *sage antique,* who rejects asceticism and retreat from the world, is perhaps the closest approximation in this list to the perspective of the others (or at least to that of Mauss and Hertz), and the Christian model is perhaps the one from which they are the most distanced. Another loose set of comparisons here can be found in Goldman's (2000) comparative analysis of the respective projects of Weber and Foucault for self-mastery. Here, Weber's ascetic and Calvinist-inspired project is roughly comparable to Durkheim's, while Foucault's aesthetics of the self, derived from the conjunction of the models of the honest man and the dandy, can be more adequately compared to the approaches of Mauss and Hertz.

A striking framework suggested by W.S.F Pickering (1998) for distinguishing the work of Mauss and Durkheim on religion offers another way of thinking about the schematization of the difference between them. He suggests that Durkheim's understanding of religion can be compared in its penchant for systematization and unity of creed to Scholastic Christianity, the pinnacle of abstract and systematic theology, while Mauss's approach can be better understood as a "Jewish" understanding insofar as both his sociology of religion and Judaism are characterized by an aversion for systematic "theologies" and dogmatic statements of creed. Pickering is clear that he intends this intriguing classificatory schema only as a provisional aid for understanding some clear differences in Durkheim and Mauss, and he would certainly acknowledge that there are serious points of weakness in this analogy stemming from, among other things, the rather too narrow definitions here provided for Christianity and Judaism. Nonetheless, there is much to be said for the endeavor to thus clarify Durkheimian thought in its several incarnations by drawing from categories of understanding in the very field the Durkheimians were primarily studying.

We can perhaps go still further down this fruitful road by considering categories from Weber's sociology of religion as applicable to the two approaches to the intellectual calling and the sacred in the Durkheimians. These categories are those of the *mystic,* who makes resignation and contemplation the foundation of religious reconciliation of worldly conflict, and the *ascetic,* who replaces resignation with notions of action and mastery. Weber further defines the two types by creating a conceptual grid in which one axis is represented by the nature of the believer's relationship to God or the sacred and the other is represented by his relationship to the established social world into which he is thrust. On the first axis, one can conceive of the relation to the sacred: 1) as of the nature of "possession," i.e., in which the believer (a mystic) is the *vessel* of the God and directly invested with the holy; or 2) as considerably more distant and doubtful, wherein the believer (an ascetic) is conceived as the *tool* of the holy and is acted upon by it without being in possession of it. The second axis yields the two opposing values of remaining in the established world, while yet pursuing the religious direction of either mystic or ascetic orientation, and of rejecting the established world for monastic seclusion (M. Weber 1946: 324–26).

Weber noted that the two types most often present themselves at neat opposites on this grid, as the most frequent outcome of the mystic orientation is toward a total contemplative withdrawal from the world, as in ideal-typical early Hinayana Buddhism, while asceticism, especially in Occidental Protestant Christian forms that achieved great expansion in Europe and the Americas, gravitated toward action directed outward toward the world, not for the sake of affirming the values of the world but in order to act as a tool of God and manifest one's status of election. But the categories can sometimes become more complicated. The ascetic mode, rather than focusing its activity on some worldly routine (as in, for example, the Calvinists Weber describes), may "confine itself to keeping down and to overcoming creatural wickedness in the actor's own nature," and mysticism, instead of fleeing fully from the world, can "give rise to communal action … characterized by the acosmism of the mystical feeling of love" (M. Weber 1946: 325; 1963: 176). Thus, the two axes give rise to *four* possible religious modes, other- and inner-worldly asceticism and other- and inner-worldly mysticism.

How then can these categories of the mystic and the ascetic help us make sense of the different projects for the intellectual pursuit of the sacred evident among the Durkheimian group? Let us begin by considering carefully an element of the Durkheimian project that was for too long overlooked by its interpreters: its fundamentally collective nature. In the past twenty-five years, the importance of this fact concerning the *Année* project has been widely recognized by historians of French sociology. Philippe Besnard (1983) was perhaps the first to begin to place long-overdue emphasis on the impossibility of thinking "Durkheimian thought" without thinking "*Année sociologique*," i.e., thinking about a group of intellectuals involved in a collaborative project. Their strong commitment to truly collective work and rejection of the then-hegemonic model of the individual scholar working alone constituted a major transgression of established intellectual convention (Besnard 1983: 84). The immense majority of the published work of several key members of the *Année* team, including Mauss, Hubert, and even Durkheim himself, consisted of work specifically for the *Année*, in the form of book reviews and articles, even if it sometimes appeared elsewhere and in other forms later. Hubert, Mauss, and Hertz rarely published books as such, but rather what appeared as their books were reworked versions of essays written initially for the *Année*. Many of these works were consummately collective projects, e.g., the essays on sacrifice and magic by Hubert and Mauss, the essay on collective representations by Durkheim and Mauss, but also numerous other works that bear the name of only one writer (e.g., Hubert's essay on time and his posthumously published volumes on Celtic history; Mauss's essay on the gift) but that were clearly the result of lengthy collective reflection and discussion, as can be seen in unpublished correspondence. Private correspondence also demonstrates how important the collective sessions at the Mauss-Durkheim family residence at Épinal, during so-called vacations, were for the overall shape and tenor of the project.[7]

But if there is much evidence for the collective nature of the project, we have perhaps not yet fully appreciated just what that means in terms of the fundamental character and implications of the work itself and of its meaning for the members of the group. The *Année* itself, and the emphasis on collective work of which it was the clearest manifestation, was seen by Durkheim as a direct realization of just the kind of modern intellectual space wherein moral and even sacred force could be generated. Durkheim speaks forthrightly of this aspect of the project in correspondence with other members of the team. Very early on, for example, in 1901, he writes to Bouglé, thanking him for an intervention on behalf of the *Année* project in another journal and clarifies the importance of the collective nature of the project: "I am ... very grateful for that act of solidarity, the moral effect of which will, I hope, be considerable. Of all the services we can render the most valuable is to show that there are in sociology workers who are more concerned with joining their efforts in order to cooperate, than with differentiating themselves in order to show their originality" (Besnard 1983: 54). With Hubert, whose commitment to the *Année* as a moral project was arguably consistently more profound than that of nearly any other collaborator, Durkheim is more frank about his notion of the importance of the collective nature of the project: "You are quite right to say that *our little group is a moral milieu as much as an intellectual one*. No one senses this more acutely than I do. But it is felt also beyond our group" (Besnard 1987: 518; emphasis added). Hubert was in many ways the central organizational member of the team besides Durkheim himself for a good stretch of the *Année*'s life, playing more important a role here even than Mauss (Besnard 1987: 484). Further evidence of the depth of Durkheim's understanding of the sacred nature of the *Année* project can be seen in the language he uses in response to Hubert's own declaration of commitment to the project: "I am very touched, my dear friend, by the terms in which you speak of *your dedication, and to employ your own expression, your devotion* to the *Année* (Besnard 1987: 490; emphasis added); and in discussing on two separate occasions the problem of the lack of "faith" of a potential *Année* recruit, Hubert's friend Emmanuel de Martonne: "I doubt he will become one of us ... He began by telling me that he didn't understand what sociology was ... *Our shared project assumes a shared faith and a great mutual confidence ... If he doesn't believe, it is better that he abstain, for when I saw him, he didn't have the faith*" (Besnard 1987: 494-95; emphasis added).

What emerges in Durkheim's discussion of the *Année* is a powerful emphasis on the moral force to be thereby produced and garnered, through a making-sacred of the collective project, i.e., the institutionalization of the discipline of sociology, which was perhaps all along Durkheim's chief intellectual goal. We have seen already how clearly devotional this project was for Durkheim, as reflected in the immense amount of his time and energy he gave to the *Année* during the formative years throughout the tenure of the first series. This sense of individual sacrifice for the collective sacred object is also well reflected in his correspondence from this period. In an exchange in 1905, at the moment of a serious crisis for the *Année*, Durkheim responds to Hubert's complaints of being overburdened with *Année* work in a language saturated with the vocabulary of moral responsibility: "If I accepted [your] devotion ... it was because I believed the *Année* was of service to you ... But I would be unable to accept a sacrifice of this magnitude, if truly you do not feel personally interested in the shared project" (Besnard 1987: 527). A few months later, Hubert apparently having responded to Durkheim's disquiet regarding his commitment to the project,[8] Durkheim restates the necessity for a full moral engagement on the part of his allies:

> What struck me was that I had quite believed I noted in you a feeling of detachment from the *Année* ... Such a state of mind did little to reassure me for the future ... you know that I too find the task heavy, the growing size of the volume adds more to it every year. I needed, to remain attached to it, to feel your own attachment to the shared labor. As I didn't feel this from you in part, I no longer myself had ... the courage that is needed. (Besnard 1987: 527–28)

These exchanges display the emergence of a mode of intellectual identity oriented to a particular kind of intellectual goal, coupled with

Durkheim's desire to guide others on the *Année* team to this same form of identity. The intellectual identity Durkheim sketches in these passages fits well with what we know of his personal demeanor from the testimonies of others. Friend and foe alike accounted him an austere, disciplined, ascetic figure, totally dedicated to the new discipline of sociology and calling for a like commitment on the part of his associates (Bourgin 1938: 216–18). This perspective was echoed by those who knew Durkheim intimately and were therefore privy to his most intimate daily life and identity. Lukes quotes Étienne Halphen, Durkheim's grandson, describing his grandfather as a "forbidding and serious" man who spoke very little (1973: 367). His life at home was organized around his work, with a family structure and a spouse who was perfectly conducive to such an arrangement. Georges Davy noted the remarkable congruence between Durkheim's scholarly concern with the family as moral center and the structure of his own family life: "His own hearth was the image of that domestic ideal. To ground it, he had the good fortune to unite himself with an admirable companion who understood him, sustained him, aided him and totally and joyfully sacrificed her own life to the austere scholarly life of her husband" (1919: 65). Mauss wrote of Durkheim's wife, Louise Durkheim née Dreyfus, that she "had given him the dignified and peaceful familial existence that [Durkheim] considered the best guarantee of morality and life. She kept every material care, all frivolity far from him" (1969: 523).[9]

But austerity and a dedicated attitude to intellectual work are not the only components of the intellectual identity I attribute to Durkheim. Still more specifically, there are in Durkheim's understanding of the *Année* collective project and the nature of collective intellectual work elements that bear closer comparison to the ascetic typology described by Weber. This ascetic Durkheimian type can be characterized as centered on a notion of intellectual labor as simultaneously sacred object and ritualistic means to that object, which is not unlike the notion of labor Weber found in the Calvinists. In Calvinist asceticism, the belief in salvation stemmed from the completely transcendent God's grace, having nothing whatever to do with human effort or deeds, and the predetermination of salvation for some and damnation for others which was also divorced from any human input. This ferociously deterministic position led to a complete rejection of sensuous and emotional culture, as these could offer no aid towards salvation. The Calvinist, who utterly rejected the value of society and other humans for their own sake, was nonetheless called through his overwhelming desire to do what was required of him by the transcendent God to contribute to a disciplined social order by means of his calling or occupation. Only through intense worldly activity in the form of work could he provide the sense of certainty of his own election, though, as Weber points out, this emergence of the possibility in Calvinism *after* Calvin of proof of election runs quite against the notion of grace and the knowledge of election found in Calvin himself (M. Weber 1930: 98–128).

The understanding of the intellectual calling that is evident in Durkheim and, in a somewhat more confused way, in Hubert (who is in this regard clearly the junior member of the cluster most like Durkheim himself in personal demeanor), can be classed as ascetic for a number of reasons. In both, we find a calling to the intellectual task that is renunciatory in the extreme, and even self-mortifying. For them, the collective endeavor by a small community of committed intellectuals, though by necessity turned to the worldly endeavor of publication and the amassing of professional capital as the by-product of the labor, was yet a quasi-monastic activity. Durkheim's paeans to self-sacrificing dedication to the scientific goals of the *Année* and to the greater good of the progressive accumulation of scientific knowledge are echoed in Hubert's own appraisal of the intellectual task:

> As for myself, *I am becoming more and more Benedictine.* I have been for several days in a period of renunciation. I feel myself incapable of happiness. I take pleasure in my old sorrows. I try to restrain myself from desiring happier days. I would be satisfied enough if I were not afflicted this week with horrible migraines. I am presently in a good disposition for work and I curse all distractions.[10]

Elsewhere, Hubert spoke to Mauss of the collective intellectual work of the Durkheimian team in the same language of his correspondence with Durkheim: "*Don't forget that we are called,* or at least I hope so, to have an influence, that we must stimulate work around us, that we will be influential less by the perfection of our own work than by the activity of our thought, than by the need, the desire, *the sacred fire of organized work that will emanate from us.*"[11] In other letters from the same period, Hubert makes still more apparent the incompatibility in his understanding of the intellectual pursuit of the sacred between its object and merely material, sensuous concerns: "I do not think of marriage as you seem to believe ... I have too many habits that make me keep to myself ... I have too much to do already, for God's sake."[12]

In the existing evidence from the lives of both Durkheim and Hubert, one is struck by the strong tone of ascetic renunciation and denial of non-intellectual activity.[13] There is an understanding of the collective, progressive pursuit of scientific knowledge as fundamentally more than an offering to social well-being. This pursuit is seen as perhaps the most powerful order-producing force in the life of the scientist and therefore as a profound psychological boon to him. Whatever scholarly or other good that might accrue to him as a result of such activity is certainly not the object of the activity, but an inconsequential by-product, much like the economic goods produced by the Calvinist's activity. There is however still more that unites them in this conception of the intellectual pursuit of the sacred in basically ascetic terms. Their understanding of the relationship between the intellectual and the sacred knowledge he or she produces is entirely in keeping with Weber's definition of the ascetic. The ascetic is a vehicle for God's will and presence; he or she does not directly participate in the being of the sacred. In both Durkheim and Hubert, a notion of intellectual knowledge production emerges that is surprisingly impersonal and disembodied. It is more about the production itself, in the form of published texts, and the regular, machine-like process by which it is produced than the producer involved in making it. In discussing their intellectual calling, both repeatedly use the language of egoless, self-sacrificial investment in a collective project (the *Année*, or science more generally) that is defined by its place in a great march toward increasingly fuller and more complete knowledge of reality. Their understanding of the production of knowledge is firmly progressive and this contributes to their capacity to detach their own existential involvement in the process of knowledge production from their conception of that process.

The intellectual's pursuit of this sacred calling in knowledge production is further characterized in two important ways that Durkheim addresses directly in his essay on intellectual elites and democracy. There, Durkheim defines the intellectual's proper involvement in political affairs as consisting of the production of "the book, the lecture, works of popular education" (1970: 280). We can see from the other evidence drawn from Durkheim's works and correspondence that this is also a delineation of the intellectual's personal mode of engagement with the sacred, which is to consist materially in the production of texts and is at root averse to active political participation. Earlier, in Chapter 7, I examined Hubert's involvement with socialism and drew comparisons of his relatively detached variety of socialism to the vastly more practically engaged positions of both Mauss and Hertz. Durkheim too considered it unfruitful for the intellectual to engage actively in political fervor, save in the most demanding of circumstances (e.g., the Dreyfus Affair). Indeed, we have already seen how he and Hubert actively worked to convince Mauss and Hertz that they should lessen their political commitment in favor of a more ascetic commitment to the scientific enterprise akin to their own.

If this characterizes the ascetic Durkheimian perspective on the intellectual calling and engagement of the sacred, what does mystic Durkheimianism look like? First, I must acknowledge that the category of mysticism into which I am attempting to place this second Durkheimianism is not thoroughly discussed in Weber's treatment, largely because Weber insinuates that this category (inner-worldly mysticism) is less consistent with the general thrust of the mystical impulse than its counterpart (other-worldly mysticism). It is essential for my purposes, though, that Weber points to a single motive that informs mystical action in the world: "the mystical feeling of love" (M. Weber 1963[1922]: 176). This looms large in defining the mystic Durkheimian tradition. We can find in other discussions of mysticism a more thorough analysis of the character of active mysticism that will help to sketch out the model for the second group of Durkheimians.

Henri Bergson examined mysticism at length in his major work on religion, and his conclusion was that "complete mysticism is action." For Bergson, the mystical disposition is fundamentally informed by a deep experience of "universal love" and this experience logically leads not to withdrawal from the world but rather to intensely active participation in the world in the form of charitable acts of kindness (1977[1932]: 226–27). From his evolutionary perspective, he found in the activist Christian mystical tradition of figures such as Teresa of Avila, Catherine of Siena, Francis of Assisi, and Joan of Arc a fuller realization of the tenets of the mystical experience than the monastic and retreatist mysticism of Hinduism or Buddhism (1977[1932]: 225–28). A more clearly sociological treatment of mysticism that also elaborates the idea of an active mysticism can be found in Clifford Geertz's discussion of Islamic mysticism in its Indonesian and Moroccan manifestations. The central thrust of Geertz's argument is that the mystical orientation can manifest itself radically differently in different contexts, as is vividly apparent in his comparison of Indonesian Islamic mysticism, which appears similar to Indian mysticism in its valorization of yoga-like quietism, and Moroccan maraboutism, in which mystical experience translates into displays of "extraordinary physical courage … [and] ecstatic moral intensity" (1968: 33). Geertz gives us a mystical *warrior* to go along with the Weberian mystical *yogi*.

The inner-worldly mysticism of the mystic Durkheimians is comparable to the attitude described by Bergson and Geertz. Here, in contrast to the ascetic Durkheimians, we find an attitude toward renunciation on the part of the intellectual pursuing the sacred that is more complex than that of the ascetics and often even explicitly hostile to the renunciatory position. One of the clearest empirical sites for viewing this difference is in the correspondence of Durkheim and Mauss regarding Mauss's personal commitment to the ascetic scholarly worldview propagated by Durkheim himself. Besnard indicates the importance of this theme in the internal politics of the Durkheimian school (Besnard 1987: 484; Durkheim 1998: 42). We can see it developing very early in the scholarly career of Mauss, as, in the dual capacity of teacher and uncle, Durkheim had invested much energy in attempting to form Mauss into a loyal disciple and he was troubled by the numerous occasions on which it became clear that Mauss's vision of the intellectual project was somewhat different from his own. Durkheim shared his doubts with Hubert: "[F]or the *Année* as it is organized, Marcel's participation is necessary. For his cooperation is for me the occasion of moral suffering; the most unbelievable irregularities take away all security from a collaboration that must have it" (Besnard 1987: 530–31). This letter came at another crisis moment in the project of the *Année*, and it is not mere chance that Durkheim speaks of Mauss's lack of commitment to the project as morally troubling. He used this language repeatedly, and what might be too easily dismissed by a careless biographer as pseudo-parental concern on the part of Durkheim becomes apparent as a fundamental difference in intellectual and personal orientation because of the intensity and the frequency of disagreements of this nature. The stakes were never clearer than in an 1898 letter, apparently in response to a letter in which Mauss voiced doubts about his desire to pursue the career of researcher prepared for him by his uncle:

> You ask that we do not seek to remake you; but, as for us [i.e., Durkheim and Mauss's mother], you cannot ask us to remake ourselves either. For it is impossible that this idolatry for your chief fault, which is much more serious than you believe, could fail to make us suffer ... if you do not resist the tendency that I am pointing out to you, you will cause much harm to yourself and you will suffer from it *unless you feel untouched by the opinion of those around you* ... I cannot permit a young man of your age to say tranquilly: it's true, that's how I am, I am wasteful, frivolous concerning my work, but you must take me or leave me as I am. At your age, it is not permissible to so easily renounce all effort ... Rather than taking pleasure in your faults, why not accept that the two of us might combat it together? (Durkheim 1998: 150–51; emphasis in original)

This moral dilemma presented to Durkheim by his nephew's insufficient attachment to his view of the intellectual calling is framed most often in the correspondence in mundane terms, e.g., Mauss's inability to finish book reviews and planned essays in timely fashion to meet *Année* deadlines, but the implications are far more important than merely to point to Mauss's tendency to procrastinate. Mauss meditates throughout his career in his intimate correspondence with his friend Hubert about his multiple desires regarding career and personal goals. As a student, he was powerfully torn between a purely political calling and that of the intellectual life, and he also clearly had an attachment to the sensuous, sentimental life that was totally alien to his uncle and his friend Hubert. He drew the line clearly on this issue in a letter to the latter:

> [F]rom the point of view of our two lives, we have the most healthy influence to exercise over one another. You have to ennoble, to idealize a certain number of my material tendencies, and I have to bring you out, from time to time, of your books, of your ideas, of your physical solitude, which you involuntarily populate with dreams.[14]

These "material tendencies" showed themselves especially during Mauss's student trips to Holland and to England. One of the most frequently mentioned features of Mauss's visit to Holland is his interest in "her pale women" and his efforts to pursue them. Early in his stay, he writes to Hubert: "I chat with a little, completely useless lawyer, take from him all I can, but have not been able to get him to introduce me to one single woman."

In a still more telling passage from another undated letter to Hubert (probably also from Holland), Mauss makes yet more clear his position on relations with women and how different it is from that of his uncle:

> I wrote you that I was going to take a trip of 10 days ... I said that I would there send for a little woman from Paris ... I was thirsty for caresses, for a delicate skin ... And that little one was delicious for 10 days. Don't talk to anyone about this. It is a necessary weakness that makes me blush. I believe, dear friend, that a pleasant mistress, without virtue but also without wickedness ... can bring, without unhappiness for her or for us, an important element of happiness at our age, or rather instead of happiness, of health and gaiety.[15]

Beyond his sometimes lusty appreciation of female charms, we should note Mauss's differences with Hubert and Durkheim here in a desire to balance the "Benedictine" tendencies of Hubert with a stronger engagement in worldly affairs. He compared Hubert to his uncle in his renunciatory intellectual attitude and distinguished his own position thus:

> In fact, my uncle and you, you two have conserved the ideal of the [École] Normale and of the *lycée*. Your entire life is turned toward intellectual things, it has as its goal only renunciation or the very highest pleasures, you have no middle ground. You have, my dear friend, the habits that a very violent education imposes on you ... [I]t is for this same reason that I see you two so often unhappy, I've said as much to Durkheim ... [Y]ou refuse yourselves those pleasures that consist of simple expansiveness ... in material pleasures ... Oh! how much I would like to give you two my serenity.[16]

Georges Dumézil, who studied with Hubert and Mauss, painted a picture of two men with radically different personal affects:

> At the time I was going to defend my thesis, Meillet wanted to know what Hubert thought and sent him a copy, asking "Dumézil just did this with me, do you want to see him?" Hubert responded "Let him come!" And I had with him one of the most unpleasant experiences of my life. I'm not sure, even today, that I've forgiven him, even though I accept nearly all of his criticisms. But one doesn't receive a student as he did, saying "You didn't want to work with us, so now you can figure it out on your own" and also "Everything I don't know, Mauss knows and everything Mauss doesn't know, I do." ... With Mauss, the introduction was completely different. He and Mauss ... were not of the same mold. Mauss was receptive, welcoming. (Bonnet 1981: 18–19)

In the mystic Durkheimians, the vision of the mode of creation of scholarly knowledge and of the relationship of the scholar to knowledge compare well to the mystic's conception of God and his relation to Him. As we saw in Chapter 7, Mauss and Hertz shared a fundamental skepticism regarding the systematic and idealist side of Durkheimian thought, distancing themselves in a number of ways from the more exaggerated manifestations of Durkheim's system-building pretensions. This distancing was part of a general stance that basically rejected the notion of efficient production of knowledge by routinized workers within the scientific apparatus, wherein a certain investment of time and energy guarantees the appearance of some amount of product, and instead considered knowledge production as something that arises as the unpredictable result of collective reflection and meditation, i.e., as the outcome of face-to-face collective work rather than the more isolated work we see in the model of Durkheim and Hubert. Whereas the collective work of the ascetic takes shape only after the individual assembly line workers have done their task in relative isolation, the notion of intellectual work of the mystic is more fundamentally dialogical, more consistently social through and through, and more embodied. Mauss's career record is a superb indication of his preference for the seminar, the conference, and the small group discussion as the chief modes of intellectual production. He also demonstrated a relative aversion to the publication model favored by the ascetic Durkheimians; he published little in his lifetime, and much of what we have now was compiled and published only after his death. In part, Mauss's failure to complete and publish many of the studies he undertook had to do with the incredible breadth of his interests (Mauss 1968a: vii), but on several occasions he made clear his privileging of a kind of scholarly activity along the lines I have outlined here. In response, for example, to an interviewer's question regarding Mauss's opinion on the most promising contemporary (in 1934) French scholars, he pointed to the "many [French] scholars who … do research for its own sake [and] are indifferent to publication, and many have published little or nothing, but they think, and they know. Their knowledge is so profound that everyone is afraid of them" (Mauss 1989:165–66). In a letter to Hubert written during his stay in Holland, Mauss was explicit about his comparison of intellectual production and artistic creative originality and spontaneity. He denigrated the simple workman-like "accuracy" he found in Dutch scholarship: "One neither thinks nor invents here … if you only knew how far one is here from that cauldron of ideas that is Paris; *the great care here is to be 'accurate,' and to be fine, to be clear, to be complete. That's all. No preoccupation at all with the truly new and original idea.*"[17]

Commentary on Mauss's seminar presence is replete with references to his guru-like character. Fournier (1994: 605) writes that he was listened to as though he were Scheherazade and Karady notes that the "rare suggestive force" and "sometimes eccentric style" of his teaching were largely responsible for his position at "the margin of the official school of sociology" and his tremendous reputation among the *coterie* of unique students he attracted (Mauss 1968a: li–ii). Dumézil spoke of a kind of disorganized genius who spontaneously blurted out great wisdom:

> I cannot exactly say what I owe him intellectually, because I only took his courses later on. He didn't prepare them in advance, he got lost in his improvisations. But as he knew an enormous amount, there were often pearls shining in what he said. It was something of an adage among his students: "On Mauss's good days, it rains thesis subjects" … We took his courses all year long, less to hear the lectures than to accompany him to his home afterwards, because he became eloquent when he left the Sorbonne; he spoke of everything, even of politics, with serenity, and it was beautiful. And he was interested in us, he was the opposite of a pontiff … Mauss was a kind of visionary, a prophet, sometimes obscure, sometimes dazzling in his expression. (Bonnet 1981: 18–19)

The metaphor of Mauss as mystical guru here should recall once more the example of Sylvain Lévi on Mauss's intellectual and personal demeanor. In keeping with the theme of mystical knowledge of the sacred, Mauss is representative of a kind of intellectual production in which it is the sage himself who is the vehicle for the sacred knowledge. Much as in the Hindu religious tradition, it is considered insufficient to merely *read* sacred texts, and instead one must encounter living, embodied examples of the enactment of the sacred principles laid out in those texts.

Hertz provides even starker evidence of the distinction between the ascetic and the mystic intellectual models. Like Mauss, he had an aversion for scholarly activity defined as the rapid production of published work and a preference for a more dialogical model of intellectual production. His avowals of these facts are frequent in his correspondence, e.g., with his ENS friend Pierre Roussel:

> The unhappy thing is that it was in vain, for I like teaching, and Science, the sacrosanct, at bottom bores me, and by the end of a few weeks in the library, I have aches in my back and elsewhere ... the pain with which I have wrenched out this little essay. Whether because of rustiness, inexperience, or constitutional inaptitude, I have had an incredibly hard time writing this study, and above all it bored me terribly. The more interested I became in uncovering data and constructing it for myself, the more the written exposition seemed tedious to me. (Riley 1999: 50, 52)

Hertz took a life-long interest in education and pedagogy, partially because this was his wife's career, and a constant point of emphasis for him in correspondence with her and others is the need for educational reform in France that would emphasize the practical and steer students away from the merely book-oriented, traditional intellectual model. During his time at the front, he was constantly stunned by and envious of the field knowledge evinced by most of the provincial soldiers. He saw this ability to think practically as sorely lacking in the city dwellers (including himself) and especially in those who had absorbed too much of traditional austere French education. He wrote frequently of his desire to escape the dustiness of the life of the researcher and even told his wife toward the end of his life that he was seriously considering giving up a life dedicated to a narrowly construed scientific calling in order to turn fully to pedagogical activism, i.e., to an embodied and engaged pursuit of collective and practical knowledge.

I discussed the mysticism of Hertz's political engagement and its parallels with religious experiences in Chapter 7, but I want to further elaborate on his understanding of the intimate interconnection between scholarly work and engaged action that together produced the sacred object he pursued by looking more closely at his ethnographic work. Hertz was in fact the sole Durkheimian to do fieldwork in this generation,[18] having accompanied a group of Catholic pilgrims in the difficult climb to the shrine to Saint Besse in the mountains of northwest Italy in the summer of 1912.[19] The central argument of this study was to demonstrate that the Churchly, hierarchical, literary tradition of the myth of Saint Besse actually had little relevance in the actual cult, which was derived much more from local and pre-Christian popular legends. Thus, the study was an effort to demonstrate the power of folk religion to live on and even exercise dominance over official institutional religious myth in the actual ideas and practice of believers. But in some ways the most compelling element of the study is the sense of Hertz's vibrant sympathy with the celebrants of the cult. This is not to say that he shared their religious faith, but he certainly had an experience of effervescence not unlike that he felt in his political activism. His language in describing the various local legends and the passion of the celebrants reveals an empathy with the profundity of their experience that distinguishes this work from some of the other Durkheimian studies of similar phenomena that were generated completely from secondary sources. In a simultaneously charming and alarming passage, Hertz describes an elderly native of one village recounting his stabbing by a resident of another village in the struggle to decide which community (and which specific version of the Besse legend) would have the privilege of carrying the statue of the saint during the procession. Hertz is eloquent in his admiration for these "worshippers so ferociously envious to serve" their saint and their "sharp tenacity" in "defend[ing] 'the honor of their commune' and the moral patrimony received from their fathers" (Hertz 1970 [1928]: 124). It is in this kind of lived experience that Hertz most fully perceived the fuzziness of the line that Durkheim readily placed between scientific knowledge and the lived personal experience of the sacred. He was powerfully moved by the prospect of the disappearance of the cult and of other such representatives of folk religious tradition: "For centuries, Saint Besse has taught his followers to raise themselves ... above the restricted horizon of their everyday lives—to joyfully place on their shoulders the heavy burden of the ideal ... When the holy rock becomes again a profane rock, completely naked and material, who will be there to remind the people of the valley of these truths?" (Hertz 1970 [1928]: 155–56).[20]

At the outbreak of war in 1914, Hertz was planning to undertake similar research in Athens, with his friend Roussel's help, on the rock cults of Mount Olympus, and he had in fact apparently written something on the topic suitable for publication that was subsequently lost (Parkin 1996: 11). This interest in the mystical properties of rocks and mountains, which was evident from early on in his life in his quasi-religious fascination with Alpinism and mountain-climbing,[21] and his desire to pursue the study of such phenomena through empirical monographs that emphasized their unique and individual character rather than attempting to systematize them under the aegis of a broader theoretical apparatus, attracted some misgivings from his Durkheimian colleagues. Hertz seemed increasingly drawn to such an understanding of his intellectual work in the later years of his young life, and this is consistent with his overall sense of intellectual pursuit of the sacred as expressed in his war correspondence.

The distinction between ascetic and mystic Durkheimians (fig. 9.1) should not obscure the strong lines of intellectual and personal connection between the two. Their shared project in the face of radically divergent and competing intellectual projects in the Third Republic was powerfully significant, not only in defining the intellectual alliances and conflicts of the period, but in shaping later interpretation and adaptation of Durkheimian thought by succeeding generations of intellectuals. But the differences I have pointed to in the mystic and ascetic Durkheimian conceptions of intellectual pursuit of the sacred are important for understanding the trajectory of Durkheimian thought after the catastrophe of World War I and the death of Durkheim. They are also essential for understanding in its fullness the Durkheimian contribution to the modern intellectual identity. In the next chapter, I draw together the two protagonists of this book, the Durkheimians and the poststructuralists, by reconstructing the trajectory of mystic Durkheimianism.

Relationship to the World

This-(inner-)worldly   Other-worldly

Vessel	Mystic Durkheimianism	
Tool		Ascetic Durkheimianism

Nature of Relationship to the Sacred

Notes

1. One can hardly expect Hertz to have been exhaustive in the single paragraph he devotes to explication of Nietzsche's position, and Mauss indicates in a footnote to the text that Hertz fully intended to fill out his reading of Nietzsche (Hertz 1994: 119); he also names specific works of Nietzsche that Hertz had consulted (e.g., *The Twilight of the Idols; The Anti-Christ; Human, All Too Human*).

2. Hertz's position is thoroughly at odds with that of liberal Christian modernists who endeavored to construct their own middle way between orthodox faith and secular reason, as he makes clear in his vigorous attack of them (1994: 64, 76, 80; see also W.S.F. Pickering's preface to this same document, 5–14). The 1911 letter Hertz wrote to his English friend Dodd from which I quoted at length in Chapter 7 (where he notes "If I was a Roman Catholic, I would certainly be with Pius X against the modernists") makes fairly clear which side of the modernist/orthodox debate in Christianity he found more attractive.

3. Hertz to Alice Bauer, 4 September 1903, FRH. In this same letter, he gives a very critical reading of none other than John Stuart Mill, one of Nietzsche's own foils, concluding that he had succeeded in rousing himself from the slumber induced by the English philosopher by turning to Nietzsche.

4. It is difficult in what follows to avoid thinking of Nietzsche's discussion of the *Kulturphilister* (see e.g., Nietzsche 1983: 7–9).

5. Mauss, in the preface to the first volume of the work on the Celts, used precisely the language of the tragic I indicate above in expressing "the *sad joy* [*la triste joie*] that we feel in saying here what an innovator we have lost" (Hubert 1974a: 13; emphasis added).

6. Examples include the following: While in Germany on a study visit in 1902, he wrote numerous letters to his wife that contain lengthy commentaries on things such as the painting of Dürer and Rubens ("There are landscapes more beautiful, more extravagant, more true even, in a sense, than nature itself, or rather than our perception of nature" (17 October 1902, FRH); and the music of Wagner (e.g., 2 October 1902, FRH). His letters from the front contain frequent references to literary and poetic works (by Tennyson, Goethe, and Sophocles) that Hertz was reading or re-reading.

7. See, for example, the excerpts from the correspondence from Durkheim to Hubert published by Philippe Besnard (1987: 483–534), which contain frequent references to this phenomenon (e.g., "Marcel is here [i.e., at Durkheim's home] and we have begun to work"; "If you should like to come and join us in the revisions, I needn't tell you that you would be very welcome").

8. Unfortunately, none of Hubert's letters to Durkheim exist today. It would seem most likely that Durkheim's correspondence was destroyed during the Occupation, either by his family or by Vichy authorities.

9. Charle (1984) suggests that the particulars of Durkheim's marriage and especially the fact that his in-laws were rising members of the Jewish petite bourgeoisie help explain his comparatively unique position among French intellectuals of the period (i.e., the rare combination of scholarly and economic capital) and even aid in the interpretation of Durkheim's complex relationship to socialism, which becomes increasingly complicated after the marriage, i.e., after

Durkheim is allied through family ties to a particularly vigorous segment of the capitalist class.

10. Unpublished letter from Hubert to Mauss, [1897?], FHM; emphasis added.

11. Unpublished letter from Hubert to Mauss, 1897, FHM; emphasis added.

12. Two unpublished letters from Hubert to Mauss, 1897, FHM.

13. Others close to Hubert noted it as well. There is a telling letter from Lucien Herr to Hubert on the happy occasion of the latter's marriage in 1910 in which Herr notes, "I have never been able to think without sorrow of what life has given you of vain and pointless suffering, of heartbreak, of anguish that exhausts and destroys your strength; it is a great happiness for me that you are finally freed from trouble, from the impossible, from the chimera that was devouring your life" (unpublished letter from Herr to Hubert n.d., FHM).

14. Undated letter, placed sometime in 1898, FHM.

15. All of these letters are located in the FHM. Mauss, unlike the other three Durk-heimians, only married very late in life (in 1934 at age 62, to a woman fourteen years his junior) and he was known throughout his life as something of a ladies' man and a "dandy" (Fournier 1994: 605, 652).

16. Mauss to Hubert, letter addressed from Leyden, 1898, FHM.

17. Letter n.d., FHM; emphasis added.

18. Henri Beauchat, who co-wrote with Mauss the essay "Morphologie des Esqui-maux," died of hunger and exposure on Wrangel Island off the northeastern coast of Siberia in 1914 during an ethnographic trip (Mauss 1969: 489), but this was several years after Hertz's fieldwork on the Saint Besse cult.

19. We might well include in his fieldwork experience the collection of stories and sayings of provincial soldiers that Hertz undertook while at the front in late 1914 and early 1915.

20. Paul Alphéndery, in an obituary on Hertz written for the *Revue d'histoire des religions* (vol. 79, 1919) wrote the following about Hertz's work on Saint Besse: "Rarely have we been given to read pages written with such a modest and full art. Under the rigor of critical investigation, one senses that the author was happy to live in the same atmosphere that he was studying, that a sympathy that went as far as emotion united him with the simple folk whose ritual gestures he was describing."

21. There are numerous letters in the FRH written by Hertz to various family members and friends recounting his almost ecstatic joy during his many mountain-climbing voyages, and even several striking photos of Hertz in the mountains. This obsession seems to have been a family characteristic; Hertz's father was killed in 1899 in a climbing accident when Hertz was a young man (Parkin 1996: 1).

10 The Line of Descent of the Mystics

The Collège de Sociologie and Critique as the Conduits to Poststructuralism

In Chapter 5, I looked at some of the reasons for the decline of Durkheimian thought in French academic institutions following Durkheim's death in 1917. The goal there was to respond to a pressing question: why this near total abandonment of an intellectual and political position that was one of the more powerful and promising ones during the middle Third Republic? Although Terry Clark's (1973) claim for a general shift in temperament in the Latin Quarter from cartesianism to spontaneism is less an explanation than a description of the effects of some other causal factors, it seems indisputable that a reaction against the perceived radical secularism of the Third Republic and its concomitant failures on several crucial domestic and international issues did begin to emerge sometime shortly after the conclusion of the Great War, and perhaps even before. In fact, the war itself and the several near-disasters it brought the French prior to the victory at the Marne in September 1914, not to mention its demographic consequences in the loss of nearly an entire generation of young men, were seen by many as a direct effect of the failure of the Republican secular ethic to properly maintain France's power position in relation to the other continental power, Germany. The wave of flight from secular Republican liberalism during this period was led in many respects by Catholics, and this was a period of intense conversion and reconversion to the Catholic faith on the part of a significant number of intellectuals (Gugelot 1998).

But even those who remained unfriendly to the Church and to other traditional religious paths often reacted violently against the Republic, its secular liberal ethics and morality, and its representative intellectuals. For many of these inter-war intellectuals, the alternatives to that lifeless and suffocating Republic, with its purported excesses of democracy, science and reason, consisted of various efforts to tie together the spirit animating three emergent forces in French society: 1) the modernist avant-garde (which, in its fascination with African and other primitive art and culture, became engaged in criticisms of both Western progressivist aesthetics and French colonialism); 2) the anti-democratic movements of communism and fascism (which saw in the rising powers of Fascist Italy and Soviet Russia the virile successors to the tired old democratic republic); and 3) a renewed mystical religious sense separated from and in fact often hostile to the Church.

If we want to understand the trajectory of Durkheimian thought after Durkheim, we need to better understand how some of these inter-war figures were able to make use of it in radical ways derived from these multiple motivations and how they then passed that tradition on to others in subsequent generations.

The Second Generation of Mystic Durkheimianism: The Collège de Sociologie

In light of the facts from French cultural history of the inter-war period laid out in Chapter 5, one might guess that the legacy of the mystic Durkheimian tradition encountered a fate considerably different from that of the ascetic strand. It is true that even on an institutional level, the star of Mauss continued to shine fairly brightly up through the beginning of World War II, in a fashion seemingly detached from the waning fortunes of orthodox Durkheimian sociology. Mauss, who had pursued a frenetic teaching schedule at three different institutions (the École Pratique, the Institut d'Ethnologie, and the Collège de France) since 1931, enjoyed a significant reputation in Parisian intellectual circles throughout the inter-war period. His election to the Collège de France in 1931 was only the most obvious testimony to his renown. Yet it was basically detached, institutionally and substantively, from the orthodox tradition of Durkheimian sociology. In 1921, at least partially at the instigation of other members of the *Année* team, Mauss made an effort to relaunch the journal that had come to represent orthodox Durkheimianism, though the first volume of the new series would not reach the press until 1925. However, it very quickly became apparent that the project would be short-lived; the second series of the *Année* ended in 1927 with the second, truncated volume. Mauss's sentiments about the burden of general editorship of the journal are manifest in a letter to Ignace Meyerson: "I am going to emerge from the nightmare of *L'Année* I to enter the nightmare of *L'Année* II. I can't go on any longer" (Fournier 1994: 482–99, 532–42). Such a project fit very neatly into the framework of the ascetic Durkheim, but Mauss proved of a constitution unamenable to this variety of intellectual undertaking. Institutionally, Mauss's affiliations were firmly in the field of ethnology or anthropology, and his students were not the philosophy and history *agrégés* and *normaliens* who had been attracted to Durkheim's work a generation earlier, but a more heterogeneous, volatile mix of orientalists, ethnologists, artists, and writers. Johan Heilbron described the circle of young intellectuals who became Mauss's first heirs as:

> outsiders in the university world; Maussian ethnology was not, in their eyes, a continuation of Durkheimian sociology, but something "new," tied to exoticism, to the world of art, or simply to archaeological studies, to the history of religion or to Oriental languages. For them, Durkheim had been "a severe professor, cold, rather rigid, truly the head of a school, while Mauss was a completely different kind of man: he was warm, expansive, he radiated." (Heilbron 1985: 230)[1]

Among these students were several of the next generation's most celebrated ethnologists: Marcel Griaule, Alfred Métraux, Denise Paulme, Georges-Henri Rivière, Jacques Soustelle, and Louis Dumont, among others. Through these students, Mauss's approach to the study of the social and at least some of the elements of the mystic Durkheimian approach to the question of the intellectual were kept alive even within French academic and administrative institutional structures.

It is however largely outside those institutions that we find the most evidence for the influence of the elements of mystic Durkheimianism on later generations. For among the students who followed Mauss's courses during the 1920s and 1930s, there were also those with distinctly different career ambitions and personal goals. Some of these were attracted by all three of the emergent cultural movements discussed above, and they saw in Maussian, i.e., mystic Durkheimian thought a consistent way of integrating the three into a lived practice as intellectuals.

Georges Bataille was the first of this group to discover Mauss's work in the fall of 1925 (through the influence of his former schoolmate at the École des Chartes, Alfred Métraux), but word would soon spread and attract a number of other similar thinkers, including Roger Caillois and Michel Leiris (Armel 1997: 219; Clifford 1988: 125; Surya 1987: 181).[2] These three shared an engagement and interest in avant-garde literary and artistic circles of the period. All had been involved to a considerable degree in André Breton's surrealist group. Bataille, who was educated as a medievalist librarian and held a librarian post at the Bibliothèque Nationale from 1923 to 1942, was the oldest of this group and in many ways he emerges as the central figure, at least in organizational terms, of the several associations and groups in which the three participated collectively in the 1930s that attempted to put into practice their reception of mystic Durkheimianism.

The first of these endeavors was the review *Documents*, established in 1929 with Bataille and Pierre d'Espezel as co-editors and intended as a kind of simultaneous destruction of the boundaries between primitive art and the avant-garde and an exploration of the status of the social sciences (Lecoq and Lory 1987: 112). The journal's intent was to "constantly place in doubt ... the proper arrangement of cultural symbols and artifacts" (Clifford 1988: 132), to engage in the kind of radical reconfiguring of cultural and political hierarchies suggested by the combination of revolutions that were simultaneously being produced in post-World War I France by the ethnographic studies fueled by colonialism and by the aesthetic and political radicalism spurred by the horror of the war. Bataille assembled a heterogeneous group of renegade surrealist writers and artists (e.g., Leiris, Robert Desnos), academic art historians (e.g., d'Espezel, Jean Babelon) and professional ethnographers (e.g., Griaule, Paul Rivet, and Pierre Mabille). He published a number of his most important articles of the period in *Documents*, including a 1930 essay on sacrificial mutilation and the severed ear of Vincent Van Gogh in which he cites the essay of Hubert and Mauss on sacrifice in a description of "insane" automutilation as the modern, Western residue of the religious sacrifice fully experienced in primitive society (Bataille 1970: 258–70). Mauss himself contributed a short article on the art of Pablo Picasso to the review for a special issue on Picasso and primitivism.

Although *Documents* lasted only two years, it was only the first significant intervention into French intellectual affairs to come from this group in the 1930s. During the height of French interest in things African, the French state intervened in an impressive way to further the ethnographic study and dissemination of knowledge of African culture. In 1931, the Exposition Coloniale attracted millions of visitors to see the vast array of cultural objects gathered from France's colonial territories. In the same year, a team of ethnological specialists was convened and funded by a combination of government and Rockefeller Foundation contributions to undertake a lengthy expedition across the African continent to study native populations and gather materials to fill the gaps in the collections of the Musée d'Ethnographie at Trocadéro. The Dakar-Djibouti mission began on the West African coast and wound its way through 20,000 kilometers in a journey that lasted from May 1930 until February 1933 (Leiris 1981 [1934]: 16). Though he did not go on the mission himself, Mauss was a central player in its organization.

His student Marcel Griaule was its director, and it included eight other young ethnologists including Leiris, who was the secretary-archivist of the mission and "investigator in charge of religious sociology" (Fournier 1994: 609). Leiris's role was to maintain a sort of general ethnographic journal of the mission. The result, his *L'Afrique fantôme*, is recognized as one of the key ethnographic field notebooks in the history of French ethnography because of the manner in which his multiple orientations as ethnologist and avant-garde writer were brought into play in his depiction of the journey. I will look more closely at this work and at Leiris shortly.

First, though, let us move to the most important of the efforts to forge a Durkheimian intellectual praxis by Mauss's students of the 1930s. This was the Collège de Sociologie, which was formed by Bataille in early 1937. By this time, Bataille had already been the founder or co-founder of a number of earlier groups that were conceived as efforts to found a new kind of intellectual project at once politically radical, aesthetically avant-garde, and existentially constitutive of the kind of effervescence spoken of by the Durkheimians. One of these groups, Contre-Attaque, which he co-founded with André Breton, spent its short life during the tumultuous period from 1935 to 1936, a period that saw political agitation in France reach levels not seen since the near-revolutionary events that preceded the founding of the Third Republic. Contre-Attaque was far more explicitly political than Acéphale (literally "headless" or "leaderless"), a secret society Bataille subsequently organized with Pierre Klossowski, Jean Wahl, Jules Monnerot, and several others in 1936. Acéphale published a review of the same name that appeared a total of four times between June 1936 and June 1939, but its central purpose was as a collective space within which a new way of constructing an intellectual identity could be pursued. This new way was consistent with the basic insights of the mystic Durkheimian tradition, albeit entangled with the avant-garde aesthetic and revolutionary political goals that had emerged in the cultural landscape of post-World War I France (Richman 2002). The group attracted a wild and sometimes dark reputation for its interest in the extreme faces of such collective effervescence and experience of the sacred. There even circulated a rumor among some of those close to the group that they intended to carry out a human sacrifice, using a member of the group, in order to reenact the foundational myth necessary to make the sacrificed individual into a founder-hero and transform the group into a new religion (Felgine 1994: 139–40).

The Collège was in some ways an extension of Acéphale to an expanded and more public arena. It held public meetings in a bookstore on rue Gay-Lussac in the heart of the Latin Quarter at which members presented papers and directed discussions, and it published its texts with the Nouvelle Revue Française, a publisher of many respected literary figures (Jamin 1980: 15). But its mystic Durkheimian orientation led it to a view of the intellectual project that was far from orthodox. The express goal of the Collège was the creation of a *sacred sociology*, i.e., an enterprise that would analyze the sacred in its effervescent role in the social *and* endeavor to construct new experiences of the sacred. In theoretical terms, the radical separation between the sociologist as subject and the social as object was put in question by the Collège. The key question posed by the Collège can be summarized as follows: "How and under what conditions can a subject position other subjects as objects of knowledge?" (Jamin 1980: 14). In responding in a fashion that denied the separation between sociological analysis of the sacred and the existential quest for the same, the Collège attempted to assert an identity as a

> moral community ... militant, interventionist ... that not only gave life to the concepts and methods ... represented by Mauss—in transferring them from the exotic to the everyday, from the distant to the near, nearly to the self ... but also made each of its members into travelers of social experiences. They became the voyagers and the actors of a sociological experiment. (Jamin 1980: 12)

Taking as their starting point the same recognition made by the Durkheimians of the dual character of the sacred, the members of the Collège followed the mystic Durkheimians in their concentration on the left or impure sacred and in their understanding of the proper manner in which to engage the sacred themselves. For them, the quest for a community that would be both intellectual and affective was a powerful motivating force. It is difficult to generalize about the work of the individuals involved as they made up such an idiosyncratic group, but there are nonetheless significant lines of common interest and orientation connecting them (Clifford 1988: 142).

Georges Bataille: Cluster Leader

Bataille's debt to mystic Durkheimianism is evident in much of his published work and in his personal trajectory. He maintained an interest in religious subjects from an early age, embracing a mystical Catholicism in his early twenties that informed his first publication, a paean to the Notre

Dame cathedral at Reims that was one of the many French cultural treasures bombed during the Great War. Even upon losing his Catholic faith, he continued an existential inquiry into the problems of the sacred, sexuality, and death that lasted for the rest of his life. All of his major works are examinations of these problems from a perspective that is indebted to two sources: Durkheimian sociology and German existentialism, with Nietzsche playing a central role in the latter category. The unifying theme in his work is itself something of a meeting point of these two influences, although terminologically it is clearly Maussian in origin. Bataille took as central the notion of expenditure, i.e., of the offering, free giving, or destroying of some capacity, force, or good. Mauss's discussion of the gift was essential to Bataille's conception, and he tied his understanding of gift-giving and expenditure even more explicitly to the sacred.

For Bataille, the crucial moments in social life are those in which society expresses itself by ritual offering and destruction of excess or surplus energy, which he called the *accursed share*. These are the moments that produce effervescence and power through a total and excessive expenditure of energy, even to the point of death. Sacrifice, war, potlatch, games, festivals, mystical fervor and possession, sexual orgies and perversions are all modes in which this kind of expenditure is carried out. This is a framework that turns traditional sociological and philosophical treatments of production and society, which take production as primary and expenditure as dependent upon it, on their heads. Bataille was among the group who in the 1930s attended the lectures at the École Pratique des Hautes Études by Alexandre Kojève on Hegel (see e.g., Boschetti 1988[1985]: 66; Surya 1987: 196), where he learned of a way to read Hegel as a radical and proto-existentialist critic of the systematizing Marxists and others who saw production and work as the keys to human society. From Kojève's Hegel, who took great pains to demonstrate "the unreasonable origins of reason" (Descombes 1980[1979]: 14), Bataille saw as basic the *desire* of man that, like animal desire, can be satiated only in destructive action that radically annihilates the object desired.

The culminating point of this position in Bataille's published work is *The Accursed Share* (1991[1947]), in which he demonstrates the centrality of this idea of excess and the necessity of its perpetual regeneration and violent expenditure in an explicitly historical and sociological manner. He invokes historical references ranging from Aztec human sacrifice to primitive potlatch, Tibetan Lamaism, and the modern West in order to extend the point made by Mauss in his essay on the gift and in his other treatments of the total social fact. Bataille demonstrates how the analysis of *general* economy (as opposed to *limited* economy, which restricts itself to production and labor) reveals the essential role played by excess and expenditure, and how this new understanding of economy enables an understanding of the centrality of the sacred. For, in its transgressive guise, the sacred is one of the central ways in which this expenditure of excess is carried out. In other discussions of eroticism, violence, and death, he echoes this point. The transgressive moment, he argues, "does not deny the taboo but transcends it and completes it" (Bataille 1986[1957]: 63); that is, an understanding of the sacred in purely *right* or pure sacred terms overlooks the necessity of the *transgressive* sacred for the completion of the sacred experience. In Bataille's view, the sacred is the experience of "the greatest anguish, the anguish in the face of death ... in order to transcend it beyond death and ruination" (1986[1957]: 87). This experience is possible only when taboos and restrictions representing protection from things and realms that can produce death are transgressed. Thus, sexual taboos are burst asunder and the participants experience the transcendent moment in which the fear of death and decay that is intimately entwined in the sexual act (for "reproduction demands the death of the parents who produced their young only to give fuller rein to the forces of annihilation") is overcome, however briefly (1986[1957]: 61). Similarly, Bataille sees as the primary element in sacrifice not the offering to the god but rather the transgression, in a violent act of collective murder, of death taboos in the interest of collectively experiencing the effervescent moment in which all perceive "the continuity of all existence with which the victim is now one" (1986[1957]: 22).

Roger Caillois and Michel Leiris: The Forgotten Ones

Caillois and Leiris were much more institutionally connected to ethnology than was Bataille. As I noted, Leiris participated in the Dakar-Djibouti expedition, and Caillois was the only one of the three central Collège de Sociologie members who studied with Mauss as a student, rather than following his courses as an *auditeur libre*. While a student at the École Normale Supérieure, Caillois was already attending Mauss's post-graduate seminars at the École Pratique and he took a diploma from its section in religious sciences in the same year he obtained his *agrégation* (1936), working closely with Mauss and Georges Dumézil on myth and later publishing a thesis on "Les Démons de midi" (Fournier 1994: 708). This early work, which remains untranslated save for a brief introduction (Caillois 2003), is vintage mystic Durkheimianism in its choice of topic. It lays out the mythical complex associated with the noon hour, a time for the premodern world marked by a peculiarly dangerous variety of demonic activity producing transgressive sexual desires.

The mature Caillois wrote several book-length studies on precisely the central themes explored by the Durkheimian religion cluster. *Le myth et l'homme* and *L'homme et le sacré* were greatly indebted to Mauss and to Durkheim. Though Mauss made some stern criticisms of the former, finding the discussion of literature as modern myth too mired in "irrationalism,"[3] it cannot be denied that Caillois's position on the foundational character that mythical thought has for social knowledge is fundamentally Durkheimian. The book on the sacred is still more obviously Durkheimian in spirit, with a great number of references to the work of Durkheim, Mauss, and Hertz. In many ways, it reads something like the textbook on the sacred that Mauss himself was undoubtedly the best suited to write but never did (Felgine 1994: 205–6). It also clearly shows the progression in the emphasis given to the sacred as transgression that we noted in Mauss and Hertz. There is a careful and elaborate discussion of the festival, the primary location of engagement with the transgressive sacred, which must be balanced with the sacred as respect in order to maintain social equilibrium. Taboo, the normative mode of engagement with the pure sacred, is observed during the bulk of the calendar, but during specific periods of festival, deliberate and systematic transgressions against the taboos are required. An example in the Christian calendar is the complementary pair of Lent and Carnival. Although contemporary Carnival has been bled of its real transgressive power in most manifestations, in the medieval Christian world, it entailed the same kind of orgiastic excess (in e.g., the dietary and the sexual) that Caillois detailed in primitive societies. Caillois here provided an elaborated theory of the festival to balance Durkheim's emphasis on the pure sacred. The ritual transgression of festival is given meaning by myths describing how the moral order must be created anew each year from the violent chaos that pre-existed it (Caillois 1959[1939]: 103–8). Caillois included a discussion of sexuality and the sacred that presaged Bataille's later work on eroticism, and he added an appendix on play and the sacred that he followed up some twenty years later with a book-length study of the same topic. The book on play provided insights into how contemporary realms of sport and entertainment might be linked into discussions of the sacred (Riley 2005).

Leiris's most important contribution to the Collège in substantive terms was a paper on "Le Sacré dans la vie quotidienne." Here, he demonstrated a concern for the sacred that was perhaps still more reflexive than even that of his comrades in the Collège. Leiris made completely explicit the connection between the ethnographer's concern with the sacred and his own participation in it by analyzing the construction of the sacred in his own childhood and the ways in which that sacred structure lived on in his adult life. We find in Leiris's personal geography of the sacred the same distinction between left and right, impure and pure sacred, or in Caillois's terms, sacred of transgression and sacred of respect; his father's top hat and revolver are examples of the latter, the bathroom and a nearby race course exemplify the former (Hollier 1979: 24–31).

The brevity of this central contribution to the Collège should not deceive us, for Leiris's notebooks in preparation for the subject demonstrate a deep and lasting concern for the subject of the sacred. More, as is the case with Bataille and Caillois, much of his work beyond the explicit connection to the Collège was also engaged with the sacred as an object of central existential importance in his own life. He continued the autobiographical investigation of the sacred he had begun in the Collège after its collapse with a work dedicated to Bataille (*L'Age d'homme*), and then a series of books that comprise his masterwork, *La Règle du jeu*. In these works, the connection between the mystic Durkheimian concern with the sacred, the ethnographic project, and the surrealist concern with literature as a profound form of self-examination is explored in depth. In the detailed exploration of his own sacred landscape through examination of dreams, childhood memories, and transgressive or limit experiences of debauchery, he hoped to create a true *littérature engagée,* in which the writer becomes *l'homme total,* "one for whom real and imaginary are one and the same" (Boyer 1974: 10), precisely in exploring the one individual in whom he can see the totality: *himself. L'Afrique fantôme* had been among the first, tentative sketchings of this quasi-scientific literature in which the methods of the ethnographer (the keeping of a "field journal" and note cards, a certain distancing from the object under investigation) are put to use on the ethnographer himself (Boyer 1974: 40–41).

The Collège's Embodied Durkheimianism

So much for a brief accounting of the ways in which the work of the Collège takes up themes that had been core concerns of the Durkheimians. In point of fact, this much was already known, as the work of Michèle Richman (2002) has masterfully explored the Collège's use of Durkheimian concepts. But what we yet do not know is, beyond this reading of texts, in what sociologically-rooted ways can we speak of the Collège as specifically shaped by *mystic* Durkheimianism? To be sure, there is to be found in the texts and in the political action of the Collège a great devotion to the impure as opposed to the pure sacred. There is also the direct, embodied connection to Mauss. It is an important fact that none of the members of the Collège knew Durkheim personally, and none took courses with Hubert, while Hertz was already dead by the time they reached intellectual maturity. All encountered the Durkheimian program directly through the teaching and person of Mauss. They would also have been exposed to the work and ideas of Hertz, as Mauss lectured from Hertz's notes on sin and expiation at the Collège de France from 1932 to 1935 and his teaching was generally peppered with references from Hertz's remaining and unfinished work during this period (Fournier 1994: 592–93). But the question of the *habitus* of Mauss is an essential one that remains unexamined in discussions of the Collège.

It seems clear that other factors I named as constitutive of the mystic Durkheimian orientation were essential in Mauss's appeal to the members of the Collège. These literary figures, each of whom was centrally interested in the connections between sociology and literature as a means for the construction and expression of self, were clearly attracted by Mauss's dandyish demeanor, his sympathies for modern art and aesthetics, his understanding that knowledge must be embodied and not idealist, his openly radical political commitments, and his aura of the quasi-religious guru. It is quite a bit more difficult to imagine men such as Bataille or Leiris, both of whom had reputations as libertines and whose aesthetic commitments were resolutely avant-garde, being attracted to the demeanor and the teaching of the austere Durkheim or Hubert with nearly the same enthusiasm with which they flocked to Mauss. I am therefore making an argument about the importance of affect and *habitus* in intellectual influence. Intellectual influence should be understood as *embodied*, not simply as a matter of the reading of texts that shape the production of other texts. It is not simply a body of thought, in ideal form divorced from its lived conditions, that attracts the members of the Collège to a certain stream of Durkheimianism, but the holistic totality of the thought and its existential manifestation in the modes discussed in earlier chapters.

The members of the Collège would have experienced this *habitus* most directly from exposure to Mauss, but there are also clear similarities between their lived intellectual projects and that of Hertz, although none of them ever met him. All of these projects were attempts to find a point of connection between the insights provided by this new social science into the nature of human existence and the deep existential yearnings gnawing internally at many intellectuals during this moment in European cultural history, i.e., the moment of the West's full entry into a modernity characterized centrally by the disappearance of traditional cultural responses to deep questions of personal meaning and the failure to locate adequate replacements for this lost symbolic treasury. Hertz is the closest thing we have to a precursor to the position taken up by Bataille and his colleagues a generation later, a position that Jean-Michel Besnier (1988) characterizes as that of *l'intellectuel pathétique,* a phrase that can perhaps be best translated as "the suffering intellectual." Why "suffering"? Precisely because of the seemingly radical contradiction between the scientific tools this figure has acquired for the exploration, and consequently the demystification, of some of the foundations of human social life and the grave difficulties one faces in attempting to constitute meaning in this demystified world.

In Hertz and Mauss, we see the struggle between their commitment to the goals of objective social science and their desire to put this science and other intellectual currents at the service of their own existential quest, but they manage to keep the combatants separated, if only with great difficulty and with more than occasional mutual intrusions. The members of the Collège are more willing for a number of reasons to allow these two realms to freely intermingle.

This difference perhaps explains some of the clear distinctions in the projects of the Collège and those of Hertz and Mauss while attesting at the same time to the parallel dilemmas they faced and the reasons they could use the same Durkheimian body of thought as a tool in facing them. The Collège coupled a Durkheimian recognition of the place of the sacred in collective life and in the perpetual renewal of the community through collective effervescence in ritualistic ecstasy with a Nietzschean tweaking of the entire edifice so as, with the aid of the injection of the will to power and the radical revaluation of moral structures, to turn the ritualistic idea of the sacred into a celebration of the transgressive moment *per se*.

From the Collège to Poststructuralism:
Passing through Structuralism

Forgotten by institutionally-centered intellectual history and, until relatively recently, all but unknown to the history of the social sciences in France, the Collège was nonetheless a significant presence in Parisian intellectual circles of the 1930s. Along with the three central members, participants in the group included Pierre Klossowski, Anatole Lewitsky (another ethnologist and student of Mauss), Jules Monnerot, Jean Wahl, Jean Paulhan, and Denis de Rougemont, while Kojève, Jean-Paul Sartre, Claude Lévi-Strauss, Julien Benda, Pierre Drieu la Rochelle, and Walter Benjamin all attended at one time or another, though more infrequently (Bataille 1985: xxi; Fournier 1994: 707). The group was very short-lived. The disintegration came in July 1939 when it became apparent that there was significant disagreement among the founding members as to the goals and methods of the group. Bataille had perhaps inadvertently prepared the way for the public surfacing of theretofore implicit differences by suggesting that the final scheduled meeting of the group during the 1939 academic year be dedicated precisely to the Collège and "its definition, its goals, its methods" and that each of the three of them speak on the subject (Bataille 1987: 103). His paper on "The practice of joy before death," which he delivered at the 6 June 1939 meeting, expressed something of the coming death-yearning that would soon engulf the entirety of Europe, and it was the formal mechanism revealing the schism in the group. Bataille addressed the difficulties Caillois and Leiris had reconciling the position he took in that paper and their own in the final meeting. Significantly, neither Caillois nor Leiris were in attendance. Caillois had left on a trip to Buenos Aires intended to last a few months; as it turned out, he remained in Argentina for the entirety of the war. Leiris announced in a letter to Bataille dated the day before the final meeting his discomfort with what was in his view an increasingly unrigorous use of sociological concepts by the group and its increasing tendency to solidify itself into a kind of literary clique rather than the open-ended "moral community that would represent something radically distinct from the usual scholarly associations" (Bataille 1987: 148). Caillois's criticisms of Bataille's position were similar. These had to do with the "the attention [Bataille] gave to mysticism, drama, madness, death," which seemed inconsistent with the more festive, orgiastic version of the sacred he saw at the root of the Collège's activities (Hollier 1979: 526).

It is easy to over-emphasize the role these differences played in the disappearance of the Collège and to thereby make too much of what was in fact not a radical difference of opinion amongst the three founders on the question of the sacred. Leiris's letter to Bataille, though critical, was also explicit in presuming the Collège, or some other version of "our movement" would continue to exist (Bataille 1987: 150), and Caillois made efforts during his extended stay in Buenos Aires to organize an Argentinian branch of the Collège (Felgine 1994: 204). The plain fact is that the outbreak of the war and the disruption of intellectual life generally in France had much to do with the dissolution. Whatever the precise reasons, the Collège did indeed disband. However, its intriguing brand of mystic Durkheimianism was passed on to a later generation of intellectuals through a rather complex set of lines of influence.

Mauss's legacy in the years following his death in 1950 is extremely complicated and often seemingly contradictory. He was appropriated by a wide range of thinkers in philosophy and the human sciences. These included phenomenologists such as Maurice Merleau-Ponty, a variety of the founding thinkers in French structuralism (Dosse 1991), and sociologists with theoretical agendas as different as Pierre Bourdieu and Georges Gurvitch (Lévi-Strauss and Eribon 1991[1988]: 70). Of these, though, it seems clear at first glance that the structuralists had the clearest case. At an explicit level of influence, several of the most important structuralists were profoundly affected in their intellectual orientations by the work of Mauss and Hertz. Lévi-Strauss, who took his *agrégation* in philosophy but quickly moved afterward toward ethnology, readily admitted his debt to Mauss and he argued fervently for an interpretation of his life-work as proto-structuralist. He noted that Mauss himself had presaged Lévi-Strauss's structuralist approach in the early essay on magic ("The unity of the whole is yet more real than each of its parts" (Mauss 1950: xxxviii)), despite the fact that he did not fully adhere to this principle in the work. Lévi-Strauss had not worked with Mauss as a student, but with his student Marcel Griaule and his *Année* colleague Georges Davy; however, by virtue of his famous introduction to Mauss's œuvre and his rising star on the academic scene during the 1950s and 1960s, his reading of Mauss became a source from which many others began. A. J. Greimas cited Lévi-Strauss's introduction to Mauss as one of the key texts in his own realization of the centrality for modern thought of "the meeting of linguistics and anthropology" (Dosse 1991: 42–43). Another *père fondateur* of structuralism, Georges Dumézil, had a direct connection to Mauss at the École Pratique, which I have previously discussed in some of its details. He spoke of Mauss's "taste for universality" as a profound influence on the need he felt in his own intellectual life to refuse intellectual borders and disciplines (Dumézil 1987: 49–50).

We should recall too that structuralism was tied to the literary avant-garde in ways not completely unlike the relationship of the Collège de Sociologie to surrealism. Lévi-Strauss met André Masson, Max Ernst, André Breton, Marcel Duchamp, Yves Tanguy, and other key members of the surrealist movement while in exile in New York during World War II and admired their art, explicitly acknowledging its influence on his own work through the surrealist interest in the structures of the unconscious (Lévi-Strauss and Eribon 1991[1988]: 31–35). Though he was often at pains to stress the scientificity of his work, many critics pointed to the literary quality of many of his writings, from *Tristes Tropiques*, which took up many of the same questions of reflexivity and self-knowledge of the ethnographer found in Leiris's field journal from the Dakar-Djibouti expedition, to his *chef-d'œuvre* on myth, *Mythologiques*. Much of the remainder of structuralism was explicitly tied to literary and artistic movements and reviews of the 1950s, 1960s and 1970s, from the writers of the *nouveau roman* movement (Alain Robbe-Grillet, Nathalie Sarraute) to the *Tel Quel* group (Philippe Sollers, Jean-Pierre Faye, Julia Kristeva, et al. (Dosse 1992: 235–42).

Yet, despite these seeming points of connection between the intellectual movement of structuralism and the Collège de Sociologie, there were substantial differences in the general understanding of intellectual work and identity and their relation to the sacred that make it impossible to understand the bulk of structuralism as an heir to mystic Durkheimianism. The structuralist incorporation of Durkheimian thought failed to follow fully the framework for the intellectual project sketched by the mystic Durkheimians. We can more properly think of their place in the lineage as *strategic* allies with Mauss and the extra-institutional Durkheimian tradition but much more broadly in line intellectually and politically with Durkheim and the ascetic line of Durkheimianism.

Reading the Structuralism/Poststructuralism Difference in Light of the Ascetic/Mystic Durkheimian Split

In some ways, the split between structuralism and poststructuralism can be understood as the same kind of family division between ascetic and mystic Durkheimians. As in the latter case, where the distinctions became most apparent in light of their reactions to certain crucial dilemmas of the identity of the intellectual of their era (e.g., the Dreyfus Affair, the War, the debates over secular morality), the divisions within structuralism that contributed to the emergence of poststructuralism were likewise linked to powerful contemporary crises of their own concerning the intellectual's identity, specifically the collapse of the model of the Communist engaged intellectual and the events of May 1968 in France. As noted in Chapter 5, we should understand the thing "structuralism" as in fact consisting of a number of related but non-identical intellectual approaches characterized by different understandings of the role of the intellectual. In Pavel's (1992) terms, moderate and scientistic structuralism have much in common with ascetic Durkheimianism, while it is speculative structuralism that gives birth to poststructuralism and upon which we should focus our attention in the construction of the genealogy of mystic Durkheimianism. In response to the crisis within structuralism that was revealed to some degree by the May 1968 events, a crisis not unlike that produced in the inter-war period by the collapse of the Popular Front (and which helped spawn the Collège de Sociologie), some descendants of Besnier's "intellectuel pathétique" again cast about for radical responses to the crisis that would enable a more holistic perspective on the compartmentalization of scientific endeavor, on the one hand, and personal experience of meaning and the sacred, on the other. If Marxism and structuralism disallowed such a holism, then another path needed to be constructed. Not coincidentally, one of the richest French sources to look to for such an effort was the mystic Durkheimian stream.

In the last several decades, some scholarly work has begun to point to a way of reading central strands in poststructuralist thought as the intellectual product of a combination of Nietzschean philosophy and Durkheimian sociology (e.g., Gane 1991a, 1991b, and 1992; Heimonet 1987; Hollier 1979; Alexander 1988). This work often alludes to the historical link in influence leading from Mauss through the members of the Collège, who were in turn read and appropriated by poststructuralist thinkers of the 1960s and 1970s. But again, as is the case with much discussion of the Collège's Durkheimianism, no distinction is made in that work among different varieties of Durkheimianism, and there is no attempt to sociologically sketch the particulars of intellectual influence and the passing along of intellectual *habitus*. In previous chapters, I have framed the macro-social fields, intellectual institutions, and local micro-networks in which poststructuralism emerged. In the next two chapters, I describe in more detail how the poststructuralists pursued a fundamentally mystic Durkheimian practice politically and intellectually. Before advancing there, however, let us look at one central institutional space where we can empirically observe the continuity from the mystic contingent of the Durkheimian religion group through the Collège and into poststructuralism.

Critique as Interaction Ritual Site for the Transmission of Mystic Durkheimianism

The journal *Critique,* which was founded by Bataille in 1946, occupied a unique place in the French intellectual landscape of the post-war period. Its "ethos" has been neatly summarized by one writer as

> a general propensity to question norms and concepts of normality. This characteristic is one of the review's two main poles, the one which leads it to explore everything new, different, and forbidden, and to approach and investigate all things magical, sacred, primitive, exotic, esoteric, unconscious, erotic, insane, and violent as openings to a "different" reality which by its very existence challenges the reasoning, values, and order that Western society has established. (Boschetti 1988[1985]:163)

During the early post-World War II period, all of the major figures in the Collège de Sociologie, with the exception of Caillois[4] (and including Pierre Klossowski and Maurice Blanchot, who also had significant personal relationships with a number of the members of our poststructuralist micro-society), were closely affiliated with the journal, Bataille and Leiris exceptionally so. Beyond them, the review benefited from the close participation of a number of other iconoclastic intellectual radicals of the era, including the "Socratic bonhomme" Eric Weil (who was co-editor with Bataille), Alexandre Kojève, and numerous others associated with the École Pratique des Hautes Études (Chaubet 2005: 159).

Anna Boschetti suggests that, during the post-war period, journals that "combine[d] literary and philosophical excellence, freedom and commitment, close reasoning and the capacity to think about everything" became dominant and journals committed either to a too-narrow intellectual or literary specialization (e.g., *Fontaine*, *Messages*) or a dogmatic orthodox political commitment (e.g., *La Nouvelle Critique*, *La Table ronde*) suffered as a result of this competition (Boschetti 1988[1985]: 144–45). Sartre's journal *Les Temps Modernes* was the big winner in this competition, but Bataille's *Critique* was an important competitor both to Sartre's journal and to his mode of intellectual engagement. For, although Boschetti classifies *Critique* as a "noncommitted review" (1988[1985]: 147), and despite Bataille's own statements to this effect,[5] there clearly is a concern for political selfhood in *Critique*. It is however a politics informed by an attention to what Boschetti unsympathetically calls "Bataille's strange, tormented quest [for] a desperate, unreasoning religion which does not meet the demand for a rationalization of reality characteristic of the demand for prophecy" (Boschetti 1988[1985]: 166). It is worth noting here that Leiris, who was closely tied to Sartre and *Les Temps Modernes* from 1945 to 1951 while at the same time intimately involved with *Critique,* put the matter rather differently in a letter to Bataille during this period: "What distinguishes Sartre from us is that he is essentially rationalist. He is a philosopher and not a poet. For me, a large part of the question finds itself expressed there" (Patron 1999: 75).

Clearly, Boschetti is correct in noting that *Les Temps Modernes* is the dominant journal of the period, and Sartre's notion of engagement is the dominant way of conceiving an intellectual's selfhood in the political world, but her overall reading of *Critique's* supposedly noncommitted status fails to reckon with some of the facts she presents. She points out, for example, that *Critique* and *Les Temps Modernes* exchanged contributors more regularly than almost any other two major reviews of the period and says this seems to indicate that "*Critique* [was] the only acceptable place during these years, besides *Les Temps Modernes,* for 'free' intellectuals" (Boschetti 1988[1985]: 148, 151). She also notes that the transgressive position of *Critique*, though dominated by *Les Temps Modernes* in the 1940s and 1950s, would give birth to the similar integration of the two poles of literary and social scientific avant-gardes represented by *Tel Quel*, which would in many ways begin to displace Sartre's journal and his form of intellectual engagement in the 1960s (Boschetti 1988[1985]: 165). Even a figure like Pierre Bourdieu, hardly an intellectual ally of Bataille and company, noted that *Critique,* "in providing access to an international and interdisciplinary culture, permitted an escape from the effect of enclosure exerted by all elite schools" and therefore allowed a mode of approaching relevant intellectual problems outside of the dominant, i.e., Sartrian mode (Bourdieu 2004: 24). The journal was a meeting ground for intellectual currents in psychoanalysis, anthropology and sociology, linguistics, philosophy, and literature (Rieffel 1993: 385). It also effused an anti-institutional energy. Even though many of the contributors were university professors and researchers, they were often working at the interstices of traditional disciplinary and university discourses, and Jean Piel is certainly correct to note the importance of the simple fact that "[t]he journal was created by Georges Bataille, who was not a professor, and neither am I" (Patron 1999: 102; Rieffel 1993: 378). But the central point we should retain here is that *Critique* clearly represents not just a vague, symbolic point of connection between mystic Durkheimian thought and poststructuralism but *an actual sociological meeting ground for the two.* It is a site in which the kinds of embodied intellectual interaction rituals Randall Collins discusses took place between men who had been present at Mauss's seminars and men who would become the representative face of French poststructuralism in the 1960s and 1970s.

   To see how this worked, I need to sketch in a bit more fully the history of *Critique.* The connection to the Durkheimianism of the Collège de Sociologie was apparent from the first issue, in which Bataille published a piece titled "Le sens morale de la sociologie" (Patron 1999: 5). His successor as editor also evinced a "preference ... for the 'sources' of sociologie, Emile Durkheim, Marcel Mauss, Gabriel Tarde, rather than for the prominent figures in the discipline ... [such as] Pierre Bourdieu" (Patron 1999: 89). Three of the four members of the poststructuralist micro-society (Foucault, Derrida, and Deleuze) had very deep affiliations to the journal throughout the 1960s and into the 1970s, as did one of the key masters of ceremonies of the group discussed in Chapter 6 (Barthes). It is not too much to talk of the *Critique* editorial board as based in a deeply familial set of relations, as the editor after Bataille's death in 1962 was his brother-in-law, Jean Piel. Piel had initially met Bataille through a series of friends of friends; he knew Jacques Prévert, who introduced him to Raymond Queneau and Robert Desnos, who knew Michel Leiris and Bataille (Rieffel 1993: 377). It was Piel who published an article by Roland Barthes in 1954, paving the way for the explicit association of *Critique* with structuralist and poststructuralist thinkers and ideas. Barthes later wrote a scintillating review of Foucault's *Histoire de la folie* for the journal in 1961, an act for which Foucault was exceptionally grateful given his sense at that time of the generally negative reception of the book (Eribon 1994: 215).

By the year after Bataille's death, in 1963, both Foucault (who had been a regular contributor to the journal since 1962) and Barthes were on the editorial board of the journal, and Derrida (who had contributed material to the journal since 1963) joined them in 1967. Deleuze, who published his first of a number of articles in *Critique* in 1967, also established a close relationship to the journal and its editorial board (Patron 1999; Rieffel 1993: 378). Piel wrote in his autobiography of the personal relationships of the editorial committee in terms we should note: "The first editorial board [i.e., Piel, Barthes, Foucault, and Michel Déguy] ... gathered from time to time for friendly and informal meetings in the cluttered office of the one Foucault called, not without irony, the 'boss'" (Piel 1982: 291). In the correspondence Piel exchanged with Foucault, Derrida and Deleuze, one sees still more intimately the close relationships that characterized the interaction site that was *Critique*. All three poststructuralists regularly include greetings to Madame Piel in their letters, a clear indication of something more than mere professional relationships in the still formal intellectual France of the early 1960s, and they make frequent mention of dinners at one or another's home. Personal matters are discussed in the letters right along with editorial matters. Deleuze, for example, speaks to Piel in frank terms about the pulmonary illness that began to seriously plague him in 1968, describes his vacations, discusses other intimate family events, and invites Piel to cocktail parties.[6] The overall sense that emerges from the correspondence is of a close-knit group working in frequent face-to-face interaction on a collective intellectual project not unlike the religion group of the *Année sociologique*. It is an "intellectual clan" (Rieffel 1993: 380) that we see at work here.

Notes

1. The quotation marks within the excerpt mark where Heilbron is quoting from remarks he gathered in interviews with Mauss's students.
2. It seems that Bataille, unlike Leiris and Caillois, did not actually attend Mauss's courses, though he distinguishes the supposed increased attention to the importance of transgression in Mauss's "oral teaching" as opposed to in his written work (Bataille 1986[1957]: 65).
3. Unpublished letter from Marcel Mauss to Roger Caillois, 22 June 1938, FHM.
4. Caillois, who created his own journal *Diogène* in returning from Argentina after the war, regretted that Bataille seemed only to want to publish "textes critiques" in his new journal, while Caillois wanted to also publish "textes originaux" (Patron 1999: 52). The two nonetheless remained friendly.

5. In a letter to Maurice Nadeau, Bataille wrote, "*Critique* is not a journal of the left. It is not a political journal" (Patron 1999: 58).

6. E.g., in a letter dated 24 August 1968, he mentions an ear operation undergone by his wife and discusses in numerous letters his treatment at a clinic in Lyon and then at the Salpetrière in Paris in the fall and winter of 1968 (unpublished correspondence, Fonds *Critique*, IMEC).

11   Being a Poststructuralist Intellectual

One of the central ideas that emerged from the discussion of the development of the personal identities of the Durkheimians (in Chapter 7) has to do with what might be called their minoritarian *habitus*. The Jewishness of Durkheim, Mauss, and Hertz is the most obvious element here. A related fact had to do with the manner in which the mystic Durkheimians Hertz and Mauss pursued a particular kind of transfigured political project that was fundamentally tied to their minoritarian identities. In this chapter, I will explore the ways in which the poststructuralist group is similarly operating from minoritarian positions, if not the same ones and if somewhat less monolithically than the Durkheimian group, and pursuing transfigured political projects of their own. Specific biographical and social facts in the construction of each of their *habitus* indicate the assembly of an identity that is excluded or Othered in some important way, and this identity is important for understanding why they used certain intellectual tools and conceptual categories to define themselves as intellectuals.

Let us recall the methodological point touched on in Chapter 2. In the investigation of the identities and early formation of the Durkheimians, correspondences were a central and abundant source of data. Unfortunately, for most of the poststructuralists, this resource is (as of yet, at least) largely unavailable to researchers. Foucault's correspondence is still held by his partner Daniel Defert and has not been made accessible to the broad research community. Derrida's extensive correspondence at the IMEC in Caen was, at the time of this writing, still being inventoried and therefore could not be consulted (Dichy and Fathy 2004). If a Deleuze correspondence exists, it is not clear where it is located; he apparently destroyed many of his manuscripts just before his suicide and it is likely that any other papers he might have kept are in the possession of his family, who have to date not been forthcoming with requests to make that information available to researchers. In the case of Baudrillard, we find a similar situation; there may be material but it has not been made available to the public at this writing. Similarly, the fact that the three most recently deceased poststructuralists died relatively recently (Deleuze in 1995; Derrida in 2004; and Baudrillard in 2007) has meant that detailed biographical works have yet to be completed for several of them. As this book was being written, a biography of Deleuze appeared (Dosse 2007), but there is still no good source on Baudrillard, and the lone biography of Derrida (Powell 2006) largely restrains itself to textual commentary and provides very few details about his life that are not already widely known. For these reasons, I rely heavily in this chapter on interviews in which the poststructuralists spoke of their own biographies.

Derrida: Algerian/Jewish/French Philosopher

Derrida occupies a unique position as the only Jew in the poststructuralist micro-group. His position is also unique in that he is the only one who has publicly and continually reflected explicitly on the question of religious identity, both with respect to his own sense of self and in more general terms. There has been significant discussion among scholarly commentators of Derrida's Jewishness in connection with his intellectual trajectory (see e.g., Caputo 1997; Ofrat 2001). It is clear that this connection must be something other than explicitly in terms of Jewish religious faith, as it is nowhere evident that Derrida is anything other than a non-practicing Jew (Caputo 1997: xvii).

Yet, just as with Durkheim, Mauss, and Hertz, leaving the discussion there without further exploration would be wrong-headed. The sociological situation of Derrida's identity-in-formation requires attention to the actual details of his social history, and those details make for an intriguing narrative. He was born in the Jewish quarter of El Biar in Algeria in 1930 and spent the first nineteen years of his life there, arriving in mainland France only in 1949. His middle name is Elie (a form of Elijah), and his father and his two Algerian grandfathers bore significant Jewish names (respectively, Haim-Aimé, Moïse and Abraham) (Ofrat 2001: 19; Derrida and Malabou 1999: 85). His original first name, Jackie, which he changed when he entered the academic world in Paris, also carries with it a very specific relationship to the Jewish community in Algeria; during the period in which Derrida was born, Algerian Jews had something of an affinity for giving newborns the names of American film stars, such as Jackie Coogan (Derrida 1995b: 344).

The cultural climate in which he spent the early years of his life was laden with information about what it meant to be Jewish, what it meant to be French, and what it meant to be both at once. Algerian Jews (Sephardim from Spain and Portugal) had suffered immensely under pre-French Islamic feudalism in Algeria. They were forced to wear clothing that marked their religion and forbidden to marry Muslim women or compete with Muslim men. There was therefore much joy among Algerian Jews when the French took Algeria in 1830 in the hope that the legacy of the Revolution would extend to them as well (Elizabeth Weber 2004: 1, 13–14). Yet, during the period of the Dreyfus Affair, there were numerous anti-Jewish pogroms in Algerian cities carried out by French colonials and the period of Derrida's youth was marked by the expulsion of Algerian Jews from state schools and institutions (Elizabeth Weber 2004: 15). Derrida directly experienced this and recalled it numerous times in interviews and other published work in the most harrowing terms. In 1942, he was, along with all other Jewish students, expelled from the *lycée* Ben Aknoun and forced to the Jewish *lycée* Maïmonide (Derrida and Roudinesco 2001: 179–82). It was a crushing, life-shaping experience for him (Derrida and Malabou 1999: 87–88). His sense was clear that the perpetrators of this and other anti-Semitic acts in Algeria were not the Nazis, but *the French themselves* (Elizabeth Weber 2004: 55–56). The full guilt could only fall on the French, whatever the efforts after the war to blame Nazism, for there had been no Germans in Algeria to enact the new "biracial" regime (Derrida and Malabou 1999: 88–89).

The difficulty Derrida experienced later in life fully culturally identifying himself as French as an extension of this early experience is clear in comments he made on his relationship to the French language. He felt "lost outside of French ... other languages, those that I more or less awkwardly read, decipher, sometimes speak, these are languages I will never inhabit." Yet, at the same time, he says, he has "never been able to call French ... my maternal language" (Derrida and Malabou 1999: 89–90). He was forever between categories, neither fully French nor fully something else that could be opposed to French, a native French speaker and writer nonetheless forever removed from the comfortable, natural relationship to the language experienced by those who have never had to face their excluded status as clearly as he did in 1942.

So Derrida was in some complex way both French and not-French; he was also both Algerian and not-Algerian. If Vichy was essential in determining the way Derrida would "inhabit" Frenchness, the Algerian war played a similar role in determining the shape of his relationship to the place of

his birth. For the first two decades of his life, he never left the Jewish sub-
urb of Algiers where he was born, not even to take the train elsewhere in
Algeria (Derrida and Malabou 1999: 41). The familial residence there, on
rue Saint-Augustin, is invoked lovingly by him as the place where he, his
older brother René and a younger brother who died in infancy the year
before Derrida, as well as a younger brother who died in 1940 at age two
from tubercular meningitis, were born and raised (Derrida and Malabou
1999: 79; Noiriel 2005: 291). He played on the street's name as a way of
invoking his sense of identification with the Christian philosopher and
saint who was also born in North Africa. Even after leaving El-Biar for the
French mainland in 1949, he returned frequently during vacations and
fulfilled his military service there, in the midst of the war, as a teacher of
French and English to French Algerian students between 1957 and 1959
(Mallet and Michaud 2004: 602). As the war intensified, Derrida's family
contemplated what seemed the inevitable: leaving Algeria. Initially, Derrida tried to convince them to stay, an indication of his attachment to
his place of birth and, given the facts of Muslim anti-Semitism in Algeria
(Elizabeth Weber 2004: 15) and the massive Algerian Jewish exodus in
the years just prior to the conclusion of the war in 1962, a remarkably
strong one. He suffered a serious period of depression toward the end
of the 1959–60 academic year, undoubtedly related to some insecurities
regarding his search for an academic post[1] but also very likely rooted in
the strain of the approach of this inevitability (Mallet and Michaud 2004:
602). By 1962, however, he was resigned and returned to Algeria to help
move his family to Nice, not subsequently returning to his country of
birth for nearly ten years. Something of the complexity of this agonized
post-Algerian war *pied noir* identity can be seen in Derrida's comments
about his Algerian accent:

> I believe I have not ... completely lost everything of my 'French Alge-
> rian' accent. The intonation of it is more apparent in certain 'prag-
> matic' situations (anger or exclamation in the midst of family, more
> often in private than in public) ... But ... I do not believe ... one can
> detect it in reading, unless I declare myself that I am 'French Algerian'
> ... accents, whatever accent it might be, and above all a strong southern
> accent, seem incompatible to me with the intellectual dignity of public
> speech. (Inadmissible, is it not? I admit it). Incompatible *a fortiori* with
> the calling of poetic speech ... hearing René Char, for example, read
> his own sententious aphorisms with an accent that seemed to me at
> once comical and obscene, the betrayal of a truth, that did much to
> ruin a youthful admiration. (Derrida and Malabou 1999: 90)

Finally, and most centrally, he was both Jewish and non-Jewish. Derrida had much of an explicit nature to say about his relationship to Juda-

ism during his life and much of what he had to say on that theme indicates the same kind of complexity of identity and non-identity that we have seen in his relationship to France and Algeria. The central figure dominating his discussion of his relationship to Judaism is circumcision. He described it as a kind of writing on the body that indicates the individual's membership in a community, an inescapable signifier that places the subject into a discourse that is not his own, whether he likes it or not (1995 [1992]: 341). His own circumcised penis, which he paralleled to the literal name that marked him with the same trace, i.e., his Jewish name Elie, signified his membership in a particular historical, ethnic, religious community in a certain manner, whatever the facts of his actual practice and belief in the tenets of Judaism. The repeated experience of seeing his father's abject submission before his Catholic employers also made apparent an evident distinction between the two identities and communities (Derrida and Malabou 1999: 35, 39). But he also discussed his inability, from early in life, to fully and willingly inhabit that neatly defined identity. He is both Jewish (as a circumcised member of this historical community bearing its literal traces on his body and life experience) and non-Jewish (as someone who does not actively embrace the explicit religious beliefs and practices of any Jewish group). But he complicates the matter yet more in discussing the fact that the Jewishness of his heritage was already something "contaminated" and impure. Though those in the El-Biar Jewish community where he lived as a youth used the term "catholic" in an uncomplicated way to refer to all non-Jewish French, the Judaism they practiced was "contaminat[ed]" by the practices and belief structures of the Christian majority among whom they lived: "We imitated the churches, the rabbis wore black cassocks, and the verger a Napoleonic cocked hat; the bar mitzvah was called 'communion' and circumcision 'baptism'" (Derrida and Malabou 1999: 84). He frequently made self-referential use of the term "*marrane*," which comes from the Spanish "*marrano*" (pig) and traditionally refers in a pejorative manner (the prohibition on pork is the allusion) to a European Jew who outwardly pretends to be a convert to Christianity in order to pass in Christian society but inwardly maintains Jewish faith, in his own reformulated manner. He is "one of these *marranes* who do not call themselves Jewish even in the secret of their hearts … because they doubt everything" (Derrida and Malabou 1999: 93).

The figure of the circumcision became for Derrida something that illuminates more than just the opposition of Jewish and non-Jewish identity. It is an example, perhaps the most profound example to be found in the history of the West, of the excluded Other that makes possible the entire philosophical and political edifice of Western society (Elizabeth Weber 2004: 48). In this sense, then, circumcision not only centrally informs his own identity; it becomes the foundational theme in his life's work: "Circumcision, that's all I've ever talked about, consider the discourse on the limit, margins, marks, marches, etc., the closure, the ring (alliance and gift), the sacrifice, the writing of the body, the *pharmakos* excluded or cut off" (Elizabeth Weber 2004: 39). The circumcised Jew becomes in Derrida's philosophical language a way of talking about the failure of all efforts to achieve pure identity owing to the inevitable exclusions necessary in such efforts (Elizabeth Weber 2004: 40–42).

In interviews in the last years of his life, Derrida spoke in still more fascinating terms of his religious identity. He acknowledged that he prayed, although prayer characterized by a "suspension of certainty ... of any expectation, any economy, any calculation" and a profound sense of "hopelessness" (Caputo, Hart, and Sherwood 2005: 31). He also addressed the complex question of whether he should be considered an atheist by arguing that neither of the terms "atheist" or "believer" adequately account for his (or anyone else's) status: "Who can say, 'I am a believer?' Who *knows* that? ... And who can say 'I am an atheist'?" (Caputo, Hart, and Sherwood 2005: 46-47).

Foucault: The Worry-Desire

A good deal of commentary on Foucault has taken his homosexuality as a central fact in understanding his personal and intellectual trajectories (e.g., Halperin 1995; Eribon 1994). Details on the early sexual experience of Foucault are hard to come by (Macey 1993: xxiii), but his own statement was that he felt sexually attracted to boys and men (an attraction he described tellingly as a "worry-desire") from as far back as he could remember. It is undoubtedly of note that Foucault was in his teen years precisely during the period of the Vichy government, since homosexuality, already taboo in respectable French society, became an object of utter horror under this regime "obsessed ... with the defense of the values of the patriarchal family" (Macey 1993: 7, 15). It is also likely that the Catholic Church's position on sexuality contributed to Foucault's alienation. His upbringing was Catholic and he took first communion and was a choirboy for some time (Macey 1993: 4). We do not know how or precisely when he left the faith. His family seems to have managed a co-existence between the basic religious observance required by bourgeois standing and a streak of anti-clericalism (Eribon 1989: 21). Foucault would seem to have drifted away from his religion fairly early; yet at the end of his life, it was discovered that he had been donating significant amounts of money to the members of the Dominican Order who ran the Bibliothèque du Saulchoir where he had frequently worked (Macey 1993: xiv).

Owing to the dual repression of Vichy and a small rural hometown (where any secrets would have been hard to keep), Foucault's first sexual experience seems not to have taken place until he was around twenty, when he left Poitiers for Paris and the École Normale (Macey 1993: 14–15). But though Paris was likely a more receptive place for his sexual orientation, it was still far from utopian in that regard. He apparently attempted suicide twice (in 1948 and again in 1950) during his time at the École Normale, and, though one can imagine the pressures involved in his study were a significant part of the reason for his depression, it is not at all unlikely that his worry-desire played a role too. ENS friends recounted episodes wherein Foucault would disappear from the school for days at a time, then return physically and emotionally worn out, implying that he had been out seeking the random and lonely sexual encounter that was virtually the only kind permitted homosexuals in proper French society during the 1950s (Macey 1993: 28).

The minoritarian, even stigmatized status of the homosexual in French society was considerable throughout Foucault's lifetime. We know of at least one specific incident of Foucault suffering personal and professional setback as a direct result of his sexuality. Toward the end of 1958, he left a position his friend Georges Dumézil had obtained for him in Sweden for Poland, where he was charged with the reopening of the Center for French Civilization in Warsaw, but the Polish authorities expelled him from the country in 1959, citing his suspicious activities in addition to the subversive nature of his work. Those activities had been revealed by an agent of the Polish police acting in a sting setup intended to round up men engaging in deviant sexual activity (Eribon 1994: 124). Louis Althusser apparently believed that Foucault's central reason for leaving the PCF had to do with the party's stance on homosexuality (Eribon 1994: 59). Even at Foucault's death in 1984, the stigma of homosexuality was revealed by the fact that even some of those inclined to be friendly to Foucault made equations of the manner of his death with shamefulness. The left newspaper *Libération* printed a story at his death denying that AIDS had been the cause, fearful that such a death somehow tainted the philosopher and his political commitments (Eribon 1989: 350–51).

One cannot write of the part of Foucault's identity that touches on his homosexuality without discussing his relationship with Georges Dumézil. The great philologist and historian of myth, and former student of Mauss,[2] must be treated here as one of Foucault's masters of ceremonies, and only in part because of the effect his work had on Foucault's intellectual perspective. Undoubtedly of more central importance was the way in which Dumézil represented for Foucault a way of being a homosexual in the upper echelon of the Parisian academic world of the mid twentieth century. Dumézil apparently first became aware of Foucault when a common acquaintance (and Foucault's former lover) alerted him to the existence of this emerging intellectual figure, who also happened to be gay, and who was seeking an initial position somewhere. Dumézil immediately wrote Foucault about a lectureship in French at the University of Uppsala in Sweden, a society even in the mid 1950s characterized by relative freedom for those judged intolerably sexually deviant in France (Eribon 1994: 110, 116). From this moment until Foucault's death in 1984 (when Dumézil wrote a striking eulogy for the *Nouvel Observateur*), the two were bonded together in a steadfast friendship. Eribon characterized it as "a nearly Romantic friendship ... of the consecrated scholar and the young philosopher" (Eribon 1994: 119), framed in the context of a larger "masculine brotherhood" surrounding Dumézil. Though they were never intimately involved, Dumézil acknowledged that their mutual homosexuality had been an inevitable element in their relationship (Eribon 1994: 125). Their seeming political differences (Dumézil was long rumored to have been politically on the right, even after thoroughly repudiating his youthful flirtation with fascism in the 1930s) never prevented them from being always in agreement on everything important (Eribon 1994: 129). Dumézil was also apparently one of the few among Foucault's friends who knew he had contracted HIV (Eribon 1989: 348).

Foucault's long-term relationship with Daniel Defert also must be mentioned. The two met while Daniel Defert was a student at the École Normale de Saint-Cloud in October 1960 (Foucault 2001a: 29). By 1963, the two men had begun living together and remained in a committed, if non-monogamous relationship that lasted until Foucault's death. The relationship was an intense one, by all accounts, and affected Foucault in many ways. Eribon has even suggested, based mostly on the account of Foucault's associate Maurice Pinguet, that his turn in the late '60s to radical populist activism was mostly a mimetic effect of Defert's radicalism rather than anything in Foucault's own intellectual project. Pinguet described this period in Foucault's life as "homosexuality lived politically ... amorous heroism lived together ... a kind of politico-heroic engagement on the foundation of romantic passion" (Eribon 1994: 206). It is an intriguing thesis that ultimately fails to account for the continuities in Foucault's scholarly program and its connection to his construction of an identity as intellectual.

Much has been speculated about Foucault's engagement in the homosexual bathhouse and sado-masochistic scenes in San Francisco and elsewhere (see e.g., J. Miller 1993). Our actual knowledge is not quite up to the intensity of the speculation. We know that he gave an interview with *The Advocate* during one of his visits in the 1980s to Berkeley in which he talked of the need to "create a gay mode of life," which apparently involved something of an embrace of the sado-masochistic "possibility of using our bodies as a possible source of numerous pleasures." He also noted that certain drugs might be of use in creating such possibilities for pleasure (Eribon 1989: 337). He certainly enjoyed Northern California life sufficiently to seriously consider leaving his post at the Collège de France in order to take up an offer from the University of California at Berkeley (Foucault 2001a: 84). In 1990, Hervé Guibert, a young gay novelist who became a close friend of Foucault late in the latter's life (and who himself died of AIDS in 1991), created something of a scandal in describing Foucault in his *À l'ami qui ne m'a pas sauvé la vie* in the guise of a character named "Professor Muzil," as a man leading a double life: by day, mild-mannered professor at the Collège de France; by night, violent and unbalanced pursuer of the most transgressive sexual pleasures imaginable in the leather bars and gay saunas hidden in the darkest corners of town.

Baudrillard: Peasant Postmodernist

Baudrillard has been something of an outlier in this study from the beginning. This is never more obvious than in the many accounts by Derrida, Foucault, and Deleuze in which they spoke of those in their generation of post-1968 thinkers with similar concerns, and named one another and a few others (Lyotard, for example) but systematically failed to mention Baudrillard. One thinks of Foucault's infamous retort to Baudrillard's *Forget Foucault* that he didn't even know who Baudrillard was.[3] However rhetorical, the response says something powerful about the respective institutional trajectories of the two, and of Baudrillard in comparison to the three other poststructuralists. Baudrillard was, in his own words, "never of the seraglio" (Baudrillard 2004: 1). Born in Reims in the year of the massive American stock market crash that brought on the greatest crisis in global capitalism of the twentieth century (Baudrillard 1990 [1987]: 144), into "a family plainly in transition from peasant farming to urban life" (Baudrillard 1993c: 1), he was neither a *normalien* nor an *agrégé*. He studied at the *lycée* of Reims until 1947, when he went off to Paris for a year of *hypokhâgne* at the *lycée* Henri-IV in Paris.

His trajectory at this point was quite similar to those of Foucault and Derrida, but somewhere along the line something significant happened and moved him elsewhere. He unexpectedly abandoned his efforts to enter the École Normale, a terrifically important biographical point about which we know almost nothing (Gane 2000: 8). He wound up returning to the Sorbonne, where he wrote a *mémoire d'études supérieures* on Nietzsche and Luther. He then took and failed the *agrégation* in German; in his account, the failure had much to do with the fact that he took the occasion of the examination to present a reading of Nietzsche (on whom he was tested in both oral and written exams) that was too unconventional for the examiners (Baudrillard 2004: 1). Blocked then from any real entrée into the French world of university positions, he taught briefly in Germany and, beginning in 1960, taught German in various Parisian and provincial lycées. Throughout his life, his institutional trajectory and influence, at least in France, remained considerably removed from that of Foucault, Deleuze, and Derrida, all of whom enjoyed much greater reputations and institutional affiliations. Even when given a chance, in the mid 1970s, at a university career in the United States, in a "revealing moment," he declined, citing a desire to "remain irresponsible" (Baudrillard 1997: 130). His way of framing his relationship to the established post-1968 French intellectual circles, among which we should count the other three poststructuralists, consistently reflected his outsider status; though he was "very friendly with Lyotard, Guattari, all of them," he was nonetheless by virtue of his educational attainment and the class habitus that had perhaps had some significant effect on it "always a little on the margins of that 'elite'" (Baudrillard 2005: 37).

Deleuze: The Sick Nomad

Deleuze was born in the 17th arrondissement in Paris to an engineer father and housewife mother. The family was politically conservative and very hostile to Léon Blum and the Popular Front of the 1930s. His father, a small business owner, was sympathetic to the Croix-de-Feu, a far right, militarist Catholic mass movement which, while not precisely fascist (Eugen Weber 1982: 134; 1996: 40), was certainly paternalistic in its understanding of the masses. Deleuze once recalled the class hatred of his parents in the pristine form of his mother's disdainful observation of the fact that, under the Popular Front, the working class too would be freed for vacation time and so "people like that" would be found on the beaches that previously had been the privileged haunts of the well-to-do (Dosse 2007: 113).

His older brother Georges was involved in the Resistance and was eventually caught by the Germans and sent to a concentration camp. He perished en route. Because of his actions, Georges was adored by their parents as a "hero" and Deleuze felt as though he were "the second, the mediocre one" (Dosse 2007: 112). One can certainly see evidence in Deleuze's personal history for his later theoretical attack on familialism and the bourgeois family. Indeed, his reluctance to talk of his family and early life were well-known among his associates and amply documented. In his words, "academics' lives are seldom interesting," and one can certainly see this in part as a justification for avoiding biographical explanations for the meaning of a philosopher's work, but it clearly also reflected his own sense that *his* biography should not be considered in an understanding of *his* ideas (Deleuze 1990: 188). We might minimally ask how much of his own political disposition was informed by the unpleasant experiences in his family that were in some ways linked to the political.

Familial issues notwithstanding, the central element in Deleuze's minoritarian *habitus* had to do with the serious health concerns he faced throughout his life. He was asthmatic and suffered from respiratory problems that began in childhood. Dosse (2007: 124) suggests that his health was a major reason for his failure at the ENS entrance examination. He began smoking heavily as a youth and this certainly worsened his condition. By 1968, he had developed a case of tuberculosis serious enough to require a major surgery to remove a lung. This is, interestingly enough, precisely the period in which his radical politics emerged; he met Guattari shortly afterward. Dosse (2007: 14) argues, following a point Deleuze himself made in his book on Samuel Beckett, that the exhausted condition of post-surgery convalescence, combined with his simultaneous struggle with alcohol abuse, opened Deleuze up to a different way of understanding his identity. His illness would nonetheless eventually serve as the defining parameter of his life; it prevented him from traveling, from leaving his flat, even from speaking on the telephone in later life, and the "tubes" of his oxygen tanks became a constant visible reminder of his status (Dosse 2007: 591). He eventually committed suicide in 1995 by leaping from his apartment window in what one of his former students characterized as his "final act of liberty" (Pinhas 2005).

Being a Political Intellectual Otherwise

Though, as I discussed in Chapter 5, the broad intellectual atmosphere in France during the years of the poststructuralists' intellectual careers was inescapably shaped by Marxist communism, they had only fleeting experiences with the PCF. Of the four poststructuralist group members, Foucault had the most direct intersection, as he was during the period of the early 1950s a PCF member while lecturing in psychology at the École Normale. His Marxism was comparatively non-doctrinaire, but still clear enough to produce citations of Stalin in some of his lectures (Dufay and

Dufort 1993: 191–92; Jeannin 1994: 238). Foucault himself accounted for his Marxist period in an interview with an Italian communist journalist by referring to his desire as a youth to be a "Nietzschean Communist ... [s]omething really on the edge of 'liveability'" (Foucault 1991[1981]: 51). He was nonetheless a member of the PCF for only a few years, roughly from 1950 to 1953.

None of the other three poststructuralists were ever Party members. Deleuze had engaged earlier in the 1960s in occasional participation in the Marxist revue *Arguments* (with which Barthes, Duvignaud, Morin, Lefebvre, and Touraine were also connected), but this was a communist journal that deviated from the PCF in its endeavor to "rethink Marxism" (Brillant 2003: 32). Derrida spoke with evident disdain of the PCF's "Stalinist and hegemonic" face at the École Normale when he was a student there and then later when he returned as an instructor (2002: 156, 164). Baudrillard seems to have been drawn to the Sartrean example early in the 1960s, when he contributed several pieces to *Les Temps Modernes*, but he moved to Maoism of a particular *gauchiste* variety in short order. He described an "uncontrollable Maoist groupuscule" called the Franco-Chinese People's Association formed with Félix Guattari and a few others that even attempted to contact Zhou Enlai in Algeria at one point but was rebuffed precisely because of the unorthodox line of the group (Baudrillard 2004: 15–16). By 1968, he had moved to the left even of the Maoists and was "very close" to the Situationist movement that was then active at Nanterre (Baudrillard 2001: 28). He was affiliated for a number of years with the journal *Utopie,* which was "evidently influenced by the bizarre cocktail of anarcho-situationism, structural Marxism and media theory" (Baudrillard 1993c: 2).

That the PCF option for political position-taking was so clearly rejected by the poststructuralist group is of a piece with the broader macrostructural changes in the political field in France during the 1950s and 1960s that I have already discussed. Nationalist positions like those taken up by some of the Durkheimians at the height of the Dreyfus Affair and during World War I were non-options owing to widespread anti-colonial sentiment in the intellectual classes, which further limited options for political position-taking. On what then could the poststructuralists base a personal politics? Much of their political activity, both at the time of May 1968 and afterward, was directed toward two figures. Both of these had to do with Otherness in the most radical way and represented categories of extreme exclusion and outsider-ness. They are 1) the prisoner, and especially the *black* prisoner, and 2) the dissident.

The focus on the prisoner is most evident in the short-lived Groupe d'information sur les prisons (GIP), which lasted only two years, from December 1970 to December 1972, but occupied a considerable amount of the energy of Foucault and Deleuze during this period. It was created in the context of the French government's heightened efforts in the wake of the May events to crack down on political radicals, especially those associated with the Gauche prolétarienne (GP). Daniel Defert has claimed that the GIP originally formed as a means of defending the GP and then expanded and autonomized; he noted that Foucault told him the very initials GIP were meant to invoke the GP, with the difference of an 'i' that stood for 'intellectuals' (Artières, Quéro, and Zancarini-Fournel 2003: 320).

In 1971, the French Interior Minister, Raymond Marcellin, introduced a law that resulted in prison terms for anyone involved in property destruction during strikes and other political actions, and the jails began to fill with radical students and workers who were often GP-affiliated (Artières, Quéro, and Zancarini-Fournel 2003: 14). But it was not solely, nor even centrally, the already radicalized intellectuals winding up inside the prison walls as a result of their actions in the streets who were the target of the GIP. It concentrated on the conceptual category of the prisoner as an entity broadly understood as anyone incarcerated in these institutions of total control and surveillance and thereby stigmatized and refashioned as something other than fully human. The point was that anyone could be made a prisoner/Other by the arbitrary power of the State; as Foucault put it in the manifesto read at the GIP's first press conference in February 1971, "None of us is certain that we will escape prison" (Artières, Quéro, and Zancarini-Fournel 2003: 43).

The GIP did surveys of prisoners and lawyers to gather a fuller understanding of the conditions of the prisons which they then made available to the public in the form of regular press conferences and a publication tellingly titled *Intolerable*. They sought to find out whether, for example, prisoners were being denied visitors, mail was being delivered, prison rules and legal options were adequately communicated to prisoners, and prisoners were fed adequately and given proper medical care and leisure activity. They also monitored and reported on prison movements both inside and outside France (Artières, Quéro, and Zancarini-Fournel 2003: 55–62, 91). At bottom of the GIP's practice was a commitment to radical democracy and the dignity of prisoners that refused to advocate positively for a new form of justice, contenting itself with negative critique of what existed (Bourg 2007: 92).

As prison strikes and revolts began to take place throughout the French system, the GIP intervened more directly in support of the rebelling prisoners. In the winter of 1971 there were riots at several prisons and the authorities, arguing that the riots had been aided by mailed weapons received by prisoners, responded by the suppression of delivery of Christmas packages. The GIP wrote an open letter of protest to the responsible minister and held a protest at the chancellery at the Place Vendôme, where they sought to deliver an enormous Christmas package (Artières, Quéro, and Zancarini-Fournel 2003: 134). Foucault wrote numerous texts explaining and supporting the revolts, arguing that what was happening was "the beginning of a new process: the first moments of a political struggle against the entire penal system led by the social stratum which is its first victim" (Artières, Quéro, and Zancarini-Fournel 2003: 155). One such piece appeared in the *Nouvel Observateur* in the wake of the September 1971 executions of two prisoners who had been involved in a revolt at Clairvaux that left two hostages dead, declaring the executions as "something physically and politically unbearable" and closing by accusing the government of murder (Foucault 2001a: 1254–57). In January 1972, just a few months before the publication of *Anti-Oedipe*, Deleuze wrote an article attacking the government's efforts to stifle the protest of a movement of prison psychiatrists and psychologists who were primary (and, in the government's view, "bothersome") witnesses to the psychological destruction of prisoners (Artières, Quéro, and Zancarini-Fournel 2003: 156). In the same month, he wrote a piece for the *Nouvel Observateur* titled "What the prisoners expect of us," in which he described the GIP's function as an organism external to the prison movement itself that would serve to more effectively communicate the movement's message and demands to the public (Deleuze 2002: 286).

With Daniel Defert, Deleuze carried out a survey on the rising problem of prison suicides in early 1973, in which they described the suicides as a radical act of resistance to the intolerable repression of the prisons (Artières, Quéro, and Zancarini-Fournel 2003: 272, 276). In the last issue of the GIP newsletter, Deleuze, again writing with Defert, chronicled the case of a specific individual prisoner who had committed suicide after being placed in solitary confinement for the offense of having sexual relations with other prisoners. Deleuze and Defert described the stigmatizing mechanisms at work against homosexuals inside the prison system, still more powerful than those that repressed them outside the institution, and declared that the prison officials were "directly and personally responsible" for the death (Artières, Quéro, and Zancarini-Fournel 2003: 302–3). Much of Deleuze's positioning here is perfectly aligned with the thrust of his criticism, elaborated in his collaborative work with Félix Guattari, of the way in which French institutions criminalized desire.

One issue of *Intolerable* was entirely dedicated to the prison killing of George Jackson. Jackson, a Black Panther activist and writer, was shot and killed by prison officials in August 1971 during an alleged escape attempt that was immediately the subject of critical investigation on the left. Deleuze was the central author of the GIP's critique of the official account of Jackson's death. He argued that Jackson was clearly a political prisoner: "Ten years in prison for 70 dollars, that is a political experience. A hostage experience, a concentration camp experience, a class war experience, an experience of colonization" (Artières, Quéro, and Zancarini-Fournel 2003: 60). His murder, Deleuze writes, was necessary because the system recognized that, as "one of the first revolutionary leaders whose entire political formation took place in prison ... [and] also the first ... who analyzed prisoners as a class and assigned them a specific role in the revolutionary process," he posed a serious threat to the racist prison system (Artières, Quéro, and Zancarini-Fournel 2003: 57, 59). Deleuze went on to note how Jackson's murder had tripped off prison rebellions "from Attica to Ashkelon" (the latter an Israeli prison for Palestinian combatants where there was a revolt just a week after the famous rebellion at Attica) because it so clearly signified a powerful reactionary countermove to the growing movement inside the prisons (Artières, Quéro, and Zancarini-Fournel 2003: 61).

Much of Derrida's political position-taking over his career was also directed toward prisoners, and especially black prisoners. Racism, both in France and abroad, was one of his constant political concerns. At a very direct level, his decision to fulfill his French military service from 1957 to 1959, in the midst of the Algerian War, by serving as a teacher of French and English to students in Algiers rather than in a capacity that would have called for wearing a uniform was a political act in opposition to a colonial war. He also intervened numerous times beginning in the 1970s in racial politics abroad. He was a staunch defender of imprisoned black militants in the United States and was engaged in the call in the 1990s to obtain a new trial for the convicted Black Panther and MOVE militant Mumia Abu-Jamal to the point of writing several letters to President Bill Clinton (Derrida 2002: 123) and a preface to one of Abu-Jamal's books that rigorously criticized the harshness of the American judicial and penal system (Derrida and Roudinesco 2001: 251). Much earlier, he had written to Jean Genet, who wrote a preface for one of the books of imprisoned Panther militant George Jackson, that "there are more 'Jacksons' than anyone can count" (Derrida 2002: 41). He was involved in the campaign during the 1980s and 1990s to free Nelson Mandela from his South African prison cell and eventually became Mandela's friend. His attachment to the politics of contestation of South African apartheid is further revealed in his dedication of his book on Marx to Chris Hani, a leader of the South African Communist Party who was murdered by a racial separatist who sought to derail the multiracial elections that eventually led to the coming to power of the ANC (Derrida and Roudinesco 2001: 163).

The dissident is the second outsider figure who shows up prominently in the political work of the poststructuralists. An important root of this political position-taking can be found in the context of the *Gulag Archipelago* affair of the mid 1970s in France. Solzhenitsyn's published account of the fate of dissident Soviet intellectuals was translated into French in 1974, and he quickly became a celebrity. This was not the moment at which French left intellectuals discovered dissidents from the communist East, of course, as the gulag had been revealed long before (Drake 2002: 149). However, the explicit movement to align with those dissidents, and often in direct conflict with the French Communists, was relatively recent; it is with the Solzhenitsyn affair that one can begin to talk of the "cult of the dissident" (Hourmant 1997: 143, 148). We should note here too the connection between the first and second Others of interest to the poststructuralists: dissidents were frequently prisoners too, so the unifying theme is imprisonment, the deep transgressions of which the imprisoned were accused, and the valorization of those transgressions by the poststructuralists.

The existing Union of the Left (which joined the PCF and Mitterrand's Socialist Party, the latter as the majority partner) made it difficult for the Socialist Party to position itself on Solzhenitsyn. The PCF attacked him violently as an anti-Soviet propagandist; Mitterrand wanted at once to defend his right to speak while maintaining skepticism about his criticism of the gulag (M. Christofferson 2003: 92, 95). Perhaps the most visible intellectual response to the whole affair was that of the *Nouveaux Philosophes*, a group of media-savvy if philosophically lightweight former 1968 radicals who had moved radically rightward and built careers by simplistically attacking the entire left as totalitarian. None of the poststructuralists took this path, though Foucault did strategically ally himself with one of the group's leaders, André Glucksmann, sufficiently to create a permanent rift with Deleuze, who attacked their thought as "worthless" (Deleuze 2003: 127; M. Christofferson 2003: 198). But the *Nouveaux Philosophes'* reading of Solzhenitsyn did reveal something of importance in the way in which the poststructuralists envisioned the figure of the dissident. It positioned him as a critic of power per se, and the poststructuralists agreed that what was called for was a critique of the very bases of power.

By 1977, the movement to support Eastern dissidents had grown. In June of that year, a reception was held for Soviet dissidents in protest against Giscard d'Estaing's meeting with Soviet premier Brezhnev, and Foucault was involved (Foucault 2001a: 70). In November of that same year another such protest took place in Venice for Eastern European dissidents as a whole (M. Christofferson 2003: 156). Foucault, along with Deleuze, Pierre Bourdieu, and others, signed a petition in December 1981 protesting the Mitterrand government's refusal to criticize or act on the situation in Poland, which by then had devolved into the government's invocation of martial law in its attempt to destroy the Solidarity movement of Walesa (M. Christofferson 2003: 270). When Lionel Jospin and Jack Lang attacked them, they formed a Solidarity committee (Foucault 2001a: 83). Foucault was interviewed in *Liberation* and the *Nouvel Observateur* in October 1982 after a visit to Poland where he saw firsthand the repression of the Solidarity movement. He acidly attacked the French communists' support of the Polish government's decision to outlaw Walesa's movement, wondering how the Socialists could conceivably align themselves with such a party and asserting the necessity not only of communicating with the Polish dissidents but also of communicating with their French fellows about the Polish situation (Foucault 2001b: 1157, 1160). Eribon (1989: 326) describes the Academie Tarnier, a group Foucault formed (named for the hospital where they met) that was intended to be a kind of GIP for political dissidents, i.e., an organization for making information available generally on international political matters (like that in Poland) about which the Mitterrand government could not be trusted to be forthright. Foucault also participated, with Sartre and others, between 1978 and 1981 in the committee "A Boat for Vietnam," which aimed to confront the communist government of Vietnam and aid its dissident refugees (M. Christofferson 2003: 267; Eribon 1989: 296).

Derrida was also centrally involved in the engagement with dissidents. Perhaps the most well-known episode concerned his efforts on behalf of Czech political prisoners. In 1981, along with J. P. Vernant and several other friends, he formed the Jan Hus Association (named after a Czech religious martyr from the fifteenth century) to that end. In December of that year, during a visit to Prague to meet with dissidents, he was set up by the state police, who planted drugs in his suitcase and arrested him. During a harrowing 24-hour period, he was subjected to an 8-hour interrogation with "terrifying State officials," during which he was threatened, insulted, and stripped naked for photographing. Finally, with the intervention of newly-elected President Mitterrand, Derrida was released and allowed to return to France. He spoke frequently of the terrifying experience in explicitly Kafka-esque terms; he even noted that one of the interrogating officials asked him if he had "the impression of living in a Kafka story" and believed that the drugs where planted while he was actually visiting the grave of the great literary resident of Prague (Derrida 1995b: 128–29).

Baudrillard avoided the concrete political work in pursuit of the dissident or the prisoner that I have just chronicled in the three other poststructuralists, and indeed he even ridiculed the concern for the Communist dissidents and the humanitarianism it evidenced in withering terms during the 1980s, calling "the anti-gulag priests ... every bit as bad as the gulag torturers" (Baudrillard 1990 [1987]: 134, 137). Yet we can see in the development of his post-1968 ideas about the political realm and the intellectual's mode of engagement in it a significant resonance with interest in the radically Other. Moreover, he managed to capture, perhaps more fully than the other three, precisely how the political interest in the Othered population of the imprisoned was in fact a translation of another, deeper motivation. He actually had a fair amount to say about racial Otherness, in both his theoretical works and in the several volumes of his journal published under the title *Cool Memories*, which I will discuss in detail in the following chapter. His chief and most sustained post-1968 political position-taking, however, was not directed in the way we have seen in the other poststructuralists. It was instead fundamentally taken up with the role of the dissident Western intellectual in his role in the political realm broadly understood, i.e., not simply as the institutionalized realm of governance, but of all other public modes of political position-taking as well. He steadfastly defined himself as "unengaged" in the post-1968 period, repeatedly and seemingly cynically noting how little influence engaged intellectuals seem to have had on the political realm. At least part of his position here might be attributed to the tremendous sense of "mourning" he described at watching the fire of the May events die away after several years: "That situation lasted until around 1973–74. I stayed a few more years, by inertia. During this work of mourning, for me, there was no more activity at all. I passed over to the side of theory. *Gauchisme*, as it had become ... there was no more possibility of that" (Baudrillard 2005: 35–36). So let down was he by the end of May that he refused to attempt to extend it by participating in the radical experiment at Vincennes that attracted Foucault and Deleuze (Baudrillard 2005: 36).

Arguably, what was going on in Baudrillard's evolution was something that became clearest in his published writings in *La Gauche divine*, a relatively forgotten collection of essays he wrote in the mid 1980s on the failure of the Mitterrand government and the institutionalized and intellectual left more generally. What he began to develop during this period was a perspective of the intellectual as the *outsider par excellence* who is destroyed completely in his capacity to do his work by efforts to insert himself into the political realm, which necessarily involve compromises of his nature: "Being on the margin is, in fact, the true position of the intellectual ... intellectuals are the carriers of negativity" (Baudrillard 1993c: 75). The context for his argument, and for the position-taking of the other poststructuralists as well, was that of the emergence of the Union of the Left and its electoral victories in the late 1970s and early

1980s, so let us rehash some of those details. The main national parties of the left, the socialists and the communists, had formed an electoral alliance in 1972 that began to pay significant dividends in the municipal elections of March 1977, where they swept a majority of the total communes of the country. In May 1981, the Union of the Left candidate François Mitterrand won the presidency. On the day of his inauguration, he led a procession up rue Soufflot (where the École Normale is found) to the Panthéon, where, in the company of renowned foreign socialist personages and intellectuals, he paid homage to Jean Moulin, Jean Jaurès, and Victor Schoelcher (the last of whom was one of the central writers in the French movement to abolish slavery). By the start of June, the new regime had begun major and radical restructuring of the French social sector. Significant raises in the minimum wage, minimum elderly pension payments, and housing allocations for the poor were initiated quickly, and later in June, 55,000 new jobs in the public sector were created (Simonin and Clastres 1989: 373). By the end of the year, nationalization of industry, finance, and banking was well underway, and in early 1982, the work week was reduced to 39 hours. By the end of that year, the death penalty and the criminalization of homosexuality were undone, and abortion was included as a reimbursable procedure under social security (Simonin and Clastres 1989: 379, 382).

By early 1984, however, a serious economic crisis had emerged, as the massive public expenditures had significantly increased the French debt. Eventually, Mitterrand appeared on television before the French public and declared, "I was wrong" (Simonin and Clastres 1989: 408). From this point, the regime turned from the seemingly radical path of the first years to an acceptance of neo-liberal capitalism and the economic status quo (T. Christofferson 1991). I cannot delve into the complexities involved in attempting to explain this shift, but it is clear that the poststructuralists distanced themselves from the government early and vigorously. Deleuze, along with Guattari and Pierre Bourdieu, was among the signatories of a call of support for the candidacy of Coluche, published in *Le Monde* on 19 November 1980. The left-wing comedian had, as a half-joking, half-serious endeavor, presented himself as a presidential candidate as a symbolic "frontal attack on the immense mess in which modern liberal society had immersed itself" (Chesneaux 2004: 230–31). He even directly addressed various excluded outsider groups in announcing his candidacy, calling for the votes of "idlers, the filthy, drug addicts, alcoholics, homosexuals, women, parasites, the young, the old, artists, prisoners, lesbians, blacks … Arabs … the mad, transvestites … all those who do not count for the politicians." The Mitterrand camp, along with the conservative administration of Giscard d'Estaing, attempted to persuade Coluche to abandon the effort, which he finally did under much media and political pressure (Bourdieu 1991[1982]: 178–79). While Foucault did not join the Coluche movement, he was frequently heard comparing Mitterrand to Pétain and was apparently planning a book, tentatively titled "The Head of the Socialists," that criticized the Mitterrand government's inability to govern effectively in the summer of 1983 (Eribon 1989: 326).

Baudrillard elaborated more fully on precisely where and how the Union of the Left failed in *La Gauche divine*, and in doing so made clear how much of the poststructuralist political position-taking we have been exploring here had to do with something beyond politics. At bottom, the Union of the Left had no understanding of the "immoral, [the] excessive" (Baudrillard 1985: 19), and they wanted "no surprise, no violence, no going beyond limits, no true passion" (Baudrillard 1985: 73). The form of socialism they advocated Baudrillard found nicely summarized by a member of Mitterrand's government, Louis Mermaz, in his explicitly anti-revolutionary politics. As Mermaz put it, "Our entire approach in the France of today is to make it so that there will be no revolutions" because an inevitable aspect of revolution involves something "unacceptable [i.e.,] the unleashing of passions, violence, impure instincts" (Baudrillard 1985: 92). Here is nothing less than the rejection of the "accursed share," an attempt to "reduce all the perverse effects, abolish all the distortions, the ambitions, the illegal passions, the game, fraud and luxury"; everything that is openly at work in the cruelty and violence of sacrifice found in other, more primitive societies is dismissed here (Baudrillard 1985: 95, 101–2). The result is "a society that is divided, ripped apart, unhappy and hypocritical in that it considers unacceptable its own foundations, its own mechanisms of functioning" (Baudrillard 1985: 102). If the Union of the Left called to the intellectuals to join them, it was calling intellectuals to a "corruption" of their function and nature (Baudrillard 1985: 85). The Socialists, like the modernist sociologists, wanted "the social," which is nothing more than the idea that every society is "solidary with its own values and coherent in its collective project" (Baudrillard 1985: 83). As the politicians give up "the duplicity of politics," they call for intellectuals to give up "the duplicity of the concept" in attaching themselves to socialism, which means giving up "the cynical ... immoral and ambiguous exercise of thought" (Baudrillard 1985: 76–77).

The suggestion here is that what calls the intellectual is not the political, or at least not the political thus defined, but something beyond the political, something that Baudrillard goes back to his days at Nanterre in order to define. The effervescent, transgressive experience that was May 1968 answered effectively to the deep yearning of the poststructuralist calling precisely in the way in which it refused institutionalization and remained "a joyous Assumption in the imaginary and … a joyful suicide … it happily remained a violent metaphor, without ever becoming a reality (Baudrillard 1985: 75). Elsewhere, Baudrillard discussed the "disappearance of politics" that had been inaugurated by the May events as a parallel to Nietzsche's pronouncement of the death of God: "[T]hose who did not live thorough [the May events] can never understand what is happening today in a diluted form, just as those who never lived through the death of God can understand nothing of the convalescence of values" (Baudrillard 1990 [1987]: 186). The fusing of intellectual and masses in his analysis here is total. Both reject representation in the political and yearn for transgression and spectacle (Baudrillard 1985: 50). The Divine Left, which Baudrillard saw personified in Laurent Fabius, the Socialist Prime Minister from 1984 to 1986, seems utterly

> ingenuous about the perverse mechanisms of popular indifference, deploring the apathy and perfidiousness of the masses, their lack of imagination and participation, the absence of a collective myth, etc … The people are bored? Then give them something to marvel at … They will seek out something to astonish them in spectacle (the spectacle of the media or of terrorism) if they cannot find it on the political stage … And this is the impression Fabius gives: sure of his ambitions and totally ignorant of the immoral ways of the world. (Baudrillard 1990 [1987]: 214–15)

What is Baudrillard sketching here? It is a perspective on the politics of the intellectual that indicates the impossibility of all the traditional options. It is, to borrow a phrase from Jean-Michel Besnier (1988), a "politics of the impossible" that oscillates, ultimately unstably, between "revolt and engagement." It is the same thing motivating the efforts of Foucault, Deleuze, and Derrida on behalf of Others, which find their origins ultimately in the sense of Otherness on the part of the intellectuals themselves. In reaching for an identity between "revolt and engagement," the poststructuralists, like the Durkheimians, are acknowledging the insufficiency of the purely political field for enactment of this identity trajectory. Something *beyond* politics is being aimed at, however incoherently and partially. Something *au-delà*.

We should also note the similarity between the very specific and limited political modes of intervention presented by the poststructuralists and the mystic Durkheimians Hertz and Mauss. Gérard Noiriel has in fact used the Foucauldian term "specific intellectual" to classify not only Foucault and Deleuze but also the Durkheimians (2005: 203–17). There is, to be sure, something going on at the level of the transformation of the relationship between political and scholarly fields in France that provides a propitious environment for the emergence of this politics of the impossible. From 1945, when the École Nationale d'Administration was created with the express goal of producing political leadership, the traditional connection of the ENS and the political field was undone, so Foucault and Derrida were faced with different political position-taking options than those their fellow *normaliens* Léon Blum and Jean Jaurès had (M. Christofferson 2003: 43). But these structural facts are not nearly enough to explain the particular tenor of the political position-taking we find among the poststructuralists. For that task, we need more nuanced information about their lived experiences, which I have summarized here, and the conceptual categories of their intellectual work. We are now prepared to turn to this latter topic.

Notes

1. In the Fonds Louis Althusser at IMEC, there are several letters from Derrida to Althusser during this period that describe the difficulties the former had convincing French authorities that his military service requirement had been met and he should be permitted to take a position at the Sorbonne offered him for the fall of 1960 (which he eventually did take).
2. Foucault wrote a letter to Roger Caillois, in response to the latter's request for an article for his journal *Diogène*, in which he pointed to their "common Dumézilian ancestry" as the reason for the similarities in their work (*Hommage à Roger Caillois* 1981: 228).
3. There exists a letter from Foucault to Jean Piel in the Fonds IMEC that, though undated, likely has to do with Baudrillard's book. Foucault writes: "I have not read Baudrillard's text. It does not seem legitimate to me to 'control' a text—all the less if it concerns me."

12 The Sacred in Poststructuralist Thought

With the Durkheimian group, it was necessary to do a significant amount of work to demonstrate the ways in which their intellectual work constituted a statement about the role and identity of intellectuals; with the poststructuralists, a good deal of that connection of the work to an autobiographical project is done by the poststructuralists themselves. Foucault spoke frequently of the connection between his intellectual work and his own experience and identity: "I have always held that my books are, in a sense, autobiographical fragments" (2001b: 1566–67). One of Derrida's close friends and colleagues has argued that "all Derrida's texts are in a way autobiographical" (Bennington and Derrida 1991: 98). Baudrillard's analysis of the failure of the Union of the Left, summarized in detail in the previous chapter, demonstrates how clearly his emerging understanding of the transgressive desires of the masses was tied to his beliefs about the task of the intellectuals. Zygmunt Bauman (1988: 225) has remarked that "intellectuals tend to articulate their own societal situation and the problems it creates as a situation of the society at large, and its, systemic or social, problems" and this seems to be especially evident in poststructuralist thought (Riley 2002).

In turning, after the historical and sociological analysis that has taken up the preceding chapters, to the intellectual work of the poststructuralists in search of evidence of the sacred, I should note an important preliminary point. I cannot and do not make claims about the entirety of their work, or even about its general tenor. Each of these four thinkers produced a vast amount of work over their lifetimes, much of it quite varied in approach and topic, and fat tomes have been written on each of the four that attempt to summarize their work. I have no such pretensions.

Each of these four thinkers covered enough ground and changed direction enough times over the course of their lives that any brief attempt to discuss their work must certainly be silent on many, many things. What I intend to do is locate and describe a significant thread running through that work that has not been sufficiently attended to previously, a thread that illuminates not only the conceptual frameworks they were devising and the intellectual trajectories in which they were working, but also their personal projects in identity construction.

Foucault: The Transgressive Sacredness of Unreason

Foucault's debt to Bataille is common knowledge among scholars of their work, and Foucault attested to it frequently in interviews, even noting that he initially read Nietzsche, commonly recognized as the single most essential source of Foucault's perspective, "because of Bataille" (Foucault 1989: 239). Much less, however, is known about the mutual rooting in Durkheimian thought of their common intellectual approach to the sacred. Foucault believed Bataille's work produced a space in which "transgression prescribes not only the sole manner of discovering the sacred in its unmediated substance, but also a way of recomposing its empty form, its absence, through which it becomes all the more scintillating" (Foucault 1977: 30). Sexuality and a number of other important subjects he explored in some detail (e.g., madness and death) become inextricably tied up with the death of God and the very possibility of the emergence of literature itself insofar as they emerge as experiences that defy language to speak of them but are nonetheless spoken of, therein enacting a violence on both language and the transgressive experience itself that Foucault read sympathetically (Foucault 1977: 51). Transgression is here not to be understood simply as "satanic denial," but rather as the "open[ing] onto a scintillating and constantly affirmed world ... without that serpentine 'no' that bites into fruits"; it is "originally linked to the divine, or rather, from this limit marked by the sacred it opens the space where the divine functions" (Foucault 1977: 37).

In his history of madness and the birth of the asylum in Europe, the theme of transgressive sacrality is still more clearly encountered. Foucault explicitly calls on the category of the sacred in his discussion of the structural space madness came to occupy as a result of the disappearance of the lazar houses:

> Leprosy withdrew, leaving derelict these low places and these rites which were intended, not to suppress it, but to keep it at a *sacred* dis-

tance, to fix it in an inverse exaltation. What doubtless remained longer than leprosy ... were the values and images attached to ... that
insistent and fearful figure which was not driven off without first being inscribed within a *sacred* circle. (Foucault 1973 [1961]: 6; emphasis
added)

The leper is the Other, the transgressive outsider who is viewed with hor-
rific awe of the power he has to rend the normal. Before the classical
period, Foucault argues, madness occupied a privileged place in the social order in that it existed "precisely at the point of contact between the
oneiric [relating to dreams] and the erroneous ... There is only one word
which summarizes this experience, Unreason" (1973[1961]: 106–7). This
vision of unreason clearly owes much to Foucault's reading of Bataille.
For the latter, the accursed share is the element of reality that transgresses
the given order and that nonetheless is necessitated by that very order,
while unreason operates conceptually in the same way in Foucault's work
here. It is not "reason diseased, or ... reason lost or alienated, but quite
simply reason *dazzled*" (1973[1961]: 108). In the classical worldview that
Foucault is trying to deconstruct, "an extremely abstract law" is at work,
and this law "forms the most vivid and concrete opposition ... of day and
night" in which "everything must be either waking or dream, truth or
darkness, the light of being or the nothingness of shadow" (1973[1961]:
109). The dazzling of unreason is something outside of those polar categories. It is not merely the darkening of reason; it is a profound transgression of the very game of either/or that has been set up in the classical
view of things.

Madness is not the only category of experience that performs this
transgression, according to Foucault. Tellingly, it is also present in tragedy
(Foucault 1973[1961]: 110). The tragedy of the Crucifixion, for example, in Renaissance Christianity partakes of this same dazzling unreason.
There, it is understood by Christians as something that "require[s] human
reason to abandon its pride and its certainties in order to lose itself in the
great unreason of sacrifice ... [of] scandal [as the] power of revelation"
(1973[1961]: 78–79). But for Christianity and the secular scientific world
alike, the Classical period sounded the death knell for unreason. For the
former, the tragic understanding of Christ on the cross was cast into the
shadows of the powerful light given off by the rational wisdom of God;
for the latter, the magic of the madman is stripped away in the asylum
through surveillance and judgment (1973[1961]: 263). Where once the
horror of madness was mingled with an "irresistible attraction [to] inac-
cessible pleasures," now it would be made the object of scientific examination and correction. Indeed, it becomes now the "object par excellence of

all the measures of confinement," no more to "cause fear," but now only to "be afraid" (1973[1961]: 208, 227, 245). Foucault argues that the attack on unreason, the province of such artistic and philosophical geniuses as Hölderlin, Nietzsche, and Artaud, threatens to completely eliminate the possibility of perhaps our last remaining access to the sacred through the experience of the "mad" work of art that, "by the madness that interrupts it," is able to raise questions about the world that would otherwise be un-available (Foucault 1973[1961]: 288). Here the realm of unreason is seen as a realm of knowledge that offers insights not provided by other knowl-edges, and scientific knowledge, far from providing any possibilities for social rejuvenation, is described as actively responsible in its psychological guises for the misrecognition and subsequent destruction of this knowl-edge. For unreason cannot be reduced to the physiological; indeed, it is the moral problem it presents in its "ethic of desire" (1973[1961]: 156) that requires its control and correction.

This engagement with the transgressive sacred as radical form of knowledge and experience of the social was not merely a fleeting phe-nomenon in Foucault's work. In *The Order of Things*, he explicitly articu-lates in his concluding remarks the possibility of the death of Man as a mutation in the fabric of knowledge that might release us from the total-izing singularity of identity and, in a paraphrase of Nietzsche, "explo[de] man's face in laughter, and [usher in] the return of masks" (Foucault 1970 [1966]: 385). Foucault speculates on this "explosion" in light of the artistic projects of Mallarmé, Artaud, Roussel, and others who worked in the region bordering transgression and the sacred "where death prowls, where thought is extinguished, where the promise of the origin intermi-nably recedes," and he finds that the "counter-sciences" of psychoanalysis, ethnology and linguistics (at least in their structuralist forms) undertake the very dissolution of Man and the turn to the dark being of Language that enables the transgressions of the poets (1970[1966]: 383).

Elsewhere, Foucault broadened his discussion of the transgressive power of the "dangerous individual" who lurks in the borderland between the moral and transgressive and "establishes the ambiguity of the law-ful and the unlawful" through his/her words and deeds (Foucault 1975 [1973]: 206). He argues that the aesthetic experience that constitutes a brushing against the sacred might go beyond the creation of a work of (traditional) art to include even acts considered vile and criminal by a horrified citizenry, like those of Pierre Rivière, the young man in pro-vincial France who murdered several members of his own family in the 1830s and subsequently wrote in a memoir of the otherworldly impera-tives that compelled him to do so. What is it about this act that, even 150 years later, "literally reduce[s] to silence" all of the purported experts of crime and madness ("criminologists, psychologists, and psychiatrists") (Foucault 1989: 131–32)? In Foucault's analysis, it is precisely "Rivière's own discourse on his act" that "so dominates … [and is] so strong and so strange that the crime ends up not existing anymore; it escapes through the very fact of this discourse held about it by the one who committed it" (1989: 132). Rivière was but one example of a multitude of infamous men who compelled Foucault's attention. He poured through the archival records of Parisian hospitals for the insane, in the interests of documenting the lives of these "obscure men" who had been judged insane, criminal, or otherwise too dangerous to be permitted to escape incarceration (Foucault 2001b: 242).

Later still, in his work on normalization and discipline (Foucault 1978 [1976]; 1979 [1975]), Foucault constructed a sociology of knowledge of specific contemporary western social spaces, in which the engagement with the sacred is increasingly structurally denied, and examined the consequences. Again scientific discourses are seen as responsible for creating as categories of deviance certain realms of knowledge and practice that offer potential possibilities for transgressive knowledges and "pleasures" (Foucault 1978 [1976]: 157). His account of the transgressive festivals that could erupt at the scene of public executions in the days before the rise of the prison and the practice of discipline could have come right from Caillois's discussion of the festival and the left sacred:

> In these [i.e., pre-modern] executions, which ought to show only the terrorizing power of the prince, there was a whole aspect of the carnival, in which rules were inverted, authority mocked and criminals transformed into heroes … executions could easily lead to the beginnings of social disturbances … the terror of the public execution created centres of illegality: on execution days, work stopped, the taverns were full, the authorities were abused, insults or stones were thrown at the executioner, the guards and the soldiers. (Foucault 1979 [1975]: 61, 63)

In a debate on the politics of popular justice, Foucault defended the "prejudicial justice" that originated in the rites of placing the head of an enemy on a pike after an execution or burning down the homes of those popularly believed guilty of crimes (Foucault 1980: 6). The carnival-esque atmosphere of such violently transgressive activities is aptly described by Orlando Patterson (1998) in his account of Southern lynchings. Borrowing explicitly from Mauss and Hubert's theoretical framework on sacrifice, Patterson shows how the practice of lynching in the mid and late nineteenth century in the American South frequently took on the characteristics of what Mauss and Hubert describe as religious ritual sacrifice. The six central elements of sacrifice in Mauss and Hubert are:

1. ritualistic "drama, celebration, and play";
2. performance in sacred places, or sacralization of the places in which they are performed by the sacrifice itself;
3. the frequent use of fire as a means of destruction and consumption of the victim;
4. the stake to which the victim is tied (and the source from which it is obtained) takes on a special sacred status;
5. moral narratives that frame the victim as a mediator between worlds of sacred and profane, with victim as representative of good, evil, or both;
6. the remains of the victim are frequently cannibalized or preserved. (Patterson 1998: 182–83)

In many cases involving both white *and* black victims (Patterson points out that the majority of Southern lynchings were of the former), ritual solidarity is produced among the participants in the raucous festival-like atmosphere through each of these six mechanisms. It is not at all difficult to apply them to the kinds of situation Foucault describes.

One of the most intriguing and unexplored locations for Foucault's engagement with the mystic Durkheimian approach to the sacred is his still unpublished final Collège de France lectures from 1984 on *parrhesia,* or truth speaking.[1] In a course on this practice in the ancient Greek and Roman world, he discussed Cynicism at great length, over several lectures, and argued that in its very scandal and transgression of the normal modes of life and philosophical being Cynicism represents a unique moment in the Western world. The Cynic's attitude, which is to reject convention, to refuse to feel shame, and to be indifferent to unimportant things, represents a kind of "non-dissimulated life" that refuses to avoid the truth of life, however depraved or horrible that truth may be. The Cynic lives in a fully public, revealed manner and he has no need to hide any part of his life from public scrutiny, not even those relating to sexuality or the cruder functions of the body. All conventions must be examined for their relation to nature and those which derive from some other (i.e., social) source must be rejected. Family, marriage, the cooking of food, all are refused as irrational dissimulations of real existence. Even the incest taboo seems to derive not from nature but from social constraints, so it too must be rejected. Foucault notes in Diogenes's account of the Oedipus myth that Diogenes rejected the tragic consequences because they do not have to be; if Oedipus had merely observed, "Well, I have killed my father and procreated with my mother, but this is what animals frequently do," he could accept and embrace what in the Oedipus cycle becomes the grounds of a crushing tragedy. Poverty and even slavery are embraced as the ideal conditions for this Cynic life.

The Cynic is, per Foucault, "the universal lookout, who watches over the sleep" of the rest of humanity. He constitutes a second crucial path of *parrhesia* in the Greek tradition, distinguishable from that sketched out by Socrates and Plato (which is taken up by the Gnostics and the early Christians as well) in so far as it constitutes "the Other life " instead of the Platonic metaphysical path of "the life which leads to the other world." The Cynic achieves, in his lived practice of philosophy according to the rules of nature, an immanent transcendence, a sacred state of release from the profane even in his embrace of objects and ideas considered fundamentally profane by the non-Cynic.

We come finally to Foucault's analysis of the Iranian Revolution in 1978, which is certainly among the most startling interventions of his intellectual life. This series of eight short pieces for the Italian newspaper *Corriere della sera,* and one article on the subject that he wrote during this same period for *Le Nouvel Observateur,* constitute a rather impressive commentary on the events in Iran. Though he admitted to knowing little about Iran prior to taking on the assignment, he did a crash course of reading on the topic and met with some of the Iranian resistance figures residing in Paris (Foucault 2001b: 662). He also spent two weeks in Iran during the fall of 1978, interviewing scholars and members of the anti-Shah movement. The situation in Iran fascinated Foucault because of its "curious" nature; this "curiosity" arose from the fact that the Iranian movement that eventually brought Khomeini to power had neither of the "two dynamics" Foucault notes Westerners recognize as constituting a "revolutionary situation": a class struggle or a revolutionary vanguard party (Foucault 1988: 212–13). The most common way Western academics tried to make sense of the Iranian situation was to label it "a crisis of modernization" in which a clumsy leader tries to pull a traditional country into the modern world too quickly and the traditional elements of the society react in revolt against him, but Foucault rejects the implicit teleology of such arguments (Foucault 2001b: 679–80). The movement against this archaic modernism is not something traditional and conservative, but new and potentially more revolutionary than the events Western academics most generally label with that term.

Foucault goes so far as to argue that something specific about Shi'ism allows it to play the role of a force that is uniquely available to popular struggles against State power. He outlined how Shi'ism was by its very structure less predisposed to some of the traits generally associated with Islamic regimes; it was characterized by an "absence of hierarchy in the clergy, their mutual independence of one another, but with dependence, even at the financial level, on those who listen to them, and the importance of purely spiritual authority" (Foucault 2001b: 688, 691). Shi'ism would perhaps, Foucault argued, permit a new spiritual dimension to enter political life, a claim he knew would be found ludicrous by many French thinkers (2001b: 693–94). The specific terms Foucault uses to describe what was happening in Iran are telling: It is an "an inner experience, a sort of constantly recommenced liturgy," involving "an absolutely collective will" that links "collective action, religious ritual, and an expression of public right … rather like in Greek tragedy where the collective ceremony and the reenactment of the principles of right go hand in hand" (Foucault 1988: 214–16). There is an almost magical quality of the phenomenon occurring in Iran, as Foucault describes it. When an oil worker's strike emerges, for example, it comes "without there being any order coming from above … the workers … coordinating among themselves … in an absolutely free way" (1988: 222). The very profundity of the event defies easy classification so "one feels a certain unease when one comes back from Iran and people, wanting to understand, ask one for an analytical schema of an already constituted reality" (1988: 221). Yet it is imaginable that what is happening in Iran is the "first great insurrection against … the weight of the entire world order" (Foucault 2001b: 716). Here again, as in the case of Cynicism in the *parrhesia* lectures, Foucault sees the proper path toward the sacred as embodied in *this* world, on a specific set of practices, rather than oriented toward another world (2001b: 716). And those practices hover around expressions of rejection, refusal, violence, and transgression.

Baudrillard: The Transgressive Sacred in Symbolic Exchange

By the early 1970s, Baudrillard had formulated a powerful critique of the productivist theory of economy, of which the Marxist theory of economy is merely one variation, and of the foundational assumptions of critical social theory generally. This critique, informed by the political events of May 1968, owed heavy theoretical debts to both Maussian ethnology and Nietzschean genealogy. The attack begins in *The Mirror of Production* (1975 [1973]), where he explicitly invokes Bataille against Marx:

> If there was one thing Marx did not think about, it was discharge, waste, sacrifice, prodigality, play, and symbolism … The social wealth produced [by Marxist labor] is material; it has nothing to do with symbolic wealth which, mocking natural necessity, comes conversely from

destruction, the deconstruction of value, transgression, or discharge ... According to Bataille, sacrificial economy or symbolic exchange is exclusive of political economy. (Baudrillard 1975 [1973]: 42–43)

He began a vigorous attack on Marxist and, indeed, *any* positions that postulate a social order fundamentally based on the existence of a mass with a rational will and a teleological place in history. It is the historical notion of the the masses, of the social as a foundational tenet of the discipline of sociology that he argued has denied the validity of the experience of surplus, sacrifice, and the sacred (Baudrillard 1983[1978]: 79). Sociology, in Baudrillard's reading, has always understood society as the result of a contract, of a utilitarian network of relations with use value as the driving force behind it. This understanding has led to the classification of the masses as alienated or mystified in their forsaking of rational communication and commerce.

But he argued it is precisely in spectacle, and in revelry in apparent meaninglessness or oversaturation with meaning that the transgressive sacred is experienced by the silent majorities. The masses, in refusing progressive political mobilization for the modern festival of e.g., a World Cup soccer match (Baudrillard 1983[1978]: 12), explode the Enlightenment mythology of the social completely. These festivals are in some sense the contemporary equivalent of Mauss's agonistic potlatch and Bataille's Aztec sacrifices. Baudrillard was here announcing not just the end of sociology as we have known it, but the end of production as the reigning paradigm of meaning and value and the arrival of a new mode of social exchange and experience. The masses are no longer the productive proletariat; they are now the silent consumers of television who systematically refuse both work and the political as the core to their identity. Their "deepest drive remains the symbolic murder of the political class ... [and] of political reality" and they contribute to this murder in their efforts to confound the work of political pollsters to bring them into the "game of information" (Baudrillard 1988: 212–13).

In *Seduction* (1991 [1979]), Baudrillard further elaborated this theory of the impure sacred. Paralleling the move to liberate sex with the move to liberate labor, he opposed the productivist paradigm again by positing a radical form of exchange, i.e., seduction, that "takes the form of an uninterrupted ritual exchange where seducer and seduced constantly raise the stakes in a game that never ends" (Baudrillard 1991 [1979]: 22). Seduction, like unreason for Foucault, is dangerous and violent. It refuses the banality of bodies and the orgasm for the play of secrets and challenges. He juxtaposes seduction to the pornographic, which "adds a dimension to the space of sex [and] makes the latter more real than the real," while seduction is about fantasy, concealment, and the veil (1991 [1979]: 28). Baudrillard took Caillois's notion of play as a fundamental mode of interaction and combined it with his interpretation of the sacred as the foundational mode of experience of the social. What emerges is at bottom agonistic and transgressive of reason and law. Baudrillard posits a form of symbolic exchange, a mode of social relations predicated not upon any rational, wealth-maximizing agents but rather upon ludic wearers of "symbolic veils," which is more fundamental than any form of exchange based upon the centrality of production (1991 [1979]: 33). The choice of specific terminology and examples here is often provocatively weighted toward the language of gender and sex because he saw this work as an expansion of his earlier critical forays against Marxist economic productivism to the realm of the productivism of desire of modern psychoanalysis and feminism, but he intended his analysis to apply to social relations *generally*.

By the late 1980s, Baudrillard's exploration of the transgressive practices of the masses took on the form of an interest in what he called "radical exoticism." Where earlier he had seen the Othering of the masses as crucial to understanding events, he now shifted in a yet more radical direction. It is the Other in racial and civilizational terms to which he now turns his attention. But this is not the non-Western Other of the liberal human rights legislators and anthropologists, not the "negotiable otherness" of "Cortes, the Jesuits, or the missionaries," but something wholly outside the power of our comprehension (Baudrillard 1993b [1990]: 133). This is an Otherness which refuses translation into the Western sphere of laws and rights altogether. Radical exoticism is based, like languages, in the notion of rule rather than law; there is no "universal principle of understanding, the regulated interplay of differences, moral, political and economic rationality" but only the "arbitrary determinants" and individual "impeccable logic" of each language or society (1993b[1990]: 140–41). His argument is that Western understanding of cultural Others is always in terms of its own basic principles, which means all actual, radical difference must ultimately be destroyed, even while the Western humanitarian discourse is cynically claiming profound interest in the recognition and preservation of difference (1993b[1990]: 125, 132). Against this false difference, he posits a truly radical Othering which denies any capacity even to begin to position or understand the Other from within one's own cultural and political framework. The very experience of discovering a people of whom one had previously been wholly ignorant carries some germ of the "shock" of radical exoticism, even if it can be quickly conquered by Western universalism (Baudrillard 1997: 138). The evidence shows that there are in fact peoples who adhere to this way of viewing others in the lens of radical exoticism; Baudrillard discusses the Alakaluf of Tierra del Fuego in Chile, a people now essentially in extinction, who saw the white European colonizers as "not even different" but "unintelligible" (1993b[1990]: 134). In Baudrillard's reading, they "perish[ed] without ever allowing the Whites the privilege of recognizing them as different ... [they] were simply irrecuperable" (1993b[1990]: 134).

This radical exoticism becomes a kind of cultural power to absorb, based in the profound belief of one's own people as the center of the universe and the refusal to include others in that same classificatory game. If "the Stranger remains foreign," he is too distant from us to threaten us; he becomes a potential threat, and a potential target of genocidal racist policy, only once he becomes "dangerously similar" to us (Baudrillard 1993b[1990]: 129). The Aztecs were destroyed not because of their radical exoticism but because they were recognized by the Christian Europeans as in fact more intensely religious than the Christians themselves, as evidenced by their sacrificial frenzies and expenditure (1993b[1990]: 134). By contrast, the perspective of radical exoticism is observable in the exchange that is hospitality:

> Hospitality represents a reciprocal, ritualized and theatrical dimension. Whom are we to receive, and how are we to receive them? ... The Other is my guest. Not someone who is legally equal, though different; but a foreigner, a stranger ... For this very reason, his strangeness has to be exorcized. But once he has been initiated in due form, my guest's life becomes even more precious to me than my own. *In this symbolic universe there is no place for the otherness of difference. Neither animals, nor gods, nor the dead, are other. All are caught up in the same cycle ...* All other cultures are extraordinarily hospitable: their ability to absorb is phenomenal. Whereas we waver between ... predation pure and simple and an idealizing recognition ... From this point of view there is not much difference between Japan and Brazil, or between either of them and Jean Rouch's "manic priests": all are cannibals in the sense that they offer a lethal hospitality to values that are not and never will be theirs. (Baudrillard 1993b[1990]: 142–43; emphasis added)

The symbolic order is precisely what was left behind by the West, in the primitive world from which we advanced; it is the order Mauss, Caillois, and Bataille describe in their accounting of gifting, potlatch, and the destruction of excess, though Baudrillard is making no argument for a return to the primitive. From this holistic social order of challenge and sacrifice, the rationality of the West produced a social order fundamentally predicated on the destruction of difference in the mad quest to apply a common ruler to all.

Baudrillard recalls many examples of the way in which the Western worldview in fact creates the racist figure of the ignorant and unredeemable savage in its classificatory efforts to make sense of the havoc it has wreaked among peoples who sought only to be left alone. "Black is the derision of White," in so far as extreme and despotic examples of purportedly authentically African leadership such as Idi Amin and Emperor Jean-Bédel Bokassa are a manner of African demonstration of "contempt" for the "authenticity" provided them by the West's classificatory system: either become fully Western (an impossibility), or remain uncivilized like the figures in Jean Rouch's famous ethnographic film *Les Maîtres Fous,* "mim[ing] in epileptic, frothing trances the white clerk, the white chief of Abidjan and even locomotives" (Baudrillard 1990 [1987]: 15). The primal savagery of the African continent of the present moment is itself a Western construct; where else but from Western colonialism have they gotten AIDS (which in the most popular existing theory was introduced into human populations as a result of mid-twentieth-century French colonial practices in central West Africa) and the weapons with which they murder one another (Baudrillard 2007 [1995]: 104–5)? In effect, we produced the primitive societies in the same way we produced the Unconscious, by discovering them as terms in our classificatory system, but once they are there, and "[e]ven when they are hounded, domesticated, pacified or obliterated, they pass into our whole arterial and cultural systems as filterable viruses ... We cannot but discover them and 'liberate' them and they cannot but destroy us" (2007 [1995]: 128). The radically exotic is transgressive of the fundamental law of the West, and thereby infects it even when the latter seems to have translated the Other into its own terms. The non-Western world as a whole might well constitute, for Baudrillard, a kind of principle of challenge (and even a prediction of what is to come) to the rationality that governs the West.

Certainly Baudrillard's most radically transgressive intervention into the language of left sacrality had to do with his numerous discussions of death and terrorism. Leaving the symbolic order and entering the modern productivist mode of exchange fundamentally shifted our relationship to the dead and death. Where once there was a sacrificial putting to death in order to "extinguish what threatens to fall out of the group's symbolic control and to bury it under all the weight of the dead," an act that is "neither violence nor an acting out of the unconscious" (Baudrillard 1993a [1976]: 138–39), death in our contemporary world is reformulated by our desire to obliterate it with rationality and science. The "natural death" has today become "the only good death" in so far as it is death "defeated and subjected to the law" (1993a[1976]: 162). Primitive death is "social, public and collective, and it is always the effect of an adversarial will that the group must absorb" (1993a[1976]: 164); here, the body is transformed into a symbolic relation in an exchange with the society of the dead. Baudrillard directly invokes Durkheim and Hertz in discussing the relationship those still immersed in the symbolic order have with their doubles and in comparing it to what emerges with the modern notion of the soul. It is a movement from a "non-alienated duel-relation with his double … [for h]e really can trade … with his shadow," while we cannot, as death has been robbed of its collective character (1993a[1976]: 141). But we recognize this, in some profound way, and are motivated to seek forms of death that transgress against this law (1993a[1976]: 165).

Baudrillard turns to two forms of contemporary transgressive death that exemplify this theoretical framework. The death of the hostage recalls sacrificial death "because we rediscover here … the ritual of execution, in the immancence of the collectively expected death" (Baudrillard 1993a[1976]: 165). Far from simply fearing the terror-related death, something deep within us is attracted by it (1993a[1976]: 166). Suicide is the other form of death that, in his exposition, escapes the logic and law of natural death; indeed, it is "the form of subversion itself" because it consists precisely in ritually destroying (in a Bataillean act of violent *dépense*) the "parcel of capital [we have] at [our] disposal" (1993a[1976]: 175–76). So radical a transgression is this act that the State will judge and condemn successful suicides in criminal trials, despite the patent ridiculousness of such acts (1993a[1976]: 176). Even when no such condemnation occurs, the contemporary order consistently endeavors to "disqualify" the suicide by "beatifying" the deceased instead of embracing the fact that such "disappearance [is] … in certain extreme situations the only true act," as did the Socialist Party when, in 1993, Pierre Bérégovoy, a failed Prime Minister in the last years of the Mitterrand administration, killed himself in disgrace (Baudrillard 2007 [1995]: 80).

If suicide at the individual level marks transgression of the dominant mode of exchange, the act of terrorism is still more radical in its turning of the principle of domination, which is normally the State's unique power to refuse the counter-gift and thereby to deny the recipient's opportunity for symbolic return, back against the State itself. In the book on seduction, Baudrillard directly juxtaposed two types of seductive "event" which parallel the pure and impure sacred. The seductive power of the cinematic star turns the masses away from the productive, but so too does the "black light" of terrorism (Baudrillard 1991 [1979]: 96). The "black magic" of terrorism derives its power from the fact that it has no goals and not even a clear enemy, as terrorists "strike at a mythical, or not even mythical, anonymous, undifferentiated enemy; a kind of omnipresent global social order" (Baudrillard 1983[1978]: 51, 55). Their acts are essentially indistinguishable from natural catastrophes (1983[1978]: 56). They are "our Theater of Cruelty" in so far as they offer "a condensed narrative, a flash ... a ritual, or that which, of all possible events, opposes to the political and historical model or order the purest symbolic form of challenge" (Baudrillard 2001a: 130).

Baudrillard's earliest discussion of terrorism focused on New Left and Palestinian terror acts of the 1970s and 1980s. The widely-discussed events in Mogadishu and Germany in October 1977 were the subject of one of his first substantive interventions on this theme. On 13 October 1977, Palestinian Arab terrorists hired by the German terrorist group the Red Army Faction hijacked a Lufthansa flight, killed the German pilot, and demanded the release of several RAF prisoners being held in Stammheim prison in Germany, threatening to blow up the plane otherwise. These terrorists were spectacularly killed by German anti-terrorist police after landing in Mogadishu, and shortly thereafter the RAF prisoners in Stammheim orchestrated a carefully planned suicide pact. The ritual their action produces and constitutes is effective, i.e., "subversive," precisely "because [it is] insoluble" (Baudrillard 2001a:130); it escapes the conventional games of signification (such as crime vs. law, or evil vs. good) by constituting a total ambivalence of meaning. There is no truth or meaning in the *dénouement* of the actions at the airfield in Mogadishu or in the cells at Stammheim, however furiously the media and other forces of power attempt to construct it. Was the hijacking botched because it did not produce the freeing of the prisoners? Did the jailers kill Baader and his comrades in Stammheim, or were they suicides? These are questions that can be asked only from within a framework that is no longer sufficient. Baudrillard suggests that the real stakes of the Mogadishu conflict are not in getting prisoners released, but rather in "oppos[ing] to the full violence and to the full order a clearly superior model of extermination and virulence operating through emptiness ... the abolition of value, of meaning, of the real ... [in a] paradoxical death which shines intensely for a moment before falling back into the real" (2001a: 132).

Baudrillard also discussed the 11 September 2001 destruction of the World Trade Center towers in New York as an act deriving its power from its contribution to symbolic exchange. Suicide terrorism of this mass and novel type challenges the system in a way well beyond even the limited suicide bombing of the Palestinians, but not because it promises an adequate military challenge to the West. On the contrary, its challenge is profound precisely because it does not attempt to take a place in that game, but instead changes the game back to a symbolic one. The goal is not to destroy capitalism, but to "humiliate" it and make it "lose face" (Baudrillard 2002: 26). It does this by attacking the "zero-death system" of capitalism in precisely the "collective sacrificial" terms to which it cannot respond, except by its own suicide and disappearance (2002: 16–17, 22). The stakes are changed and raised once the terrorists place their own deaths into the game as stakes (2002: 19). In combining the "twentieth century's two elements of mass fascination ... the white magic of the cinema and the black magic of terrorism," the September 11 attacks achieved what a purely military response could never achieve (2002: 29–30). The terrorists managed to exploit both Western capitalism's obsession with the control of death and a vertigo-inducing fact that very few of us are willing to acknowledge: that we have ourselves wished for this kind of spectacular, cataclysmic event (while watching its cinematic simulation in a dozen action films) as an escape from the tentacles of the very system to which we pledge our allegiance. The wager made by the terrorists is effective precisely because the response of the West would have to address our own desire for the symbolic violence they performed, which it can never do (2002: 5–6).

Derrida: The Transgressive Sacred and Deconstruction

During the academic year 1977–78, Derrida gave a series of lectures at the ENS devoted in large part to a reflection on Mauss's essay on the gift, later published as a book (Derrida 1992 [1991]). The book begins with a typically Derridean piece of analysis. The gift is introduced in the person of Madame de Maintenon, the famous mistress of Louis XIV, the Sun King. In her writings, de Maintenon claims that the King takes up all her time, while she would like to give it all to Saint-Cyr, the institution for the education of young women with which she was associated. The King's death in 1715 made possible her gift of her time, so, Derrida suggests playfully, might we not say that the question of the gift is "secretly linked to the death of the king," or the deconstruction of the traditional metaphysical realities of philosophy (1992 [1991]: 4)?

What is the institution of the gift, in philosophical terms? It is "aneconomic," that is, outside of the circle of exchange generated and sustained by economic relations, according to Derrida (1992[1991]: 7). Gift is that which "interrupts" this system, precisely because it refuses the rules of the system (1992[1991]: 13). There is a paradox built into gift-giving in so far as a gift, to exist as such, must not be experienced or perceived as a gift. It is an event that "does not belong to the economy of time" (1992[1991]: 18). In fact, the gift is so far outside of the normal categories of our consideration of exchange and social relation that "a consistent discourse on the gift becomes impossible" (1992[1991]: 24). All of the outside-ness of the gift makes it akin to other interstitial, marginal states and experiences, such as madness (1992[1991]: 35, 38).

Derrida situates his own contribution here explicitly in light of the earlier effort of Mauss, who, Derrida argues, had set as his task to demonstrate the originary nature of gift in exchange, thereby suggesting a more holistic ("the total social fact") way of understanding exchange than provided by traditional economic understandings. Mauss's position is that of a "liberal socialist," opposing both capitalist and Marxist communist economies, and it endeavors to a kind of rational finality. Yet, ultimately, Derrida finds that Mauss's analysis "go[es] a little mad" in so far as it has to come to terms with the radical uncertainty of the very definition of gift (1992[1991]: 46). As is true frequently for Derrida, the problem ultimately reduces to a problem of language. Mauss in fact also comes to this realization in his essay, perhaps without fully being aware of it. The term "gift" descends from a Germanic root that has the dual meaning of "offering" and "poison," the former preserved in modern English's "gift," the latter in modern German's "gift" (Mauss 1969: 46). There seems a vast amount of slipperiness in the terms "to give" and "gift"; what precisely does it mean to "give time," or for a window to "donne sur la vue," as it can in French, or to "give an order" (Derrida 1992[1991]: 52–54)? Mauss's essay, which is intended to be an essay on the gift, becomes by necessity an essay on the word "gift" (Derrida 1992[1991]: 55).

This was not the only, or even the first time that Derrida mediated on the concept of the gift and its radicality. At the 1972 Nietzsche conference at Cerisy, he presented a paper on the subject of woman in the work of Nietzsche that actually went to the heart of the question of interpretation and meaning. In Nietzsche's various invocations of woman and the sexual difference throughout his œuvre, something curious emerges: Woman manifests herself as woman *both "in giving herself,* while man takes, possesses, takes possession of … [and when she] in giving herself *gives herself for,* simulates, and thus assures for herself possessive mastery" (Derrida 1978a: 90, emphasis in original). Submission and domination are thus interchangeable according to Nietzsche, as female subordination is in fact also the means to domination of men (Derrida 1978a: 92). Derrida then demonstrates that what Nietzsche is up to here is something more systematic than a commentary on gender relations; he is describing the radical instability of the oppositions we presume metaphysically, given in the concepts of giving and taking (1978a: 92, 98).

Beyond this direct engagement with Mauss, we can locate broader connections in Derrida's philosophical project to the mystic Durkheimian interest in the transgressive sacred. For at the core of Derrida's work is a preoccupation with the aspect of western metaphysics that requires foundational binary categories that, in Derrida's analysis, are actually undone by certain crucial concepts and categories that can invoke both poles of a contradictory binary and that demonstrate the ultimate instability of seemingly firmly constructed philosophical systems of reasoning. Derrida spent considerable time examining the role played in foundational texts and writers of the western philosophical tradition by these unstable concepts and categories in order to unveil the holes in binary thought that they represent, and to criticize what he saw as a systematic classification of writing as somehow more radically separated from real metaphysical presence than is speech. Notable examples are *pharmakon* (which can mean both "poison" and "remedy") in Plato (Derrida 1981 [1968]); *supplément* (which, Derrida argued, means both "addition to" and "replacement of," with reference to writing's relationship to speech) in Rousseau (Derrida 1974 [1967]: 141–64); and, as we have just seen, "gift." In the essay on Rousseau's use of *supplément,* Derrida notes that Rousseau uses this term to allude not only to writing, but also to masturbation. In this latter case, he explicitly names the *supplément* "dangerous," as something secondary that also usurps the rightful place of that which it replaces, and Derrida suggests that writing is transgressive and "seductive" in that "it leads desire away from the good path ... guides it toward its loss or fall and therefore it is a sort of lapse or scandal" (1974 [1967]: 151). And yet, he adds, "there have never been anything but supplements" (1974 [1967]: 159).

The highly ambivalent and troubling character of the *pharmakon* is articulated neatly in Plato's *Phaedrus.* In that Platonic dialogue, Socrates tells the story of Thoth, the Egyptian deity who invented writing, passing this discipline, which he characterizes as a *pharmakon,* to the Egyptian king (Derrida 1981 [1972]: 75). It is Plato's intention to attack writing, but Derrida masterfully shows how the very term he uses to characterize it undoes the dualistic opposition that he seeks to construct (1981 [1972]: 103). Even in the figure of Thoth, Derrida shows, Plato invokes the ambivalence and transgression of the categories that one finds in *pharmakon.* For this deity "is at once his father, his son, and himself [and] cannot be assigned a fixed spot in the play of differences"; he is "[s]ly, slippery and masked, an intriguer and a card, like Hermes ... neither king nor jack, but rather a sort of joker, a floating signifier, a wild card, one who puts play into play" (1981 [1972]: 93). This is hardly the only such term to emerge in Plato, and therefore to play an important role in the very founding of philosophy. In the *Timaeus,* the term *khôra* (literally "place," "region," or "country") plays a key role; according to Derrida, it eludes binary logic altogether and "one cannot even say that it is neither this nor that or that it is both this and that at once" (1993: 16). It exceeds the *logos* while yet being unclassifiable as *mythos* (Derrida 1993: 18).

Derrida's project, in the context of what he saw as the dangerous rigidity and oppressive hierarchical character of traditional western metaphysics and logic, was to offer a new, radical kind of thought and writing that undoes this rigidity by refusing the binary categories, exposing their limitations and reveling in transgression of the hierarchical rules of traditional thought. Deconstruction aims to do precisely this, and in several works he noted the efforts of others he sees as exemplary in this regard. In a reading similar to that of Foucault, Derrida sees in Bataille's work a radical effort at "a sovereign form of writing" that embraces "the poetic or the ecstatic," which is defined by Bataille as "that *in every discourse* which can open itself up to the absolute loss of its sense, to the (non-)base of the sacred, of nonmeaning, of un-knowledge or of play, to the swoon from which it is reawakened by a throw of the dice" (Derrida 1978b [1967]: 261, 266). With Bataille, Derrida follows the Hegelian dialectic right up to the point at which it breaks down, which is when it comes up against its "blind spot," i.e., "the point at which destruction, suppression, death and sacrifice constitute so irreversible an expenditure, so radical a negativity … that they can no longer be determined as negativity in a process or a system" (1978b[1967]: 259). At this point, one must pass beyond Hegel, or must one? For the transgression enacted by Bataille's sovereign writing cannot simply obliterate the discourse or the law that it exceeds, but rather it must "conserve or confirm" it. Only in relation to that which is transgressed can it be defined as transgression and thereby gain access to the impure sacred (Derrida 1978b[1967]: 274).

Derrida interpreted the Theater of Cruelty of Artaud, which excluded from its ranks "all non-sacred theater," as analogous to his own efforts in a similar vein (1978b[1967]: 243). Jean-Michel Heimonet (1987) has carefully demonstrated the direct links between the treatment of the sacred in modern poetry by members of the Collège de Sociologie and Derrida's theory of *différance*. As we have already seen, Leiris, Caillois and Bataille were determined in their efforts to attach the Durkheimian theory they had encountered in Mauss's work to what they and others (especially the various members of the Surrealist movement) saw as a contemporary crisis in literature that was in their view linked, like the political and broader cultural crises of inter-war France, to the disappearance of myth and the sacred (see also Rieusset 1983: 67–123). Derrida had simultaneous theoretical, philosophical, political, and literary crises to address, and his response was calculated to speak to all of them at once.

Derrida directly addressed the topic of religion in a number of his writings of the 1990s. In fact, an early essay, "Violence and Metaphysics," on Levinas's criticism of Heidegger shows Derrida already concerned at the start of his career with this question: Can a religion or an ethics without violence at its core be imagined (1978b[1967]: 79–153)? We should note too that this early piece shows Derrida already thinking about the place of Jewishness in Western thought, which he would turn to with decidedly more urgency in the 1990s, in his attention to the Jewish theological origins of Levinas's thought. In *The Gift of Death* (1995a [1992]), an essay by the Czech Christian philosopher Jan Patocka, provides his starting point. Patocka sought to define the relationship of religion and ethical responsibility by removing from the former all traces of "the demonic … that which confuses the limits among the animal, the human, and the divine, and which retains an affinity with mystery, the initiatory, the esoteric, the secret or the sacred" (Derrida 1995a[1992]: 2). Religion for Patocka thus becomes nothing more or less than ethical responsibility. But Derrida questions this argument at its most fundamental level:

> One must never forget … that the mystery that is incorporated, then repressed, is never destroyed … Orgiastic mystery recurs indefinitely, it is always at work: not only in Platonism … but also in Christianity and even in the space of the *Aufklärung* and of secularization in general … every revolution, whether aesthetic or religious, bears witness to a return of the sacred in the form of an enthusiasm or fervor … Given the affinity between the sacred and secrecy, and the practices of sacrifice in initiation ceremonies, it might be said that all revolutionary fervor produces its slogans as though they were sacrificial rites or effects of secrecy. (1995a[1992]: 21)

He then notes Patocka's citation from Durkheim's *Formes élémentaires*, where the latter invoked the reemergence of the sacred in secular forms in the early years of the French Revolution, and argues that the paradox that Patocka seeks to leap over (the inescapability of the orgiastic, even in the most seemingly secular, rational, and ethical of societies) literally bursts from his own analysis. In the core of the book, Derrida turns to a consideration of the singular case in the Judeo-Christian tradition that best illustrates the paradox: the demand Yahweh makes of Abraham to sacrifice his son Isaac. Are the ethical and the sacred separable here? Only, says Derrida, if we fail to adequately understand the requirements of the two. What is required for my responsibility? Contrary to "common sense, just as for philosophical reasoning," I can only be responsible if my duty applies to me only, singularly, that is, if no one else can take my place and perform the required act. In speaking and making public my responsibility, I "renounce at the same time my liberty and my responsibility" (Derrida 1995a[1992]: 60). Paradoxically, ethical responsibility requires secrecy and silence, the realm of the sacred. Abraham does not speak of Yahweh's command that he sacrifice his son, and he does not reveal the intended act to anyone, precisely because he recognizes an absolute, singular duty before his God that he cannot compromise through discourse with others. The ethical is thus something he pursues and resists as a temptation at the same time: "He keeps quiet in order to avoid the moral temptation which, under the pretext of calling him to responsibility, to self-justification, would make him lose his ultimate responsibility along with his singularity, make him lose his unjustifiable, secret, and absolute responsibility before God" (1995a[1992]: 61).

Though it is crystallized in Abraham's dilemma, this scandalous paradox shows through the entirety of the Abrahamic religions. The message of Jesus that his disciples must come to hate their own parents, children, and indeed, their own lives, is nothing more than the sacrificial requirement to "hate and betray what is most lovable" (Derrida 1995a[1992]: 64). Ethics and ritual violence wind up not in neat opposition but in collusion. Abraham sacrifices ethics in moving to put his son to death, at the same time as he fulfills the letter of ethical responsibility in the same act (1995a[1992]: 66). In thus acting, he is at once "the most responsible and the most irresponsible of men," an ethical paragon and a monster (1995a[1992]: 72). All ethical acting, Derrida adds, is condemned to the same paradox. That which most radically transgresses against responsibility and ethics is always in fact entailed by ethical action.

This same idea of the inescapable presence of the orgiastic at the very heart of Western secular Enlightenment can be found in the paper Derrida wrote for a 1995 conference on religion. Titled "Foi et Savoir," it denied the radical separation of religion and the secular reason of the Enlightenment and argued that in the Western world, the very parameters for thinking the thing "religion" have from the earliest moment been irrevocably intertwined with the knowledge and reason of the Enlightenment. This is most strikingly evident in the fact that the Indo-European term for "god" (*deiwos*) means "luminous," the same light and luminosity alluded to by the various European terms for "Enlightenment" (Derrida 1998 [1996]: 7). He returns here to the same question raised in *The Gift of Death:* Can religion be freed from the orgiastic, the sacrificial, the violent, the secret and mysterious—in short, the sacred? His answer is the same:

> [T]he divided law, the double bind, also the dual foci, the ellipsis or originary duplicity of religion, consists therein, that the law of the unscathed, the salvation of the safe, the humble respect of that which is sacrosanct (*heilig*, holy) both requires and excludes sacrifice, which is to say, the indemnification of the unscathed, the price of immunity. (1998 [1996]: 52)

This is all of tremendous import given the emphasis in much of Derrida's late work on ethics and responsibility. If the religious is inseparable from the ethical, and the holy/*heilig*/sacred is inseparable from the religious, then the holy/*heilig*/sacred must be inseparable from the ethical.

Deleuze: The Transgressive Sacred and Schizoanalysis

In perhaps his lengthiest published reference to Durkheim, Deleuze (with Guattari)[2] is explicit in siding with Durkheim's old rival, Gabriel Tarde, against the founder of the *Année sociologique*. Yet a little investigation reveals that Deleuze's discussion of Durkheim hinges on precisely the distinction of ascetic and mystic Durkheimianism I have been elaborating. What distinguishes Durkheim and Tarde, according to Deleuze, is the fact that Durkheim's

> preferred objects of study were the great collective representations, which are generally binary, resonant, and overcoded. Tarde countered that collective representations presuppose exactly what needs explaining, namely, "the similarity of millions of people." That is why Tarde was interested instead in the world of detail, or of the infinitesimal: the little imitations, oppositions, and inventions constituting an entire realm of subrepresentative matter ... The Durkheims answered that what Tarde did was psychology or inter-psychology, not sociology. But that is true only in appearance ... a microimitation does seem to occur between two individuals. But at the same time and at a deeper level, it has to do with not an individual but with a flow or a wave. Imitation is a propagation of a flow; opposition is binarization, the making binary of flows; invention is a conjugation or connection of different flows ... in the end the difference is not at all between the social and the individual (or interindividual), but between the molar realm of representations, individual or collective, and the molecular realm of beliefs and desires in which the distinction between the social and the individual loses all meaning since flows are neither attributable to individuals nor overcodable by collective signifiers. Representations already define large-scale aggregates, or determine segments on a line; beliefs and desires, on the other hand, are flows marked by quanta, flows that are created, exhausted, or transformed, added to one another, subtracted or combined. (Deleuze and Guattari 1987 [1980]: 218–19)

We should note immediately the resonance of some of what Deleuze classifies here as oppositional to Durkheimianism with the positions Mauss, Hubert, and Hertz articulated regarding the thought of Bergson and Nietzsche and the category of *mana* and its absorption of the binarism of the sacred, which I discussed at length in earlier chapters. It is also telling that, in the first volume of *Capitalism and Schizophrenia*, Deleuze solidly situates the study in a Durkheimian framework, if with reference to Mauss instead of Durkheim. The notion of the "inscribing socius" is at least as pro-Durkheimian as it is anti-Marxian; the idea here is that society is fundamentally based in "inscription" and the "essential thing is to mark and to be marked" (1977 [1972]: 142). The Maussian discussion of gifting and potlatch is explicitly taken up and championed here (1977[1972]: 149–50). Still later in the same text, Deleuze deliberately links the desire that is the fundamental conceptual core of the book to the Maussian theoretical apparatus: "Desire knows nothing of exchange, it knows only theft and gift, at times the one within the other under the effect of a primary homosexuality" (1977[1972]: 186).

It has sometimes been remarked by commentators on Deleuze that his is an anti-binarist theoretical framework, fundamentally opposed to something like the Durkheimian reliance on the opposed categories of sacred and profane. It is of course easy to find hostility to dialectical thinking, which has a certain relationship to binary structures, in Deleuze, but it is also easy to find him constructing binaries himself. One can argue with much evidence that the entire project of *Capitalism and Schizophrenia* is based on binary opposing categories, those Deleuze rejects and those he embraces. There are, for example, "two poles of social libidinal investment," the one "reactionary and fascisizing," the other "revolutionary"; there is the socius opposed to the body without organs; the molar opposed to the molecular (Deleuze and Guattari 1977[1972]: 366). There are, he writes, "two sorts of unconscious ... the one schizoanalytic, the other psychoanalytic; the one schizophrenic, the other neurotic-Oedipal ... the one really concrete, the other symbolic; the one machinic, the other structural; the one molecular, microphyscial and micrological, and the other molar or statistical ... the one productive, the other expressive" (1977[1972]: 381). Often, just after an argument rejecting some binary, Deleuze gives us another that he apparently accepts; for instance, after rejecting that of "vitalism vs. mechanism," he presents a "real" binarism of the "two states of the machine," i.e., molar and desiring (1977[1972]: 286).

I should also address the idea that Deleuze's theory cannot adequately be called transgressive because he denies the binary relation law/transgression and rejects law altogether (see e.g., Bourg 2007: 120). Deleuze himself provided considerable fuel for this engine in his caustic remarks about Bataille's fixation on transgression, which he once called "a concept too good for seminarists under the law of the Pope or a priest" (Deleuze and Parnet 2007 [1977]: 47), although we should also note that he cites Bataille approvingly in the same discussion of Mauss and the gift just discussed above (Deleuze and Guattari 1977[1972]: 190). Yet there is much in Deleuze's elaboration of the "schizorevolutionary" and the various other concepts that accompany it that looks remarkably like the remade versions of the transgressive sacred we have seen in the other poststructuralists. There is a powerful concentration on destruction that resonates in the same way as Baudrillard's call to symbolic violence that shatters the frame of productivism, or Foucault's embrace of the unrecuperable violence of Rivière and other "infamous men":

> Destroy, destroy. The task of schizoanalysis goes by way of destruction ... Destroy Oedipus, the illusion of the ego, the puppet of the superego, guilt, the law, castration. It is not a matter of pious destruction, such as those performed by psychoanalysis under the benevolent neutral eye of the analyst. For these are Hegel-style destructions, ways of conserving ... Destroying beliefs and representations, theatrical scenes. And when engaged in this task no activity will be too malevolent. (Deleuze and Guattari 1977[1972]: 311, 314)

Deleuze, like Foucault, wants to retheorize madness, to "undo ... all the reterritorializations that transform madness into mental illness" through an explicit kind of "antipsychiatry"; he foresees "an age when madness would disappear ... because the exterior limit designated by madness would be overcome by means of other flows escaping control on all sides, and carrying us along" (1977[1972]: 321). Is this the complete escape from an existing framework or the revaluation of an element of that framework?

We find some particularly powerful evidence of Deleuze's engagement with the transgressive sacred in his intriguing book on Sade and Masoch. This study, which is not often foregrounded in discussions of Deleuze's œuvre, presents both of the two pornographic writers named in the title as "great anthropologists, of the type whose work succeeds in embracing a whole conception of man, culture and nature" (Deleuze 1971 [1967]: 16). Both are read as essentially involved in constructing theories for the construction of ecstatic social spaces/situations through "subversion of the law" (1971[1967]: 75). Masochism is a theory of contracts "which, once established, becomes ... increasingly cruel and restrictive towards one of the parties," who yet derives sensual or experiential satisfaction from the relationship characterized by "waiting and suspense ... pleasure ... delayed and preceded by pain, punishment or humiliation" (1971[1967]: 62, 66–7). Sadism, in contrast, is a theory based, in Deleuze's reading, on the "deepest hostility for contract and law" (1971[1967]: 67). It is institutions that interest Sade because, unlike contract and law, they elude the reciprocal, equalizing perspective of rights and duties and instead encompass "a long-term state of affairs which is both involuntary and inalienable

... [They] render laws unnecessary [by replacing] the system of rights and duties by a dynamic model of action, authority, and power" (1971[1967]: 67–68). This is a social theory not unlike that proposed by St. Just during the French Revolution, a state of "free, anarchic action, in perpetual motion, in permanent revolution, in a constant state of immorality," precisely because no laws will be permitted to rigidify the flux of social relations into some sedentary state (1971[1967]: 69). Institutions are in this sense deeper than law and contract, which is of course an essentially Durkheimian position, although clearly the emphasis here is on the transgressive power of the energy in those institutional sites.

Deleuze also discusses the distinct visions of social utopia presented by Sade and Masoch. For the former, it is "rationalistic and atheistic Masonic and anarchistic societies" (Deleuze 1971[1967]: 80), certainly not the totalitarianisms that careless readers of Sade infer must be his ideal. He even favorably cites Bataille's reading of Sade as the best proof "to invalidate all theories relating Sade to Nazism" since Bataille noted that "the language of Sade ... is essentially that of the victim," not that of the victimizer (1971[1967]: 16). For Masoch, the utopia is to be found in "mystical agrarian sects" in which contract and law ultimately lead to the creation of ritual and myth, subjection to a "terrible Tsarina ... [wielding] the most sentimental but at the same time the coldest and severest law" naturally leading to the emergence of ritualistic cults for said Tsarina (1971[1967]: 80, 84). The transgressive pleasure of Sadism and Masochism come at bottom, for Deleuze, from the particular way in which they transform the relationship between repetition and the pleasure principle. Both theories of interaction or exchange consist in a process of movement between desexualization and resexualization, and this "instantaneous leap" from one to the other is what permits what we should ordinarily experience as pain to be experienced instead as voluptuous pleasure (1971[1967]: 104). Tellingly, Deleuze describes this whole process as a kind of "mysticism" (1971[1967]: 104–5). It is perhaps not too much to argue that Deleuze reads the visions of Masoch and Sade as representative of pure and impure sacred, respectively, both oriented to experiences that are ecstatic (ex-stasis) but the one centered on "draw[ing] up contracts" and the other on "abominat[ing] and destroy[ing] them" (1971[1967]: 20).

A central theoretical image in the second volume of *Capitalism and Schizophrenia* also resonates significantly with the Durkheimian mystic tradition. The central thrust of Deleuze's effort here was to theorize an experience he compared to Gregory Bateson's notion of plateau, which are "continuing regions of intensity ... a piece of immanence" (Deleuze and Guattari 1987 [1980]: 158). These experiences of intensity are generated, as they are in Mauss, Hertz, Bataille et al., not in isolation but socially; they emerge in situations in which the individual disappears completely into the social in the form Deleuze named the "body without organs": "Where psychoanalysis says 'Stop, find your self again,' we should say instead, 'Let's go further still, we haven't found our BwO [body without organs] yet, we haven't sufficiently dismantled our self'" (1987[1980]: 151). Whereas in the first volume, Deleuze had emphasized destruction, here he describes in positive terms the kinds of experiences that will challenge what he calls the socius; these experiences are nonetheless of a clear relation to the experiences the mystic Durkheimian tradition elaborated. The plateaus alluded to in the title are an effort directed at once at the levels of biological and social realities. They are predicated on the idea that a theoretical model based on the notion of the root, which presumes relationships and experiences defined by clear beginning and ending points, is inferior to one based instead on the rhizome, which "connects any point to any other point, and ... brings into play very different regimes of signs, and even nonsign states" (1987[1980]: 21). The rhizome is made up not of clear beginning and ending points, but instead consists of an infinite number of in-between points that Deleuze describes as "continuous self-vibrating region[s] of intensities whose development avoids any orientation toward a culmination point or external end" (1987[1980]: 22). The body without organs and the process of "becoming-intense" that it involves is tied, in the molar, repressive social and moral order of capitalist relations, to experiences that are just the sort of transgressive, extreme experiences we find in the impure sacred, and especially in the work of Bataille. The bulk of the empirical examples Deleuze provides are examples of deviant sexual and erotic practices, from masochism to Chinese Taoist methods of prolonged intercourse, i.e., varieties of sexual pleasure not linearly directed toward orgasmic finality but instead to a kind of elaborate sexual mysticism (1987[1980]: 151, 155, 157, 241). In keeping with the prevalent political tenor of the movement of May 1968, various kinds of radical political action are also included as examples of "becoming-intense"; Deleuze even names "crime societies" and "riot groups" as examples (1987[1980]: 247). Despite a general antipathy toward molar religion, Deleuze also recognized in the prophetic personality a propensity toward the nomadic and the "becoming-intense" (1987[1980]: 382–83).

Notes

1. The source of the discussion that follows are cassette tapes of the lectures in the Foucault archives at IMEC.
2. A brief intervention on a complex topic: I take the work published collectively by Deleuze and Guattari as more indicative of the overall intellectual tenor and tra-

jectory of the former than of the latter, and therefore proceed in the discussion of that collective work as essentially compatible with an overall Deleuzian project. There is considerable evidence as to the relative status of the contributions of the two to their group project to back up this reading; in his journal, Guattari noted during their collaboration that Deleuze "works a lot. We are truly not of the same dimensions!" (Dosse 2007: 24), and it was apparently even the case that one of the books bearing the names of both men was actually entirely the work of Deleuze, and Guattari was brought in only in the last stage of preparing the book (which was *Qu'est-ce que la philosophie?*) as a personal favor by Deleuze to help bring his friend out of a depression (Dosse 2007: 27).

13 Godless Intellectuals, Then? Or … Something Else?

At the conclusion of *Formes élémentaires*, Durkheim posed a question: What shape will religion take in the future, as secularization, already well underway in his time, continues its expansion? I have argued that he was posing this question for the intellectuals as much as for everyone else, and that the echoes of that fact resounded in some ways that have not been fully understood. Mystic Durkheimianism, in its incarnations among the young *Année* members, in the Collège de Sociologie, or in some varieties of the poststructuralism that emerged in France in the 1960s, constitutes a fascinatingly nuanced intellectual response to secularization and the question of the sacred. This intellectual tradition forces us perhaps to think a bit harder about what we imagine we already know well, and indeed about what structures almost all our discourse on the issue, academic as well as popular. Ask just about anyone what they think about religion, God, or the supernatural, and you will frequently get a response fitted to an assumed binary framework: "Yes, I am religious/spiritual" (side A of the binary), or "No, I am not" (side B of that schema). One is either religious or one is secular; one simply cannot be both at once, or neither the one nor the other, that is, something else. Not only do we build this into the framework of our surveys of the population, thus perhaps creating a set of categories rather than reflecting what is already there; but we also frequently apply it as an unquestioned category of knowledge about ourselves, even when it rubs hard against our actual experience of our identities.

The mystic Durkheimian tradition addresses this question in a complex manner, succinctly summarized by Derrida in a response to an inquiry regarding his own status *vis-à-vis* the religious object of his intellectual interest: "Who can say, 'I am a believer?' Who *knows* that? ... And who can say 'I am an atheist'?" (Caputo, Hart, and Sherwood 2005: 46–47). Implied in each purported state, Derrida went on to argue, are characteristics of the other. The strongest faith is always troubled by radical doubt; who believes that Abraham, standing before Isaac with the knife, or Jesus on the cross crying out, "Father, why have you forsaken me?" were not terrified to their core that the one in whom they had put their trust in fact did not exist and therefore would not help them in their hour of direst need? The most rigorous critic of religious belief experiences the same complex reality of a constant oscillation between the two points; how else to explain the frequency of foxhole or aging atheists spontaneously emerging in those moments of crisis as members of the faithful, or the antagonist of supernatural beliefs who nonetheless still engages in ritualistic finger-crossing or mumbled prayers in moments of suspense? In fact, the ascetic Durkheim had already long ago alluded to just the nuance to which Derrida was speaking in describing what he saw as the existential requirement for the scholarly approach to religion. To those who called themselves "free thinkers," Durkheim defended the necessity of approaching the study of religion with religious sentiment: "[W]hoever does not bring to the study of religion a sort of religious sentiment cannot speak of it! He would be like a blind man who would speak of color!" (1970: 309). But this did not mean entering into the religious perspective in the holistic way generally described by its proponents, for it had to be accepted, Durkheim went on to argue, that "humanity is abandoned, on this world, to its own powers and it cannot count on anything beyond itself to direct its destiny" (1970: 313). But how can the materialist remain a materialist and at the same time adapt to "the state of mind of the believer" (1970: 309)?

Durkheim did not expand on his view, but we find the answer developed in the subsequent tradition of mystic Durkheimianism. Bataille put this position admirably well in an interview conducted a little more than a year before his death:

> Everyone knows what God represents for the mass of men who believe in him, and what place he occupies in their thought, and I think that when the personage of God is suppressed from that place, there nonetheless remains something, an empty place. It is that empty place that I have wanted to speak of. (Chapsal 1973: 30–31)

Here then is the emergence of the possibility of an intellectual and personal position with respect to religion that cannot be reduced to either of the two options assumed by most observers. This is a position outside the either/or imperative presented by the two positions just described, which are mirrored in two contemporary social scientific perspectives on the question of religion: We might call them the crude materialist and the New Age postmodernist. The first of these (common in sociology departments) rejects religious knowledge as mere delusion, generally linked to illegitimate hierarchy and power, and champions a mechanistic worldview wholly devoid of anything that cannot be fully reduced to inert matter. The second (encountered among some cultural anthropologists) endeavors to correct the lacunae of the first, an admirable intention inaptly handled by assuming there are important hidden verities in religious knowledge that the researcher must seek to discover by initiating herself into the mysteries of this way of knowing, for example, by becoming a Yaqui shaman (Castaneda 1968), a Songhay sorceror (Stoller 2004), or an astrologer (Teissier 2001); instead of the crude materialist's "Down with religion!," the response here is "Down with crude materialism—and therefore *back* to religion!"

The mystic Durkheimian escape from the dilemmas of these two positions on religious knowledge can be compared to the position Bruno Latour stakes out on the question of how best to understand knowledge claims more generally. Latour describes and criticizes two common, opposed positions on epistemology, "particular universalism" and "cultural relativism," which line up well with the two social scientific positions on religion just described. In both of Latour's categories, the natural world is seen as outside of society, but the epistemological relationship between nature and social groups is different in the two. In particular universalism, one culture (the Western, scientific one) has a superior, privileged perspective on nature that raises it epistemologically above all other cultural groups. In cultural relativism, on the contrary, all cultures have precisely the same perspective on and insight into nature, and no superior knowledge claims can be made (Latour 1993[1991]: 105). In Latour's third way, which he calls "symmetrical anthropology," both nature and society are entities that must be constituted by particular collectivities in action, and cultural groups differ in exactly how they undertake this constitutive action through the mobilization of networks and resources. In his terms:

> [T]he differences are sizeable, but they are only of size. They are important (and the error of cultural relativism is that it ignores them), but they are not disproportionate (and the error of universalism is that it sets them up as a Great Divide). The collectives are all similar, except for their size, like the successive helixes of a single spiral. The fact that one of the collectives needs ancestors and fixed stars while another one, more eccentric, needs genes and quasars, is explained by the dimensions of the collective to be held together. (Latour 1993[1991]: 108)

Like the crude materialists, the universalists believe there is a way out of the process of mobilizing forces for epistemological claims; they believe some such claims carry epistemological superiority inherently in their very structure. And as with the New Age postmodernists, the cultural relativists, in their desire to equalize all epistemological claims, fail to attend to meaningful differences in how particular knowledges are articulated; moreover, they commit an unconscionable sin against their own relativist doctrine by forgetting that they too are members of a tribe (that of Western social scientific intellectuals), and that tribe has established rules for constructing and evaluating knowledge that they flout in attempting to join other tribes, whether those of the Yaqui, the Songhay, or the astrologers, and use their strategies. But we Western intellectuals are not members of those tribes, and we therefore cannot purport to use their tribally-rooted modes of knowledge production, because our networks, our collectives are not the same.

For Latour, the most promising way to attack the knowledge problem is through an anthropology that has "come home from the tropics" (Latour 1993: 100), that is, an anthropology that will (finally) effectively account for its own knowledge perspective and fully renounce the Romantic project of identification with the mobilization strategies and systems of Rousseau's noble savage. In a turning that they perhaps did not and could not anticipate, the cultural relativists find themselves guilty of the same crime with which they vehemently (and correctly) charge the universalists: They want to occupy a view from nowhere, not that of scientific knowledge, to be sure, but instead that of the pure, innocent, and naturally-attuned Other. The constructivist vision must be brought to bear on all religious knowledge, indeed on all knowledge, but this cannot mean that we Western social scientists thereby become capable of throwing off our own positionality and tribal location. Our tribe simply has no space for shamans, or magical faith healing, or astrology as a predictive art; it operates according to a logic of the rejection of such resources and an embrace of others, and it is all that we have to work with, just as the space of magical faith healings is the limit of the tools available to some other cultural groups. At the same time, we accept, precisely because of our own particular set of cultural prejudices and values, that our local gods are not God, and our local strategies for forming collectives and making knowledge claims stick are not universally accepted or useful strategies. Like Hertz confronting the faithful of Saint Besse, ours must be the position not of the scientific imperialist who would impose our truth on the highlander seeking magical stones from the sacred rock, nor of the fellow cult celebrant who happily joins the highlander to look for his own sacred stones, but of the humble and eternal skeptic who wants to understand how the sacred rock seeker's strategy is useful to him because that is the business of our work, and we desire to carry it out despite the inevitable doubts we have, as an inescapable element of our condition, about even the claims *we* will make.

As we have seen described throughout the book, at the root of this quest to reinvent the sacred is an attempt by the intellectual class to speak to a problem of consuming social importance, which they believed was applicable not only to themselves but to the rest of society as well, but that historical developments seem to indicate was and still is to very large degree a problem specifically of the intellectuals. That problem was the threat of disappearance of the sacred, and the response from the Durkheimians was to endeavor to find a way to reconstruct it and thereby retain its primordial social energy, not simply to destroy it, as contemporary materialist intellectuals suggested. The Durkheimians especially were acutely attuned to the great complexities and seeming contradictions of the status of the sacred in the modern world. It seemed at one and the same time an anachronism (especially for the educated classes) and an indispensable source of social effervescence (especially for the less well-educated classes), and they realized, perhaps better than any other group of thinkers then or since, that the modern project for intellectuals entailed a continuing struggle with this paradoxical problem. The real roots of the paradox become apparent when one examines the status of the sacred outside of intellectual circles, for the evidence that the sacred is in danger in its traditional forms and discourses there has proven somewhat less than convincing, to say the least, as even those intellectuals sympathetic to radical secularization admit (see e.g., Gellner 1992). This is particularly so in the United States and in large segments of the global East and South, where very large majorities of people respond to questions on their relationship to these traditional sacred objects and systems of belief affirmatively; even in the former Soviet Bloc, where traditional religious faiths have re-emerged since the fall of communism, and in Western Europe, where post-1960s new religious movements are making significant advances to the dismay of many governments in the region, we see clear evidence of the limits of secularization theory.

So, to use the categories that emerge in Ernest Gellner's work on postmodernism and Islam (1992), if it seems relatively clear that the two positions he names as fundamentalist (i.e., religious fundamentalism, on the one hand, and Enlightenment, rationalist, and materialist foundationalism, on the other) still clearly remain options for large segments of the population, even in the West, then we should probably be quite careful in advancing the kinds of simple claims about a generalized postmodern condition, wherein relativism reigns, that appear in some treatments of the subject. As Zygmunt Bauman argues, it is a fact that "intellectuals tend to articulate their *own* societal situation and the problems it creates as a situation of the society at large, and its, systemic or social, problems" (1988: 225; emphasis added). Recognition of this fact has some important consequences for our understanding of much in the landscape of intellectual development and history. Most centrally, it requires suspicion of simple distinctions between so-called modern and postmodern theories of the social (which are, respectively, frequently propounded by intellectuals in one or the other camp on the issue of religious experience and identity described above) at least in so far as it is understood that both kinds of theories are created by intellectuals with just the biases Bauman notes, and that, indeed, the very idea of a postmodern condition has something important to do with the emerging crisis in the intellectual class related to its relationship to the sacred. This is not, however, to say that the entirety of what is labeled postmodern theory (which often includes the work of the poststructuralist group discussed in this book) can or should be discarded as irrelevant, as Gellner and some others seem inclined to suggest; we ought to be careful, though, in attempting to generalize its applicability too readily. This caution will better enable us, in my view, to understand the ways in which some varieties of classical sociology and some varieties of postmodern and/or poststructuralist theory, far from being necessarily antagonistic to one another, can in fact mutually benefit one another if one recognizes their commonalities. Those theses and claims from postmodern theory on the purported death of the social, on the implosion or irrelevance of the central categories of sociological inquiry (e.g., social class, ideology, status, anomie, social differentiation, authority, alienation, community) and their necessary replacement by new categories created for theorization of this new postmodern world (e.g., spectacle, simulacra, fatal strategies, rhizomes, war machines, bodies without organs, emotive tribes, the hyperreal) must be viewed skeptically (Turner and Rojek 1993: 72). Even if one accepts a definition of sociology as "a social science having as its main focus the study of social institutions [and processes] brought into being by the industrial transformations of the past two or three centuries" (Giddens 1982: 9) and therefore believes that sociology is fundamentally the study of the social consequences of modernity, there is absolutely no need to see it as superceded by postmodernism. In fact, the very phenomenon involving some groups of intellectuals that I have discussed here is nothing if not a consequence of modernity, and we should be able to examine it with the tools of sociology. But, at the same time, we must be careful to be critical of sociological pronouncements on the futility or ridiculousness of all postmodern theory, as it seems clear that the rise of this perspective offers unique tools and self-reflexive possibility for the sociologists to more fruitfully account for their own activity and engagement in their work. As much interesting sociological theory in recent years has been centrally concerned with this problem of reflexivity and the sociology of sociology, one should be attentive to using new tools for this endeavor.

The postmodern moment thus remains compelling and of the greatest importance for those of us who are centrally concerned with the situation of the intellectual. In the opening chapter, I reiterated Edward Shils's argument concerning the intellectual as the figure in any social order most involved in the realm of transcendent and universal manufacture and manipulation of symbols that he identified as the engagement with the sacred. Even some seemingly clearly secular intellectuals, in Shils's view, are in fact centrally engaged with the sacred; for example, science and philosophy are as deeply implicated in the exploration of ultimate and transcendent realms of value as is religion (Shils 1972: 16). My work in this book might be seen as something of a limited confirmation of this theory, as it has revealed the parallels between classical sociology and poststructuralist theory, both seemingly secular in the extreme, in terms of their mutual interest in re-theorizing and preserving the sacred and their common alliance against the challenge of a materialist reductionism that is in its essence the most powerful enemy of difference. We would do well to recall too Szakolczai's description of the self-reflexive sociological engagement he finds in the work and lives of Weber and Foucault, and which we can see in the Durkheimians as well. This engagement considers the sociological enterprise to be centrally involved in the project of intellectual identity-construction and self-understanding, and not limited to more one-sided analysis of an inert external social world. In this definition, the sociological enterprise can be fruitfully linked to the self-reflexive project that is poststructuralist theory, which is centrally engaged in understanding the effect on the theorist of producing theory.

I have a final observation on the perspective of this book, which runs the risk of a radical misreading from both sides of the divide described between crude materialists and New Age postmodernists. In discussing the book's argument with colleagues during the time it was being written, I received more or less scandalized responses from some fellow social scientists and other university professors and researchers who found it at best strange, and occasionally altogether distressing, that one would consider comparing, in any terms, the Durkheimians to the poststructuralists, or the poststructuralists to the Durkheimians, or either group to people who actually believed in the existence of supernatural beings. Postmodern sociologists and anthropologists who snicker at the stereotype of the positivist Durkheimians that they learned about in their graduate courses have chided me for wanting to show connections between their heroes and the hated social *scientists*, though at the same time some have (equally incorrectly) presumed that, because I have argued here for the depth of the mystic Durkheimian concern for religious knowledge, the argument being presented is that Mauss, Hertz, Hubert et al. must have shared their own belief that there are no crucial differences between religious and scientific knowledge and that therefore social scientific intellectuals owe no greater allegiance to the one or the other. On the other hand, some traditional partisans of Durkheim (often armed with an array of misconceptions and prejudices concerning Baudrillard, Derrida et al.) have assured me that the thesis of this book could not possibly be right, and the second-generation mystic Durkheimians must certainly, and probably willfully, have misunderstood what Mauss and Hertz were saying.

The case, of course, must ultimately be made in the twelve chapters preceding this one. I would not make so bold as to follow Bourdieu's statement about his *Homo Academicus* and call this "a book for burning," but I believe it safe to say that, like Bourdieu's book, it will in some quarters raise questions about the author's fidelity to the tradition. Along these lines, Derrida once spoke about his place in the philosophical tradition as both "faithful and unfaithful":

> [I]t is necessary to know how to reaffirm that which comes "before us" … Reaffirm, what does this mean? Not only to accept this heritage, but to recast it otherwise and keep it alive … My desire resembles that of a lover of tradition who would like to free himself from conservatism. Imagine someone mad about the past … but mad in a way that fears the dated, the nostalgic, and the cult of memory. (Derrida and Roudinesco 2001: 15, 16–17)

His infidelity to that tradition, i.e., his interest in reading Plato, Rousseau, and Heidegger in ways that stretched and even contradicted existing frameworks for understanding that work, made him more than a few enemies, although he believed this infidelity was as important as the continuation of a static orthodoxy. I have adopted a similar faithlessness in reading Derrida himself, and all the other key players in this study, against orthodox readings in order to stretch the parameters of our understanding of their work and the meaning of their lives. But I would insist that this inquiry too has been, precisely in the sense of Derrida's remark, *faithful.*

Bibliography

Afary, Janet and Kevin B. Anderson. 2004. "The Seductions of Islamism: Revisiting Foucault and the Iranian Revolution," *New Politics*, 10, no. 1 (Summer).

Alexander, Jeffrey. 1988. "Introduction: Durkheimian Sociology and Cultural Studies Today." In *Durkheimian Sociology: Cultural Studies*, ed. Jeffrey Alexander. Cambridge: Cambridge University Press:.

———. 2003. *The Meanings of Social Life: A Cultural Sociology*. Oxford: Oxford University Press.

Alibert, François-Paul. 1928. *Terre d'Aude*. Carcassonne: Louis Gally.

Althusser, Louis. 1993[1992]. *The Future Lasts Forever: A Memoir*, ed. Olivier Corpet and Yann Moulier Boutang, trans. Richard Veasey. New York: New Press.

———. 1998. *Lettres à Franca, 1961–1973*. Paris: Stock/IMEC.

Andler, Charles. 1977[1932]. *La Vie de Lucien Herr (1864–1926)*. Paris: François Maspero.

Armel, Aliette. 1997. *Michel Leiris*. Paris: Fayard.

Aron, Jean-Paul. 1984. *Les Modernes*. Paris: Gallimard.

Aron, Raymond. 1955. *L'Opium des intellectuels*. Paris: Calmann-Lévy.

Artières, Philippe, Laurent Quéro, and Michelle Zancarini-Fournel, eds. 2003. *Le Groupe d'Information sur les Prisons: Archives d'une lutte 1970–72*. Caens: Éditions de l'IMEC.

Azéma, Jean-Pierre and Michel Winock. 1976. *La Troisième République (1870–1940)*. Paris: Calmann-Lévy.

Barrès, Maurice. 1925. *Scènes et doctrines de nationalisme*, 2nd vol.. Paris: Plon.

Barrett, William. 1962. *Irrational Man*. Garden City: Doubleday Anchor.

Barthes, Roland. 1981. *Le Grain de la voix: entretiens 1962–1980*. Paris: Éditions du Seuil.

Bataille, Georges. 1970. *Oeuvres Complètes I*. Paris: Gallimard.

———. 1985. *Vision of Excess: Selected Writings, 1927–1939*, trans. Allan Stoekl. Minneapolis: University of Minnesota Press.

———. 1986[1957]. *Erotism: Death and Sensuality*, trans. Mary Dalwood. San Francisco: City Light Books.

———. 1987. *Lettres à Roger Caillois, 4 août 1935–4 février 1959*, ed. Jean-Pierre Le Bouler. Paris: Éditions Folle Avoine.

———. 1991[1949]. *The Accursed Share (1. Consumption)*, trans. Robert Hurley. New York: Zone Books.

Baudelaire, Charles. 1995. *Les paradis artificiels/Le spleen de Paris*. Paris: Bookking International.

Baudrillard, Jean. 1975. "Au- delà de l'inconscient: le symbolique." *Critique* 31, no. 333. ((February)): 196–216.

———. 1975[1973]. *The Mirror of Production*, trans. Mark Poster. St. Louis: Telos Press.

———. 1983[1978]. *In the Shadow of the Silent Majorities ... or the End of the Social and other essays*, trans. Paul Foss, Paul Patton, and John Johnston. New York: Semiotext(e).

———. 1985. *La Gauche divine: chronique des années 1977–1984*. Paris: Grasset.

———. 1988. *Jean Baudrillard: Selected Writings*, ed. Mark Poster. Palo Alto: Stanford University Press.

———. 1990[1987]. *Cool Memories*, trans. Chris Turner. London: Verso.

———. 1991[1979]. *Seduction*, trans. Brian Singer. New York: St. Martin's Press.

———. 1993a[1976]. *Symbolic Exchange and Death*, trans. Iain Hamilton Grant. London: Sage.

———. 1993b[1990]. *The Transparency of Evil: Essays on Extreme Phenomena*. New York: Verso.

———. 1993c. *Baudrillard Live: Selected Interviews*, edited by Mike Gane. London/ New York: Routledge.

———. 1997. *Le Paroxyste indifférent: entretiens avec Philippe Petit*. Paris: Grasset.

———. 2001a. *The Uncollected Baudrillard*, ed. Gary Genosko. London: Sage.

———. 2001b. *D'un fragment l'autre: entretiens avec François L'Yvonnet*. Paris: Albin Michel.

———. 2002. *The Spirit of Terrorism and Requiem for the Twin Towers*, trans. Chris Turner. London: Verso.

———. 2004. *Fragments: Conversations with François L'Yvonnet*. London: Routledge.

———. 2005. *À Propos de l'Utopie*. Paris: Sens & Tonka.

———. 2007[1995]. *Fragments: Cool Memories III, 1990–1995*, trans. Emily Agar. London: Verso.

Bauman, Zygmunt. 1988. "Is there a Postmodern Sociology?" *Theory, Culture & Society*, 5: 217–37.

Beaud, Michel. 1971. *Vincennes An III: Le Ministère contre l'université*. Paris: Éditions Jérôme Martineau.

Bélanger, André. 1997. *The Ethics of Catholicism and the Consecration of the Intellectual*. Montréal: McGill-Queen's University Press.

Bellah, Robert. 1970. *Beyond Belief: Essays on Religion in a Post-Traditional World*. New York: Harper and Row.

Benda, Julien. 1975. *La Trahison des clercs*. Paris: Grasset.

Bennington, Geoffrey and Jacques Derrida. 1991. *Jacques Derrida*. Chicago: University of Chicago Press.

Berger, Peter. 1963. *Invitation to Sociology: A Humanistic Perspective*. Garden City: Doubleday.

———. 1969. *The Sacred Canopy: Elements of a Sociological Theory of Religion*. Garden City: Anchor.

Bergson, Henri. 1977[1932]. *The Two Sources of Morality and Religion*, trans. R. A. Audia and C. Brereton. Notre Dame: Notre Dame University Press.

Besnard, Philippe. 1982. "L'Anomie dans la biographie intellectuelle de Durkheim." *Sociologie et société*, 14, no. 2: 45–54.

———, ed. 1983. *The Sociological Domain: The Durkheimians and the Founding of French Sociology*. London and Paris: Cambridge University Press/Éditions de la Maison des Sciences de l'Homme.

———. 1986. "L'Impérialisme sociologique face à l'histoire." In *Historiens et sociologues aujourd'hui. Journées d'études annuelles de la Société française de sociologie*. Paris: CNRS.

———, ed. 1987. "Lettres de Emile Durkheim à Henri Hubert." *Revue française de sociologie*, 38: 483–534.

———. 1993. "De la datation des cours pédagogiques de Durkheim à la recherche du thème dominant de son oeuvre." In *Durkheim, sociologue de l'éducation, journées d'étude, 15–16 octobre 1992*, eds., François Cardi and Joëlle Plantier. Paris: L'Harmattan.

Birnbaum, Pierre. 1972. "Du Socialisme au don." *L'Arc* 48.

Blum, Antoinette, ed. 1992. *Correspondance entre Charles Andler et Lucien Herr (1891–1926)*. Paris: Presses de l'Ecole Normale Supérieure.

Bompaire-Evesque, Claire-Françoise. 1988. *Un Débat sur l'université au temps de la Troisième République*. Paris: Aux Amateurs de Livres.

Borlandi, Massimo and Laurent Mucchielli, eds. 1995. *La Sociologie et sa méthode. Les Règles de Durkheim un siècle après*. Paris: L'Harmattan.

Boschetti, Anna. 1988[1985]. *The Intellectual Enterprise: Sartre and Les Temps Modernes*, trans. Richard McCleary. Evanston: Northwestern University Press.

Bouglé, Célestin et al. 1921. *Du sage antique au citoyen moderne*. Paris: Librarie Armand Colin.

Bourdieu, Pierre. 1990[1980]. *The Logic of Practice*, trans. Richard Nice. Cambridge: Polity Press.

———. 1984. *Homo Academicus*. Paris: Éditions de Minuit.

———. 1987. *Choses dites*. Paris: Minuit.

———. 1988. *L'Ontologie politique de Martin Heidegger*. Paris: Éditions de Minuit.

———. 1991[1982]. *Language and Symbolic Power*, trans. Gino Raymond and Matthew Adamson. Cambridge: Harvard University Press.

———. 1993. *The Field of Cultural Production*, trans. New York: Columbia University Press.

———. 2004. *Esquisse pour une auto-analyse*. Paris: Éditions Raison d'agir.

Bourg, Julian. 2007. *From Revolution to Ethics: May 1968 and Contemporary French Thought*. Montreal: McGill-Queen's University Press.

Bourgin, Hubert. 1938. *De Jaurès à Léon Blum. L'École Normale et la politique*. Paris: Librairie Arthème Fayard.

Boyer, Alain-Michel. 1974. *Michel Leiris*. Paris: Éditions Universitaires.

Braunstein, Jean-François. 2000. "Canguilhem avant Canguilhem." *Revue d'histoire des sciences*, 53, no. 1: (January–March): 9–26.

Brillant, Bernard. 2003. *Les Clercs de 68*. Paris: PUF.

Cahm, Eric. 1972. *Péguy et le nationalisme français, de l'Affaire Dreyfus à la Grande guerre*. Paris: Cahiers de l'Amitié Charles Péguy.

Caillois, Roger. 1959[1939]. *Man and the Sacred*, trans. M. Barash. New York: Free Press.

————. 2003. *The Edge of Surrealism*. Claudine Frank, ed. Durham: Duke University Press.

Calvet, Louis-Jean. 1990. *Roland Barthes*. Paris: Flammarion.

Canguilhem, Georges. 1976. *Vie et Mort de Jean Cavaillès*. Villefranche d'Albigeois: Les Carnets de Baudasser.

Caputo, John. 1997. *The Prayers and Tears of Jacques Derrida: Religion without Religion*. Indianapolis: Indiana University Press.

Caputo, John, Kevin Hart, and Yvonne Sherwood. 2005. "Epoché and Faith: An Interview with Jacques Derrida." In *Derrida and Religion: Other Testaments*, eds. Yvonne Sherwood and Kevin Hart. New York: Routledge: 27–52.

Cardi, François and Joëlle Plantier, eds. 1993. *Durkheim, sociologue de l'éducation: journées d'étude 15–16 octobre 1992*. Paris: L'Harmattan.

Castaneda, Carlos. 1968. *The Teachings of Don Juan: A Yaqui Way of Knowledge*. Berkeley: University of California.

Chapsal, Madeleine. 1973. *Les écrivains en personne*. Paris: Union Générale d'Éditions.

Charle, Christophe. 1983. "Le Champ universitaire parisien à la fin du 19e siècle." *Actes de la recherche en sciences sociales*, 47/48: 77–89.

————. 1984. "Le Beau marriage d'Émile Durkheim." *Actes de la recherche en sciences sociales*, 55: 45–49.

————. 1987. *Les Elites de la République (1880–1900)*. Paris: Fayard.

————. 1990. *Naissance des "intellectuels" 1880–1900*. Paris: Éditions de Minuit.

————. 1994. "Les Normaliens et le socialisme (1867–1914)." In *Jaurès et les intellectuels*, eds. Madeleine Rebérioux and Gilles Candar. Paris: Éditions Ouvrières: 133–68.

————. 1998. *Paris fin-de-siècle: culture et politique*. Paris: Seuil.

Charlton, D.G. 1963. *Secular Religions in France (1815–1870)*. London: Oxford University Press.

Chesneaux, Jean. 2004. *L'engagement des intellectuels 1944–2004: itineraire d'un historien franc-tireur*. Toulouse: Éditions Privat.

Christofferson, Michael Scott. 2003. *French Intellectuals Against the Left: The Antitotalitarian Moment of the 1970s*. New York: Berghahn.

Christofferson, Thomas. 1991. *The French Socialists in Power, 1981–1986: From Autogestion to Cohabitation*. Newark: University of Delaware Press.

Clark, Terry. 1973. *Prophets and Patrons: The French University and the Emergence of the Social Sciences*. Cambridge: Harvard University Press.

Clifford, James. 1988. *The Predicament of Culture: Twentieth-Century Ethnography, Literature and Art*. Cambridge: Harvard University Press.

Colquhoun, Robert. 1986. *Raymond Aron: Volume 2, The Sociologist in Society 1955–1983*. London: Sage.

Collins, Randall. 1998. *The Sociology of Philosophies*. Cambridge: Harvard University Press.

————. 2004. *Interaction Ritual Chains*. Princeton: Princeton University Press.

Comité national d'évaluation des établissements publics à caractère scientifique (CNE). 2005. *Rapport d'évaluation de l'Université Paris X- Nanterre*. Paris.

Crossley, Nick. 2001. *The Social Body: Habit, Identity and Desire*. London: Sage.

Czarnowski, Stefan. 1919. *Le Culte des héros et ses conditions sociales, Saint Patrick, héros national de l'Irlande*. Paris: Alcan.

Davy, Georges. 1919. "Émile Durkheim." *Annuaire de l'Association amicale des anciens élèves de l'École normale supérieure.*

Debray, Regis. 1981[1979]. *Teachers, Writers, Celebrities: The Intellectuals of Modern France,* trans. David Macey. London: NLB.

Debru, Claude. 2004. *Georges Canguilhem, Science et non-Science.* Paris: Éditions Rue d'Ulm.

Delannoi, Gil. 1989. "Mai et les sciences sociales dans l'évolution idéologique de l'après-guerre." *Les Cahiers de l'Institut d'Histoire du Temps Present,* no. 11 (April): 27–38.

Deleuze, Gilles. 1971[1967]. *Masochism: An Interpretation of Coldness and Cruelty.* New York: George Braziller.

———. 1988[1962]. *Nietzsche and Philosophy,* trans. Hugh Tomlinson. New York: Columbia University Press.

———. 1990. *Pourparlers, 1972–1990.* Paris: Éditions de Minuit.

———. 2002. *L'île déserte et autres textes.* Paris: Minuit.

———. 2003. *Deux régimes de fous et autres textes.* Paris: Minuit.

Deleuze, Gilles and Claire Parnet. 2007[1977]. *Dialogues II,* trans. Hugh Tomlinson and Barbara Habberjam. New York: Columbia University Press.

Deleuze, Gilles and Félix Guattari. 1977[1972]. *Anti-Oedipus: Capitalism and Schizophrenia,* trans. Robert Hurley, Mark Seem and Helen R. Lane. New York: Viking Press.

———. 1987[1980]. *A Thousand Plateaus: Capitalism and Schizophrenia,* trans. Brian Massumi. Minneapolis: University of Minnesota Press.

Deploige, Simon, ed. 1912. *Le Conflit de la morale et de la sociologie.* Louvain: Institut supérieur de philosophie.

Derczansky, Alexandre. 1990. "Note sur la judéité de Durkheim." *Archives de Sciences Sociales des Religions,* 35, no. 69 (January–March): 157–160.

Derrida, Jacques. 1974[1967]. *Of Grammatology,* trans. Gayatri Spivak. Baltimore: Johns Hopkins University Press.

———. 1978a. *Spurs: Nietzsche's Styles,* trans. Barbara Harlow Chicago: University of Chicago Press.

———. 1978b[1967]. *Writing and Difference,* trans. Alan Bass. Chicago: University of Chicago Press.

———. 1981[1968]. "Plato's Pharmacy." In *Dissemination,* trans. Barbara Johnson. Chicago: University of Chicago Press.

———. 1992[1991]. *Given Time: 1. Counterfeit Money,* trans. Peggy Kamuf. Chicago: University of Chicago Press.

———. 1993. *Khôra.* Paris: Éditions Galillée.

———. 1994[1993]. *Spectres of Marx: The State of the Debt, the Work of Mourning, and the New International,* trans. P. Kamuf. London: Routledge.

———. 1995a[1992]. *The Gift of Death,* trans. David Willis. Chicago: University of Chicago Press.

———. 1995b. *Points: Interviews, 1974–1994,* trans. Peggy Kamuf et al. Palo Alto: Stanford University Press

———. 1998[1996]. "Faith and Knowledge: The Two Sources of 'Religion' at the Limits of Reason Alone." In *Religion,* eds. Jacques Derrida and Gianni Vattimo. Palo Alto: Stanford University Press.

————. 2002. *Negotiations: Interventions and Interviews, 1971–2001*. Palo Alto: Stanford University Press.

Derrida, Jacques and Catherine Malabou. 1999. *Contre-allée*. Paris: La Quinzaine littéraire.

Derrida, Jacques and Élisabeth Roudinesco. 2001. *De quoi demain … dialogue*. Paris: Flammarion.

Descombes, Vincent. 1980[1979]. *Modern French Philosophy*, trans. L. Scott-Fox and J. M. Harding. Cambridge: Cambridge University Press.

Dichy, Albert and Safaa Fathy. 2004. "Les archives de JD à l'IMEC." In *Derrida*. eds. Marie-Louise Mallet and Ginette Michaud Paris: L'Herne.

Dosse, François. 1991. *Histoire du structuralisme: le champ du signe*, vol. 1. Paris: Éditions la Découverte.

————. 1992. *Histoire du structuralisme: le chant du cygne*, vol. 2. Paris: Éditions la Découverte.

————. 2007. *Gilles Deleuze et Félix Guattari: biographie croisée*. Paris: La Découverte.

Drake, David. 2002. *Intellectuals and Politics in Post-War France*. New York: Palgrave.

Drouard, Alain. 1982. "Réflexions sur une chronologie: le développement des sciences sociales en France de 1945 à la fin des années soixante." *Revue française de sociologie*, 23: 55–85.

Dubar, Claude. 1972. "Retour aux texts." *L'Arc* 48.

Dufay, François and Pierre-Bertrand Dufort. 1993. *Les Normaliens: De Charles Péguy à Bernard-Henri Lévy, un siècle d'histoire*. Paris: Jean-Claude Lattès.

Dumézil, Georges. 1987. *Entretiens avec Didier Eribon*. Paris: Gallimard.

Durkheim, Émile. 1898. "Preface," *Année sociologique* 1.

————. 1899. "Preface." *Année sociologique*, 2.

————. 1916. Letters 1, 5, 10 and 11 in *Lettres à tous les Français*. Paris: Comité de publication.

————. 1950[1894]. *The Rules of Sociological Method*. Glencoe: Free Press.

————. 1951[1897]. *Suicide*. Glencoe: Free Press.

————. 1953. *Sociology and Philosophy*, trans. D. F. Pocock. Glencoe: Free Press.

————. 1958[1893]. *The Division of Labor in Society*, trans. George Simpson. New York: Free Press.

————. 1963. *L'Éducation morale*. Paris: Presses Universitaires de France.

————. 1969. *L'Évolution pédagogique en France*. Paris: Presses Universitaires de France.

————. 1970. *La Science sociale et l'action*, ed. Jean-Claude Filloux. Paris: Presses Universitaires de France.

————. 1975 a and b, *Textes (1. Éléments d'une théorie sociale 2. Religion, morale, anomie 3. Fonctions sociales et institutions)*, vols. 1 and 2, ed. Victor Karady. Paris: Les Éditions de Minuit.

————. 1976[1901]. "The Role of Universities in the Social Education of the Country," trans. George Weisz. *Minerva*, 14, no. 3: 377–388.

————. 1991[1912][. *Les Formes élémentaires de la vie religieuse: le système totémique en Australie*. Paris: Librairie Générale Française.

————. 1998. *Lettres à Marcel Mauss*, eds. Philippe Besnard and Marcel Fournier. Paris: Presses Universitaires de France.

Eribon, Didier. 1989. *Michel Foucault, 1926–1984*. Paris: Flammarion.

———. 1994. *Michel Foucault et ses contemporains*. Paris: Fayard.

Eyerman, Ron. 1994. *Between Culture and Politics: Intellectuals in Modern Society*. Cambridge: Polity.

Fabiani, Jean-Louis. 1988. *Les Philosophes de la République*. Paris: Les Éditions de Minuit.

———. 1993. "Métaphysique, morale, sociologie: Durkheim et le retour à la philosophie," *Revue de métaphysique et de morale*, 98, nos. 1–2: 175–192.

Feenberg, Andrew and Jim Freedman. 2001. *When Poetry Ruled the Streets: The French May Events of 1968*. Albany: SUNY Press.

Felgine, Odile. 1994. *Roger Caillois, biographie*. Paris: Éditions Stock.

Filloux, Jean-Claude. 1977. *Durkheim et le socialisme*. Geneva: Librairie Droz.

Foucault, Michel. 1970[1966]. *The Order of Things: An Archaeology of the Human Sciences*, trans. New York: Vintage.

———. 1973[1961]. *Madness and Civilization: A History of Insanity in the Age of Reason*, trans. Richard Howard. New York: Vintage.

———, ed. 1975[1973]. *I, Pierre Rivière, having slaughtered my mother, my sister, and my brother: a case of parricide in the 19ᵗʰ century*, trans. New York: Penguin.

———. 1977. *Language, Counter-Memory, Practice: Selected Essays and Interviews*, trans. Donald Bouchard and Sherry Simon. Ithaca: Cornell University Press.

———. 1978[1976]. *The History of Sexuality: Volume 1: An Introduction*, trans. Robert Hurley. New York: Vintage.

———. 1979[1975]. *Discipline and Punish: The Birth of the Prison*, trans. Alan Sheridan. New York: Vintage.

———. 1980. *Power/Knowledge: Selected Interviews and Other Writings, 1972–1977*, trans. Colin Gordon, Leo Marshall, John Mepham and Kate Soper. New York: Pantheon.

———. 1988. *Politics, Philosophy, Culture: Interviews and Other Writings, 1977–1984*, trans. Alan Sheridan et al. New York: Routledge.

———. 1989. *Foucault Live (Interviews 1966–1984*, ed. Sylvère Lotringer, trans. John Johnston. New York: Semiotext(e).

———. 1991[1981]. *Remarks on Marx: Conversations with Duccio Trombadori*, trans. R. James Goldstein and James Cascaito. New York: Semiotext(e).

———. 2001a and b. *Dits et écrits I–II, 1954–1988* (two volumes). Paris: Gallimard.

Fournier, Marcel. 1994. *Marcel Mauss*. Paris: Fayard.

Frazer, James George. 1960. *The Golden Bough, A Study in Magic and Religion*, abridged ed. New York: Macmillan.

Fustel de Coulanges, Numa Denis.1956[1864]. *The Ancient City: A Study on the Religion, Laws, and Institutions of Greece and Rome*, trans. Garden City: Doubleday Anchor.

Gane, Mike. 1991a. *Baudrillard's Bestiary: Baudrillard and Culture*. London: Routledge.

———. 1991b. *Baudrillard: Critical and Fatal Theory*. London: Routledge.

———, ed. 1992. *The Radical Sociology of Durkheim and Mauss*. London: Routledge.

———. 2000. *Jean Baudrillard: In Radical Uncertainty*. London: Pluto Press.

Geertz, Clifford. 1968. *Islam Observed: Religious Development in Morocco and Indonesia*. New Haven: Yale University Press.

Gellner, Ernest. 1992. *Postmodernism, Reason and Religion.* London: Routledge.

Giddens, Anthony. 1982. *Sociology: A Brief but Critical Introduction.* New York: Harcourt Brace Jovanovich.

Goffman, Erving. 1982. *Interaction Ritual.* New York: Pantheon.

Goldman, Harvey. 1988. *Max Weber and Thomas Mann: Calling and the Shaping of the Self.* Berkeley: University of California Press.

———. 2000. "The Philosophy of Foucault's Practices of the Self." In *Identità, riconoscimento e scambio: Saggi in onore di Alessandro Pizzorno,* eds. Donatella Della Porta, Monica Greco and Arpad Szakolczai. Florence: La Terza.

Gouldner, Alvin. 1979. *The Future of Intellectuals and the Rise of the New Class.* New York: Seabury Press.

Gramsci, Antonio. 1971. *Selections from the Prison Notebooks,* eds. Quintin Hoare and Geoffrey Nowell Smith. London: Lawrence and Wishart.

Greenberg, Louis M. 1976. "Bergson and Durkheim as Sons and Assimilators: The Early Years." *French Historical Studies,* 9, no. 4: 619–34.

Grogin, R. C. 1988. *The Bergsonian Controversy in France, 1900–1914.* Calgary: University of Calgary Press.

Gugelot, Frédéric. 1998. *La Conversion des intellectuels au catholicisme en France (1885–1935).* Paris: CNRS Éditions.

Guibert, Hervé. 1990. *Á l'ami qui ne m'a pas sauvé la vie.* Paris: Gallimard.

Hadot, Pierre. 1981. *Exercices spirituelles et philosophie antique.* Paris: Études augustiniennes.

Halévy, Daniel. 1979. *Péguy et les Cahiers de la quinzaine.* Paris: Livre de poche.

Hayward, J. E. S. 1961. "The Official Social Philosophy of the Third Republic: Léon Bourgeois and Solidarism." *International Review of Social History,* 6: 19–48.

Hazareesingh, Sudir. 1991. *Intellectuals and the French Communist Party.* Oxford: Oxford University Press.

Healy, Ellen Louise. 1995. "Tel Quel and the Formation of a Postmodern Avant-Garde: French Intellectual Culture Since 1950." Doctoral dissertation, University of California, Los Angeles.

Heilbron, Johan. 1985. "Les Métamorphoses du durkheimisme, 1920–1940." *Revue française de sociologie,* 26: 203–37.

Heimonet, Jean-Michel. 1987. *Politiques de l'ecriture, Bataille/Derrida: le sens du sacré dans la pensée française du surréalisme à nos jours.* Chapel Hill: University of North Carolina Press.

Héran, Jean-Michel. 1989. "De *La Cité antique* à la sociologie des institutions," *Revue de synthèse,* 4: 3–4: 363–90.

Hertz, Robert. 1970[1928]. *Sociologie religieuse et folklore.* Paris: Presses Universitaires de France.

———. 1994. *Sin and Expiation in Primitive Societies,* ed. and trans. Robert Parkin. Oxford: British Centre for Durkheimian Studies, Occasional Papers 2.

———. 2002. *Un ethnologue dans les tranchées, août 1914–avril 1915, lettres de Robert Hertz à sa femme Alice,* eds. Alexander Riley and Philippe Besnard. Paris: CNRS Éditions.

Hirsch, Arthur. 1981. *The French New Left: An Intellectual History from Sartre to Gorz.* Boston: South End Press.

Hollier, Denis, ed. 1979. *Le Collège de sociologie.* Paris: Gallimard.

Hommage à Roger Caillois. 1981. Paris: Centre Georges Pompidou, collection Cahiers pour un temps.

Hourmant, François. 1997. *Le Désenchantement des clercs: figures de l'intellectuel dans l'après–Mai 68.* Rennes: Presses Universitaires de Rennes.

Hubert, Henri. 1904. Introduction to P.-D. Chantepie de la Saussaye. *Manuel d'histoire des religions,* trans. Henri Hubert et al. Paris: A. Colin.

———. 1974a. *Les Celtes et l'expansion celtique jusqu'à l'époque de La Tène.* Paris: Albin Michel.

———. 1974b. *Les Celtes et la civilisation celtique depuis l'époque de La Tène.* Paris: Albin Michel.

Hubert, Henri and Marcel Mauss. 1929. *Mélanges d'histoire des religions.* Paris: Félix Alcan.

Huisman, Denis, ed. 2002. *Histoire de la philosophie français.* Paris: Perrin.

Huizinga, Johan. 1950[1938]. *Homo Ludens: a Study of the Play Element in Culture.* Boston: Beacon Press.

Isambert, François-André. 1969. "The Early Days of French Sociology of Religion." *Social Compass,* 16, no. 4: 435–52.

———. 1979. "Henri Hubert et la sociologie du temps." *Revue française de sociologie,* 20: 183–204.

———. 1983. "At the frontier of folklore and sociology: Hubert, Hertz and Czarnowski, founders of a sociology of folk religion." In *The Sociological Domain,* ed. Philippe Besnard. London and Paris: Cambridge University Press/Éditions de la Maison des Sciences de l'Homme.

Isambert-Jamati, Viviane. 1971. "Une réforme des lycées et collèges: essai d'analyse sociologique de la réforme de 1902." *Année sociologique,* 3rd series, 20: 9–60.

Jamin, Jean. 1980. "Un sacré collège, ou les apprentis sorciers de la sociologie." *Cahiers internationaux de sociologie,* 68: 5–30.

Janet, Paul. 1895. *Victor Cousin et son oeuvre.* Paris: Alcan.

Jaspers, Karl. 1964. *Spinoza,* ed. Hannah Arendt. New York: Harvest.

Jeannin, Pierre. 1994. *Deux siècles à Normale Sup': Petite histoire d'une Grande École.* Paris: Larousse.

Jones, Robert Alun. 1993. "Durkheim and *La Cité antique:* An essay on the origins of Durkheim's sociology of religion." In *Emile Durkheim: Sociologist and Moralist,* ed. Stephen Turner. New York: Routledge.

Judt, Tony. 1992. *Past Imperfect: French Intellectuals, 1944–1956.* Berkeley: University of California Press.

———. 1998. *The Burden of Responsibility: Blum, Camus, Aron, and the French Twentieth Century.* Chicago: University of Chicago Press.

Juillard, Jacques and Michel Winock, eds. 1996. *Dictionnaire des intellectuels français: les personnes, les lieux, les moments.* Paris: Éditions de Seuil.

Karady, Victor. 1976. "Durkheim, les sciences sociales et l'Université: bilan d'un semi-échec." *Revue française de sociologie,* 17, no. 2: 267–311.

———. 1979. "Stratégies de réussite et modes de faire-valoir de la sociologie chez les durkheimiens." *Revue française de sociologie,* 20: 49–82.

———. 1983. "Les Professeurs de la République: le marché scolaire, les réformes universitaires et les transformations de la fonction professorale à la fin du 19e siècle." *Actes de la recherche en sciences sociales,* 47/48: 90–112.

Kaufmann, Walter. 1956. *Nietzsche: Philosopher, Psychologist, Antichrist.* New York: Meridian.

Kauppi, Niilo. 1996. *French Intellectual Nobility: Institutional and Symbolic Transformations in the Post-Sartrian Era.* Albany: SUNY Press.

Khilnani, Sunil. 1993. *Arguing Revolution: The Intellectual Left in Post-War France.* New Haven: Yale University Press.

LaCapra, Dominick. 1972. *Emile Durkheim: Sociologist and Philosopher.* Ithaca: Cornell University Press.

———. 1978. *A Preface to Sartre.* Ithaca: Cornell University Press.

Lacroix, Bernard. 1981. *Durkheim et le politique.* Montréal: Presses de l'Université de Montréal.

Lantier, Raymond. 1928. "Hommage à Henri Hubert." *Revue archéologique,* 28.

Latour, Bruno. 1993[1991]. *We Have Never Been Modern,* trans. Catherine Porter. Cambridge: Harvard University Press.

Lautman, Jacques. 2000. "Un Stoïcien chaleureux." *Revue d'histoire des sciences,* 53 no. 1 (January–March): 27–45.

Lecoq, Dominique and Jean-Luc Lory, eds. 1987. *Écrits d'ailleurs. Georges Bataille et les ethnologues.* Paris: Éditions de la Maison des Sciences de l'Homme.

Le Goff, Jean-Pierre. 2006[1998]. *Mai 68: L'héritage impossible.* Paris: La Découverte.

Leiris, Michel. 1981[1934]. *L'Afrique fantôme.* Paris: Gallimard.

Lemire, Laurent. 1998. *Cohn-Bendit.* Paris: Éditions Liana Lévi.

Lenin, V. I. 1966. *Essential Works of Lenin* ed. Henry Christman. New York: Bantam.

Lepenies, Wolf. 1988[1985]. *Between Literature and Science: The Rise of Sociology,* trans. R. J. Hollingdale. Cambridge: Cambridge University Press.

Le Rider, Jacques. 1999. *Nietzsche en France, de la fin du XIXe siècle au temps présent.* Paris: PUF.

Lévi-Strauss, Claude and Didier Eribon.1991[1988]. *Conversations with Lévi-Strauss,* trans. Paula Wissing. Chicago: University of Chicago Press.

Lindenberg, Daniel. 1990. *Les Années souterraines (1937–1947).* Paris: Éditions la Découverte.

Llobera, Joseph. 1994. "Durkheim and the National Question."In *Debating Durkheim,* eds. W.S.F. Pickering and H. Martins. London: Routledge.

Lukes, Steven. 1973. *Emile Durkheim, His Life and Work: A Historical and Critical Study.* London: Allen Lane.

L'Yvonnet, François, ed. 2004. *Jean Baudrillard.* Paris: Éditions de l'Herne.

Macey, David. 1993. *The Lives of Michel Foucault: A Biography.* New York: Pantheon.

Mallet, Marie-Louise and Ginette Michaud, eds. 2004. *Jacques Derrida.* Paris: L'Herne.

Marx, Karl. 1972. *The Marx-Engels Reader,* ed. Robert Tucker. New York: Norton.

Massis, Henri and Alfred de Tarde (Agathon). 1911. *L'Esprit de la nouvelle Sorbonne. La crise de la culture classique.* Paris: Mercure de France.

Mauss, Marcel. 1900. Review of B. Spencer and F. Gillen, *The Native Trives of Central Australia.* London: Macmillan, 1899. *Année sociologique,* 3: 205–215.

———. 1913. Review of *The Golden Bough,* J.G. Frazer. *Année sociologique,* 12: 75–79.

———. 1925, "In Memoriam. L'oeuvre inédite de Durkheim et de ses collaborateurs." *L'Année sociologique,* 1.

———. 1930. "Hommage à Pablo Picasso." *Documents,* 2: 177.

———. 1950. *Sociologie et anthropologie.* ed. Claude Lévi-Strauss. Paris: Presses Universitaires de France.

———. 1968a and b, *Oeuvres (1. Les Fonctions sociales du sacré 2. Représentations collectives et diversité des civilisations),* ed. Victory Karady. Paris: Les Éditions de Minuit.

———. 1969. *Oeuvres (3. Cohésion sociale et divisions de la sociologie),* ed. Victor Karady. Paris: Les Éditions de Minuit.

———. 1979. "L'oeuvre de Mauss par lui-même." *Revue française de sociologie,* 20, no. 1 (January–March): 209–20.

———. 1989. "A 1934 Interview with Marcel Mauss." Stephen Murray, ed. *American Ethnologist,* 16, no. 1: 163–68.

———. 1997. *Écrits politiques,* ed. Marcel Fournier. Paris: Fayard.

Mauss, Marcel and Henri Hubert. 1899. "Essai sur la nature et la fonction du sacrifice." *Année sociologique,* 2

———. 1904. "Esquisse d'une théorie générale de la magie." *Année sociologique,* 7.

May, Rollo. 1969. *Love and Will.* New York: Dell.

Mazon, Brigitte. 1988. *Aux origins de l'Ecole des hautes études en sciences sociales: le rôle du mécénat américain (1920–1960).* Paris: Éditions de CERF.

Mendras, Henri. 1994. *La Seconde revolution française, 1965–1984,* 2nd edition. Paris: Gallimard.

Mergy, Jennifer. 1988. "On Durkheim and Notes critiques." *Durkheimian Studies,* 4: 1–7.

Miller, James. 1993. *The Passion of Michel Foucault.* New York: Simon and Schuster.

Miller, W. Watts. 1996. *Durkheim, Morals and Modernity.* Montréal: McGill-Queen's University Press.

Molnar, Thomas. 1961. *The Decline of the Intellectual.* New York: Meridian.

Morin, Edgar. 1975. *L'Esprit du temps, nécrose,* vol. 2. Paris: Bernard Grasset.

———. 1991. *La Méthode: 4. Les idées.* Paris: Seuil.

Moulier-Boutang, Yann. 1992. *Louis Althusser, une biographie: tome 1, la formation du mythe (1918–1956).* Paris: Bernard Grasset.

Mucchielli, Laurent. 1998. *La Découverte du social: naissance de la sociologie en France (1870–1914).* Paris: Éditions la Découverte.

Mucchielli, Laurent and Massimo Borlandi, eds. 1995. *La Sociologie et sa méthode. Les Règles de Durkheim un siècle après.* Paris: L'Harmattan.

Musselin, Christine. 2001. *La Longue marche des universités françaises.* Paris: PUF.

Nadeau, Maurice. 1989[1948]. *The History of Surrealism,* trans. Richard Howard. Cambridge: Belknap Press.

Nielsen, Donald. 1999. *Three Faces of God: Society, Religion and the Categories of Totality in the Philosophy of Emile Durkheim.* Albany: State University of New York Press.

Nietzsche, Friedrich. 1969. *On the Genealogy of Morals/Ecce Homo,* trans. Walter Kaufmann. New York: Vintage.

———. 1974[1887]. *The Gay Science,* trans. Walter Kaufmann. New York: Vintage.

———. 1990a. *Twilight of the Idols/The Anti-Christ,* trans. R.J. Hollingdale. London: Penguin.

———. 1990b[1886]. *Beyond Good and Evil: Prelude to a Philosophy of the Future,* trans. R.J. Hollingdale. London: Penguin.

Nisbet, Robert. 1966. *The Sociological Tradition.* London: Heinemann.

Noiriel, Gérard. 2005. *Les fils maudits de la République: L'avenir des intellectuels en France.* Paris: Fayard.

Ofrat, Gideon. 2001. *The Jewish Derrida.* Syracuse: Syracuse University Press.

Parkin, Robert. 1996. *The Dark Side of Humanity: The Work of Robert Hertz and its Legacy.* Amsterdam: Harwood Academic Publishers.

Parodi, Maxime. 2004. *La Modernité manquée du structuralisme.* Paris: PUF.

Passeron, Jean-Claude. 1986. "1950–1980: l'Universite mise à la question: changement de décor ou changement de cap ?" In *Histoire des universités en France,* ed. Jacques Verger. Toulouse: Bibliothèque historique Privat,

Patron, Sylvie. 1999. *Critique 1946–1996: Une encyclopédie de l'esprit moderne.* Caen: Éditions de l'IMEC.

Patterson, Orlando. 1998. *Rituals of Blood: Consequences of Slavery in Two American Centuries.* New York: Basic Civitas.

Pavel, Thomas G. 1992. *The Feud of Language: A History of Structuralist Thought.* London: Blackwell.

Peyrefitte, Alain. 1998. *Rue d'Ulm: chroniques de la vie normalienne.* Paris: Fayard.

Pickering, William S. F. 1984. *Durkheim's Sociology of Religion: Themes and Theories.* London: Routledge and Kegan Paul.

———. 1993. "The Origins of Conceptual Thinking in Durkheim: Social or Religious?" In *Emile Durkheim: Sociologist and Moralist,* ed. Stephen Turner. New York: Routledge.

———. 1998. "Mauss's Jewish background: a biographical essay." In *Marcel Mauss: A Centenary Tribute,* eds. N.J. Allen and Wendy James. New York: Berghahn.

Piel, Jean. 1982. *La Rencontre et la différence.* Paris: Fayard.

Pinto, Louis. 1986. *Les Philosophes entre le lycée et l'avant-garde. Les métamorphoses de la philosophie dans la France d'aujourd'hui.* Paris: L'Harmattan.

———. 1995. *Les Neveux de Zarathoustra: la réception de Nietzsche en France.* Paris: Seuil.

Poulat, Emile and Odile.1966. "Le Développement institutionnel des sciences religieuses en France." *Archives de sociologie des religions,* 21: 23–36.

Powell, Jason. 2006. *Jacques Derrida: A Biography.* London: Continuum.

Prendergast, Christopher. 1983–84. "The Impact of Fustel de Coulanges' *La Cité antique* on Durkheim's Theories of Social Morphology and Social Solidarity. *Humboldt Journal of Social Relations,* 11, no. 1: 53–73.

Prochasson, Christophe. 1993a. "Philosopher au XXe siècle: Xavier Léon et l'invention du "système R2M" (1891–1902)." *Revue de métaphysique et de morale,* 98, nos. 1–2: 109–140.

———. 1993b. *Les Intellectuels, le socialisme et la guerre, 1900–1938.* Paris: Éditions du Seuil.

———. 1997. *Les Intellectuels et le socialisme, XIXe-XXe siècle.* Paris: Plon.

Prost, Antoine. 1968. *Histoire de l'enseignement en France, 1800–1967.* Paris: Armand Colin.

———. 1992. *Éducation, société et politiques. Une histoire de l'enseignement en France, de 1945 à nos jours.* Paris: Éditions du Seuil.

Racine, Nicole and Michel Trebitsch, eds. 1992. "Sociabilités intellectuelles." *Cahiers de l'institut d'histoire du temps présent.* (March).

Reader, Keith and Khursheed Wadia. 1993. *The May 1968 Events in France: Reproductions and Interpretations.* New York: St. Martin's Press.

Reinach, Salomon. 1927. "Henri Hubert." *Revue archéologique*, 26.

Rémond, René. 1979. *La Règle et le consentement: gouverner une société*. Paris: Fayard.

Richman, Michèle. 2002. *Sacred Revolutions: Durkheim and the Collège de Sociologie*. Minneapolis: University of Minnesota Press.

Rieffel, Rémy. 1993. *La Tribu des clercs: les intellectuels sous la Cinquième République, 1958–1990*. Paris: Calmann-Lévy/CNRS Éditions.

Rieusset, Isabelle. 1983. "Fonction et signification du mythe dans le "Collège de sociologie."" Doctoral dissertation, Université de Paris VII.

Rigby, Brian. 1994. "Intellectuals, education and culture at the Liberation: the opposition to 'la culture scolaire.'" *French Cultural Studies*, 5, no. 15: 241–251.

Riley, Alexander. 1999. "The Intellectual and Political Project of Robert Hertz: The Making of a Peculiar Durkheimian Intellectual, as seen through selected correspondence with Pierre Roussel." *Durkheimian Studies/Études durkheimiennes*, 5: 29–59.

———. 2002. "Durkheim contra Bergson? The Hidden Roots of Postmodern Theory and the Postmodern 'Return' of the Sacred." *Sociological Perspectives*, 45, no. 3: 243–265.

———. 2005. "The Theory of Play/Games and Sacrality in Popular Culture: The Relevance of Roger Caillois for Contemporary Neo-Durkheimian Cultural Theory." *Durkheimian Studies/Études durkheimieénes*, 11: 103–14.

Ringer, Fritz. 1992. *Fields of Knowledge: French Academic Culture in Comparative Perspective, 1890–1920*. Cambridge and Paris: Cambridge University Press and Éditions de la Maison des Sciences de l'Homme.

Rioux, Jean-Pierre and Jean-François Sirinelli. 1991. *La Guerre d'Algerie et les intellectuels français*. Paris: Éditions Complexe.

Roudinesco, Élisabeth. 1998. "Georges Canguilhem, de la medicine à la resistance: destin du concept de normalité." In *Actualité de Georges Canguilheim: Le normal et le pathologique*, Georges Canguilhem et al. Paris: Empêcheurs Penser en Rond: 13–41.

———. 2005. *Philosophes dans la tourmente*. Paris: Fayard.

Rubenstein, Diane. 1990. *What's Left?: The École Normale Supérieure and the Right*. Madison: University of Wisconsin Press.

Sartre, Jean-Paul. 1968[1960]. *Search for a Method*, trans. Hazel Barnes. New York: Vintage.

Schmaus, Warren. 1994. *Durkheim's Philosophy of Science and the Sociology of Knowledge: Creating an Intellectual Niche*. Chicago: University of Chicago Press.

Schrift, Alan. 2006. *Twentieth-Centure French Philosophy: Key Themes and Thinkers*. Oxford: Blackwell.

Shils, Edward. 1972. *The Intellectuals and the Powers and other essays*. Chicago: University of Chicago Press.

Simonin, Anne and Hélène Clastres. 1989. *Les Idées en France, 1945–1988: Une chronologie*. Paris: Gallimard.

Sirinelli, Jean-François. 1990. *Intellectuels et passions françaises: Manifestes et pétitions au XXème siècle*. Paris: Fayard.

Smith, Robert J. 1982. *The École Normale Supérieure and the Third Republic*. Albany: State University of New York Press.

Smith, Philip. 2004. "Marcel Proust as Successor and Precursor to Pierre Bourdieu: A Fragment." *Thesis Eleven*, 79: 105–111.

Sorum, Paul Clay. 1977. *Intellectuals and Decolonization in France*. Chapel Hill: University of North Carolina Press.

Soulié, Charles. 1998. "Le Destin d'une institution d'avant-garde: histoire du département de philosophie de Paris VIII." *Histoire de l'éducation*, 77 (January): 47–69.

Stock-Morton, Phyllis. 1988. *Moral Education for a Secular Society: The Development of Morale Laïque in Nineteenth Century France*. Albany: State University of New York Press.

Stoekl, Allan.1992. *Agonies of the Intellectual: Commitment, Subjectivity, and the Performative in the Twentieth-Century French Tradition*. Lincoln: University of Nebraska Press.

Stoller, Paul. 2004. *Stranger in the Village of the Sick: A Memoir of Cancer, Sorcery, and Healing*. Boston: Beacon Press.

Strenski, Ivan. 1987. "Henri Hubert, Racial Science and Political Myth." *Journal of the History of the Behavioral Sciences*, 21: 353–67.

———. 1995. "Émile Durkheim, Henri Hubert et le discours des modernistes religieux sur le symbolisme." *L'Ethnographie*, 91, no. 1: 33–52.

———. 1997. *Durkheim and the Jews of France*. Chicago: University of Chicago Press.

Sullivan, John W. N. 1960. *Beethoven: His Spiritual Development*. New York: Vintage.

Surya, Michel. 1987. *Georges Bataille. La mort à l'oeuvre*. Paris: Librarie Seguier.

Szakolczai, Arpád. 1998. *Max Weber and Michel Foucault: Parallel life-works*. London: Routledge.

Teissier, Élisabeth. 2001. "Situation épistémologique de l'astrologie à travers l'ambivalence fascination/rejet dans les sociétés postmodernes." Doctoral thesis. Université de Paris V.

Tiryakian, Edward. 1962. *Sociologism and Existentialism: Two Perspectives on the Individual and Society*. Englewood Cliffs: Prentice Hall.

———. 1978. "Emile Durkheim," in Tom Bottomore and Robert Nisbet, eds. *A History of Sociological Analysis*. New York: Basic Books.

———. 1979. "L'École durkheimienne à la recherche de la société perdue: la sociologie naissante et son milieu culturel." *Cahiers internationaux de sociologie*, 66: 97–114.

———. 1981. "Durkheim's 'Elementary Forms' as 'Revelation.'" In *The Future of the Sociological Classics*, ed. Buford Rhea. Boston: Allen and Unwin, 114–135.

Tonquédec, Joseph de, et al., eds. 1926. *Ce que je sais de Dieu*. Paris: Éditions Montaigne.

Tourneur-Aumont, J.M. 1931. *Fustel de Coulanges (1830–1889)*. Paris: Boivin et Compagnie.

Tuilier, André. 1994. *Histoire de l'université de Paris et de la Sorbonne, De Louis XIV à la crise de 1968*, vol. 2. Paris: G. V. Labat.

Turner, Bryan and Chris Rojek. 1993. *Forget Baudrillard?* London: Routledge.

Turner, Victor. 1980. "Social Dramas and Stories about Them." *Critical Inquiry*, 7: 141–168.

Vogt, W. Paul. 1976. "The Uses of Studying Primitives: A Note on the Durkheimians, 1890–1940." *History and Theory*, 15: 33–44.

Weber, Eugen. 1962. *Action Française: Royalism and Reaction in Twentieth-Century France*. Palo Alto: Stanford University Press.

———. 1982. *Varieties of Fascism: Doctrines of Revolution in the Twentieth Century.* New York: R. E. Krieger Publishing.

Weber, Elizabeth. 2004. *Questioning Judaism: Interviews by Elisabeth Weber,* trans. Rachel Bowlby. Palo Alto: Stanford University Press.

Weber, Max. 1930. *The Protestant Ethic and the Spirit of Capitalism.* London: G. Allen and Unwin.

———. 1946. *From Max Weber.* Hans Gerth and C. Wright Mills eds. New York: Oxford University Press.

———. 1963[1922]. *The Sociology of Religion,* trans. Ephraim Fischoff. Boston: Beacon Press.

Weill, Georges. 1925. *Histoire de l'idée laïque au dix-neuvième siècle.* Paris: Alcan.

Weisz, George. 1983. *The Emergence of Modern Universities in France, 1863–1914.* Princeton: Princeton University Press.

Wilson, Colin. 1957. *The Outsider.* New York: St. Martin's Press.

Winock, Michel. 1997. *Le Siècle des intellectuels.* Paris: Seuil.

Index

Abarvanel, Leo Judah (Léon
  L'Hébreu), 131–32, 150n4
Abraham, 261–62
Abu-Jamal, Mumia, 235
Academie Tarnier, 237
Acéphale, 205, 206
Action Française, 46
Agathon, 45–46
Alain, 106
Alakaluf society, 253
Alexander, Jeffrey, 35–36, 168
Algerian War, 79, 80, 91, 112, 120–21
Alliance Israélite Universelle, 130
Althusser, Louis, 95, 98, 100–104, 111,
  121nn1–2, 227, 242n1
Andler, Charles, 62, 180
Année sociologique, L' (journal), 85, 147,
  168, 170, 185–90, 192, 202–3
Arguments (journal), 232
Aron, Jean-Paul, 89, 120
Aron, Raymond, 4, 76, 80
Austin, J. L., 28
Aztec society, 253

Bachelard, Gaston, 100
Barrès, Maurice, 67, 133, 142, 145
Barrett, William, 171
Barthes, Roland, 87–88, 90, 95,
  108–12, 115, 218, 219, 232
  Barthes/Picard affair, 87–88
  on politics, 110–11
Bataille, Georges, 203–4, 206–8, 209,
  210, 212–13, 216, 219n2, 219n4,
  220n5, 244, 245, 250, 253, 260,
  264–65, 270

influence on Baudrillard,
  Deleuze, Derrida, and Foucault,
  244, 245, 250, 253, 260, 264–65
Baudrillard, Jean, 14, 104, 109–10, 118,
  222, 229–30, 232, 237–39, 240–41,
  242n3, 243, 250–57, 265
  on May '68, 118, 237–38, 240–41
  relationship to Roland Barthes,
  14, 109–10
  on the sacred, 250–57
  on terrorism, 255–57
  on Union of the Left, 238–39,
  240–41
Bauman, Zygmunt, 243, 274
Beauvoir, Simone De, 75, 116
Bélanger, André, 8
Bérégovoy, Pierre, 255
Bergson, Henri, 48–53, 191, 263–64
  élan vital, 48, 52
Berque, Jacques, 120
Berr, Henri, 147
Besnard, Philippe, 13, 123, 146–47,
  170, 185, 191, 199n7
Besnier, Jean-Michel, 211–12, 241
Blanchot, Maurice, 216
Blum, Léon, 63, 230, 242
Boat for Vietnam committee, A, 237
Boudon, Raymond, 88–89
Bouglé, Célestin, 183, 186
Bourdieu, Pierre, 17–18, 23–24, 27, 84,
  87, 97, 106, 218, 276
  on field and *habitus*, 17–18
  heteronomous and autonomous
  principles, 18
Brasillach, Robert, 75